THE ULTIMATE MOTORCYCLE ENCYCLOPEDIA

THE ULTIMATE MOTORCYCLE ENCYCLOPEDIA

Harley-Davidson, Ducati, Triumph, Honda, Kawasaki and all the great marques

Roland Brown & Mac McDiarmid

JG PRESS

Published by World Publications Group, Inc.

140 Laurel Street

East Bridgewater, MA 02333

www.wrldpub.net

Produced by Anness Publishing Ltd

Hermes House

88–89 Blackfriars Road

London SE1 8HA

tel. 020 7401 2077; fax 020 7633 9499

www.annesspublishing.com

If you like the images in this book and would like to investigate using them for publishing, promotions or advertising, please visit our website www.practicalpictures.com for more information.*Publisher* Joanna Lorenz
Project editors Polly Willis and Felicity Forster
Designers Michael Morey and Dave Jones
Illustrator Stephen Sweet
Production controller Lee Sargent
Editorial consultant Shaun Barrington

ETHICAL TRADING POLICY
Because of our ongoing ecological investment programme, you, as our customer, can have the pleasure and reassurance of knowing that a tree is being cultivated on your behalf to naturally replace the materials used to make the book you are holding. For further information about this scheme, go to
www.annesspublishing.com/trees

© Anness Publishing Ltd 2000, 2008

A CIP catalogue record for this book
is available from the British Library

ISBN-10: 1-57215-521-3

ISBN-13: 978-1-57215-521-3

Printed and bound in China

Previously published in two separate volumes,
The Encyclopedia of Motorcycles and *The Ultimate Harley-Davidson*

Publisher's note regarding pages 254–503
In recognition of the uniquely American pedigree of
Harley-Davidson motorcycles, their engine capacity is generally expressed in
imperial units (cubic inches) with
the metric equivalent (cc) in brackets. However, even
Harley-Davidson employs units somewhat arbitrarily, favouring cu in for
heavyweight twins, but ccs for Sportster models, a practice we have also adopted.

The capacity of Harley engines should also be treated
with some care. Even from the early days, the inch sizes quoted and used by
Harley fans were a sort of numeric shorthand, relating only approximately to
measured reality. More recently, even the "80-inch" Evo engine actually
measured 81.8cu in – a difference of no less than 29cc.
In general, where an engine is referred to as something-inch, this refers to
popular usage. Dimensions expressed in
cu in and/or cc are as accurate as records permit.

We trust that this historical ambiguity will not reduce
the reader's enjoyment.

Contents

INTRODUCTION

■ BELOW *A reconstruction of the first motorcycle ever built, by Gottlieb Daimler, in 1885.*

Gottlieb Daimler was a sensible man, as well as a brilliant engineer. Having invented the motorcycle in 1885 (although as his wooden-framed contraption had stabilizers, it rather raises a question mark over the definition of the first two-wheel machine) he pretty quickly abandoned the project and became famous for producing Daimlers. Not everyone was so sensible, thank goodness, and hundreds of tiny companies went bankrupt in the 1910s and 1920s trying to build motorcycles.

It was the sheer impracticality of the motorcycle that was its chief glory, leading to tremendous diversity around the basic layout. In the first instance this meant putting the engine between the wheels – even that took some time to figure out – and led to the triumph of hope over adversity as well as to an entire motorcycling philosophy that was based upon individuality, rebellion and fun. If you like motorcycles, as you probably do if you are reading this book, you will know that they do not appeal to everyone, which makes them even more appealing, and that they have given rise to so many types of competition – dramatic, dangerous and sometimes not entirely sane – from the TT to ice racing. This book gives details of all of those crazy competitions, and a whole lot more. Written by experts and enthusiasts, the first half of the book guides you not only through the most important examples of the two-wheel product in history, but also gives a rider's eye view, explaining just what motorcycle culture is all about.

The second half follows the history and analyzes the output of just one company – Harley-Davidson. It is the oldest motorcycle marque in the world (Norton used to claim that honour, but no more) so we follow the company's history, and see it rise to every challenge presented to it over the last century, including two world wars, a

■ LEFT *This CCM 604E 1999 "supermotard" is a far cry from the rather more basic model built by Daimler.*

■ LEFT *Unmistakable: Harley-Davidson is a legend in motorcycling.*

Depression and competitors who, several times, seemed to have sunk H-D for good. Harley-Davidson also embodies so much of the motorcycle ethos. Not only have people been adding things on and stripping things off their Harleys since the very beginning (representing that all-important individualism) but also the basic layout – the 45-degree V-twin engine – has survived for many decades, representing the continuity and essential simplicity of motorbike culture. The very sound of a Harley is extraordinary. To understand Harley-Davidson is to understand motorcycles.

Bikes are for looking at as well as riding, and what a superb collection of models awaits in this book: the bespoke glamour of the Bimota Tesi, the world-beating blur of the Yamaha YZR500 and the 170mph (273kph) Turbo Ecomobile. What was the world's first mass-produced four-cylinder bike? What do you know of the Lanying CJ750F? You may know a lot about motorcycles, but there is much here to enlighten and surprise. Put on your leathers and enquire within.

■ BELOW *Yamaha has produced some of the fastest bikes on the racing circuit: pictured is the four-cylinder 1998 Fazer.*

THE WORLD OF MOTORCYCLING

Two wheels and an engine. The basic ingredients of the motorcycle are so simple;
but its attraction, stronger than ever after more than a century of relentless development,
is so hard to explain. Part of the reason for this is that motorcycling means so many
things to so many different people. More than merely a form of transport, it
incorporates everything from an ancient Scott roadster to a modern MotoGP racer,
from a simple Velocette single to a fully equipped grand tourer.

This section of the book takes a winding ride from the first ever motorcycle – Gottlieb Daimler's
Einspur – to the fastest ever – Dave Campos's 322mph (518kph) Harley-Davidson – via Chelsea
Bridge, Hollywood and the Nürburgring. But if it is the machines that form the outline of the
motorcycling picture, then it's the people who design, build, modify, pose, commute or tour on,
race, crash, repair, fight or save lives on them who add the colour.

The World of Motorcycling is their story: from Valentino Rossi pulling a wheelie on his factory
Honda to Marlon Brando leaning on a Triumph Thunderbird in *The Wild One*; from a medical
worker delivering supplies in the African Bush to a Sunday-morning superbiker cranking a
Ducati 999 through a turn. Different people, on different motorcycles, and in very different
situations, united by a shared appreciation of two wheels and an engine.

The Evolution of the Motorcycle

By all accounts it was a short and slow journey. With a 0.5 horsepower engine, wooden frame and no suspension, that was inevitable. But when Paul Daimler rode his engineer father Gottlieb's new contraption named Einspur – "One track" – around the countryside near Stuttgart in Germany on 10 November 1885, he was taking what is commonly accepted to be the world's first ride on a motorbike.

Bikes have come a long way from those days to the present, when even ordinary middleweights exceed 100mph (160kph) reliably and with ease. But when comparing the earliest bikes of this century to the sophisticated, powerful machines of today, in many respects it's noticeable not how much but how little motorcycles have changed. Of course, there is a huge difference between the 1901 New Werner and Honda's latest Grand Prix racer – but the two are unmistakably related. This chapter is the story of how the former evolved into the latter.

EARLY DAYS

Gottlieb Daimler wasn't much of a motorcycle man, and soon after producing Einspur in 1885 he gave up bikes to make his name in the newly-developed car industry. But Daimler had made a major breakthrough. Although steam-powered railways and ships were already well established by the 1880s, steam was ill-suited to smaller vehicles. With Einspur's 265cc internal combustion engine, Daimler, who had previously worked as an assistant to Dr Nikolaus Otto, inventor of the four-stroke engine, had shown the way forward for personal transport.

Steam-powered bikes had been tried before, notably the Michaux-Perreaux velocipede built in France in 1869, but they were gradually abandoned as petrol-burning engines gained

■ LEFT *The Werner brothers of Paris sold several hundred of their light and practical 1898 model "motocyclette" which had its engine mounted above the front wheel.*

■ BELOW *In 1901, the French firm patented the New Werner layout, with engine positioned between the wheels for improved handling, which motorcycles have used ever since.*

■ ABOVE *It is said that the first ever bike race took place when two motorcyclists met on the road for the first time — these two road riders certainly look to be enjoying a bit of friendly competition in 1903.*

■ TOP *The De Dion Bouton tricycle, powered by the same firm's reliable four-stroke single engine, was raced very successfully in the final years of the last century.*

■ ABOVE *Indian's single, with its engine inclined to the rear in American fashion, was very successful in 1902 – over 100 were built and there was a reported 17-year waiting list.*

■ RIGHT *Such was the pace of change in motorcycling's early years that Daimler's Einspur, with its huge wooden frame, was totally outclassed by bikes of 15 years later.*

popularity. Among the earliest converts were the German brothers Hildebrand, who with their partner Wolfmüller produced the world's first production motorcycle in 1894. The Hildebrand & Wolfmüller held a watercooled, 1500cc twin-cylinder four-stroke engine in a specially made steel frame. Among other high-tech features, it benefited from John Boyd Dunlop's recently invented pneumatic tyres. Its top speed of about 25mph (40kph) was quite fast enough consider-ing the rear emergency brake consisted of a simple metal bar that dragged on the ground.

The next big step in motorcycling's development came soon afterwards when two Frenchmen, Count Albert De Dion and Georges Bouton, produced a single-cylinder, four-stroke engine of about 125cc. The De Dion unit was rated at 0.5bhp but in reality produced more, revved reliably to 1800rpm, and was very compact. It was originally used to power the De Dion tricycle, which was raced successfully in the late 1890s. Frustratingly for its manufact-urers, the design was blatantly copied by

numerous other firms as motorcycle production spread across Europe.

Few of the new firms could agree on the best place to locate the engine until the Paris-based Werner brothers, whose original bike used a De Dion-style unit above the front wheel, revised their design in 1901. The New Werner's engine was placed low, between the wheels, in a steel frame, and drove the rear wheel via a leather belt. With its bicycle-style saddle, wheel-rim brakes, and improved handling due to its lower centre of gravity, the New Werner set the pattern for 20th-century motorcycle design.

■ LEFT *The Wall Autowheel, pictured here in 1910, was an engine and auxiliary wheel that clamped to a bicycle — very useful for well-laden bikes.*

■ BELOW *Lawrence of Arabia was the most famous rider of the fast and sophisticated Brough Superior V-twin of the 1920s.*

Development from that point was rapid, as enthusiasm for bike production spread across Europe and America. In that same year of 1901, Americans George Hendee and Oskar Hedstrom produced the first Indian motorbike. Three years later, as Indian was pioneering the twistgrip method of throttle control and planning its first twin-cylinder model, the firm gained a new rival named Harley-Davidson. During the next ten years, Indian, Harley and other firms including Excelsior adopted the V-twin engine layout that remains America's favourite to this day.

■ LEFT *The world's first kick-start, situated alongside the rear wheel, was just one of the features pioneered by Yorkshire firm Scott on its two-stroke parallel twin in 1910.*

American firms Indian and Pierce both launched four-cylinder models as early as 1909, but by then the ultra-sophisticated four from Belgian manufacturer FN had already been on the market for four years. Benefiting from an aircooled, 363cc in-line four engine with shaft final drive, the FN was a remarkably smooth and classy device – undoubtedly an early superbike! During two decades of FN production the four's engine capacity was increased to 750cc, and further refinements including a clutch, gearbox and leading-link forks were added to the original design.

Elsewhere, too, technology was leaping ahead. By 1910 the British-built Scott featured not only a watercooled, two-stroke twin engine

■ RIGHT *Despite some faults, Ariel's smooth Square Four of 1937 represented the pinnacle of two-wheeled sophistication before the Second World War.*

but also a kick-start, chain final drive and telescopic front forks. Early four-stroke advances included Harley's use of all-mechanically operated valves, in place of the early inlet-over-exhaust (IOE) design whereby the inlet valve was simply sucked open by the piston. In 1913, another American firm, Cyclone, produced a big V-twin roadster with overhead camshafts. Only a year later, French firm Peugeot had a vertical-twin racebike with twin cams and four-valve cylinder heads.

The American motorcycle industry suffered badly in the years after the First World War, partly due to competition from Henry Ford's ultra-cheap Model T motor car, but in Europe the bike business boomed in the 1920s. English firms such as Matchless, Triumph and Velocette, German marques BMW (whose first flat-twin, the 493cc R32, appeared in 1923) and Zündapp, and Italian manufacturers

■ BELOW *Early BMW flat-twins, such as this 482cc R52 from 1928, established a reputation for cleanliness and reliability that the firm would benefit from for many years.*

Benelli and Moto Guzzi all produced a variety of increasingly sophisticated bikes.

By the late 1930s, motorcycles had evolved into reasonably fast, reliable and easily ridden machines. At the top end of the market was Ariel's Square Four, a luxurious 1000cc tourer. Triumph's 500cc Speed Twin had been launched in 1937, with a parallel twin engine layout that would serve for over 50 years. Glamorous, large-capacity V-twins were being produced by Brough and Vincent in Britain, and by Harley and Indian in America. Barely half a century after Einspur's first faltering trip, motorcycling had well and truly arrived.

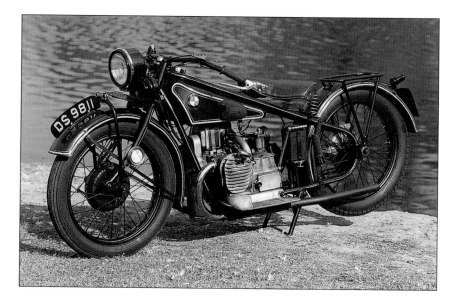

■ OPPOSITE *Several decades of progress are clear in this 1935 London Motorcycle Show publicity shot of a 500cc New Imperial with an 1897 Holden, the world's first four-cylinder bike.*

THE GOLDEN AGE

Motorcycling's rate of progress slowed considerably in the decades following the end of the Second World War. In contrast to those inventive early years, the period spanning the 1940s, 1950s and early 1960s was characterized by numerous singles and twins from the dominant British industry.

In those days, machines like the Norton Dominator, BSA Gold Star, Triumph Thunderbird and Velocette Venom ruled the road. Now these names are enough to arouse misty-eyed nostalgia for an era of blood-and-thunder biking, when traffic was light, noise regulations and speed limits were much less rigorously enforced than today's, and motorcycling was an all-year-round pursuit whose benefits included social alienation and ingrained dirt under the fingernails.

For all the lack of revolutionary change, there was nevertheless a gradual refinement in two-wheeled design. A typical roadster of the late 1940s had no rear suspension, crude girder front forks, a bicycle-style single saddle, a manual ignition advance-retard lever, and a sluggish, low-compression engine that had been designed to run on low-octane wartime fuel. Paint finish was dull, frequently army-surplus camouflage green. Items such as a speedometer, brake light and pillion footrests were still optional extras.

■ BELOW *The Brough Superior's image and reputation for performance lived on through the 1940s and 1950s, long after production of models such as the SS100S had come to an end.*

■ RIGHT *Indian ceased production of its Chief V-twin in 1953, but the firm's subsequent attempt to produce British-style parallel twins was unsuccessful.*

Throughout the 1950s that format was modified through the adoption of brighter colours, telescopic forks, plunger and swing-arm rear suspension, speedos, dual-seats and more sophisticated electrics. Four-stroke engines adopted shorter-stroke dimensions, higher compression and aluminium barrels for added performance and reduced weight. A mid-1950s Triumph or BSA 650cc twin was good for a genuine 100mph (160kph), and handled reasonably well besides.

Britain's bike industry went from strength to strength in the 1950s, with domestic sales rising to a peak of 330,000 in 1959. The Brits also made a big impression in America, where the home industry – suffering from poor direction and lack of small-capacity models – was in serious decline. Of the last two great American manufacturers, Indian built its final big V-twin in 1953, and Harley sold fewer than 10,000 bikes in 1955.

■ RIGHT *This 750cc Norton, shown being given as the prize in a raffle organized by the London-based 59 Club, was a typical British parallel twin of the mid-1960s.*

■ FAR RIGHT *Motorcycling clergyman the Reverend Bill Shergold, pictured here buying a new Triumph, founded the 59 Club and was a prominent figure during British biking's heyday in the 1960s.*

The British firms, however, had more competition from Europe, where German firms BMW and NSU made rapid post-war recoveries. Italian manufacturers including Ducati, Gilera and MV Agusta built rapid 100 and 125cc sportsbikes that were raced in road events such as the Milano-Taranto and Giro d'Italia. Scooters also became increasingly popular, the modest performance of the Vespas and Lambrettas being offset by the advantages of weather protection and, more subjectively, style. By comparison, British small-capacity rivals, mostly powered by two-stroke Villiers engines, were considered terribly dull.

■ OPPOSITE MIDDLE
Triumph's 650cc Bonneville was the most famous British twin.

■ OPPOSITE BELOW
Soichiro Honda, pictured (left) with co-founder Takeo Fujisawa, led Japan's assault on British dominance of the motorcycle market.

■ RIGHT *Triumph's "bathtub" full rear enclosure, introduced on this 350cc Model 21 in 1957, was later used on bigger twins but was unpopular.*

■ LEFT *Velocette's*
500cc Venom carried
the British single-
cylinder tradition into
the 1960s.

In 1965 Honda launched the CB450 twin,
which competed almost head-on with Britain's
traditional parallel twins. Following hard on
Honda's heels Kawasaki, Suzuki and Yamaha
would soon release big motorcycles of their own
– and there was nothing the British firms could
do to stop the erosion of their market lead.

Italy also spearheaded the attack on British
dominance on the racetrack following the
introduction of the world championship series
in 1949. AJS, Norton and Velocette, successful
in the first few seasons, gave way to fours from
Gilera and MV Agusta; in the smaller classes
Moto Guzzi and Mondial battled with
Germany's NSU. On the street Britain was still
in the lead in the mid-1950s, but disaster was
looming for firms whose complacency had led
to a lack of investment and innovation.

As the 1960s arrived, it was the growing
challenge from Japan that held the real danger
to Britain's long-dominant industry. In 1960,
Triumph boss Edward Turner made a now
famous visit to several factories in Japan,
returning to warn – to little avail – of what he
termed as the somewhat frightening spectacle
of its hugely promising and fast-growing
motorcycle firms. By then Honda had already
made a successful first trip to compete in the
Isle of Man TT.

In the showrooms, an expanding range of
well-built and sophisticated small-capacity
motorcycles had been enhanced by the 50cc
C100 scooter, whose famous "You meet the
nicest people on a Honda" slogan would help
attract annual sales of over half a million for
years. Despite what many in the European
industry vainly continued to believe, the
Japanese would not remain content to build
small bikes for long.

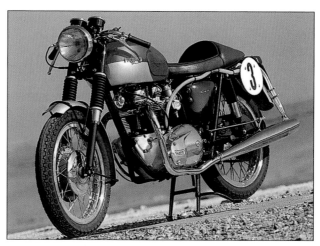

THE MODERN ERA

When Honda introduced the CB750 in 1969, it was not just the Japanese machine's four-cylinder, overhead-cam engine and 120mph (193kph) top speed that heralded the start of motorcycling's modern age. Equally important was the Honda's lavish specification, including an electric starter and front disc brake, and its general air of sophistication. Ironically, Triumph's three-cylinder, 750cc Trident T150, which was launched at the same time, handled at least as well and was slightly faster. But the British bike's pushrod engine, kick-start and drum brakes – plus its dubious reliability and need for frequent maintenance – marked the Triumph as a machine from an earlier era.

Japan had shown the way forward, and the 1970s would belong not just to Honda but to Kawasaki, Suzuki and Yamaha too. Kawasaki

■ LEFT *Ducati's 750 Super Sport (left) and its successor the 900SS, both singleminded race-replicas, were among the fastest and best Italian superbikes of the mid-1970s.*

■ LEFT *Honda's sophisticated CB750 four caused a sensation when it was revealed at the Tokyo Show in late 1968, and again when it was displayed at the Brighton Show shortly afterwards.*

■ BELOW *Suzuki's GS1000 of 1978 proved that the Japanese manufacturers were learning to build chassis strong enough for their mighty engines.*

■ ABOVE *Britain's crumbling hold on the bike market came under further attack in the 1970s when Triumph's Bonneville (left) was faced by Yamaha's XS650.*

■ BELOW LEFT *The Japanese firms' race to build bigger and more powerful superbikes climaxed in 1979 with the massive, six-cylinder Kawasaki Z1300.*

■ BELOW RIGHT *Moto Guzzi's 850 Le Mans Mk.1 V-twin (left) and Kawasaki's 900cc Z1 four offered contrasting brands of 1970s superbiking.*

raised the stakes again in 1973 with the launch of the 900cc Z1, whose muscular twin-cam engine gave 130mph (209kph) top speed with unburstable reliability. The bike they nicknamed the King and its descendants would dominate superbiking for much of the decade.

Not that the Japanese had it all their own way. Britain's industry might have been dying but Italy, in particular, had much to offer. Ducati and Moto Guzzi, each with a distinctive brand of V-twin engine, and Laverda, with powerful 1000cc triples headed by the legendary Jota, all produced memorable mid-1970s superbikes. The Italian bikes' biggest advantage was in handling, for the Japanese firms found chassis harder to perfect than engines. Not until the Suzuki GS1000 appeared in 1978 did Japan build a superbike

that could hold its own in the bends – and even then poor wet-weather performance remained.

Japanese manufacturers also had a "bigger is better" fixation that reached a peak in 1979 with Kawasaki's massive Z1300 six. But there were some excellent small bikes too, including Yamaha's long-running RD series of middleweight two-stroke twins. Smelly strokers fell foul of emission regulations in America, but thrived elsewhere throughout the 1980s. That decade saw Japanese aircooled fours take over the large and medium capacity market to such an extent that the term UJM – Universal Japanese Motorcycle – was coined to describe them. But there were more imaginative designs, too – notably the turbocharged models tried and then abandoned by each of what, by now, were termed as the Big Four.

■ LEFT *Ducati's 916 V-twin and Honda's 750cc V-four, the RC45, updated the two firms' traditional formats to produce stunning mid-1990s superbikes.*

■ BELOW LEFT *Kawasaki's ZZ-R1100 — the ZX-11 in America — was the world's fastest production bike for five years following its launch in 1990.*

More successful 1980s' developments included the increasing fitment of fairings (and luggage systems for tourers), and the adoption of chassis features such as single-shock rear suspension and radial tyres. Aluminium became frequently used in frame construction, following the dynamic arrival of Suzuki's ultra-light GSX-R750 race-replica in 1985.

By 1990 the Japanese had almost univers-ally adopted liquid-cooling for engines, partly to satisfy tightening emission laws. Kawasaki's awesome new ZZ-R1100 had a 16-valve engine producing over 140bhp, a twin-beam alumin-ium frame, a top speed of 175mph (281kph) and levels of handling, roadholding and

■ BELOW *Naked, large-capacity "retro bikes" proved popular with 1990s' riders, and Yamaha's XJR1200 was arguably the pick of the Japanese bunch.*

■ RIGHT *Honda's aggressive CBR600RR four, styled after the firm's MotoGP racer, contrasted with its more versatile CBR600F predecessor. The RR's arrival reflected many riders' desire for high-performance machines for use on circuit track days.*

braking that would have been unthinkable ten years earlier. The best bikes' all-round excellence meant that developments were less dramatic than before, but outstanding machines continued to appear. Honda's CBR900RR of 1992 combined superbike power with light weight. The FireBlade dominated the super-sports world until Yamaha's YZF-R1 and Suzuki's GSX-R1000 arrived on the scene with even more power and less weight.

But not every rider simply wanted speed. From Honda's mighty Gold Wing tourer – introduced as a basic 1000cc flat-four in 1976, now a lavishly equipped 1500cc six – to scooters via sports-tourers, trail-bikes and cruisers, the Japanese built something for almost everyone. As bikes were increasingly used for leisure rather than mere transport, and the average age of riders rose to above 30 in many countries, what some bikers wanted was an unfaired retro-style machine whose appeal was based on simplicity and nostalgia.

One thing most riders seemingly did not want was technology at a premium price.

■ BELOW RIGHT *Trail bikes such as Triumph's Tiger 955i are very popular in some countries. Although capable of being ridden off-road even in difficult conditions, their size and weight ensure that most are used as roadgoing tourers.*

■ BELOW *Rock star Paul Young's custom Harley-Davidson, pictured in London's King's Road, epitomizes the American machines' shift in image from outlaw hog to fashionable accessory.*

Anti-lock brakes were introduced with some success, notably by BMW. But expensive technical tours de force such as Bimota's Tesi and Yamaha's GTS1000 – each with non-telescopic front suspension – and Honda's oval-pistoned NR750 sold in small numbers. That remained true into the 21st century, when manufacturers continued increasing performance,

while sticking to conventional engine and chassis layouts. Technical advances included more sophisticated fuel-injection systems and new aluminium frame casting techniques. But inline four and V-twin engines continued to dominate.

Not that this resulted in a lack of choice for the motorcyclist. Japanese offerings ranged from middleweight fours to giant cruisers that rivalled Harley's ever-popular V-twins. Meanwhile V-twins from Europe's Aprilia and Ducati, triples from Triumph, and flat-twins from BMW offered all-important character to the image-conscious motorcycle market.

INTO THE FUTURE

■ BELOW *Honda's EXP-2 racer did not lead to the production of similar clean-burning two-stroke roadsters.*

Futuristic concept machines appear at many international bike shows. With names like Morpho, Nuda or New American Sports, they attempt to point the way forward for motorcycle design. But while some concept-bike features do eventually make it into real life, predicting the future of the powered two-wheeler is a risky business.

In the near future, bikes are likely to incorporate many of the features already seen in limited numbers. Catalytic converters and fuel-injection systems, rare in the last millennium, are now commonplace. Similarly variable valve timing and programmable, smart-card engine-management systems, as seen on Honda's VFR800FI and the Japanese market NSR250 race-replica have already hit the street and seem likely to become more and more common.

Electric power has been used for several small bikes, including scooters that combine a petrol engine for open roads and batteries for use in town. But batteries are heavy and give limited performance. Their wide-spread adoption in larger motorcycles is still years away.

■ ABOVE *The power characteristics of this Honda NSR250 could instantly be varied by putting a different memory card, which also acted as the ignition key, into the slot in its dashboard.*

■ LEFT *Yamaha's Morpho concept bike, pictured at the Cologne Show in 1990, had futuristic features including forkless front suspension — which was introduced on the GTS1000 two years later.*

■ LEFT *Honda's stunning New American Sports concept bike, unveiled in 2002, combined advanced technology with a fresh approach to styling.*

■ BELOW LEFT *"Showdown" was Spanish student Cesar Muntada's award-winning idea of what a Harley-Davidson roadster might look like in 2020.*

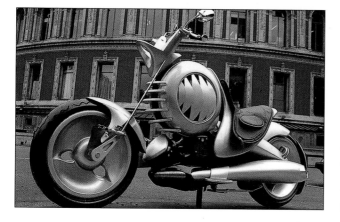

Other firms have been more cautious. In the mid-1990s, Honda debuted an experimental two-stroke racer called the EXP-2 in the Grenada-Dakar Rally. At the time the EXP-2's 402cc, environmentally friendly engine was thought likely to appear in roadgoing form, but this did not happen.

Yamaha learned a hard lesson about advanced chassis technology in the 1990s with the failure of the forkless GTS1000 sports-tourer. More recently Yamaha has developed a promising two-wheel drive system, which has been successfully used on off-road prototypes. But like active suspension, which reacts to bumps using a computer instead of springs, it has yet to feature on production bikes.

Advanced concepts including two-wheel drive, two-wheel steering and hydraulic steering may yet be introduced to showroom models. But motorcycling's immediate future is likely to be based on more down-to-earth factors such as lightness, simplicity and individuality.

More promising is the direct-injection two-stroke engine, which dramatically cuts emissions by injecting fuel directly into the combustion chamber after the exhaust port has closed. Italian firm Aprilia has led the way, but its direct injection engines have so far been restricted to small-capacity scooters.

Bimota, the small Italian firm whose reputation was built on advanced chassis engineering, highlighted the risks involved in putting futuristic technology into production. Having already suffered a financial blow with the failure of its forkless Tesi in the early 1990s, Bimota pressed forward with production of the 500 Vdue, a V-twin two-stroke with direct injection. The Vdue ran poorly, and its failure bankrupted the company.

■ ABOVE *The weight and performance of batteries has so far limited their two-wheeled use, but the 1994 special "Violent Violet" was fast.*

The Rider's View

There is a lot more to motorcycling than simply riding a bike. Owning and using a motorcycle gives a different perspective on life to that of the average pedestrian or car driver. Depending on the rider, the machine and the moment, you are an individual – free, rebellious, fast-moving, glamorous, somehow above the dull troubles of the normal world. You're also mistrusted, maybe persecuted, even pitied, always vulnerable.

Those shared emotions produce a bond between motorcyclists that can sometimes bridge the huge gaps between the many different types of rider. Many's the time that the owner of a superbike has pulled up to help a novice with a broken moped. But within the overall two-wheeled scene is a vast number of diverse subgroups and cultures, reflecting the variety of experience that motorcycling has to offer.

MODS, ROCKERS & ANGELS

The bad boy image has been an integral part of motorcycling for years, and probably always will be. Bikes are a potent symbol of speed, rebellion and youthful aggression. And despite the ever-increasing numbers of respectable, leisure-time riders, many people still view motorcyclists as undesirable and outside the law.

In the 1960s the main cause of the bad reputation, particularly in Britain, were the Rockers. Generally dressed in studded black leather jackets, jeans and black boots, they met at cafés such as the Ace, in north London, and Johnsons, near Brands Hatch circuit in Kent, to drink tea, talk bikes and go street-racing. Favoured machinery included BSA Gold Stars,

■ LEFT *Probationary patch-club members have to earn the right to wear full colours on their backs.*

■ BELOW *The Ace Café in north London was the famous meeting-place of café racers and Rockers in the 1960s.*

Triumph Bonnevilles, Norton Dominators and the legendary Triumph/Norton hybrid the Triton, generally with tuned motors, lightened chassis and turned-down Ace handlebars.

When the Ace regulars were not racing against each other or outrunning a Daimler V-eight police car, a popular trick was to put an Elvis or Eddie Cochran single on the jukebox, then run out to the bike and attempt to complete a pre-set road circuit before the disc ended. Despite plenty of brushes with the law, the Rockers were more into bikes than violence. Even so, their bank-holiday seafront battles with their rivals the Mods – scooter riders dressed smartly in suits and anoraks – made national news regularly in the 1960s.

The Hell's Angels, whose notoriety peaked at about the same time, were a different and much more dangerous proposition. Formed in 1950 in San Bernardino, California, but later best known through the chapter based in Oakland, near San Francisco, the Angels were by far the biggest and most powerful of the many American outlaw bike groups that included Satan's

■ RIGHT *Most British café racers of the 1960s wore open-face helmets and leather jackets, and rode singles or parallel twins with low "Ace" handlebars.*

■ BELOW *A leather-jacketed Rocker is led away by a policeman after a clash with scooter-riding Mods at Margate, on England's south coast, in 1964.*

■ OPPOSITE
America's veterans of the Vietnam War have their own motorcycle club, complete with Angel-style colours and regalia.

Slaves, Gypsy Jokers and Commancheros.

Angel fever spread worldwide, and numerous chapters still exist in Europe and elsewhere. But their profile is much lower than it was in the 1960s when the Angels, famously dirty, wearing their ever-present colours – the winged-and-helmeted skull symbol – and riding chopped Harley-Davidsons, became a feared force through clashes with police and civilians. They were immortalized in films including *Hell's Angels on Wheels* and *Hell's Angels '69*, both of which starred genuine members of the Oakland Angels, and in Hunter S Thompson's memorable book *Hell's Angels*.

■ RIGHT *The film* Hell's Angels '69 *starred members of the Oakland Angels, the most powerful and best-known of California's numerous groups, or "chapters".*

MOTORCYCLES IN THE MOVIES

There's no more vivid way of charting motor-cycling's changing image than through its portrayal on film. Bikes have starred in the movies since the likes of *No Limit*, improbably featuring ukulele-playing George Formby at the Isle of Man TT, and *Motorcycle Squad*, about a bike cop who joins a gang of criminals, were released in the 1930s.

The most famous bike film is *The Wild One*, Stanley Kramer's 1953 classic starring Marlon Brando and Lee Marvin. Triumph-riding Brando and Harley-mounted Marvin played rival bike-gang leaders in a film loosely based on the events that occurred in 1947 at Hollister, California, where a minority of motorcyclists at a big rally caused trouble. The film was controversial enough to be banned in Britain for 15 years. It inspired teenagers, horrified their parents and formed attitudes that last to this day.

Later films featuring dubious biking characters include *The Leather Boys*, a British period piece from the 1960s, and *Girl On A*

Motorcycle, starring Marianne Faithfull. The 1960s also produced *Easy Rider*. The story featured Peter Fonda, Dennis Hopper and Jack Nicholson riding across America on a pair of chopped Harleys, complete with drugs, rednecks and music by Steppenwolf and others, and remains a classic biker film.

Another of the better efforts is the 1974 Australian production *Stone*, which features excellent street-race footage as well as outlaw gang fights. *Mad Max*, the Australian film that shot Mel Gibson to stardom in 1979, also has

■ LEFT *Jack Nicholson (left) and Peter Fonda rode a Harley across America with Dennis Hopper in Easy Rider, the ultimate 1960s' bike movie.*

■ ABOVE *Marianne Faithfull turned plenty of heads in the 1968 film* Girl on a Motorcycle, *also released with the title* Naked Under Leather.

■ ABOVE *Marlon Brando, here with co-star Mary Murphy and his 650cc Triumph Thunderbird, caused outrage as bike-club leader Johnny in* The Wild One.

■ RIGHT *Silver Dream Racer combined a couple of songs from lead star David Essex with road-race action footage shot at Brands Hatch and Donington Park in Britain.*

its share of bike action. Other big names in films with two-wheeled interest include Mickey Rourke and Don Johnson, stars of *Harley-Davidson and the Marlboro Man*. A Harley also makes the title of the 1973 movie *Electra Glide in Blue*, which stars Richard Blake as a bike cop with an attitude problem.

Films about bike sport are headed by *On Any Sunday*, which stars Steve McQueen, already the veteran of a bike chase in *The Great Escape*, plus racers Malcolm Smith and Mert Lawwill, and conveys the thrill of dirt-track and desert racing. Robert Redford makes a fair off-road racer in *Little Fauss and Big Halsy*. Motorcycling has no road-race movies to compare with four-wheel epics such as *Grand Prix* and *Le Mans*. But both *Silver Dream Racer*, the 1979 British film starring David Essex, and *Race For Glory*, its 1989 American equivalent, include some reasonable action footage.

RIDING THE CLASSICS

Of all the two-wheeled trends of recent years, the growth of classic biking is perhaps the most dramatic. For most of the motorcycle's life, the classic concept has barely existed. To most riders, old bikes have simply been that: old bikes. Interesting and useful to a degree, but generally less desirable than the superior machines of the day.

That attitude began to change in the 1970s, as Japanese bikes took over the motorcycle market and an increasing number of enthusiasts became nostalgic for the old-fashioned, mainly British, machines of the past. The launch of *Classic Bike* magazine in 1979 reflected a growing demand, although at that time few people could have imagined the way in which interest would snowball.

These days classics are a major part of the motorcycling scene, above all in the UK. There is a wide choice of specialist magazines, each

full of advertisements from firms who sell, maintain, restore, make bits for or insure classic machinery. Complete Nortons – Manx racers and Commandos – are built from new parts. Many European dealers specialize in importing British and Japanese bikes from

■ ABOVE *Veteran machines from motorcycling's earliest years set off on the annual Pioneer Run, from London to Brighton on England's south coast.*

■ LEFT *The annual Classic Bike Show at Stafford, England has become a huge event, with club and trade stands, an autojumble, auction and concourse contest.*

■ **ABOVE LEFT** *Some modern-day classic riders prefer to dress in period fashion, although old-style headgear offers little protection from injury or the law.*

■ **ABOVE RIGHT** *Recreations of long-distance classic events such as Italy's Milano-Taranto give owners of old machines a perfect opportunity for a run.*

■ **RIGHT** *Demand for classics such as this Indian Chief has led to the emergence of many firms specializing in the restoration of bikes and production of spares.*

American states where the combination of consistently high sales figures and a kind climate has left clean old machines in abundance.

And there is a huge choice of events for classic bikes, too, from club runs and race meetings to shows and concourse contests. At the latter, fanatical officials dock points for a restoration that uses over-polished alloy or slightly the wrong shade of maroon on a side-panel. Bikes restored to factory standard – or, better still, with a verifiably interesting history – are highly desirable and change hands for vast sums of money.

The question of how to define a classic bike causes much heated discussion. To some hard-liners only British bikes qualify; others accept American and European machines too. One of the fastest-growing organizations of all is the Vintage Japanese Motorcycle Club, which caters for owners of Japanese bikes over 15 years old and has more than 4,000 members.

Things are more precisely defined for really old bikes, for which long-running organizations such as the Vintage Motor Cycle Club have established rules. Veteran bikes are defined by the VMCC as those built before 1915; vintage as made between 1915 and 1930; and post-vintage as between 1931 and 1945.

At the other end of the scale are those riders who prefer their classics straight out of a crate. They can choose from most Harley-Davidsons, numerous retro-styled Japanese bikes, and Triumph's classic models including the Bonneville parallel twin. All combine the advantages of modern engineering with the look and at least some of the nostalgic appeal of the originals.

THE GEAR

Modern motorcycle clothing is almost as sophisticated as the bikes themselves. These days a serious rider wears a full-face helmet made from lightweight composite materials, and brightly-coloured, one-piece protective leathers. The well-dressed motorcyclist is likely to draw some suspicious looks if found wandering around on foot.

■ ABOVE *Marlon Brando's role in the controversial movie* The Wild One *stamped the image of a tough biker in jeans and black leather jacket on the public consciousness.*

■ LEFT *Although it's expensive, the best of modern racing (left) and touring clothing is stylish, comfortable and provides protection from head to toe.*

■ ABOVE *This leather suit's neck hump, designed to smooth the air-flow, gives a tiny speed increase to a 125cc racer but is of dubious benefit for road use.*

■ ABOVE *A two-piece touring suit usually has a zip to hold jacket and trousers together, reducing draughts and increasing protection.*

Riding gear was very different in biking's early years, when motorcyclists wore cloth caps and tweed jackets, just as they had for riding the bicycles from which many early machines were developed. Before the Second World War many riders' kit comprised nothing more specialized than a back-to-front cap and pair of goggles. Others would wear a leather flying helmet, and maybe a leather trenchcoat, heavy leather gauntlets and thick boots.

After the War, motorcyclists began to adopt a uniform of ex-airforce flying jackets and boots, with various items of army-surplus clothing being used for bad-weather gear. Crash

■ RIGHT *Modern off-road and bad-weather riding gear makes use of man-made fabrics such as Goretex and Kevlar to provide strength and weather protection.*

■ BOTTOM *The black leather jacket is the classic biker uniform — often customized with badges, patches, lettering and studs.*

■ ABOVE *Geoff Duke was among the first of the racers to wear wind-cheating one-piece leathers in the 1950s.*

■ ABOVE *Before the Second World War bike riders usually wore goggles, a cap, a coat, leather gauntlets and a pair of stout shoes.*

Leather suits became increasingly popular in the 1970s. Full-face helmets were common by then but their easily-scratched visors made night riding difficult, and waterproofs that lived up to their name were rare.

By the 1990s full leathers were common-place among serious riders, with many firms offering wide ranges of colourful one- and two-piece designs. Many modern suits incorporate sophisticated body armour; racers and some road riders wear spine-protectors too. Helmets feature sophisticated air vents and long-lasting anti-scratch visors.

Bad-weather clothing ranges from simple unlined waterproofs to elaborate suits, made from breathable, man-made fibres, featuring high-visibility reflective patches, detachable linings and padding of their own. In cold weather riders can switch on electrically heated gloves, vests or full suits. Modern motorcycling gear isn't cheap, but the best of it is extremely effective.

helmets, which had been used for racing since the 1930s, became more common among road riders, and the early leather-sided pudding-basin design was gradually superseded by a more protective open-face style.

Black leather jackets were popular with American motorcyclists by the early 1950s, and hit the big time with the release of *The Wild One* in 1953. Marlon Brando's character Johnny, in his turned-up jeans and double-breasted Schott jacket, epitomised this classic style along with James Dean, Elvis and others. Over the years the basic item has been added to and modified with various tassels, patches, badges and metal studs, but its essential appeal – and attitude – remains.

TOURING

Motorcycle touring means different things to
different people. From a gentle weekend trip to
an epic journey around the world; from a
professionally planned expedition involving
dozens of riders, to the result of one person's
sudden urge simply to get on a motorbike and
ride. The beauty of touring by motorbike is that
the journey itself is as much a part of the
experience as the stops.

■ BELOW *Big cruisers
are not the most
comfortable or practical
way to travel, but they
can cover long distances
enjoyably if you don't
mind taking your time.*

With its unique ability to cover reasonably
large distances while immersing its rider in his
or her surroundings, the motorcycle is perfect
for explorers. Ted Simon, author of *Jupiter's
Travels*, the best-selling story of a four-year
trans-world ride on a 500cc Triumph twin in
the 1970s, wrote of his gut feelings about how
he wanted to travel. He instinctively knew his
transport had to be a motorcycle, even though
he had neither bike nor licence before
planning his trip.

Simon chose the Triumph Tiger partly out of
patriotism and partly because it was fairly light
while relatively simple and solid—a positive
boon when it came to repairs. Similar thinking
has led many more recent two-wheeled
explorers to use single-cylinder trail bikes
such as Honda's XL600 and Yamaha's XT600
Ténéré. Others accept the extra weight of
BMW's long-running boxer twins, notably the
dual-purpose R80 and R100GS models, to gain
the benefits of increased comfort and shaft
final drive. Husband and wife team Richard
and Mopsa English also opted for an old

■ ABOVE *Many riders' favourite touring mount is a big BMW fitted with fairing, top-box and panniers.*

■ RIGHT *Norway provides tourers with some excellent roads, and breathtaking views.*

■ BELOW *Ireland's charm makes it a great country for touring, and a big slow-revving Moto Guzzi California is an ideal bike on which to travel.*

Triumph twin for the round-the-world trip described in their book *Full Circle*, but they added a large sidecar too.

Choosing the basic motorcycle is merely the first step in preparing for a very long tour, particularly one through difficult terrain. Any bike will require modification, notably to enable it to carry the large amount of luggage necessary. Solid fibreglass or preferably aluminium panniers may be fitted, in conjunction with soft luggage of leather, plastic or canvas. Many riders fit home-made metal racks that hold cans for spare fuel and water. Other common modifications include large-capacity fuel tanks, oil-coolers and protective engine bash-plates, extra fuel filters and heavy duty wheel-rims and spokes.

■ ABOVE *Many riders would argue that America's wealth of magnificent scenery is best appreciated from the saddle of a well-laden Harley-Davidson.*

Purpose-built tourers such as Honda's Gold Wing, Yamaha's Venture or Harley's Electra Glide make life easier with fairings, big seats and easily detachable luggage facilities, and often provide accessories such as stereos, electrical sockets, cruise control and foot-boards. But small and apparently unsuitable bikes can be used successfully – provided factors such as route, daily distances and luggage are chosen accordingly.

Riders wishing to venture further afield without the time and expense of buying, preparing and possibly transporting a bike can turn to a growing number of specialist firms. Some offer just bike hire, but many provide complete motorcycling package tours for which the cost usually includes a local guide, food and accommodation, plus a following vehicle to carry excess luggage and deal with problems. Whether you want to ride a BMW in the Alps, a Harley-Davidson across America or an Enfield Bullet through India, there is a firm that can arrange it.

Several manufacturers have seen the potential for organized excursions, too. Honda's Transalp Rallies provided a good excuse for European owners to test their XL600Vs' dual-purpose ability, and Honda has also arranged longer, more road-oriented trips for the ST1100 sports-tourer. Harley-Davidson tours have included an 80-strong excursion to Norway's Nordkapp, deep inside the Arctic Circle. Best of all were the series of Spirit of Adventure trips organized by Yamaha for owners of Ténéré and Super Ténéré trail-bikes. These were demanding treks, in Egypt, Mexico, America and Australia, which gave owners the opportunity to ride through harsh and often beautiful terrain, with organization, riding gear, machinery and back-up – including a medical helicopter – taken care of.

None of those things is necessary for an average bike tourer, whose trip maybe lasts for two weeks in Europe or America and is all on tarmac roads. Most medium or large-capacity bikes can be pressed into service for an annual touring holiday, merely with the addition of a tank-bag, a set of throw-over panniers and perhaps a rucksack either worn by the pillion passenger or strapped to the empty seat.

■ RIGHT *A tank-bag and pair of throw-over panniers can transform even a simple unfaired roadster such as Triumph's Trident 900 into a capable tourer.*

■ BELOW *Yamaha's series of Spirit of Adventure trips gave owners of the firm's trail bikes the opportunity to ride them in remote places such as central Australia.*

Motorcycles and their Anatomy

Few motorcyclists are prepared simply to ride their bikes and leave them alone the rest of the time. Most riders are enthusiasts, far more knowledgeable about their machines than the average car driver. The majority positively enjoy maintaining, tuning, customizing or adapting their bikes in some way, whether to improve performance, enhance looks or to make theirs different from everyone else's.

In the early years regular work was absolutely unavoidable, as bikes were mostly used as a cheap form of transport, and needed frequent maintenance that in most cases only the rider was able to provide. As bikes improved, and basic servicing was increasingly carried out by professionals, keen owners could always think of ways to improve their machines. Even now, with standard bikes better and more reliable than ever before, the opportunity to spend large amounts of time and money on them is undiminished.

CAFE RACERS AND SPECIALS

Specials are arguably the most exciting and glamorous bikes of all. The term essentially means something hand-built, either a one-off or a small series of similar machines. Some are notable mainly for their unusual design – bikes with two engines or radical suspension, some created as much for the engineering challenge as for pure performance. But most specials are built for speed, and that certainly goes for café racers. The tuned-up sportsbike with low handlebars and a single seat remains one of motorcycling's most vivid images.

BSA's Gold Star Clubman of the late 1950s and early 60s was arguably the first café racer, although the legendary 500cc single was not

■ ABOVE *In 1974, when superbike riders wore open-faced helmets and flared jeans, Dunstall's Honda and Kawasaki fours were among the ultimate café racers.*

■ LEFT *The most successful 1960s special was the Triton, a fast and fine-handling blend of Triumph parallel twin engine and Norton Featherbed frame.*

■ BELOW *Some specials,
such as this four-cylinder
Triumph powered by a
side-by-side pair of
750cc Bonneville
engines, are built more
for show than for go.*

■ RIGHT *BSA's 500cc
Gold Star, complete
with "Ace" handlebars
and filterless Amal
carburettor, had few
rivals as a café racer
during the early 1960s.*

■ BELOW *The
handsome red special
built by German firm
AMC was among the
best of many recent
sportsbikes powered by
Harley-Davidson's
V-twin engine.*

actually a special but a standard factory-built model. Twins from BSA, Norton and Triumph took over in the 1960s, and were frequently modified with clip-on handlebars, rear-set footrests, alloy fuel tanks and free-breathing exhaust systems. Many parts were provided by engineers such as Paul Dunstall, whose Norton-powered Dunstall Dominator was a 1960s classic.

The archetypal café racer was the Triton, the blend of Triumph engine and Norton Featherbed frame that gave the best of British power and handling. Some riders combined Triumph motor and BSA chassis to form a Tribsa, or housed a Vincent V-twin engine in a Featherbed frame to produce the exotic Norvin.

The era of the café-race special continued when Japanese bikes took over in the 1970s. Honda's CB750 and then Kawasaki's Z900 and Z1000 provided seemingly endless four-cylinder horsepower, but early models were let down by their handling. Established British chassis specialists such as Dresda and Dunstall, plus others including Rickman, Harris, Fritz Egli from Switzerland, Bimota of Italy and Georges Martin from France, developed racy chassis kits for the big fours.

Engine tuning also featured highly in the café-racer cult over the years. State-of-the-art motors progressed from Bonneville lumps with ported heads and open-mouthed Amal carbs, via Yoshimura-tuned GS1000 Suzukis to modern turbocharged Kawasaki ZZ-R1100s. Harley-Davidson's long-standing lack of a sportsbike led to dozens of firms building V-twin sportsters of their own in a variety of styles.

■ BELOW *By far the most popular custom bike powerplant is Harley-Davidson's V-twin, here used to good effect by Dutch chassis specialist Nico Bakker.*

CUSTOM CYCLES

To some riders, the way a bike looks is far more important than the way it rides. A motorcycle can be an art form – a sculpture on two wheels – a chrome-plated, custom-painted, elaborately engraved celebration of style and individuality that may be difficult to control due to over-long forks, a hard-tail rear end, a massively wide rear tyre or a combination of all three.

The best custom bikes, built by visionaries such as California-based legend Arlen Ness, challenge existing concepts with intricate engineering and new images. Their influence can be seen in the thousands of less radical customized bikes at Daytona Beach or Sturgis, each sporting aftermarket parts chosen to make a machine stand out from the crowd.

Ironically, the custom movement began in America in the 1940s and 1950s when Harley riders began to strip their bikes of unnecessary accessories, mainly in search of improved performance, to produce machines known as bobbers. Modifying the chassis by kicking out the front forks for extra stability became popular, and in the 1960s this was increasingly taken to extremes with longer and longer forks,

■ RIGHT *Much of a custom bike's appeal is in the quality of its finish, and paintwork is often done by experts such as Californian Jeff McCann.*

■ BELOW *The Harley ridden by Peter Fonda in Easy Rider, with its ape-hanger bars, long forks and lack of front brake, summed-up the late 1960s custom style.*

often holding a bicycle-thin front wheel with no brake. The classic late 1960s custom was the chopped Harley with high, pull-back handlebars, massively extended forks and hard-tail (ie, unsprung) rear end, as ridden by Peter Fonda's character, Captain America, in the film *Easy Rider*.

In the mid-1970s Ness, who had progressed from painting bikes to building complete machines, was central in popularizing a new custom look, with lower handlebars, short forks and a long, low-slung chassis reminiscent of a drag-racer's. Ness's Bay Area style (his shop was in San Leandro, near San Francisco)

■ LEFT *Arlen Ness has become known as the master Harley customizer, having repeatedly introduced new styles with a string of imaginative machines.*

■ BELOW *Sometimes custom bikes are treated as art, as when British customizer Uncle Bunt's Yamaha formed part of a Birmingham exhibition in 1994.*

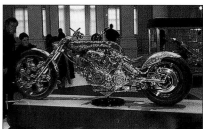

■ ABOVE *Harley-Davidsons are frequently referred to as hogs, but this customized V-twin looks as though it would be more at home in a cattle market.*

■ BELOW *For those who don't like fancy paint and shiny chrome, building a ratbike provides the perfect opportunity to let the imagination run wild.*

normally centred on a tuned Harley V-twin engine with open-mouthed carburettors, intricate exhaust pipes and names like Kwik Silver, Accel Bike and Strictly Business. Harleys have always been the most popular bikes for customizing, with Honda's CB750 making an impression in the 1970s and Triumph twins retaining a loyal following.

That remains true today, as Harley-Davidson itself has recognized in recent years with a wide variety of niche models and an array of factory accessories. Specialist customizing shops have thrived, too, offering everything from chrome-plated footpegs to hard-tail frames and complete machines. And although most modern custom bikes are merely Harleys with a few bolt-on parts, there will always be individuals dedicated to building motorcycles with a radical and eye-catching look.

SIDECARS AND TRIKES

Many modern motorcyclists regard sidecars as strange contraptions that lack both the motorbike's advantages of mobility and performance, and the car's benefits of comfort and convenience. In these days of relatively cheap cars, it certainly is difficult to make a logical argument for three-wheeled travel. But both sidecars and three-wheelers are still popular — albeit with a minority — not for practical reasons but simply because they are different and fun.

The three-wheeler's attraction has traditionally been more down-to-earth. Very early examples included Edward Butler's pioneering Petrol-Cycle of 1888. In the 1920s, three-

■ **LEFT** *This BSA's large sidecar provided generous, fairly weather-proof and relatively cheap transportation in 1924, when the outfit was employed as a taxi.*

■ **FAR LEFT** *Many solo riders consider sidecars rather dull, but they can provide plenty of entertainment, even when bolted to a humble 500cc BSA trials bike.*

transport was a big single-cylinder Panther bike weighed down by an enormous double-adult unit alongside, loaded with children. The same decade saw the bubble cars, tiny enclosed three-wheelers made by firms including German aircraft manufacturers

■ **BELOW** *A Princess sidecar was a popular addition to Indian's Chief V-twin in 1936, and treated its passenger to a leather seat and a very comfortable ride.*

wheelers such as the Morgan and Coventry Victor, generally with two wheels up front and one behind, offered good performance at a low price and even led some observers to predict that they would take over from bikes altogether. In the 1930s the opposite layout became more popular in America, where Indian's Despatch Tow and Harley's Servicar — basically a 45ci model with a large box between two rear wheels — served as small-scale pick-up trucks.

In Britain the sidecar's popularity peaked in the 1950s, when the typical mode of family

■ BELOW *Custom trikes powered by big V-eight car engines are a frequent sight at gatherings such as Daytona — for some owners, the bigger the better.*

■ ABOVE *The Californian-made Flexit sidecar, here fitted to a Triumph Trophy 1200, featured a linkage system that allowed it to lean with the bike in bends.*

Heinkel and Messerschmitt. Cheap cars spelt the beginning of the end for three-wheeled travel by the 1960s. But machines such as the Bond Bug and Reliant Robin, increasingly car-like in looks if not stability, were produced for some years afterwards.

These days the only three-wheelers still in production are enthusiasts' machines, such as the Triking, whose transverse V-twin Moto Guzzi engine, exposed between two front wheels, gives the look of an early Morgan. Other idiosyncratic offerings along similar lines are the JZR, powered by Honda's CX500 V-twin, and the Lomax, which uses the engine, chassis and suspension from Citroen's 2CV car. More upmarket is the sporty Grinnall Scorpion, whose four-cylinder BMW K1100 engine gives a top speed of 130mph (208kph).

True sidecars remain popular in Continental Europe, especially Germany, where fully-enclosed and often lavishly equipped modern devices can be seen alongside colour-matched superbikes such as Honda's CBR1000 or Yamaha's FJ1200. Among the most exotic is the Krauser Domani, a futuristic and expensive BMW-powered device that resembles a Grand

Prix kneeling sidecar. Perhaps the most unlikely – and exciting – is the Flexit, a Californian creation whose linkage system allows bike and sidecar to lean in parallel through corners, in similar fashion to the Flxicar racers of the 1920s.

BELOW *In the 1920s, when it was not done for a young lady to ride pillion, a chap's best hope was to fit his Triumph with a Gloria sidecar.*

ARMY BIKES

The motorcycle's speed and manoeuvrability has made it an important tool in wartime, and the "iron horse" has been used to good effect from the First World War to recent times. Bikes of many types and nationalities have been converted for fighting use with camouflage paint schemes, modifications for extra strength and reliability, and even fitment of machine-guns – sometimes in a sidecar alongside, sometimes on a solo for use by the rider alone.

British forces in the First World War used a variety of bikes, mainly for reconnaissance and communications work. Triumph supplied the Army with 30,000 units of its three-speed Model H; Douglas built almost as many of its sturdy horizontal twin; and P&M supplied the Royal Flying Corps with its 3.5bhp, two-speed single. German forces also used bikes, notably after production of the four-cylinder Belgian

FN had been taken over by the occupying German Army.

Germany's best-known bike in the Second World War was the BMW R75, which normally came fitted with a sidecar and later starred in many war films. Moto Guzzi also produced several military models such as the Alce and

■ ABOVE *A Canadian rider and his Harley WLC are the centre of youthful interest in 1941, in the grounds of an English country house used as a Brigade headquarters.*

■ LEFT *These British Army riders, splashing their single-cylinder machines through a ford, are taking part in a training exercise in Essex in 1941.*

■ LEFT *This captured Second World War BMW flat-twin and sidecar gave three British RAF mechanics the chance of a ride at Sidi Rezegh, Libya in 1942.*

■ RIGHT *BSA's M20 was useful for delivering copies of an Army newspaper to South African troops based in a remote part of the Western Desert in 1942.*

■ LEFT *A military bike enthusiast poses in suitable attire with his neatly restored Triumph Model C, built in 1914 and a veteran of the First World War.*

■ BELOW *French Army troops, waiting for embarkation orders at a British port in June 1944, on Harleys with rifles mounted alongside the front wheel.*

Airone, which were flat-singles of 500 and 250cc. The bigger bike often dragged a sidecar, and was also made as a three-wheeler called the Trialce. An early predecessor of Guzzi's current transverse V-twin engine was used to power a small armoured car.

Most of the bikes produced for the Second World War were simple 350cc singles from Matchless, Norton and Triumph, but the best-known Allied bikes were the American-made V-twins: Indian's 500cc Model 741 Military Scout and Harley's 750cc WLA 45. The Harley, in particular, was churned out in huge numbers – at one point in 1942 the Milwaukee factory was building 750 a week, for use by Russian and Chinese armies as well as by the Americans, Canadians and British. After the war many ex-army 45s were converted to civilian use, and did much to increase Harley's worldwide popularity.

Even in these days of ultra-sophisticated weaponry, many forces still have a role for the humble motorbike. Harley-Davidson's 350cc military machine, powered by a single-cylinder Rotax two-stroke engine, is exported to forces including the British Army. Basically a sturdy trail bike with panniers around its front wheel and a rifle rack on the back, the Harley is mainly used for reconnaissance work and convoy duties. Its predecessor, the 500cc Armstrong, played a role in the Gulf War, as did Italian-made Cagivas and Husqvarnas.

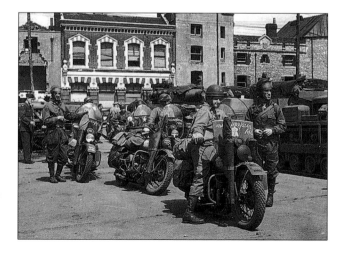

THE MOTORCYCLE AT WORK

For many riders motorcycling is not just a hobby but a job. Bikes are used for a variety of work – in most cases because their combination of open-road speed and ability to cut through traffic is unmatched by any other form of transport. The attraction of being paid to ride a bike draws many enthusiastic motorcyclists to try despatch riding, although for many the reality of riding all day in all weathers fails to match the dream. Some riders in cities around the world have found alternative employment as a two-wheeled taxi service whose journey times beat those of any conventional cab.

Police motorcyclists are some of the most visible two-wheeled workers, and use a huge variety of specially adapted bikes. Best known is the Harley-Davidson V-twin, as used by American forces for many years, including in a lead role in the film *Electra Glide in Blue*.

■ LEFT *The comfort, performance and reliability of BMW's boxer twins helped make them popular with police forces in many countries for years.*

■ LEFT *American forces, such as the California Highway Patrol, have traditionally used Harleys, although Kawasaki fours were popular in the 1980s.*

■ **ABOVE LEFT** *Grand Prix stars and Riders for Health charity workers Randy Mamola (hidden, left) and Kevin Schwantz (right) visit Lesotho in 1992.*

■ **ABOVE RIGHT** *Many national organizations such as Britain's Post Office run fleets of small-capacity bikes, like Honda's single-cylinder RS250, for city-centre use.*

■ **FAR RIGHT** *Despatch riders are a familiar sight on many city streets, normally loaded with luggage and carving through the traffic with practised ease and confidence.*

Traditionally a large-capacity road model converted with a single seat, radio equipment, extra identification lights, first-aid kit, fire extinguisher and weather protection, the police bike often ends up being rather heavy – although small bikes are commonly used for urban duties.

Almost every major manufacturer produces at least one model aimed at the lucrative police force market. Among the most common have been the Triumph Saint 650cc parallel twin of the 1960s; the Kawasaki Z1000 four that was popular in America in the 1980s and featured in the popular *CHiPs* television series about the California Highway Patrol; and the BMW flat-twin, which in various guises has been in police use, in Germany and other countries, for many decades.

Other two-wheeled workers include those from the motoring rescue services, whose first response to a breakdown call is often by bike, and the organizations that transport blood and other urgently needed medical supplies to hospitals. Motorcycling paramedics, carrying a wide range of life-saving equipment, can often reach road-crash or heart-attack victims before an ambulance – sometimes with life-saving results. It has been known for local midwives to find mopeds or motorcycles to be the quickest and most efficient way to travel.

Motorcycles also perform a vital service in less developed countries, where they provide otherwise impossible mobility to health workers and teachers. Riders For Health, the motorcycling charity backed by leading Grand Prix racers including Randy Mamola, works in African countries teaching local riders how to use and maintain their machines so that they can reach remote areas whenever needed.

■ **RIGHT** *Motorcycling paramedics can reach emergencies quickly on machines such as this Norton rotary, fitted with a variety of life-saving equipment.*

ANATOMY OF A MOTORCYCLE

A motorcycle's essential ingredients may simply be two wheels and an engine, but its design can go in any direction from there. Bikes vary from the latest Grand Prix missile to the earliest roadster; from a high-tech sports-tourer to a humble commuter machine. Over the years motorcycles have been powered by batteries, by rockets, even by the sun. They have used vastly different frames, bodywork, suspension, seating and engine positions.

But that's only a tiny minority, and most motorbikes are essentially very similar. Since the New Werner in 1901, the predominant layout of motor and riding position has been unchanged. Piston engines, in both two-stroke and four-stroke form, have powered the vast majority of bikes since even before then. A handful of basic systems has been adapted and updated over the years to provide suspension, braking, roadholding, and sometimes weather-protection or luggage-carrying ability.

The days when all motorcyclists needed to be knowledgeable about the workings of their temperamental machines are gone. Modern technology and production efficiency ensures that most modern bikes are reliable, oil-tight and require minimal maintenance. They increasingly feature sophisticated electronics, engine-management systems and parts requiring specialist tools – so it's not surprising that many modern riders rely on a professional for all but the most simple mechanical work. But beneath the neon-coloured plastic and the manufacturers' publicity claims, most bikes work in much the same way they have for years.

Ducati's World Superbike racing championships have played a big part in the firm's recent sales success

Removing the cover reveals a pillion seat — and unusually for a sports-bike, the 900SS has a passenger grab-rail too

Ducati's tubular steel ladder frame uses the engine to add rigidity

Like the front forks, the single shock absorber is made by Japanese specialist Showa, and is adjustable for spring preload plus both compression and rebound damping

The cantilever style aluminium swing-arm operates the shock unit directly, rather than via rising-rate linkage as used by many modern bikes

A small single brake disc is adequate at the rear, as forward weight transfer under hard braking makes the back wheel lock up very easily

Tyres are both low-profile radials, the rear being much wider than the front to cope with the forces of acceleration

Twin silencers are large to meet strict noise limits — although the 900SS retains Ducati's traditional V-twin exhaust note

■ BELOW *Ducati's 900SS, here with the lower part of its fairing removed, combines the Italian marque's traditional V-twin engine and tubular steel frame with many features typical of a modern sportsbike.*

Handlebars are set low to give a wind-cheating riding position

Fairing and screen protect the rider from the elements, and help give a top speed of over 135mph (216kph) despite the engine's fairly modest 80bhp output

A large airbox is crucial to engine performance, with the result that much of what looks like a large fuel tank contains only air

Twin Mikuni carburettors are situated in the crook of the engine's Vee

The Ducati's fork angle, or rake, is 25 degrees — fairly steep, to give quick and light steering, but not dramatically so by modern sportsbike standards

Front forks are the "upside-down" type currently fitted to most sports machines, with the thicker and more rigid outer section at the top

Twin discs are large at 320mm in diameter, can "float" on their mountings to allow for expansion when hot, and are gripped by four-piston calipers whose large pad area provides maximum braking power

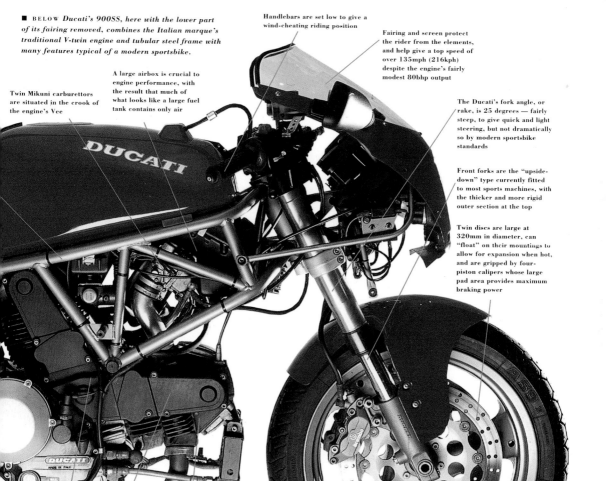

An oil-cooler helps control the temperature of the engine, which is cooled by a mixture of air and oil

Drive to the desmodromic engine's single overhead camshaft is by toothed rubber belt

The longitudinal V-twin engine's cylinders are spaced at 90 degrees, with the front "pot" angled almost horizontally to aid cooling

The 900SS's cylinder heads have two valves each, instead of the four-valves-per-cylinder layout more common on high performance bikes, and feature Ducati's desmodromic system of positive valve closure

Like most sportsbikes' front wheels, the Ducati's is made from cast aluminium and is 17 inches in diameter

Anatomy of a Motorcycle

SUCK-SQUEEZE-BANG-BLOW

The four-stroke engine is named after its four basic operations: induction, compression, combustion and exhaust. Invented by Dr Nikolaus Otto and also known as the Otto Cycle, the four-stroke principle has been motorcycling's mainstay throughout this century. While such elements as valve train

■ RIGHT *This four-cylinder, 16-valve cylinder head from BMW's K1 is disass-embled to show its twin camshafts and valves, their springs and the "buckets" operated by the camshaft lobes.*

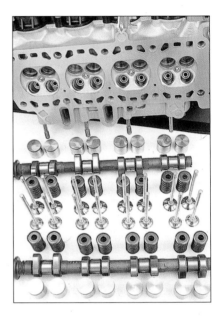

THE FOUR-STROKE CYCLE

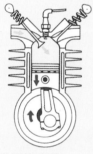

1 INDUCTION (SUCK)
As the piston descends, the inlet valve opens, allowing fuel/air mixture to be drawn into the cylinder

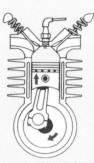

2 COMPRESSION (SQUEEZE)
The inlet valve then closes and the piston travels upwards, compressing the mixture

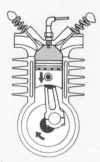

3 COMBUSTION (BANG)
Just before the piston reaches the top of its stroke (known as Top Dead Centre), the spark plug ignites the compressed fuel/air mixture, forcing the piston down on its power stroke

4 EXHAUST (BLOW)
As the piston rises again the exhaust valve opens, allowing the burnt gases to be released through the exhaust port

design and materials used have changed greatly since early motors that produced just a few horsepower, the basic suck-squeeze-bang-blow sequence remains the same.

Road-going four-stroke multis now run reliably to as high as 15,000rpm, and provide phenomenal performance. The best Japanese four-cylinder 600cc engines deliver 100bhp, more than most car units, while the biggest bikes are so powerful that in many countries their 140bhp-plus motors have to be restricted for legal purposes.

■ **TYPES OF FOUR-STROKE ENGINE**
The earliest and simplest four-stroke layout, the single, dominated in the 1950s and is still used for various motorcycles ranging from mopeds to racebikes. In spite of increasingly

■ RIGHT *On this cut-away of Honda's CBR600F it is possible to follow how air travels from the duct above the front wheel to the airbox, through the air-filter and carburettors to the engine, and then out via the exhaust system. Note also the cross-section of the steel frame beams visible at the steering head.*

sophisticated balancing arrangements, its practical limit remains about 650cc. Parallel twins took over in the 1960s, and can be used in either 360-degree — both pistons rising together — or 180-degree layouts. BMW's classic flat-twin, or boxer, layout is generally smoother and ideal for cooling, if not for ground-clearance. V-twins vary in the angle of their cylinders, and can be longitudinal, like the 45-degree Harley and 90-degree Ducati, or transverse, as favoured by Moto Guzzi.

Three-cylinder engines can be arranged either across the frame, as with Triumphs and Laverdas, or along the line of the bike like BMW's K75. Likewise with in-line fours, where BMW's K series follows the old Henderson/ Indian longitudinal layout, but with horizontal instead of vertical cylinders. Many modern bikes use the familiar Japanese transverse format popularized in 1969 by Honda's CB750.

Honda fours also include the V-four of the VFR750 and the flat-four of the earlier Gold Wing models. Ariel's legendary Square Four was named after its unusual engine layout.

Five-cylinder bikes are rare, the most original being the amazing 1922 Megola,

■ RIGHT *Different approaches to four-stroke valve design are highlighted by pistons from (clockwise from top left): a two-valves-per-cylinder Moto Guzzi; a two-valve Harley-Davidson; a four-valve Suzuki GSX-R; and a five-valve Yamaha FZ750.*

whose 640cc five-pot engine was arranged radially inside the front wheel. The modern 1500cc Gold Wing is a watercooled flat-six; other six-cylinder designs include the straight-six Honda CBX1000, Kawasaki Z1300 and Benelli 750 of the 1970s.

Laverda raced a V6 in 1978, and fellow Italian firm Morbidelli has produced an exotic 850cc V-eight to power a prototype sports-tourer. Meanwhile the mighty Boss Hoss makes do with the V-eight Chevy unit commonly found in American cars.

Anatomy of a Motorcycle

TWO-STROKES AND ROTARIES

Two-stroke motors are lighter and potentially more powerful than four-strokes of similar capacity, which is why they are used for Grand Prix racebikes. They are also mechanically simpler and generally cheaper to produce, which is why they are popular for small commuter bikes. But the two-stroke's workings are more complex. Instead of having mechanical valves, a two-stroke uses the underneath of the piston to force the incoming mixture of fuel and air into the combustion chamber, via the crankcase and connecting transfer ports.

This allows the engine to fire with every rotation of the crankshaft (ie, every two strokes), rather than every two rotations (or four strokes), which gives the "stroker" its power advantage. But it means that lubricating oil cannot sit in the crankcases, and must be carried in the fuel/air mixture and burnt,

■ ABOVE *Suzuki's RG500 features rotary disc valve induction. Its carburettors are mounted on the side of the crankcase, and induction is controlled by slotted discs that spin with the crankshaft.*

■ ABOVE RIGHT *A piston-ported two-stroke such as Yamaha's TZ750 has a non-return reed valve between each carburettor and the engine. This allows mixture in, and prevents it from being blown back.*

adding to pollution. And despite the modern two-stroke tuner's skill in selecting the correctly shaped expansion chamber for the exhaust system, some of the mixture goes down the exhaust without being burnt – further increasing emissions. These problems are being addressed by the new wave of clean two-strokes under development.

■ **TYPES OF TWO-STROKE ENGINE**

Many of the best two-strokes have been parallel twins, from the Scott Squirrel of motorcycling's early years to Yamaha's recent RD350LC. Kawasaki's late 1970s KR250 and 350 Grand Prix racers were tandem twins, with one cylinder behind the other. Modern Grand Prix 250s are in-line V-twins, as are several roadsters including Aprilia's RS250. Two-stroke triples have included 1970s classics such as Kawasaki's aircooled 750cc H2 and 500cc H1, and Suzuki's watercooled GT750.

Freddie Spencer's 1983 world championship winning Honda NS500 was a V-triple, as was the NS400 roadster it subsequently spawned. Four-cylinder two-strokes have included

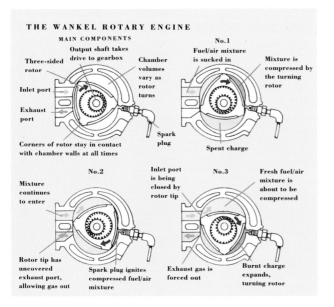

THE WANKEL ROTARY ENGINE

MAIN COMPONENTS

Three-sided rotor

Output shaft takes drive to gearbox

Chamber volumes vary as rotor turns

Inlet port

Exhaust port

Corners of rotor stay in contact with chamber walls at all times

Spark plug

No.1
Fuel/air mixture is sucked in

Mixture is compressed by the turning rotor

Spent charge

No.2
Mixture continues to enter

Inlet port is being closed by rotor tip

No.3
Fresh fuel/air mixture is about to be compressed

Rotor tip has uncovered exhaust port, allowing gas out

Spark plug ignites compressed fuel/air mixture

Exhaust gas is forced out

Burnt charge expands, turning rotor

■ BELOW LEFT *Kawasaki's 750cc H2 aircooled triple of the early 1970s was smelly, thirsty, noisy, inflexible — and very powerful indeed.*

■ BELOW RIGHT *Most two-strokes have followed Suzuki's GT750 triple in using watercooling for a more controlled operating temperature.*

THE TWO-STROKE CYCLE

A INDUCTION
As the piston rises, the fuel/air mixture in the cylinder is compressed, while fresh mixture is being drawn into the crankcase

B TRANSFER
As the piston descends on the power stroke, it first compresses the fuel/air mixture in the crankcase, and then uncovers the transfer port (on right of diagram) through which the mixture is forced into the cylinder

C COMPRESSION
The piston's upward movement compresses the charge in the combustion chamber

D COMBUSTION
As the piston nears the top of its stroke the mixture is ignited, after which the piston begins its downwards, or power, stroke

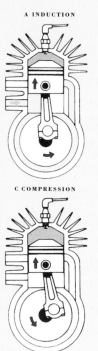

A INDUCTION   B TRANSFER

C COMPRESSION   D COMBUSTION

E EXHAUST

E EXHAUST
Near the bottom of the power stroke, the piston uncovers the exhaust port. The burnt gases escape due to their own pressure and by being displaced by the fresh charge being forced through the transfer port. Despite two-stroke tuners' best efforts, some fresh mixture is inevitably lost through the exhaust port

Yamaha's straight-four TZ750 racer and Suzuki's racing and road-going square-four RG500. Recent 500cc Grand Prix racers have been V-fours. Honda's NSR500 has a single crankshaft while Suzuki's and Yamaha's V-fours use two geared-together cranks.

■ **THE ROTARY ENGINE**
The smoothest engine of all is the Wankel rotary, named after its inventor, Felix Wankel. A figure-of-eight shaped chamber holds a three-sided rotor, which turns in such a way that its corners always remain in contact with the sides. The rotor's movement forms three compartments of varying volume, in which the suck-squeeze-bang-blow cycle takes place. The Wankel engine can be powerful, compact and light although fuel consumption is high. Rotary roadsters from DKW, Suzuki and Norton have not, however, been commercially successful.

■ ABOVE *Norton's Classic roadster proved that a rotary bike engine could be neat, reasonably powerful, and very smooth.*

■ BELOW *Honda's*
2002-model FireBlade
featured a twin-spar
aluminium frame
designed to allow
flex in certain areas.

Anatomy of a Motorcycle

FRAMES AND SUSPENSION

The motorcycle's basic layout may have changed little during the last 100 years but chassis performance has improved hugely – as a ride on most classic bikes, with their heavy, flexible frames and crude suspension, confirms. Handling depends on many variables, notably frame strength and geometry, weight distribution, suspension type and adjustment. All have been affected by advances in chassis technology, leading to modern machines that are stable, well-balanced and comfortable over a wide range of speeds and road conditions.

Until the 1950s, many bikes had thin steel frames and springer front forks with no damping or a simple friction arrangement. Rear suspension was provided by a crude plunger set-up or was non-existent leaving the rider cushioned only by the back tyre and a sprung saddle – not surprisingly this was known as a hard tail. Later models had sturdier frames, either of pressed steel or, in the case of the legendary Norton Featherbed, braced and often triangulated steel tubes designed to hold a pair of hydraulically damped rear shock absorbers. Sometimes, as with Honda's four-cylinder racers of the 1960s, the engine was an integral stressed member of the frame.

The increases in superbike engine's power and weight in the 1970s left many chassis

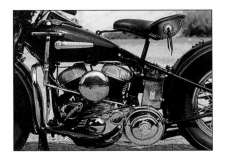

unable to cope – leading to wobbles and weaves – but technology has moved fast in recent years. A typical modern sportsbike has a rigid frame, particularly in the crucial link between steering head and swing-arm pivot. Frame design may incorporate a traditional tubular steel cradle, a large diameter main spine as used by Triumph, a space-frame or ladder of thinner tubes – a recognizable Ducati trademark – or the common sports and racing format of twin aluminium spars.

■ SUSPENSION DESIGN

Front forks and rear shock units work in essentially the same way. They absorb shocks with a coil spring, using a hydraulic damper – oil forced through holes of various sizes – to control the rate of its compression (bump or compression damping) and, more importantly, of its return (rebound damping). Suspension action produces heat, so many modern shock units have remote oil reservoirs, situated alongside or away from the main unit, to aid cooling.

The more sophisticated front and rear units are adjustable, both for spring preload – which controls the amount of weight needed to

■ LEFT *Many modern*
Harleys use hidden
suspension units to give
the look of a genuine
hard-tail such as the
1949 model WL45.

little trail and plenty of weight over its front wheel for quick and light steering – often at the expense of marginal stability.

At the other extreme, a cruiser is set up for stability, with raked forks, lots of trail, a long wheelbase and more weight over the rear wheel. Most roadsters fall somewhere in-between, and some chassis can be fine-tuned using adjustable fork yokes to vary rake and trail, plus various methods to raise or lower the front or rear suspension.

compress the unit further – and for compression and rebound damping. Multiple springs of different rates can be used to give a progressive effect. At the rear, rising rate suspension is more commonly provided by a mechanical linkage system at one end of the shock. This allows a light action for small bumps, and a firmer response nearer the end of the spring's travel to prevent bottoming out.

■ ALTERNATIVE FRONT SUSPENSION

Many engineers argue that telescopic forks are a poor solution – because they are affected by braking, and acted upon by forces in directions they are not designed for. Alternative hub-centre designs, in which the front wheel pivots on a bearing inside its hub, get over these pro-blems and separate the processes of steering and braking. Bimota's Tesi and Yamaha's GTS1000 used different forkless systems to provide a high degree of stability, particularly under braking. But neither proved commercially successful, partly because of high costs but mostly because modern front forks actually work very well indeed.

■ CHASSIS GEOMETRY

The way a bike handles is greatly affected by the geometry of its chassis. A modern racebike has a short wheelbase, steep front forks, very

■ RIGHT *Bimota's Yamaha-engined YB4 and YB6 were among the first sportsbikes to use the now-common alloy beam frame format.*

■ BELOW *Ducati's 999 features the Italian firm's traditional tubular steel frame construction, which uses the engine as a stressed member.*

Anatomy of a Motorcycle

WHEELS, TYRES AND BRAKES

The motorcycle's inherent instability makes its tyres and brakes all the more important, especially as the need to lean in corners means that even the biggest and most powerful bikes have tyres whose footprint is precariously narrow by car standards. Until the 1960s most bikes wore tubed front and rear tyres of crossply construction and roughly similar size. In contrast, modern sports machines achieve incredible cornering angles – well in excess of 45 degrees – due largely to the high levels of grip provided by their sticky, low-profile, tubeless radial tyres, the rear of which is much wider than the front to cope with high levels of power. Soft-compound superbike rear tyres are often worn out after less than 2000 miles (3218 kilometres) of hard road use.

Increasingly specialized demand has led to an extraordinary variety of tyre types, from treadless racing slicks designed to put down maximum surface area in dry conditions, but useless in the wet, to heavily treaded knobbly tyres for trials or motocross events. In-between come sports tyres which are lightly treaded (because tread flex increases heat build-up, thus reducing performance) and harder, more comprehensively patterned tyres for commuting or touring. Dual-purpose tyres, designed for trail bikes, are generally biased towards road riding and of limited use in heavy mud. Road-racing wet tyres, with block-pattern tread and ultra-soft compound, can wear out literally in minutes if used on a dry track.

The most notable advance in motorbike wheels has been the move from wire-spoked to cast-construction, something which happened gradually through the 1970s and 1980s. Cast wheels, normally made of aluminium but sometimes of lighter magnesium, are generally stronger and can accept modern tubeless tyres.

■ LEFT *This shows only part of the huge collection of wheels and tyres that Yamaha's Grand Prix team required for each race.*

■ BELOW *The Manx Norton's combination of Roadholder forks, wire front wheel and twin-leading-shoe brake was impressive in the 1960s.*

■ BELOW *A front disc brake with single-piston caliper was a very soph-isticated feature when Honda's CB750 four was released in 1969.*

■ BELOW *This Suzuki RGV500 racer is fitted with upside-down forks and huge carbon-fibre brake discs, gripped by four-piston calipers.*

■ BELOW *The rear end of Ducati's 916 features a single-sided swing arm and an ultra-wide, 190-section radial tyre for maximum roadholding.*

■ BELOW *Racing-style radial front brake calipers appeared in 2003 on several super-sports bikes including Kawasaki's ZX-6R.*

Wire wheels, however, are still fitted to some new bikes, mainly to emphasize their retro look. Sportsbike wheel diameter has become standardized at 17 inches front and rear, with rear tyre width increasing to cope with rising power outputs. In the early 1980s the fashion was for 16-inch front wheels – led, as with much in roadster chassis design, by developments in Grand Prix racing.

■ **BRAKE DESIGN**

Until fairly recently most motorbikes were stopped by drum brakes, and some small bikes still are. This consists of a pair of semi-circular shoes which are forced open against the inside of the drum when the brake is applied. Some drums, such as those fitted to the otherwise magnificent Brough Superior, were notably poor, and prone to overheating and fading with hard use. Others, such as the big, ventilated four-leading-shoe Grimecas used by specials and racebikes in the 1960s, were very powerful although they required regular adjustment to give optimum performance.

Disc brakes began to take over the motorcycle world in the early 1970s, led by Honda's CB750. A simple system consists of a single steel disc gripped by the twin pads of a hydraulically operated caliper. Discs don't

■ BELOW *This Michelin rack in a roadrace paddock holds (from left) two front slicks; a wider rear slick; heavily treaded rear and front wets; a lightly treaded front intermediate; and two more front slicks.*

require adjustment for wear and tend to cope better with the heat generated by braking, but early systems worked very poorly in wet weather. Modern superbikes use twin front discs, with another at the rear, gripped by calipers each containing four or six individual pistons for improved power and feel. Some bikes, mainly larger tourers and sports-tourers, use a variety of hydraulic systems to link front and rear brakes.

Several manufacturers have anti-lock brake systems. But the complexity and expense is such that fitment is again restricted mainly to long-distance bikes from firms including BMW, which also has a car-style servo brake system.

Sport on Two Wheels

The Olympic motto, *citius*, *altius*, *fortius*, meaning faster, higher, stronger can equally be applied to competition aboard motorcycles.

Almost as long as bikes have been built, people have been holding contests to see who could make them go quickest, last longest – even get to the top of the biggest hill.

Motorcycle competition does not have to be all about speed. The sport of trials, for example, produces champions as skilful as any on two wheels. Endurance often plays a part, whether in a 24-hour road-race or the three-week slog from Paris to Dakar. But mostly it's the thrill of high velocities that attracts riders and spectators to bike sport. This is true wherever they are in the world, and on whatever surface they compete – from the steep, man-made banking at Daytona to the sand of the Baja desert; from frozen ice-race ovals to the unforgiving public roads of the Isle of Man.

EARLY RACERS

■ OPPOSITE *Top Texan racer Eddie Hasha poses in front of a steeply banked board-track, or motordrome, with Indian's new eight-valve V-twin in 1911. In the following year he and seven others died following a crash at Newark in New Jersey.*

When motorcycle racing began, at the end of the last century, riders had to contend not only with their rivals but with the fragility of their crude bikes and the often appalling condition of the roads. Many early racing machines were tricycles, some with engines as large as two litres. Riders competed in gruelling inter-city marathons on temperamental bikes with no suspension, typically wearing clothing no more protective than a woolly jumper, plus-fours, stout shoes and a peaked cap.

Continental Europe was the birthplace not just of the motorcycle but also of bike racing, with the first major event being held between Paris and Rouen in July 1894. The next year saw pioneering races in both Italy and America. Other, even longer, events around the turn of the century included Paris-Vienna and

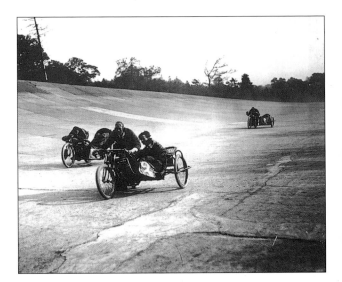

■ ABOVE *The width and banking of the concrete Brooklands track are clear in this shot of a Zenith outfit leading a race "for cycles and sidecars" in 1913.*

■ LEFT *The stopwatch is running as Sunbeam rider HR Davies gets under way at Caerphilly in Wales on a hill-climb, a popular early form of competition.*

■ RIGHT *Flying Merkel factory racer Maldwyn Jones won second place in a 300-mile (480 kilometre) race, at Savannah, Georgia in 1913.*

■ BELOW *These Indian V-twins hit 100mph (160 kph) with no suspension or brakes, and tyres prone to coming off the rims.*

Paris-Madrid. In the early 1900s short-circuit races became popular, often held on banked cycle tracks such as those at Lille and Paris's *Parc des Princes* in France, and at Plymouth and Crystal Palace in Britain.

The first big international race took place in France in 1904. The Coupe International was a 170-mile (273-kilometre) event in which a maximum of three bikes from each country was allowed. French rider Demester won on a Griffon, at an average speed of 45.1mph (72.5kph), but the race was declared void due to the dubious legality of the winning bikes, and after it became clear that tyres had been sabotaged by nails sprinkled by spectators.

The year 1907 was notable for two momentous events in Britain, one of which was the first-ever Tourist Trophy meeting in the Isle of Man. The other was the opening of Brooklands, the world's first artificially constructed race circuit. Surfaced with concrete and 2.8 miles (4.5 kilometres) in length, the egg-shaped Surrey track included two high and wide banked turns, remains of which are still visible today. Brooklands' layout allowed high speeds and attracted bike racers, record-breakers and testers until its closure at the start of the Second World War.

■ ABOVE RIGHT *Rem Fowler overcame mechanical problems to win the twin-cylinder class of the first TT in 1907 on this Peugeot-engined Norton.*

■ BELOW *Three competitors get under way side-by-side in this 1913 shot of the Brighton Speed Trials, an event that still takes place today.*

Banked tracks of a different kind became popular in America, where big V-twins from Indian, Thor and Flying Merkel thundered round narrow wooden circuits with sides as steep as 60 degrees. These were thrilling and highly dangerous events, at which professional racers with names like "Fearless" Balke and "Dare Devil" Derkum raced head-to-head, reaching speeds of 100mph (160kph), in front of crowds of 10,000 people. Board-racing's decline can be traced almost exactly to the day when two riders and six spectators were killed in a crash at Newark, New Jersey in 1912.

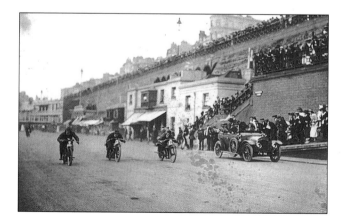

RACING   ON   THE   ROADS

For many years the Isle of Man Tourist Trophy was the world's greatest motorcycle racing event. Even today there are those who maintain that the legendary 37.7-mile (60.6-kilometre) Mountain course makes the TT the supreme test of rider and machine. And although purpose-built circuits now dominate the sport from amateur to world championship level, pure road racing continues at places as far apart as Ireland, Belgium and New Zealand.

The TT's history dates back to 1907, when the Isle of Man was chosen as a race venue because competing on public roads was banned on mainland Britain. The event was known as the Tourist Trophy because machines had to be fitted with brakes, mudguards and a toolbox. Rem Fowler averaged just 36.2mph (58.2kph) when he won the twin-cylinder class on a Peugeot-engined Norton, pedalling up hills and stopping several times to repair punctures and broken drive-belts.

By the early 1920s, winning riders were averaging over 50mph (80kph) in gruelling

■ RIGHT *Charlie Collier, who ran the Matchless firm with his father and brother, won the single-cylinder class of the first TT in 1907, and won again three years later.*

■ BELOW *Mike Hailwood crashed his MV Agusta in the 1965 Senior TT, but got back on again to win with a bleeding nose, a broken fairing and flattened exhaust megaphones.*

races of five or more laps. On his TT debut in 1922, Stanley Woods had time to have his clothes catch fire while refuelling, stop to mend his engine and then crash and remount – yet still finish fifth. Woods went on to win a total of ten TTs between 1923 and 1939. Speeds had risen sharply by 1950, when Norton's Geoff Duke raised the lap record to 93.33mph (150.19kph) on the way to his first victory. Duke dominated the TT during the 1950s with six wins, but it was Bob McIntyre who set the first 100mph (160kph) lap – riding a four-cylinder Gilera in 1957.

Heroes in the 1960s included Giacomo Agostini, who scored ten wins, and Mike Hailwood, whose total of 14 victories included the 1967 Senior in which ":Mike the Bike" beat "Ago" in the race that many fans still consider to be the greatest TT of all time.

Hailwood's most famous win came in 1978 when he returned from retirement to take the Formula One race on a Ducati. By then the TT had lost its world championship status, and

■ BELOW *Hailwood returned from retire-ment to ride a Ducati to an emotional Formula One TT win in 1978.*

■ RIGHT *Joey Dun-lop's exploits at the TT and his native Ireland earned him the title "King of the Roads".*

■ BELOW *The beauty and danger of the TT circuit are clear as Scottish star Steve Hislop ignores the speed limit on the exit of Ginger Hall.*

stars such as Barry Sheene and Kenny Roberts refused to risk the obvious dangers of racing at speed between stone walls.

But the TT continued to produce its own breed of heroes. Men like Joey Dunlop, winner of a record 26 TTs, Steve Hislop and David

Jefferies all lapped at average speeds of over 120mph (193kph). Racing on the roads will never regain its former prestige, but events continued to take place at circuits including the TT, Ireland's North West 200 and Belgium's Chimay.

GRAND PRIX 500s

Grand Prix racing's 500cc class is the most prestigious in motorcycling. In the modern era, whoever has worn the 500cc crown has been entitled to call himself the best motorcycle racer in the world. As the most powerful and fastest bikes, the 500s have generally attracted the top riders, the biggest budgets, the greatest interest and the most publicity.

Modern 500 stars battle in a true world championship that in recent years has included rounds as far apart as Australia, America and Argentina. The situation was very different in 1949, when the world championship was first formed from the "Continental Circus" – the band of riders who, with their bikes and a few spares in small vans, followed a winding route around Europe from one race to the next. Britain's Les Graham won the 500cc title after six rounds, all of which were in Europe.

Graham won that first 500cc crown on a British twin, the AJS Porcupine, and Geoff Duke took the championship two years later on a single-cylinder Norton. But for the rest of the

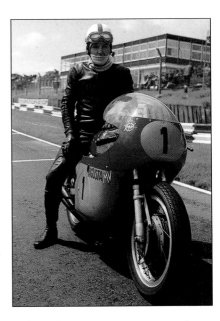

■ RIGHT *John Surtees began MV Agusta's domination of the 500cc world championship in 1956, with the first of his four titles for the Italian factory.*

■ BELOW *The AJS Porcupine was originally designed for supercharging, but in "unblown" form took Les Graham to the first 500cc title in 1949.*

1950s, 1960s and early 1970s, racing's premier class was dominated by multi-cylinder Italian four-strokes, firstly from Gilera – whose six championships included a hat-trick from Duke between 1953 and 1955 – and then from MV Agusta.

MV's red and silver machines set records that will probably never be equalled, winning 17 consecutive world 500cc championships between 1958 and 1974 as well as a total of 38 riders' world titles and 37 manufacturers' championships. The so-called "Gallarate Fire Engines" reigned supreme in the 500cc class, winning the championship with John Surtees in 1956 and then, after a year's break, regaining it with Surtees, Gary Hocking and Mike Hailwood, who won four in a row.

Competition between numerous Italian factories was intense until the mid-1950s. But

■ BELOW *Giacomo Agostini's haul of eight 500cc and seven 350cc world championships makes him the most successful Grand Prix rider of all.*

■ LEFT *Gilera's DOHC four changed the face of 500cc Grand Prix racing, winning six titles and providing the ins-piration for MV Agusta's similar machines.*

■ BELOW *Guzzi withdrew from Grands Prix before the legendary 500cc V-eight, pictured in the factory museum, could prove its worth.*

■ BELOW *The changing face of 500cc racing is summed-up in this 1975 shot of Barry Sheene, on a two-stroke Suzuki, coming up behind reigning world champion Phil Read riding the four-stroke MV Agusta.*

Mondial, Moto Guzzi and Gilera quit the arena in 1957, Guzzi without ever realizing the full potential of their exotic and super-fast V-eight. MV's next serious works challenge came from Mike Hailwood who left for Honda in 1966 and twice came desperately close to taking the title, with Agostini just beating him each time. Honda then quit racing, and Ago went on to

take seven consecutive championships for MV.

Phil Read retained the 500cc title for MV in 1973 and 1974 but the Japanese two-stroke challenge was looming. Ironically though, it was Italian hero, Agostini, who in 1975 won the title for Yamaha, ending Agusta's glory years and confirming the two-stroke as the dominant force in 500cc Grand Prix racing.

GP 500s: The Two-stroke Era

Multi-cylinder two-strokes ruled Grand Prix racing for almost three decades. They arrived in the 1970s as an unstoppable force, with more power and less weight than the suddenly uncompetitive four-strokes. When their era ended at the start of the 21st century, these pure-bred racing projectiles had evolved into 190bhp V-four missiles with top speeds of up to 200mph (322kph). Ultra-rigid frames, sophisticated suspension and fat slick tyres allowed incredible angles of lean. The 500s' performance was so violent and demanding that only a select band of talented and highly-paid professionals – men like 500cc

champions Eddie Lawson, Wayne Gardner, Wayne Rainey, Mick Doohan, Alex Criville, Kenny Roberts Jnr and Valentino Rossi – were able to master them.

■ LEFT *Factory honour is at stake as Shinichi Itoh (Honda, 7), Alexandre Barros (Suzuki, 6), Daryl Beattie (Yamaha, 3) and Doug Chandler (Cagiva, 10) battle in the 1994 Italian Grand Prix.*

■ BELOW *Kevin Schwantz, world champion in 1993, retired two years later after a Grand Prix career that contained many victories and almost as many injuries.*

■ LEFT *Honda's Freddie Spencer and Yamaha's Kenny Roberts, here at the Italian Grand Prix, clashed many times during the 1983 season.*

■ BELOW *The Suzuki RG500s of Barry Sheene and Dutch star Wil Hartog lead Kenny Roberts' Yamaha in the French Grand Prix at Nogaro in 1978.*

■ ABOVE *Freddie Spencer won two 500cc titles in the 1980s.*

■ BELOW *Australian ace Michael Doohan won five 500cc titles before his career was ended by injury in 1999.*

The two-stroke revolution began with Yamaha who, in the early 1970s, first built a 500cc four: basically two twins combined, with the cylinders set in line across the frame. With double the number of power strokes for a given engine speed, a two-stroke should always produce more power than an equivalent capacity four-stroke, and Yamaha's format was immediately a major success. Jarno Saarinen won the French Grand Prix on the four's debut in 1973. Although the Finnish star was killed later that year, Yamaha's Giacomo Agostini went on to win the Daytona 200 in 1974 and the 500cc world title the following season.

Suzuki's more compact square-four RG500 took Barry Sheene to the championship in 1976 and 1977. Kenny Roberts then arrived on the scene to win three consecutive titles on his straight-four YZR Yamaha, redefining the art of riding a 500cc Grand Prix bike with a power-sliding style developed from American dirt-track racing. Suzuki and the RG hit back, with championships for Italians Marco Lucchinelli and Franco Uncini, before Freddie Spencer finally won Honda's first 500cc title in 1983 on the NS500 two-stroke triple.

From then on the dominant 500cc engine layout was the V-four, with Honda's NSR, Yamaha's YZR and Suzuki's RGV each taking championships. The Honda was the most successful, winning ten world titles in 18 years, including five in a row for Australia's fearsomely fast and committed Mick Doohan.

When Italian star Valentino Rossi won that tenth NSR title in 2001, the 500cc class had in many ways never been healthier. Factory teams were highly professional; worldwide television coverage brought the sport to millions; racing was close; and tracks were safer than ever before. But none of those things could keep the two-strokes competitive in 2002, when the new MotoGP class was opened to a fresh generation of 990cc four-strokes, led by Honda's RC211V, that were more powerful and faster still.

MotoGP: Four-strokes Return

Motorcycle racing entered a new era in 2002 with the introduction of the MotoGP class, which allowed multi-cylinder four-strokes of up to 990cc capacity. The change was instigated by the major manufacturers, who regarded the old 500cc two-stroke format as an expensive sideline with little relevance to road bike development. Although MotoGP had drawbacks, including the cost of creating new bikes and the initial dominance of Honda, the series brought new interest to racing.

The MotoGP rules, which combined a 990cc four-stroke limit with a variable minimum weight dependent on the number of cylinders, generated a variety of engine designs, in contrast to the uniformity of the 500cc two-stroke V-fours. Suzuki developed a V-four, Aprilia an in-line triple, Yamaha and Kawasaki stuck to in-line fours, and Honda created an ambitious 20-valve V-five, with cylinders at 75.5 degrees.

Honda's RC211V engine revved to 14,000rpm, produced 220bhp and gave the bike a top speed of over 200mph (322kph). To nobody's great surprise Honda dominated MotoGP from its first race, especially in the

■ LEFT *Honda's RC211V engine was a compact, 20-valve V-five with a capacity of 990cc. Three cylinders were angled forwards and two to the rear. Honda refused to disclose the 20-valve engine's cylinder dimensions; the maximum output was approximately 220bhp.*

■ BELOW *First-lap action from Assen in Holland in 2002 shows the MotoGP class's variety, as Max Biaggi (Yamaha) leads Tohru Ukawa and Valentino Rossi (Honda), and Kenny Roberts (Suzuki, 10). Loris Capirossi, No. 65, is riding a Honda NSR500 two-stroke.*

■ LEFT *A typically colourful MotoGP scene as bikes
including Loris Capirossi's new Ducati V-four (left)
line up on a dummy starting grid during a pre-season
practice session at Barcelona in 2003.*

hands of charismatic Italian Valentino Rossi,
who had won the previous year's title on the
NSR500 two-stroke. Rossi finished outside
the first two places only once all year to be
crowned the first MotoGP champion, as the
RC211V won 14 of the season's 16 races. Only
Yamaha's YZR-M1, on which fellow Italian
Max Biaggi won twice, came even close.

Honda showed no sign of relinquishing its
grip as MotoGP continued from strength to
strength, having relegated the rival World
Superbike championship, for production-based
bikes, to a distant second best. Some Japanese
factory teams proved surprisingly uncompetitive
while European challengers Ducati, who in
2003 entered the Grand Prix championship for

■ BELOW LEFT
*Valentino Rossi brought
a welcome touch of
glamour and good
humour to the MotoGP
scene, along with the
riding skill and bravery
that made him the first
MotoGP world champion.*

■ BELOW RIGHT
*Honda had done much
to create the MotoGP
four-stroke format, and
immediately dominated
the series with the
RC211V, which won the
first nine races. Here,
typically, Rossi leads
his Repsol team-mate
Tohru Ukawa.*

the first time in many years, impressed with a
powerful 16-valve V-four, the Desmosedici.

The Desmosedici's engine layout differed
from Ducati's traditional V-twin format; and
similarly, Honda seemed in no hurry to produce
a roadgoing V-five based on the RC211V. But
in other ways, MotoGP was succeeding in
connecting Grand Prix racing with showroom
machines. The Desmosedici featured a tubular
steel frame, like Ducati's roadsters; while
Honda's production CBR600RR followed the
RC211V in its styling, as well as its low-level
fuel tank and tailpiece-mounted exhaust silencer.

Increased marketing potential was one
reason why MotoGP was generally regarded as
a success. Equally importantly, the series had
other vital ingredients: the world's best riders,
locked in fierce battle aboard light, loud and
insanely fast bikes. With other factories
planning involvement, and spectator interest
high both live and via television, racing's
premier class had an exciting future.

THE SMALLER GP CLASSES

■ BELOW *Phil Read keeps his two-stroke Yamaha twin ahead of Jim Redman's Honda four-stroke twin in a 350cc race at Mallory Park in 1964.*

The smaller Grand Prix categories can't match the straight-line speed or the sheer glamour of MotoGP – but they often more than make up for that with even closer racing and more potential winners. The thrilling sight of six or more tiny 125s and riders slipstreaming each other down straights and clashing fairings through bends for lap after lap has long been commonplace.

Racing regulations limit Grand Prix 125s to a single cylinder and 250s to two, with six gears apiece. But rules were less restrictive in the past, which inspired some remarkable bikes. The Suzuki RK66 on which Hans-Georg Anscheidt won the 50cc world title in 1966, for example, had two cylinders, 14 gears and made 17.5bhp at 17,300rpm. Honda and MV Agusta built many multi-cylinder 250s and 350s in the 1960s. In 1964 the Japanese factory unveiled the legendary 250cc, six-cylinder RC166, which revved to 16,500rpm and reached 150mph (241kph). The next season Honda's Swiss star Luigi Taveri won the 125cc title on an exotic five-cylinder machine.

■ BELOW *Haruchika Aoki (No.12), one of several outstanding Japanese 125cc riders, screams his Honda into the lead in the 1995 Spanish Grand Prix.*

■ ABOVE *Germany's Hans-Georg Anscheidt, a triple world champion in the 1960s, leaps Ballaugh Bridge on his 50cc, 14-speed Kreidler during the 1964 TT.*

In recent years the smaller Grand Prix classes have comprised just 250s and 125s, but in the past there have also been races for 350 and 50 or 80cc bikes. Riders commonly used to contest more than one class. In 1967 Mike Hailwood rode works Hondas in the 250, 350 and 500cc classes. At Assen, after winning his third Dutch TT of the day, Hailwood almost fell off the 500 through sheer exhaustion. Riders often contested both 250 and 350cc championships until the larger class

was dropped in 1983. Both Kork Ballington and Anton Mang scored double championship wins aboard Kawasaki's tandem twins.

One of racing's most spectacular achievements was Freddie Spencer's 250 and 500cc championship double for Honda in 1985. Since then the increasingly competitive and demanding nature of Grand Prix racing, and the contrasting technique required to get the best from machines with dramatically different power outputs, has kept riders to one class.

Although Grand Prix racing has become more concentrated on the premier class in recent years, the smaller categories have provided exciting racing as well as a stream of talented riders. Valentino Rossi won world titles on 125s and 250s before moving to bigger bikes, where he resumed battle with former 250cc champions Max Biaggi and Loris Capirossi. Following the demise of the 500cc class, the future of the smaller two-strokes is unclear. But the sight and sound of a swarm of tiny bikes, screaming round a track like angry hornets, is as vivid as ever.

SUPERBIKES

Superbikes have provided some of the closest and most spectacular bike racing of all. Visually similar to, and directly derived from, road-going machines, the big four-strokes are strictly limited in the modifications allowed. Over the years, Ducati V-twins and numerous Japanese bikes, backed by the major factories and ridden by stars including Carl Fogarty, Colin Edwards and Troy Bayliss, have generated many memorable racing battles.

Superbike racing began in America, where the tradition of competing on modified streetbikes dates back to the 1970s. Then riders such as Reg Pridmore, Wes Cooley and Steve McLaughlin locked high handlebars on BMW flat-twins and 1000cc fours from Suzuki and Kawasaki. In the 1980s, rising American stars Freddie Spencer, Eddie Lawson, Wayne Rainey and Kevin Schwantz raced four-strokes

in spectacular style before moving into Grands Prix. But the so-called "diesels" were considered the poor relation of pure racing machines.

That attitude began to change in 1988, when the World Superbike Championship was established by McLaughlin, the former rider who had been instrumental in starting the US series. Another flamboyant American, "Flyin' Fred" Merkel, won the first two titles on a factory-backed Honda RC30, and the roadster-based series was an immediate success. Italy's

■ ABOVE *The Ducatis of Carl Fogarty, champion Doug Polen and Frenchman Raymond Roche emphasize the Italian factory's Superbike strength at Donington Park in 1992.*

■ LEFT *Californian Fred Merkel, riding for an Italian-based team, won the first World Superbike championship on an RC30 fitted with factory race-kit parts.*

■ LEFT *In 1994 Carl Fogarty fought a season-long battle with Kawasaki's reigning champion Scott Russell (No.1) before recapturing the title for Ducati.*

■ BELOW *Freddie Spencer, pictured at Daytona, 1980, rode a four-cylinder Honda Superbike before graduating to Grands Prix.*

■ BOTTOM *Colin Edwards won two Superbike world titles on Honda's 999cc V-twin before leaving to race in the MotoGP series.*

Ducati then took over – aided by rules allowing twins a capacity and weight advantage over fours – with championship victories for Frenchman Raymond Roche and America's Doug Polen.

The sales success of Ducati's red race-replica V-twins highlighted the commercial potential to be gained from Superbike success, and the factories stepped up their involvement. Scott Russell won on a Kawasaki ZXR750 before Carl Fogarty regained the crown for Ducati in 1994. The Englishman dominated Superbikes in the 1990s, winning four championships for the Italian marque.

The new Millennium saw a fresh injection of excitement as Texan Colin Edwards took the title on Honda's new 999cc SP-1 V-twin. Australian Troy Bayliss snatched the title back for Ducati in 2001, setting up a showdown the following year in which Edwards regained the crown in a sensational finale at Imola.

Both riders then left to take factory rides in the MotoGP class, whose high-profile introduction had left the Superbike series looking distinctly second-best. But new rules allowing participation by the latest breed of 1000cc four-cylinder roadsters looked set to restore the excitement and close racing for which Superbike racing has long been known.

ENDURANCE RACING

Long-distance racing adds an extra dimension to the spectacle of high-speed motorcycling. Modern endurance events are run at a furious pace, and races of up to 24 hours contain fuel-stops, rider and tyre changes – all conducted in just a few seconds – and hours of hard riding through the night. For riders who crash or break down, the race can include a long push back to the pits, after which a team of well-drilled mechanics works flat-out to get a damaged bike back onto the track.

Things were less hectic but even more tiring when the Bol d'Or, the oldest and most famous 24-hour event, was first held on the outskirts of Paris in 1922. The winning rider – only one

was allowed per machine – covered over 750 miles (1206 kilometres) on a 500cc Motosacoche. By 1930 the Bol, held on a different road circuit near Paris, was attracting over 50,000 spectators and had become an important showcase for manufacturers. Best and toughest of the early racers was Gustave Lefèvre, who had five solo wins on a 500cc Norton, and then two more after co-riders were allowed in 1954.

In the 1970s endurance became a demanding proving ground for large-capacity roadsters. BSA/Triumph triples won in 1970 and 1971, before big four-cylinder Hondas and Kawasakis took over. Bikes raced by legendary

■ BELOW *Riders run across the track to their bikes in the traditional Le Mans start, with fastest qualifiers on the left, as the famous 24-hour race gets under way at the French circuit in 1987.*

■ **LEFT** *The pit lane stays busy at night during the Spa 24-hour race in Belgium, as lap-scorers signal times to riders, and bikes arrive for refuelling or repair.*

■ **RIGHT** *French endurance ace Jean-Claude Chemarin won races for both Honda and Kawasaki, on whose 1000cc four he is pictured at the Bol d'Or in 1983.*

■ **FAR RIGHT** *Honda's factory 750cc V-four RVF dominated endurance racing in the mid-1980s, and formed the basis of the Japanese firm's RC30 roadster.*

French pairings such as Godier/Genoud and Chemarin/Léon housed factory-tuned 1000cc motors in specially built chassis. Many innovative engineering solutions were tried and endurance trends were often copied on road-going superbikes.

In more recent years three riders have been allowed in 24-hour races, and bikes have been limited first to 750cc and then to Superbike format, reducing cost but also outlawing the technically interesting prototypes. Although endurance is unpopular in many countries, and has often failed to support a full-scale world championship, the French 24-hour classics at Le Mans and the Bol d'Or feature top-level factory teams and are unbeatable for atmosphere and drama. The Suzuka eight-hour in Japan, which regularly attracts over 100,000 spectators, is regarded by the Japanese factories as the year's most important race.

■ **RIGHT** *Works endurance bikes can be refuelled and given fresh tyres in just a few seconds, and every moment can be vital — as Kawasaki's Scott Russell discovered when he lost the 1994 Suzuka eight-hour race to Honda by less than a third of a second.*

MOTOCROSS

Today, a top-level off-road race is almost as likely to take place in a covered arena as in its natural habitat of a dusty, sandy or muddy outdoor track. The old sport of scrambling has developed into motocross and its descendent, supercross, which sees colourfully clad riders – astride tall, lightweight single-cylinder two-stroke or four-stroke machines with long-travel suspension and knobbly tyres – fly over gravity-defying jumps on courses constructed in city stadia.

The link to racing a motorbike around a field remains, but the sport has seen more than the odd change of name since the first off-road meeting was organized in 1924. In that year, a group of riders from Surrey decided to run an adaptation of Yorkshire's Scott trial, excluding the observed sections where points co. lost. Without these the event couldn't be called a trial, and one competitor's comment that the

race would be a fair old scramble led to the new form of racing being called scrambling.

Scrambling's popularity spread from Britain to continental Europe in the 1940s, and in 1947 the first international Moto-Cross des Nations was contested between five-man teams from France, Belgium, the Netherlands and England. In the 1960s and 1970s the sport was dominated by Belgian and Scandinavian riders including Joël Robert, Roger De Coster and Heikki Mikkola.

The sport had become known as motocross but was otherwise essentially little changed when it reached America in the late 1960s. Americans had

■ ABOVE *Kurt Nicholl, a leading Grand Prix star and British multiple motocross champion in the 1990s, takes a jump in typically effortless style on his factory Honda.*

■ LEFT *Greg Albertyn's 1994 world championship-winning Suzuki RM250 shows off the massive suspension travel it requires for landing from high jumps.*

■ RIGHT *Three-times former world champion Dave Thorpe kicks up the sand as he uses a berm, or bank, to get round a left-hand turn at maximum speed.*

other ideas, and in 1972 the Olympic Coliseum in Los Angeles was converted into an indoor motocross circuit with dramatic jumps.

Supercross had been born, and four years later it had grown into an eight-round national championship, was attracting huge crowds and was on the way to taking over as the most important branch of the sport in the States.

In recent decades America has produced many spectacular riders including Bob Hannah, Rick Johnson and Jeremy McGrath. Americans have proved they can ride outdoors, too, winning the Motocross des Nations on numerous occasions. Meanwhile, supercross has in turn been adopted by countries as far apart as Scandinavia, Japan and France. Indoor races at venues such as Bercy in Paris provide an extravaganza of laser-shows, fireworks, huge leaps and wheel-to-wheel racing action.

■ LEFT *The French sport of supermoto, a combination of motocross and road-racing, demonstrated by Gilles Salvador at Paris's Circuit Carole.*

■ BELOW *The first turn of a top-level motocross race is no place for the faint-hearted, as a gang of snarling, dust-throwing motorcycles aims for the same piece of land.*

TRIALS, ENDUROS AND DESERT RACING

Trials bikes' light weight and knobbly, low-pressure tyres allow them to navigate terrain that looks impossible for a mountain goat, let alone a motorcycle. These range from sheer rock faces and deep gullies in traditional outdoor trials, to artificial hazards such as huge pipes or a series of tables in the indoor events that often attract huge crowds.

Modern courses test mainly the skill and balance of the riders within a time limit, but when the sport began after the turn of the century it was the bikes' reliability that was on trial. Among the most famous events is the Scottish Six Days Trial, which dates from 1910 and attracts a large number of riders ranging from club riders to top professionals, although it is not a world championship event. Another famous trial, the Scott, takes place on the Yorkshire Moors and began as a closed event for workers at the nearby Scott factory.

The most famous trials rider in the 1950s and 60s was Sammy Miller, the Irishman who won over 1000 events, including five Scottish Six Days, on bikes including his famous Ariel with its registration GOV132. In the mid-60s Miller rode for the Spanish firm Bultaco and helped develop the two-stroke 250cc Sherpa that led the move away

from four-stroke singles, known as thumpers. Spain has other leading marques in Gas Gas and Montesa and has also produced many outstanding riders including multiple world champion Jordi Tarrés. The Spaniard's domination was more recently matched by Dougie Lampkin, from the famous Yorkshire trials family, who won a string of world titles both indoors and out.

■ LEFT *Until the 1960s, trials were dominated by four-strokes such as the 250cc Greeves Anglian on which Bill Wilkinson won the Scottish Six Days Trial in 1969.*

Enduro competition lies somewhere between motocross and trials, being essentially an off-road race against the clock for street-legal machines with lights. No points are lost for putting a foot down in sections; instead, riders must make sure to arrive at a series of checkpoints within strict time limits. The most prestigious event is the International Six Day Enduro, a punishing marathon fought out by teams from all over the world.

The other main form of off-road competition is desert racing, of which the best-known event is the legendary Paris-Dakar Rally. Bikes are highly specialized single- or twin-cylinder four-strokes with long travel suspension, extra fuel in rear pannier tanks and sophisticated computerized navigation equipment. The Paris-Dakar crosses the Sahara Desert and covers thousands of miles in three weeks. Other desert races include the Pharaohs in Egypt, and the Baja in Mexico.

Over the years the Dakar has inspired desert-race replica roadbikes including Yamaha's Super Ténéré and Honda's Africa Twin. More recently the race has been dominated by Austrian firm KTM's fast and rugged machines.

■ OPPOSITE *Spaniard Jordi Tarrés established himself as one of the all-time great trials riders with seven world championships, dominating the sport in a manner more recently matched by Englishman Dougie Lampkin.*

■ RIGHT *Top desert racer Stéphane Peterhansel stands high on the footpegs as he blasts his works Yamaha through the Sahara Desert in the 1994 Paris-Dakar Rally.*

SPEEDWAY, LONG TRACK AND ICE RACING

Speedway bikes have little in common with other motorcycles, being purpose-built for short, four-lap races on quarter-mile (400 metre) dirt ovals. Their engines are 500cc, single-cylinder four-strokes that run on methanol and have just one gear. Their chassis have minimal front suspension and none at the rear, no front brake, and a right footrest set low to take the rider's weight as the bike power-slides through the left-hand bends.

The sport became popular in Australia in the 1920s and took off in Europe after the first British meeting was staged in Essex in 1928. Speedway is essentially a team sport, with meetings consisting of heats between four riders from two rival teams. But the year's biggest event has traditionally been the individual World Final. Sweden's Ove Fundin and New Zealander Barry Briggs each won five

times in the 1950s and 1960s. Ivan Mauger, another New Zealander, won a record sixth title in 1979.

Several other types of racing share speedway's basic format of competing on a tight, anti-clockwise oval. The closest to speedway is long track, a German-dominated sport, also run on shale, whose longer straights

■ LEFT *Denmark's
Tommy Knudsen shows
typical speedway style
as he remains perfectly
in control while
broadsiding out of a
bend on his single-
cylinder Weslake.*

and higher speeds demand engines with two
gears. Ivan Mauger won three world titles in
the 1970s but the most successful rider is
Britain's Simon Wigg, who won his fifth in
1994. Grass-track and sand racing are related
but less high-profile sports that require tyre-
sliding skills on different surfaces.

The maddest form of bike sport is ice racing
on bikes whose tyres bristle with scores of
sharp steel spikes. These give excellent grip on
the ice, allowing near-horizontal cornering
angles, but they can turn a crash into an even
nastier experience despite protective wheel-
guards that extend part-way around the tyre.
Ice racing has generally been dominated by
Russians, but is also popular in parts of
Eastern Europe and Scandinavia.

Japan has its own brand of speedway called
autorace. Held solely to allow the large crowds
to bet on the outcome, this takes place on
concrete ovals. Eight riders contest each race,
on 600cc single or twin-cylinder bikes, which
are capable of 120mph (193kph). Prize money
levels are high, and leading riders can earn as
much as top Grand Prix stars. Nevertheless the
temptation to fix results necessitates the
imposition of strict rules to ensure that riders
are kept away from the crowd before racing.

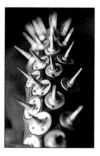

■ ABOVE *Three battling ice-racers demonstrate the
radical cornering angles and aggressive, knee-down
styles that are possible despite the slippery track.*

■ LEFT *Ice-race bikes do not slide in bends like
speedway machines, but grip the track with long
metal spikes fitted to their tyres, which can injure
riders in a crash.*

■ BELOW *Speedway's short races and tight tracks
combine to make the start particularly important;
many races are won by the rider who gets away first.*

DIRT-TRACK AND HILL-CLIMBING

America's most spectacular bike sport takes place on one-mile (1.6-kilometre) ovals, where up to 16 riders thunder round on big Harleys with no front brakes. Through the turns they hold the bikes sideways under power from 100 horsepower V-twin engines, rear tyres throwing up dirt, and on the straights they slipstream or draft at speeds up to 130mph (209kph). The American Motorcycle Association (AMA) Grand National Championship also includes half-mile (800 metre) races, and quarter-mile (400 metre) short tracks, where 600cc single-cylinder bikes are used, and also steeple-chases, which combine elements of dirt-track and motocross.

Dirt-track began on horse tracks at country fairs across America before the First World War. Harley-Davidson's first official race entry was at

■ ABOVE *Jay Spring-steen (No.1) takes his XR750 wide through the "cushion" of loose dirt, while rivals use the firmer "groove" on the inside of the turn.*

the big 300-mile (482-kilometre) event at Dodge City, Kansas, on July 5 1914. The sport was America's most popular in the 1930s but it wasn't until 1946 that the AMA held a one-off championship race at the Springfield Mile, won by Norton-mounted Chet Dykgraff. Harley rider Joe Leonard was the winner in 1954, when the championship was first decided over a series of races, and the American marque has been the most successful ever since.

The most famous dirt-track bike is Harley-Davidson's XR750 V-twin, which was introduced in 1970 and has been taken to victory by dozens of riders, including multiple champion Scott Parker. Honda mounted a successful challenge with the RS750 V-twin, which took four consecutive titles after its introduction in 1984. But the Japanese firm pulled out after the AMA changed the rules to limit the RS's power.

A similar fate met the most outrageous dirt-track bike of all, the four-cylinder, two-stroke Yamaha TZ750 on which Kenny Roberts won the Indianapolis Mile in 1975. Bikes with more than two cylinders were banned at the end of that year and even Roberts didn't complain. The season-long battle for the champion's No.1

■ LEFT *European hill-climbing traditionally takes place on steep and twisty tarmac courses, often with spectacular backdrops such as this one in Devon, England.*

■ BELOW *Harley's in-line V-twin has been dirt-track's dominant engine for years partly due to its controllable power delivery.*

■ OPPOSITE *Scott Stump's left hand is tucked in to improve his XR750's aerodynamics as he enters a straight at the Sacramento Mile, one of the fastest dirt-track venues.*

plate included road races as well as dirt-tracks until separate series were set-up in 1986. Racing dirt-track from a young age has contributed to the road-racing success of many American riders including Roberts, Eddie Lawson and Wayne Rainey.

The other peculiarly American sport is that of hill-climbing – basically a test to see which rider can go furthest and fastest up a dirt-covered slope that starts steep and gets steeper. Hill-climbing has a long tradition at events such as the famous Widowmaker, and produces long bikes with heavily-treaded rear tyres. An event called hill-climbing also takes place in Europe but this contest is based on timed sprints up a short, twisty tarmac course.

■ ABOVE *Ricky Graham, Bubba Shobert and others were successful on the RS750 before Honda quit after a rule-change made the V-twin less competitive.*

■ RIGHT *Kenny Roberts won the Indianapolis Mile on the TZ750 two-stroke, but still supported its ban.*

DRAG RACING

The quickest and most violent form of bike competition is drag racing – a straight duel of acceleration over a standing-start quarter-mile (0.4-kilometre). The fastest top fuel dragsters produce almost 1000bhp and reach over 220mph (354kph) in just 6.5 seconds – roughly the time a top sports car takes to reach 60mph (96kph). To keep the front wheel down and deliver maximum traction, drag bikes are built long and low, with massively wide rear tyres, and often using wheelie bars that extend far beyond the back of the machine.

Drag racing began in America, where most of the fastest times are still set, although the sport is popular in Europe and elsewhere too. In the early days, Indian and Harley V-twins raced against lighter Triumphs. Japanese motors took

over in the 1970s, when Californian Russ Collins built double and even triple-engined monsters using 750cc Honda power. Another star of the 1970s was Dutchman Henk Vink, known as the "Big Spender", who won many races on a 400bhp twin-engined Kawasaki. The extreme stresses that top fuel engines are exposed to make blow-ups frequent and big budgets essential.

Top fuel bikes have been limited to single engine since the 1980s, but speeds have increased and in recent years riders including Larry McBride have posted times below 6 seconds.

Harley-engined dragsters are also now faster than ever – and are often enlarged to over two litres, supercharged and fuelled by nitromethane. The Harley class has increased

■ **ABOVE** *Instant reactions are vital when the lights change.*

■ **BELOW** *Terry Vance takes his place on the start-line on one of the ultra-quick Suzukis with which he had much success in the 1980s.*

■ **BELOW** *Twin-engined bikes such as the Weslake-powered machine of top British rider John Hobbs dominated drag racing in the 1970s, but are no longer permitted.*

in popularity to such an extent that some American racers are well-sponsored professionals.

Modern drag meets include numerous classes such as Funny Bike, for machines with roadster-based looks and power aids such as turbochargers or nitrous oxide, and Pro Stock, for highly tuned, near-standard-looking bikes that run on petrol. The cheapest and most basic class is one which allows riders to race on almost any motorcycle including standard or lightly modified roadsters.

RECORD BREAKING

The fastest motorcycles of all are the record-breakers: long, low and highly specialized machines built purely to reach phenomenal top speeds in wide open spaces. Aerodynamics are as vital as horsepower at very high speed, and the fastest machines run at places such as the Bonneville salt flats in Utah are streamliners, cigar-shaped projectiles in which the rider reclines with feet forward.

Bikes were much more simple when William Cook took his Peugeot-engined NLG to a recorded 75.9mph (122.14kph) at Brooklands in 1909, setting what is generally accepted as the first speed record. Indian's Jake de Rosier raised the figure to 88.9mph (143.06kph) at the same track two years later, only to be beaten by Matchless founder Charles Collier, who was recorded at 91.3mph (146.92kph) shortly afterwards. In 1920 Indian regained the

■ LEFT *In the 1930s Ernst Henne made use of Germany's autobahns to set a series of world records on streamliners powered by super-charged BMW twins.*

crown when Ernie Walker was timed at 104mph (167.36kph) at Daytona Beach. This is regarded as the first official world record, as by now contestants had to make two-way runs within a set time limit.

The 1930s were a great time for record-breaking in Europe, where Germany's Ernst Henne set several new marks on BMWs,

■ OPPOSITE *Bob Leppan at the 1966 London Motorcycle Show in Gyronaut X-1, the twin 650cc engined Triumph on which he set a record of 245.6mph (395.2kph).*

■ LEFT *Don Vesco poses on the Bonneville salt with Lightning Bolt, the twin-engined Kawasaki on which he set a record speed of 318.5mph (512.5kph) in 1978.*

culminating in 173.5mph (279.21kph) in 1937. Henne's great rival was Britain's Eric Fernihough, who earlier the same year had set a 169.7mph (273.09kph) record on his supercharged, JAP-engined Brough Superior. A year later Fernihough was killed when his bike got into a wobble at 180mph (290kph).

The 200mph (321kph) barrier was finally breached in 1956, when Wilhelm Herz

■ ABOVE *Bert Munro's streamlined Munro Special, based on a Model 596 Indian Scout built in 1920, set a class record of 183.5mph (295.3kph) at Bonneville in 1967.*

■ RIGHT *Bert Le Vack on a Brough Superior SS100 Pendine V-twin, on which he set several speed records in the early 1930s.*

■ BELOW *NSU's 1956 Delphin III's size is emphasized in an aerial shot of the streamliner alongside a conventional racing machine.*

(427.26kph) on a 1480cc Harley. In 1978 Vesco set a record of 318.5mph (512.5kph) on his Lightning Bolt streamliner, powered by two turbocharged, four-cylinder Kawasaki Z1000 engines. Harley reclaimed the record in 1990 when Dave Campos, riding a twin-engined, 2400cc streamliner – sponsored by readers of the American magazine *Easyriders* – raised the record to 322mph (518.19kph).

recorded 211.4mph (340.2kph) on a supercharged 500cc NSU. A year earlier Johnny Allen had taken a 650cc Triumph twin to 193.3mph (311kph) at Bonneville. The run was not recognized by the FIM, because no official observers were present, but Allen's exploits led to Triumph's most famous roadster being named the Bonneville.

In recent years the fight on the salt has been between Japan and Harley. American Don Vesco recorded 251.6mph (404.8kph) on a twin-engined, 700cc Yamaha two-stroke streamliner in 1970; a month later fellow road racer Cal Rayborn was timed at 265.5mph

A-Z OF MOTORCYCLES

The A-Z section that follows is a guide to the major manufacturers and the models they have produced since Gottlieb Daimler first fired-up Einspur back in 1885. No attempt has been made to cover all the makes: that would have been impossible. Motorcycling's history is littered with names of firms that built a few bikes and then went out of business, many of them before 1930. Names such as Abako, Abbotsford, ABC Scootamota, Abendsonne, Aberdale, Abe-Star.

The most important marques and their greatest hits, plus a few misses, are here, from AJS and Bimota to Yamaha and Zündapp. Between them they tell the story of an industry that has had many ups and downs, but which has produced many fine machines for the benefit of millions of riders worldwide. Some bikes have been cleverly engineered, others are simply beautiful to look at. The best have combined both style and performance, giving their riders the feeling of exhilaration and freedom that only a great motorcycle can provide.

AJS

■ BELOW *Although it looked uninspiring,
the AJS Model 30 handled well and was
comfortable and reliable.*

■ AJS MODEL 30

Like most AJS roadsters, the 600cc
Model 30 of the late 1950s suffered
from a case of dual personality. Almost
exactly the same bike, differing only in
paint colour, badges and exhaust system,
was also sold as the Matchless G11 – a
result of the Wolverhampton-based AJS
firm having been taken over by
Matchless of London in 1931. The
combined firm in turn became part of
Associated Motor Cycles (AMC) in
1938, but the AJS and Matchless names
were retained and used in an attempt to
attract the continued support of each of
the brand's enthusiasts.

AJS had originally been founded by
Albert John Stevens in Wolverhampton

AJS MODEL 30 (1957)	
Engine	Aircooled 4-valve OHV pushrod parallel twin
Capacity	593cc (72 x 72.8mm)
Power	33bhp @ 6800rpm
Weight	180kg (396lb)
Top speed	95mph (152kph)

around the turn of the century, and won
the Junior TT in 1914. But AJS's
greatest racing feats came later, notably
when Les Graham won the first ever
500cc world championship on the
Porcupine twin in 1949.

The most popular AJS racebike was

the single-cylinder 350cc 7R, known as
the "Boy Racer". Introduced in 1948,
the 7R was hugely successful and was
later enlarged to 500cc to make the
Matchless G50.

Most of AJS's roadsters were less
spectacular singles and parallel twins
such as the Model 30, whose 600cc
engine had almost square dimensions,
and gave a smoother ride than most
other models. Peak output was only
33bhp but the twin was capable of
cruising fairly smoothly at 70mph
(112kph). Handling was predictable and
made for a relaxed, comfortable bike
over distances. The Model 30 was also
well-made, reliable and economical.
Unfortunately such attributes were not

■ BELOW *AJS "Boy Racers" such as this 1954-model 7R/3 remained competitive at international level for many years.*

■ BELOW *Notable early AJS models included the 350cc "Big Port" single-cylinder racer of the 1920s.*

enough to keep AJS in business. Poor sales led to parent company AMC becoming part of Norton Villiers in 1967. Some AJS bikes were then built incorporating Norton parts, but they were not successful and the factory ceased production shortly afterwards.

OTHER MAKES

■ ABC

Best known of several ABCs in the 1920s was the 398cc flat-twin built by British aircraft firm Sopwith. Regarded as the predecessor of the first BMW, the engine's unreliability led to ABC's collapse.

■ ACE

American Bill Henderson set up ACE after selling his Henderson firm to the Schwinn cycle company in 1917, and produced bikes with a similar in-line four-cylinder layout. Best known was the XP-4, which set a record speed of 130mph (209kph) in 1923. Rights were later sold to Indian, who built a similar four.

■ ADLER

Germany's Adler built motorbikes for a short time from 1902, then concentrated on cars and bicycles before making a comeback in 1949. The firm's most popular model was the M250, a twin-cylinder two-stroke roadster released in

■ ABOVE *Four-cylinder ACE racers such as this were among the world's fastest bikes in 1923.*

1953. Adlers were ridden successfully in road races and enduros, but sales declined. Finally in 1958 the firm was taken over by the Grundig Corporation, who abandoned bikes to concentrate on producing typewriters.

■ AERMACCHI

The former aircraft factory at Varese in northern Italy built some fine 250 and 350cc single-cylinder four-strokes in the 1950s and 1960s, most notably racebikes such as the 100mph (160kph) Ala d'Oro 250 introduced in 1959. Aermacchi turned to two-strokes after being bought by AMF Harley-Davidson in the 1960s. Walter Villa rode Varese-built Harleys to four 250 and 350cc world titles between 1974 and 1976, but two years later the firm was declared bankrupt and sold to Cagiva.

■ ABOVE *A 350cc Aermacchi single from the mid-1960s in racing action.*

APRILIA

■ BELOW *Aprilia's fast and agile Tuono brought a new level of performance to the naked V-twin class in 2002.*

■ APRILIA RSV MILLE

Aprilia built its reputation with fine small-capacity roadsters and a string of road-racing titles in the 250 and 125cc classes. Eventually, in 1998, the firm from north-eastern Italy entered the superbike market with the RSV Mille. Combining a 998cc V-twin engine with a chassis that owed much to Grand Prix racing experience, the RSV was a fast and fine-handling sportster.

The Mille's engine echoed rival Italian firm Ducati in its liquid-cooled, eight-valve V-twin layout, but differed in having its cylinders set at 60 instead of 90 degrees. This allowed the motor to be very compact but necessitated two vibration-reducing balancer shafts.

APRILIA RSV MILLE (1998)	
Engine	Watercooled 8-valve DOHC 60-degree V-twin
Capacity	998cc (97 x 67.5mm)
Power	128bhp @ 9250rpm
Weight	189kg (416lb)
Top speed	165mph (265kph)

Chassis design was based on a rigid twin-spar aluminium frame, which held high-quality cycle parts. Although its bodywork was more efficient than elegant, the Mille was well finished and included neat touches including a lap-timer in the instrument console.

■ LEFT *Its light weight and superb chassis made the RS250 almost unbeatable for fast cornering.*

■ BELOW *The title-winning 250cc Grand Prix racebike provided inspiration for the RS250 roadster.*

For an all-new machine the RSV was stunningly competitive in every respect. Its fuel-injected motor was smooth and reliable, with abundant midrange torque plus a peak output of 128bhp that gave a top speed of more than 160mph (257kph). Additionally, its chassis delivered high-speed stability plus very taut, responsive handling. The Mille quickly established Aprilia as a superbike manufacturer and formed the basis of a racebike that competed with some success in the World Superbike Championship.

Aprilia soon enlarged the RSV range with models including the super-sports Mille R, the versatile Falco, and a purpose-built sports-tourer called the Futura. In 2002 these were followed by a pair of naked bikes, the Tuono Fighter and limited-edition Tuono R, each combining the same 998cc V-twin engine and aluminium frame with high handlebars and a small headlamp fairing. Both were fast, handled well, and were very entertaining to ride.

Meanwhile Aprilia had quietly ceased production of the V-twin that had led its attack on the streetbike market just seven years earlier: the RS250. Essentially a roadgoing replica of the bike on which Italian idol Max Biaggi had won the 1994 250cc world title, the RS two-stroke was quick and brilliantly agile, but very much a bike from a previous era. Aprilia boss Ivano Beggio clearly had ambitious plans for the future, following his purchase of two famous old Italian marques, Moto Guzzi and Laverda.

OTHER MAKES

■ **AJW**
British firm AJW built numerous parallel twins and singles dating back to the 1920s, and carried on after the Second World War with its best-known model, the 500cc, JAP-engined Grey Fox.

■ ABOVE *In the 1930s AJW built 500cc singles, such as this one, using engines from Stevens and JAP.*

■ **AMAZONAS**
Notable for its size but not for its performance, the Brazilian-made Amazonas of the mid-1980s was powered by the flat-four VW car engine. Its astonishing vital statistics were an engine capacity of 1584cc, producing just 56bhp that needed to propel a massive 385kg (848lb).

■ RIGHT *Aprilia's 1995-model Motò 6.5 roadster was created by brilliant French designer Philippe Starck.*

■ OPPOSITE *The original 1998-model RSV Mille quickly established Aprilia as a leading super-bike manufacturer.*

ARIEL

■ ARIEL RED HUNTER

One of the oldest manufacturers of all, Ariel was known for its bicycles before they started to build motorcycles around the turn of the century. By the early 1930s, the firm from Selly Oak in the Midlands was one of Britain's most influential, and at that time employed Edward Turner, Val Page and Bert Hopwood – who would eventually

become known as three of the British bike industry's greatest designers.

Ariel hit financial problems during the 1930s and the factory was closed for a time until Jack Sangster, son of founder Charles, bought the firm and restarted production of Page-designed single-cylinder four-strokes including the Red Hunter. These were handsome machines, built in 350 and 500cc sizes, that were produced from 1932 to the late 1950s, and were even successful in sidecar trials into the 1970s. Sammy Miller's successful GOV132 trials bike was based on a 1955 Red Hunter 500.

■ BELOW *A 1954 redesign failed to make the 500cc KH twin a success.*

A late 1930s Red Hunter 500 was among the best bikes of its day, capable of well over 75mph (120kph) and reliable with it. Handling provided by

ARIEL VH500 RED HUNTER (1937)	
Engine	Aircooled 2-valve OHV pushrod single
Capacity	497cc (81.8 x 85mm)
Power	26bhp @ 5600rpm
Weight	170kg (375lb)
Top speed	82mph (131kph)

■ BELOW *The unfaired Arrow two-stroke cornered very well.*

the combination of girder forks and rigid rear end was respectable too; rear suspension was not to be introduced until 1939. The Hunter was refined throughout the 1930s, gained telescopic forks when production recommenced after the Second World War and was kept going with an alloy cylinder head and new frame in the early 1950s.

After the firm's sale to BSA in 1944, Ariel built two main types of twin, firstly the softly-tuned 500cc KH, which was introduced in 1949 but sold poorly. More powerful and successful was the Huntmaster, which was powered by a slightly modified version of the 650cc twin-cylinder engine from BSA's A10. There was more to the Huntmaster than mere badge engineering, since most parts, including the frame, were its own.

The result was a pleasant bike, good for 100mph (160kph) that was particularly popular with sidecar enthusiasts in the late 1950s.

If Ariel's most famous bike is undoubtedly the Square Four, then the bravest must be the Leader, the innovative, fully enclosed 250cc two-stroke released in 1959. With an 18bhp, twin-cylinder engine based on that of the German Adler, a pressed steel frame, effective weather protection and optional panniers, the Leader was intended to be a proper motorcycle with the convenience of a scooter.

The Leader actually worked rather well, with a top speed of about 70mph (112kph) and excellent handling. But the public didn't take to it, partly because the new Mini car offered cheap four-wheeled travel, and the bike had temperamental starting and poor brakes and finish. Ariel later stripped off the bodywork to produce the Arrow, tuning the engine to 20bhp to produce Super Sports and Golden Arrow versions. But although the Arrow sold quite well it wasn't enough to save Ariel, and the firm eventually ceased trading in 1967.

■ RIGHT *Leader was a sales flop.*

ARIEL

ARIEL SQUARE FOUR

One of the most famous roadsters of all, Ariel's Square Four was also one of the longest lived, remaining in production in various forms from 1931 to 1958. The Square Four, whose powerplant was effectively a pair of geared-together parallel twins, was designed by Edward Turner shortly after the future Triumph boss had joined Ariel in 1928. The Four's capacity of 500cc was soon afterwards increased to 600cc and then 997cc. In all three forms the "Squariel" was superbly smooth, but suffered from overheating problems with its rear cylinders. Although the biggest model was capable of more than 100mph (160kph), its performance was severely handicapped by its excessive weight.

After the Second World War the Square Four was comprehensively updated, first with a lighter aluminium engine and then, in 1954, with a new cylinder head and striking four-pipe exhaust system. By this time the Ariel had also gained telescopic front forks and plunger rear suspension. Despite this, the heavy Four was a soggy handler. Even in its final, more sophisticated guise the engine was prone to overheat. But the Square Four's smoothness, relaxed high-speed cruising ability, comfort and looks made the bike much loved by those who could afford one.

ARIEL SQUARE FOUR (1958)	
Engine	Aircooled 8-valve OHV pushrod square four
Capacity	997cc (65 x 75mm)
Power	45bhp @ 5500rpm
Weight	211kg (465lb)
Top speed	105mph (168kph)

■ BELOW *The looks of the later Square Fours, such as this 1958 model, were enhanced by a four-pipe exhaust system.*

■ OPPOSITE
Handling was never
the big, heavy
Square Four's
forte, but it could
still be made to
corner rapidly.

■ BELOW *Square*
Fours such as this
model from 1937
were supremely
smooth and good
for almost 100mph
(160kph).

■ RIGHT AND
BELOW RIGHT *The*
997cc Square Four
from 1937 – with
instruments set into
fuel tank –
produced 36bhp.

OTHER MAKES

■ ARMSTRONG

The motorcycle arm of British car components giant Armstrong produced motocross, trials, road racing and military bikes in the 1980s, after taking over Barton Engineering and CCM. Most were powered by engines from Rotax of Austria. Armstrong's CF250 road-racer, introduced in 1983, featured a tandem-twin Rotax engine in an innovative twin-spar carbon fibre frame. Niall Mackenzie and Donnie McLeod dominated British racing, and scored some impressive results in Grands Prix. Armstrong also built a very successful single-cylinder, four-stroke military bike, rights to which were later sold to Harley-Davidson.

■ ATK

Utah-based ATK made its reputation building motocross bikes with both two-stroke and four-stroke engines, most of which were sold in the States. Following a

■ ABOVE *Future 500cc Grand Prix star*
Niall Mackenzie rose to prominence on
Armstrong's rapid 250cc twin.

change of ownership, the firm introduced a pair of purposeful street legal Dirt Sports machines in 1994.

■ BAKKER

Many superb specials and racebikes have emerged from Nico Bakker's workshop in northern Holland, most with innovative chassis, and with engines ranging from Yamaha's TZ350 to BMW and Harley-Davidson four-strokes. His radical QCS (Quick Change System) sportsbike, most commonly powered by Yamaha's FZR1000 engine, used an advanced non-telescopic front suspension system. Bakker has also done much chassis development work for manufacturers including BMW and Laverda.

■ BELOW *Bakker's Bomber used*
BMW's R1100 flat-twin engine.

BENELLI

■ BENELLI 750 SEI

With its smart styling, Italian racing-red paintwork and the unique attraction of its six-cylinder engine — emphasized by an array of gleaming chromed exhaust pipes — the Benelli 750 Sei looked set to be a world-beater when it was

BENELLI 750 SEI (1975)	
Engine	Aircooled 12-valve SOHC transverse six
Capacity	748cc (56 x 50.6mm)
Power	71bhp @ 8900rpm
Weight	220kg (485lb) dry
Top speed	118mph (189kph)

■ LEFT *The Sei was supremely smooth and comfortable, but its straight-line performance was unexceptional.*

■ BELOW AND BOTTOM *The Sei's big aircooled engine and its six exhaust pipes dominate from every angle.*

launched in 1975. Instead the Sei turned out to be softly tuned and no faster than Honda's CB750-four of six years earlier. Its modest performance led to the Benelli being overshadowed by more powerful superbikes,

particularly its Italian rivals from Ducati, Guzzi and Laverda.

Not that the Sei was a bad bike, for in most respects it was a very good one. The engine, criticized for closely resembling one-and-a-half Honda CB500 units, was commendably narrow

■ RIGHT *Benelli's stylish Tornado Limited Edition roadster was very closely related to the Italian firm's World Superbike racer.*

for a six. But the maximum output of 71bhp gave a top speed of less than 120mph (193kph), and even the Sei's excellent handling and braking could not make up for that in the eyes of most riders looking for an Italian superbike.

The Sei's lack of blood and thunder was surprising given Benelli's racing pedigree. The firm was founded by six Benelli brothers from Pesaro, and produced its first bike in 1921. Racing success soon followed, culminating in Dario Ambrosini's victory in the 250cc world championship in 1950.

Ambrosini's death a year later shook Benelli, but the firm returned to racing with a four-cylinder 250cc machine that Australian Kel Carruthers rode to the 250cc world championship in 1969.

Shortly afterwards the Benelli family sold out to Argentinean car baron Alejandro de Tomaso, whose attempt to relaunch the marque with the 750 Sei and its 900cc successor ended in failure. The Benelli name faded until being acquired in the late 1990s by Andrea Merloni, a young motorcycle enthusiast who was backed by his family, owners of

one of Italy's largest industrial groups. Merloni revived Benelli first with scooters, then with a 900cc three-cylinder superbike, the Tornado.

As well as being an innovative roadster, the Tornado Limited Edition formed the basis of a World Superbike racer. Both the Limited Edition and the Tornado Tre that followed used a 12-valve motor whose 143bhp output gave a top speed of 165mph (265kph). The chassis featured an under-seat radiator with cooling fans in the tailpiece. Racing success proved elusive, but Benelli was back in style.

OTHER MAKES

■ BARIGO

Founded by Patrick Barigault at La Rochelle on the west coast of France, Barigo was a small firm with a background in supermoto racing. In 1992 Barigo produced the Supermotard roadster – basically a street-legal version of the firm's competition machine – with a 600cc Rotax single-cylinder engine, aluminium twin-beam frame and long-travel suspension. Two years later came the Onixa, which combined a similar motor and frame with sportsbike cycle parts and striking, fully-faired bodywork. But few were built before Barigo ceased production.

■ LEFT *Barigo's 600cc Onixa sportster looked peculiar but was very light and handled well.*

BIMOTA

■ BIMOTA SB6

The small Italian firm Bimota produced
relatively few bikes during its turbulent
30-year life, but made an impact out of
all proportion to its size. At its best the
firm from Rimini produced glamorous,
technically advanced superbikes of high
performance and minimal compromise.
One such was the 1994-model SB6,
which was powered by a 156bhp four-
cylinder Suzuki GSX-R1100 engine that
gave a top speed of 170mph (273kph).
The SB6 featured a state-of-the-art
frame, self-supporting seat unit and
top-quality cycle parts, and was a hugely desirable sportsbike.

Seventeen years earlier, exactly the
same had been true of another Bimota,

BIMOTA SB6 (1994)	
Engine	Watercooled 16-valve DOHC transverse four
Capacity	1074cc (75.5 x 60mm)
Power	156bhp @ 10,000rpm
Weight	190kg (418lb)
Top speed	175mph (280kph)

the GS750-powered SB2 of 1977. This
was the first purpose-designed roadster
produced by Bimota after the firm had
been formed by Messrs BIanchi, MOrri
and TAmburini (hence the name). Its
75bhp GS750 motor was held in a
beautifully made tubular steel frame.

OTHER MAKES

■ BETA

Italian firm Beta built a rapid 175cc roadster in the late 1950s, but in recent years has concentrated on the off-road market, particularly trials bike.

■ BFG

Powered by the 70bhp, 1300cc flat-four engine normally found in a Citroën GS car, the French-built BFG was intended

as a grand tourer. Strange styling and excess weight meant that sales were limited mainly to the French police, and BFG went bust in the mid-1980s.

■ BIANCHI

Best known for some impressive Grand Prix performances in the early 1960s, Bianchi built bicycles before becoming one of the first Italian motorcycle manufacturers in 1897. Bianchi won many races in the 1920s, built a spectacular supercharged four-cylinder 500cc race r in 1938, and sold motocross bikes as well as small-capacity roadsters before motorcycle production ended in 1967.

■ LEFT *In the early 1960s Bianchi produced both racing bikes, and roadsters such as this 300cc MT61.*

■ ABOVE *Bimota's Tesi could be made to handle very well, but its complex non-telescopic front suspension system sometimes gave problems.*

■ RIGHT *With its sculpted bodywork and state-of-the-art chassis, Bimota's SB2 was a sensation in 1977.*

■ LEFT *The stylish and rapid SB6, powered by Suzuki's GSX-R1100 engine, was a great success for Bimota.*

Suspension, brakes and tyres were the best available, and the swoopy seat-tank unit's fibreglass was lined with aluminium, meaning no rear subframe was needed. In 1977 the fine-handling, 130mph (209kph) SB2 was the ultimate roadster sensation.

These and models including the Kawasaki-engined KB1, Yamaha-powered YB6 and Ducati V-twin based DB1 and DB2 were successful despite.

Bimota's high prices, but the firm's adoption of new technology ultimately proved fatal. The forkless Tesi 1D of the early 1990s was an expensive flop, and a more serious failure came at the end of the decade with the 500 Vdue, a sportster powered by Bimota's own direct-injection two-stroke engine. The Vdue was stylish and light but its engine ran poorly. Bimota, heavily in debt, ceased production in 2000.

BMW

■ BMW R60/2

In recent years BMW has produced bikes with one, three and four cylinders, but the German firm's name is synonymous with flat-twins. The very first BMW motorcycle, the R32 of 1923, was powered by a boxer engine that produced 8bhp at 3300rpm and used shaft final drive. The R32 was rather expensive – but it was cleverly designed, nicely finished and sold well. Some things really don't change.

Among the most popular BMW twins during the 1950s and 1960s were the 600cc R60 and its successor the R60/2, which was launched in 1960. These models, and also the slightly slower 500cc R50 and R50/2 bikes of the same period, were hugely successful due to their relaxed, fuss-free nature, reliability and general ease of use. The R60/2 used a slightly tuned version of the 28bhp

BMW R60/2 (1960)	
Engine	Aircooled 4-valve pushrod flat-twin
Capacity	494cc (68 x 68mm)
Power	26bhp @ 5800rpm
Weight	195kg (430lb)
Top speed	87mph (139kph)

aircooled boxer motor from the R60, which gave superbly smooth running and a top speed of about 90mph (145kph). Although BMW had been among the first firms to use telescopic forks in the 1930s, the R60/2 was fitted with leading-link Earles forks which were particularly well suited to sidecar work. Heavy steering and soft suspension at both ends made the 60/2 ill-suited to sporty solo riding, but the

BMW had few equals for comfortable long-distance touring.

BMW has had little involvement in top level competition in recent years, but has a long and impressive history of racing and record-breaking. One of the most famous early stars was Ernst Henne, who set a number of speed records on streamlined, supercharged boxers in the 1930s. Schorsch Meier became the first foreign rider to win an Isle of Man TT when he took the 1939 Senior race on a supercharged 500cc flat-twin. Works BMW pilot Walter Zeller won many international races for BMW in the 1950s, finishing second in the 500cc world championship in 1956. And BMW flat-twins dominated sidecar racing for two decades, winning 19 out of 21 world championships between 1954 and 1974 with drivers including Max Deubel and Klaus Enders.

■ LEFT *The 494cc R50/2, seen here in 1955 with a single saddle, shared many parts with the 60/2.*

■ BELOW LEFT *Schorsch Meier's 1939 TT-winning supercharged twin had a top speed of over 125mph (201kph).*

■ BELOW *Fritz Scheidegger's world titles in 1965 and 1966 continued a long run of BMW sidecar success.*

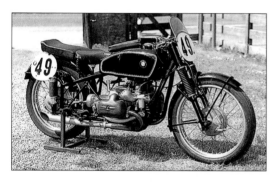

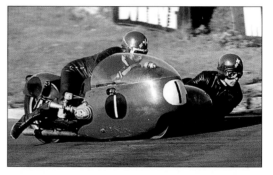

■ RIGHT
This 500cc, 12bhp R52 flat-twin dates from 1928, the first year BMW fitted lights as standard.

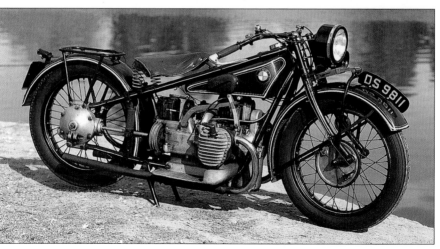

■ OPPOSITE
With its Earles forks, smooth 30bhp engine and all-round comfort, the R60/2 made a fine tourer.

BMW

■ BMW R90S

BMW's traditional flat-twins were gradually refined over the years and reached new heights of performance and desirability with the R90S of 1974. The basis of the R90S was the familiar 898cc boxer lump from the R90/6, tuned slightly to give 67bhp at 7000rpm. To the normal specification the R90S added a neat bikini fairing, stylish smoked paintwork, twin front disc brakes and even the luxury of a clock in the dashboard.

The R90S couldn't match the sheer

■ RIGHT
Although it was built for comfort as well as speed, the R90S was a match for most bikes in the corners.

■ BELOW
With its fairing and smoked orange paintwork the R90S had the looks to match its superb performance.

■ ABOVE *Increased compression ratio and 38mm Dell'Orto carburettors gave the R90S an output of 67bhp.*

■ OPPOSITE *The R1100S was the sportiest BMW boxer for years, and handled well thanks to an innovative chassis layout.*

BMW R90S (1974)	
Engine	Aircooled 4-valve OHV pushrod flat-twin
Capacity	898cc (90 x 70.6mm)
Power	67bhp @ 7000rpm
Weight	215kg (474lb)
Top speed	125mph (201kph)

■ BELOW *The sophisticated, fine-handling R1100RS sports-tourer heralded a new era for BMW flat-twins.*

■ BELOW *The R1200C Independent featured a solo seat, smoked speedster windsheild and two-tone paintwork.*

power of Kawasaki's four-cylinder Z1 but it accelerated smoothly to a top speed of 125mph (201kph), handled very respectably, and was superbly comfortable, well-finished and reliable. Unfortunately, in many markets the exotic German machine cost twice as much as Honda's CB750.

In the early 1980s the future looked bleak for the flat-twins, as BMW released its new range of watercooled K-series fours and triples. But demand for the traditional twins remained strong, and BMW's management thought again. Eventually, in 1993, came the new-generation boxer, the R1100RS, powered by a 1085cc fuel-injected, air/oilcooled, four-valves-per-cylinder, high-cam motor producing 90bhp.

The R1100RS's chassis featured Telelever front suspension, consisting of hollow fork legs, a horizontal arm pivoting on the engine, and a single suspension unit. Telelever worked well, and the rest of the RS was equally impressive. With plenty of midrange power, a 135mph (217kph) top speed, a protective fairing, and powerful, anti-lock brakes, the R1100RS was a sports-tourer in the finest BMW tradition.

In 1997 BMW produced a modern equivalent of the R90S in the R1100S,

which combined a more powerful, 98bhp version of the boxer motor with a lighter and sportier chassis based around an aluminium frame. With a top speed of 140mph (225kph), excellent handling and powerful brakes, the R1100S was the sportiest BMW yet, though it was still comfortable enough for everyday or touring use. The R1100S gave BMW's image a big boost and the same was true

of a very different boxer that arrived in the same year. The R1200C cruiser was refreshing in its departure from the V-twin format adopted by almost every other firm. As well as the 1170cc flat-twin engine layout and Telelever suspension, it featured a host of distinctive styling touches plus some neat details including a pillion seat that converted into a rider's back-rest.

BMW

■ BMW K1

With its brightly-coloured, all-enveloping bodywork, the K1 was a startling bike by any manufacturer's standards when it was launched in 1989, let alone by the standards of traditionally conservative BMW. In conjunction with the huge front mudguard, the K1's fairing and large rear section combined to give a wind-cheating shape unmatched even by Japanese sportsbikes.

Behind the plastic was a tuned, 16-valve version of the watercooled,

BMW K1 (1989)	
Engine	Watercooled 16-valve DOHC longitudinal four
Capacity	987cc (67 x 70mm)
Power	100bhp @ 8000rpm
Weight	234kg (468lb) wet
Top speed	145mph (233kph)

987cc four-cylinder engine that had been introduced five years earlier in the K100. The K-series four aligned its

cylinders horizontally, in contrast to the transverse layout favoured by the Japanese. In K1 form the fuel-injected four produced 100bhp, sufficient to send the aerodynamically efficient BMW to a top speed of over 140mph (225kph). A strong steel frame, based on that of the K100, firm suspension (with the Paralever system to combat the effect of the drive-shaft) and powerful triple-disc braking gave good handling and stopping power. The K1 was too big and heavy to be a true sportsbike, but it did much to boost BMW's image.

■ BELOW *With its aggressive styling, the K1 was a radical departure for traditionally conservative BMW.*

■ LEFT *The 1997-model K1200RS featured 130bhp maximum output, aluminium frame and adjustable riding position.*

■ BELOW *By 2003 the K1200GT came with linked brakes, large touring fairing, as well as panniers and an optional GPS system.*

OTHER MAKES

■ **BÖHMERLAND**

Notable for its vast length and for being designed to carry three people, the Böhmerland was produced in Czechoslovakia between 1923 and 1939. Designed and built by Albin Liebisch, the Böhmerland was powered by a 600cc, 16bhp single-cylinder engine. As well as the long wheelbase "Langtouren", with its rear pannier fuel tanks, there was a shorter Jubilee model, and a sportier bike called the Racer.

■ **BOSS HOSS**

Originally named Boss Hog until Harley-Davidson objected, and powered by America's ubiquitous Chevrolet V-eight engine – typically with a capacity approaching six litres and output of 300bhp – the Boss Hoss was arguably the biggest, heaviest and most powerful bike in series production. Final drive was by chain and there was only one gear: fast forward. Claimed top speed was over 150mph (241kph) but the Hoss's handling, with 450kg (992lb) of weight and a square-section rear tyre, made for just as much excitement. During the 1990s the Hoss was refined with automatic transmission plus a much improved chassis, and was joined by a slightly lighter V-six model.

■ ABOVE *The amazing Böhmerland had a top speed of over 70mph (112kph).*

■ ABOVE AND RIGHT
Its awesome Chevy V-eight powerplant made the Boss Hoss very fast – in a straight line!

BRITTEN

■ BRITTEN V-1000

Impressive displays in international twin-cylinder races in recent seasons confirmed the Britten V-twin's status as one of the world's most exotic and brilliantly engineered motorbikes. Designed and almost totally hand-built by New Zealander John Britten and his small team, the Britten was powered by a watercooled, fuel-injected 60-degree V-twin motor. After the original V-1000 had made its mark at Daytona in 1991, its engine was enlarged to 1108cc, producing a phenomenal 171bhp. To allow the bike to compete in Superbike racing, Britten then developed a new V-1000 with a 985cc, short-stroke engine.

The rigid power unit acted as the V-1000's frame, supporting girder forks and the huge rear swing-arm, both of which were formed from lightweight Kevlar and carbon fibre. Front and rear

suspension systems were multi-adjustable and used Öhlins shocks. The rear unit was situated in front of the engine for optimum cooling. The Britten

BRITTEN V-1000 (1995)	
Engine	Watercooled dohc 8-valve 60-degree V-twin
Capacity	985cc (99 x 64mm)
Power	155bhp @ 12,400rpm
Weight	145kg (320lb) wet
Top speed	185mph (296kph)

featured an advanced, computerized engine-management system that recorded and could adjust the engine's performance as it ran. To top it all, the V-1000 was beautifully styled; its narrow width and sensuous curves contributed to recorded speeds of more than 180mph (289kph) at Daytona.

As well as the bikes raced successfully by Britten's own riders including Paul Lewis and Andrew

Stroud, small numbers of production racebikes were sold for sizeable sums of money. The V-1000's elaborate construction made the prospect of a road-going version appear remote.

In 1995, when the racebike was again successful at Daytona, John Britten's collaboration with the Indian marque's new Australian owner, Maurits Hayim-Langridge, looked likely to result in elements of the V-1000 being incorporated in Indian streetbikes due for release within a few years. When Britten tragically died of cancer only six months later, at the age of 45, the motorcycle world lost one of its greatest engineering talents.

■ ABOVE *Its engine-management system allowed the Britten, ridden here by Jim Moodie, to be fine-tuned to suit the conditions.*

■ OPPOSITE *The sculpted V-1000 was one of the most beautiful bikes ever built, as well as one of the fastest.*

OTHER MAKES

■ BRIDGESTONE

Motorcycle production was never any more than a sideline for the Bridgestone rubber company, which remains a major tyre manufacturer to this day. But in the 1950s and 1960s Bridgestone built a range of bikes, from mopeds to twin-cylinder two-stroke sportsters, the best of which was the 350GTR. Powered by a disc-valve, parallel-twin engine that produced a claimed 40bhp, the GTR was a quick and stylish motorcycle that was capable of over 90mph (145kph).

The six-speed Bridgestone was a sophisticated machine when it was launched on the American market in 1966. Its rubber-mounted motor was reasonably smooth, and its blend of steel twin-downtube frame, gaitered forks and twin shocks gave good handling with a plush ride. But the high price limited export sales and at the end of that year Bridgestone, who had declined to take on important tyre customers Honda, Kawasaki, Suzuki and Yamaha by selling bikes on the home market, quit motorcycle manufacture altogether.

■ LEFT AND INSET *The disc-valve 350GTR was fast and refined, but Bridgestone abandoned it to concentrate on tyre production.*

BROUGH SUPERIOR

■ BELOW AND BOTTOM *The final, 1939-model Superior SS100 was arguably the world's finest motorcycle.*

■ BROUGH SUPERIOR SS100

George Brough combined his own frames with bought-in engines and other parts to produce bikes which were innovative, exclusive, expensive and, above all, fast. Never one to sell his products short, he named his first machine the Superior to the displeasure of his motorcycle engineer father, William Brough, who built flat-twins and who commented that he supposed his was now to be known as the Inferior.

But superior George's bikes were – as they proved with a string of race wins and speed records in the 1920s and 1930s – ridden by Brough himself and other legendary figures such as Eric Fernihough, Freddie Dixon and Bert Le Vack. The machines built by the small

■ LEFT *By 1939,
the SS100 was
powered by a 50-
degree Matchless
V-twin engine,
fitted with a four
speed gearbox.*

■ BELOW *Earlier SS100s, such as this
1926 example, used powerplants from JAP
of Tottenham, north London.*

■ BOTTOM *Had not the Second World
War intervened, Brough's flat-four Dream
might have proved an outstanding machine.*

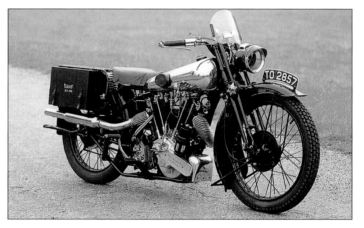

BROUGH SUPERIOR SS100 (1939)	
Engine	Aircooled 4-valve OHV pushrod 50-degree V-twin
Capacity	988cc (85.5 x 86mm)
Power	45bhp @ 5000rpm
Weight	180kg (396lb) dry
Top speed	100mph (160kph)

team from Nottingham were regarded by many as the best in the world. When *The Motor Cycle* summed up a test by saying a Superior was the Rolls Royce of motor-cycles, Brough seized on the line for his advertising – and Rolls didn't object.

The SS100, produced between 1925 and 1940, was Brough's most famous model. It was powered initially by a 980cc V-twin from JA Prestwich (JAP), the big engine-making firm from north London, and came with a signed guaran-tee from Brough that the bike had been timed at over 100mph (160kph) for a quarter of a mile (0.4 kilometres). Brochures also boasted of the hands-off stability at speeds of 95mph (152kph).

Fewer than 400 SS100s were built, most using the JAP engine but the last 100 or so models powered by a Matchless V-twin. The bike's specification was constantly changed, with the result that no two SS100s were identical. Optional rear suspension was

introduced in 1928, foot gearchange in 1935 and a four-speed Norton gearbox a year later. Brough's numerous innovations included flyscreens, twin headlamps, crashbars and panniers.

TE Shaw, alias Lawrence of Arabia, owned a series of Superiors (the last of which cost him his life in a crash), each of which he fitted with a special stainless steel petrol tank.

The Brough Superior that might have topped even the SS100 was the Dream, an exotic 990cc flat-four roadster that George Brough revealed in late 1938. Its engine featured twin crankshafts, linked by gears, and a firing arrangement that made it supremely smooth. Development of the promising Dream was halted when the Second World War broke out, and Brough Superior production was never restarted.

BSA

■ **BSA GOLD STAR DBD34**
For most of its life the Birmingham
Small Arms Company was Britain's
biggest motorcycle manufacturer, and in
the years after the Second World War it
was the largest in the world, producing
over 75,000 bikes in some years during
the 1950s. At that time BSA was an
industrial giant, involved in producing
guns, taxi-cabs and metal plate, and had
also taken over Ariel and Sunbeam.

The firm's origins in armaments manufacture stretched back to 1863. Bicycle
production followed in the 1880s and
the Small Heath factory built its first
motorcycle, powered by a Minerva
engine, in 1905. BSA's reputation grew,
notably with a series of reliable and
successful V-twins in the 1920s.

BSA's best-loved early model was the
S27, universally known as the Sloper

■ BELOW AND
BOTTOM *Lean,
functional and
stylish, the DBD34
did the most to
make the Gold Star
badge famous.*

BSA GOLD STAR DBD34 (1956)	
Engine	Aircooled 2-valve OHV pushrod single
Capacity	499cc (85 x 88mm)
Power	42bhp @ 7000rpm
Weight	159kg (350lb)
Top speed	110mph (177kph)

■ BELOW *This 1930s Champion spark plug advertisement featured the Sloper in an unflattering manner.*

■ LEFT *Over 125,000 of BSA's 500cc M20 singles were supplied to allied forces during the Second World War.*

■ BELOW LEFT *This off-road Gold Star competed successfully in the International Six Days Trial in 1954.*

■ BOTTOM *Slopers such as this model from the early 1930s were refined, quiet and good for 65mph (104kph).*

due to its angled-forward single cylinder. Introduced with a 500cc engine in 1927, and later available in 350 to 595cc versions, the Sloper was stylish, sophisticated and notably quiet. It quickly became popular and was frequently updated through its ten years in production.

The Second World War was a particularly busy time for the BSA factory which, despite suffering heavy bomb damage that claimed 53 workers' lives, produced huge numbers of both guns and bikes.

The most famous BSA was the legendary Gold Star single, which was hugely successful as a roadster and as a competition bike in road racing, motocross and trials in the 1950s. The "Goldie" had its origins in 1937, when racer Walter Handley earned a Brooklands Gold Star award for lapping the banked track at over 100mph (160kph) on BSA's 500cc Empire Star. The next year's model was named Gold Star in recognition, and after a break for

the War it was relaunched, initially as a 350. Several tuning options were available, with power outputs ranging from 18bhp for the trials version, to over 30bhp for the track racer. Each bike was supplied with a factory certificate testifying to the machine's power.

Numerous revisions kept the Gold Star in top position throughout the 1950s. The archetypal model was the 500cc

DBD34 introduced in 1956, with its clip-on handlebars, polished tank and finned engine. An open-mouthed Amal carburettor and swept-back exhaust combined to give 110mph (177kph) top speed. The Gold Star dominated the Isle of Man Clubmans TT in that year and was successful in many unofficial burn-ups, remaining prized as a café racer after production ended in 1963.

BSA

■ BSA 650cc A10

BSA built two main versions of the trademark British parallel twin: the 500cc A7, which was introduced in 1946 and updated five years later, and the 650cc A10 that appeared in 1950. Both the A7 and A10 were sold in many forms in the 1950s, earning a reputation more for oil-tightness, economy and reliability than for looks or performance. In 1962 they were replaced by the 500cc A50 and the 650cc A65, which featured updates including a unit-construction engine and gearbox.

The original A10 was the Golden Flash, whose flexible, 35bhp single-camshaft engine gave a top speed approaching 100mph (160kph). In 1954 the Flash was updated with swing-arm rear suspension, instead of the old plunger design. Other A10s including

■ BELOW *The 646cc A10 of the mid-1950s was a handsome machine, and a big-selling success for BSA.*

BSA 650cc A10 GOLDEN FLASH (1958)	
Engine	Aircooled 4-valve OHV pushrod parallel twin
Capacity	646cc (70 x 84mm)
Power	34bhp @ 5750rpm
Weight	195kg (430lb)
Top speed	96mph (154kph)

the Super Flash and Road Rocket provided a little more power and speed, and in 1958 BSA produced the A10S Super Rocket, with a 43bhp engine and top speed of 105mph (168kph).

The best and rarest of the bunch was the Rocket Gold Star introduced in 1962. This consisted of a slightly tuned Super Rocket engine in a frame based on that of the Gold Star single. Forks, brakes and wheels also came from the

■ OPPOSITE PAGE, TOP *This A65L
Lightning twin provided good performance
by mid-1960s' standards.*

■ LEFT *John Cooper rode BSA's 750cc
triple to some famous victories.*

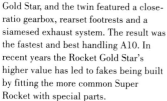

■ ABOVE *BSA's smaller twin was
the 500cc A7, like this 1956-model
Shooting Star.*

Gold Star, and the twin featured a close-ratio gearbox, rearset footrests and a siamesed exhaust system. The result was the fastest and best handling A10. In recent years the Rocket Gold Star's higher value has led to fakes being built by fitting the more common Super Rocket with special parts.

BSA's last great roadster was the 750cc Rocket Three triple, which appeared at the same time as the Triumph Trident in 1969. The two models shared a 58bhp engine that owed more to Triumph than BSA, although the Rocket Three unit was angled at 15 degrees in a different twin-downtube frame. Like the Trident, the Rocket Three was a fast, competent bike, but by 1971 BSA was in financial trouble, recording a massive loss. The once mighty firm was swallowed up by the new Norton Villiers Triumph company, and the last batch of triples – wearing the well-known Triumph badges – left BSA's famous Small Heath factory in 1973.

■ BELOW *The ultimate BSA parallel twin
is a genuine Rocket Gold Star such as this
immaculate 1963 model.*

BUELL

■ BELOW *Twin headlamps gave the Lightning XB9S an aggressive look.*

■ BOTTOM *The Firebolt was one of the most innovative bikes for years.*

■ BUELL FIREBOLT XB9R

Erik Buell had been building quirky, cleverly engineered bikes around Harley-Davidson engines for years when the Firebolt XB9R was launched in 2002, but even by Buell's standards this bike was unusual. Its aluminium frame held a tuned, 984cc version of Harley's V-twin Sportster powerplant, and looked conventional. But the frame spars also acted as the fuel tank, while the aluminium swing-arm doubled as the oil tank. Add to that the single perimeter front brake disc, bolted to the wheel rim instead of the hub, and the result was one of the most innovative bikes for years. With an output of 92bhp from its heavily modified 45-degree pushrod

BUELL FIREBOLT XB9R (2002)	
Engine	Aircooled 4-valve OHV pushrod 45-degree V-twin
Capacity	984cc (88.9 x 79.8mm)
Power	92bhp @ 7200rpm
Weight	175kg (385lb) dry
Top speed	130mph (209kph)

V-twin, the Firebolt had a top speed of 130mph (209kph) so was not particularly fast. But that unique, light and compact chassis gave top-class handling and braking. And the stylish Firebolt, which was soon followed by an aggressive naked model called the Lightning XB9S

■ RIGHT *The RS1200 was one Harley-engined bike that encouraged hard riding on twisty roads.*

■ BELOW *Buell's S2 Thunderbolt was developed and sold in collaboration with Harley-Davidson itself.*

which shared its major chassis parts, was great fun to ride.

Buell was founded by former Harley engineer and racer Erik Buell, who designed and built an innovative, Harley-engined racebike called the RR1000, which was successful in twin-cylinder racing in the 1980s. The RR was followed in 1989 by the RS1200, a half-faired roadster that used a similar engine and tubular steel frame incorporating Buell's ingenious rubber-mounting system, and a rear shock set horizontally beneath the engine.

Buell's big break came in 1993, when Harley bought a 49 per cent stake in the firm, later taking a controlling interest. Added investment led to a new range of steel-framed 1200cc V-twins including the S2 Thunderbolt and X1 Lightning. These and the Firebolt that followed in 2002 confirmed that Erik Buell's talent for innovative engineering was undiminished.

OTHER MAKES

■ BULTACO

Francisco Bulto founded Bultaco near Barcelona in 1958 after splitting from Montesa, which he had co-founded, due to that firm's reluctance to go racing. The new firm built a series of rapid small-capacity two-stroke racers through the 1960s, and had many high finishes in Grands Prix. Roadsters included the rapid 250cc Metralla, which had a claimed top speed of more than 100mph (160kph). Bultaco also specialized in off-road bikes. Sammy Miller's win on a Sherpa in the 1965 Scottish Six Days Trial heralded the two-stroke's takeover in trials. After the trials world championship was started in 1975, Bultaco won five years in a row. In road racing, Angel Nieto

■ LEFT
Angel Nieto won two 50cc world titles for Bultaco.

■ FAR LEFT
Bultaco's trials stars have included world champion Yjrio Vesterinen.

and Ricardo Tormo won a total of four 50cc world titles in the years up to 1981. But by then a series of strikes had crippled Bultaco, and production ended shortly afterwards.

■ CABTON

One of several Japanese firms that built bikes heavily based on British singles and parallel twins in the 1950s, Cabton failed to survive the more competitive decade of the 1960s.

CAGIVA

CAGIVA V-RAPTOR

Cagiva has had a turbulent history since the Castiglioni brothers, Claudio and Gianfranco, founded the firm on the site of the former Aermacchi Harley-Davidson factory at Varese in northern Italy in 1978. Owner of first Ducati and then MV Agusta, Cagiva also raced successfully at 500cc Grand Prix level and has produced some high quality street bikes, notably the Raptor and V-Raptor with which the marque entered the superbike market in 2000.

Styled by Miguel Galluzzi, the creator of Ducati's Monster, the Raptors were striking naked machines powered by the 996cc V-twin engine from Suzuki's TL1000S. Previous large-capacity Cagivas were trail bikes including the 900 and 750cc Elefant, derivatives of which were successful in desert racing. Cagiva's earlier growth was based on

■ ABOVE *John Kocinski won the US Grand Prix in 1993, and briefly led the championship in 1994.*

CAGIVA V-RAPTOR (2000)	
Engine	Watercooled 8-valve DOHC 90-degree Suzuki V-twin
Capacity	996cc (98 x 66mm)
Power	105bhp @ 8500rpm
Weight	197kg (433lb)
Top speed	150mph (241kph)

125cc two-strokes, notably the Mito, an agile 100mph (161kph) screamer with cutting-edge style and performance.

The last years were the best ones for Cagiva's 500cc Grand Prix challenge, as the small Italian team that had dared take on the Japanese factories finally won races in 1992 and '93 – and saw John Kocinski briefly lead the 1994 500cc world championship on the C594 V-four. Then Cagiva quit racing, amid financial problems that resulted in the sale of Ducati. Seven years later in 2001, financial trouble severely delayed production again.

OTHER MAKES

■ CASAL

When Casal began production of its small-capacity two-strokes in the mid-1960s it relied on Zündapp engines. The Portuguese firm has since developed its own powerplants, and continues to build mainly 50cc bikes for the home market.

■ CCM

After building big-single motocross bikes based on BSA's B50 in the 1970s, British

■ LEFT *Cotton's Telstar racer of the mid-1960s used a 30bhp Villiers single-cylinder engine.*

■ BELOW LEFT *Trials star Dave Thorpe in action on a 250cc CCM in 1979.*

specialist CCM was taken over by the Armstrong car components firm. Founder Alan Clews bought the company back in the mid-1980s and produced Rotax-engined motocross and trial bikes. Recent enduro and supermoto models such as the quick and versatile R30 and 644 Dual Sport have used 644cc single-cylinder Suzuki engines.

■ COTTON

Most of Cotton's production in the 1950s and 1960s consisted of modest roadsters with Villiers two-stroke engines. The firm had some racing history, though, and its "coTTon" badge was inspired by Stanley Woods' Isle of Man win in 1923.

■ CYCLONE

Famous for its exotic 1000cc, overhead-camshaft V-twins, Cyclone began to build bikes in 1913 and won many races with them. But the American firm's roadsters were not profitable, and Cyclone production lasted only for a few years.

■ CZ

Czech firm CZ began building bikes in the 1930s, and won several motocross world titles with its single-cylinder two-strokes in the 1960s. After the Second World War CZ was nationalized and produced utility roadsters in collaboration with Jawa, before Cagiva took control of the company in 1992.

■ ABOVE *The 1994 version of Cagiva's 125cc Mito featured a 30bhp two-stroke engine, aluminium beam frame and styling inspired by Ducati's 916.*

■ OPPOSITE *The stylish V-Raptor added a headlamp fairing to the basic naked V-twin format of the Raptor.*

■ RIGHT *Cagiva's Elefant 900 was a sophisticated trail bike powered by a Ducati V-twin engine.*

DOUGLAS

■ DOUGLAS DRAGONFLY

The flat-twin engine was Douglas's trademark, and the firm from Bristol concentrated on that layout from 1906 – when the Douglas family began building bikes previously known as Fairys – until its demise in the late 1950s. Early

DOUGLAS DRAGONFLY (1955)	
Engine	Aircooled 4-valve OHV pushrod flat-twin
Capacity	348cc (60.8 x 60mm)
Power	17bhp @ 6000rpm
Weight	166kg (365lb)
Top speed	75mph (120kph)

models had boxer engines in line with the bike, including the banked sidecar outfit that versatile racing star Freddie Dixon used to win the 1923 sidecar TT. Roadsters such as the K32 were among the most sophisticated of the 1930s.

Later boxers such as the 350cc T35 of 1947 mounted the cylinders across the frame in BMW style, but although performance was good Douglas gained a reputation for dubious quality of both workmanship and materials. The last and best model was the 350cc Dragonfly, which was launched in 1955 and featured a headlamp nacelle that blended into the fuel tank. Aided by stout Earles forks and well-damped twin

rear shock units, the handling was excellent. But although the Dragonfly cruised smoothly and comfortably at 60mph (96kph), its low-rev performance and 75mph (120kph) top speed were moderate, and sales were not enough to keep Douglas in business.

■ ABOVE *The Dragonfly's 348cc flat-twin engine was not highly successful, lacking real smoothness at low revs.*

■ LEFT *Flowing styling and a Reynolds-Earles pivoted front fork gave the Dragonfly a distinctive look.*

■ RIGHT *Early*
Douglas twins,
such as this
2.75bhp model
from 1914, had
cylinders in line
with the bike.

■ FAR RIGHT
Douglas introduced
the disc brake on
this 6bhp racebike
in 1922.

OTHER MAKES

■ DAIMLER
German engineer Gottlieb Daimler is credited with building the world's first motorcycle, the wooden-framed Einspur that was first ridden by his son Paul in 1885. Daimler had no great interest in motorcycles, and shortly afterwards abandoned the project to concentrate on automobile development.

■ DERBI
Barcelona firm Derbi's name showed its roots, DERivados de BIcicletus meaning "derivative of bicycles" – which is what they had built until the 250cc Super was released in 1950. Early motorcycles included a 350cc twin but in the 1960s Derbi concentrated on small-capacity bikes such as the racy 49cc and 74cc Grand Sports. The firm's successful challenge in Grand Prix racing's smaller classes culminated in Angel Nieto winning five 50cc and 125cc world titles between 1969 and 1972, when Derbi pulled out to concentrate on road bikes and motocross. Over a decade later the firm returned to Grands Prix to win a string of titles with another legendary Spanish rider, Jorge "Aspar" Martinez.

■ DKW
Founded by Danish-born Joerge Rasmussen, two-stroke specialist DKW began building bikes in 1920 and by 1928 had become the world's largest manufacturer with a production of over 100,000 machines. In 1932 DKW merged with Audi, Horsch and Wanderer to form Auto Union, giving the four-circle logo still

■ ABOVE *Daimler's 265cc Einspur had a*
top speed of about 8mph (12kph).

■ ABOVE *Spanish stars and Derbi team-*
mates Jorge Martinex and Alex Criville were
closely matched at Jerez in 1988.

■ ABOVE *The SB500 Luxus became the*
300,000th DKW bike to be built when it
rolled off the German firm's line in 1935.

used by Audi. Numerous racing successes included Ewald Kluge's 1938 Junior TT win on a supercharged 250cc split-single. After the Second World War the Zschopau factory was taken over by MZ, and DKW moved to Ingoldstadt in West Germany. In 1957 the firm joined the Victoria and Express companies in the Zweirad Union, but in 1966 this was bought by two-stroke engine manufacturer Fichtel & Sachs, who dropped the DKW name.

■ DMW
Wolverhampton-based DMW was founded during the Second World War to make suspension systems for rigid framed bikes, and progressed to building complete machines in 1947. Most were Villiers-engined two-strokes, notably the 250cc twin-cylinder Dolomite. Roadster production ended in 1966, although DMW continued to build trials bikes on a limited basis.

■ DNEPR
For many years Ukrainian firm Dnepr has built shaft-driven flat-twins based on BMW designs from the 1940s. The Dnepr 11 was a 649cc twin, producing 36bhp. Designed for use with a sidecar, it had a reverse gear and a top speed of about 75mph (120kph). The broadly similar military-style Dnepr 16 outfit featured drive to both rear wheels.

■ DOT
DOT's Lancashire factory built Villiers-engined trials and motocross two-strokes in the 1950s and 1960s. The firm's best decade was the 1920s, when DOT riders competed in the TT and its roadster range included a 1000cc JAP-powered V-twin.

DUCATI

■ DUCATI 250 DESMO

In 1926 the Ducati brothers, Adriano
and Marcello, founded a company in
Bologna to produce electrical components. Badly damaged in the Second
World War, the factory was taken over by
the government in exchange for their
investment. Ducati looked for new
opportunities, and in 1946 began
producing the Cucciolo, a 50cc four-
stroke engine that clipped onto a bicycle
frame and sold in huge numbers. In
1954 the firm appointed a new chief
designer, Fabio Taglioni, who would be
responsible for many great bikes, and

DUCATI 250 DESMO (1975)	
Engine	Aircooled 2-valve SOHC desmodromic single
Capacity	249cc (74 x 57.8mm)
Power	30bhp @ 8000rpm
Weight	132kg (290lb) wet
Top speed	95mph (152kph)

for adopting the desmodromic system of
valve operation – that is valves closed
by a cam, rather than springs – that has
become the company's trademark.

■ ABOVE
*Taglioni's classical
single, featured
bevel shaft, single
overhead cam and
desmo valvegear.*

■ LEFT *The 250
Desmo single's
uncompromising
approach was
emphasized by its
simple and
elegant styling.*

■ ABOVE LEFT *Ducati's first engine was the 50cc Cucciolo, or "little pup", which clipped to a bicycle.*

■ ABOVE RIGHT *The 450cc desmo engine was also used to power a successful Street Scrambler model.*

■ ABOVE *The 100cc Grand Sport, Taglioni's first design for Ducati, set the tone for many future models.*

By 1955 Taglioni had produced the 100cc Grand Sport, known as the Marianna, whose single-cylinder engine, with overhead camshaft driven by bevel shaft, would provide Ducati's basic format for the next 20 years. The single was very successful in events like the Giro d'Italia, and in 1958 a 125cc desmo racebike won several Grands Prix and finished second in the world championship. Ducati's range grew with singles like the 175cc Sport of 1957, and the 1964 model 250cc Mach 1 – fast, light, stylish and successful on road and track.

The fastest and best singles of all were the Desmo roadsters, produced in 250, 350 and 450cc versions from the early 1970s. With sleek, simple styling by Leo Tartarini, they were sportsters with clip-on bars, rearset pegs and single seats. Both larger models were capable of over 100mph (160kph), and even the smallest Desmo came close, with reasonable smoothness and fine handling to match. Ducati also built a Street Scrambler version of the single, which sold well and was a predecessor of modern trail bikes.

■ RIGHT *Fine handling was always one of the light, firmly suspended Ducati singles' assets.*

■ OPPOSITE *Top-class suspension and a rigid frame gave the 900SS excellent handling at speed.*

DUCATI

■ DUCATI 900SS

Lean, loud and built purely for speed, Ducati's 900SS was the most single-minded and arguably the finest of the great Italian sportsters of the 1970s. The 900SS combined a potent V-twin engine

DUCATI 900SS (1975)	
Engine	Aircooled 4-valve SOHC desmodromic 90-degree V-twin
Capacity	864cc (86 x 74.4mm)
Power	79bhp @ 7000rpm
Weight	188kg (414lb)
Top speed	132mph (211kph)

with a taut chassis, top-class cycle parts and a racy riding position to provide performance that few rivals could approach. Its gaping, filterless 40mm (1.5in) Dell'Orto carburettors, free-breathing Conti pipes and lack of such niceties as electric start or pillion seat, left no doubt about its aggressive nature.

Ducati had released its first V-twin, the 750GT, in 1971 and followed it shortly afterwards with the tuned 750 Sport, an unfaired roadster with bright yellow paintwork. Paul Smart's victory in the 1972 Imola 200 inspired the Bologna firm to build a street-legal replica called the 750SS with desmo-dromic valve operation like the racer's. In 1975 the engine was enlarged to

864cc to produce the 900SS, whose maximum of 79bhp and generous mid-range torque gave great acceleration and a top speed of over 130mph (209kph).

The 900SS carried virtually no components that were not strictly necessary,

■ ABOVE *Big Dell'Orto carbs and thunderous Conti pipes helped the desmo V-twin produce 79bhp.*

■ LEFT *The original 900SS was the most singleminded of all 1970s superbikes – a pure-bred racer on the road.*

and the bike's light weight, strong tubular steel frame and firm Marzocchi suspension parts gave unshakeable high-speed handling. A useful cockpit fairing, Brembo brakes and elegant styling added to the charm of a bike that could be raced successfully in production events with few modifications.

Ducati's success in the 1970s owed much to two racing victories, both by Englishmen but in very different circumstances. Paul Smart's unexpected win at the prestigious Imola 200 in April 1972 was a landmark. Smart finished just ahead of team-mate Bruno Spaggiari, beating several factory entries including MV Agusta's Giacomo Agostini, for a result that did much to establish the Ducati name worldwide.

Six years later came another famous day, when Mike Hailwood returned from retirement to win the Isle of Man Formula One TT. Hailwood's emotional victory on the red and green Sports Motorcycles V-twin, at an average speed of 108.51mph (174.6 kph), led to Ducati producing a limited edition

Hailwood Replica of the 900SS in 1979. Like the standard 900, it remained in production until 1984, steadily losing its performance edge due to tightening emissions laws and Ducati's growing financial problems, which led to the state-owned firm being taken over by Cagiva in 1985.

■ TOP *Paul Smart's legendary victory at the Imola 200 in 1972 gave the reputation of Ducati's V-twins a big boost.*

■ ABOVE *Ducati celebrated Mike the Bike's 1978 TT win with a successful Hailwood Replica V-twin.*

■ BELOW *The 750 Sport of the early 1970s featured a 56bhp V-twin engine.*

DUCATI

■ DUCATI 916

Rarely has a new motorcycle generated as much excitement as Ducati's 916 did on its launch in 1994. The bike's styling was gorgeous, from the sleek nose of its fairing, via a single-sided swing-arm to the tailpiece from which emerged twin silencers. Its fuel-injected V-twin engine was magnificent, churning out midrange torque and a peak of 114bhp. And its chassis was sublime, combining state-of-the-art suspension technology with the strength and simplicity of Ducati's traditional tubular steel frame.

The 916, designed by a team headed by former Bimota co-founder Massimo Tamburini, was the ultimate development of the watercooled, eight-valve desmodromic V-twin series that had begun with Massimo Bordi's 851 Strada in 1988. The 851, which was subsequently enlarged to 888cc, had brought Ducati, revitalized under Cagiva's control, roaring into the 1990s, combining the V-twin's traditional torque and charm with a new-found refinement.

The 916 raised the stakes again, with a top speed of 160mph (257kph), even more midrange acceleration and the addictive feel that only a V-twin can provide. Its uprated chassis gave light steering with impeccable stability, plus huge amounts of cornering clearance and grip. The 916 was a hit, and was soon followed by a smaller-capacity

DUCATI 916 (1994)	
Engine	Watercooled 8-valve DOHC desmodromic 90-degree V-twin
Capacity	916cc (94 x 66mm)
Power	114bhp @ 9000rpm
Weight	195kg (429lb)
Top speed	160mph (256kph)

■ BELOW *The 916 was beautiful, from its
sharp nose to its high-level silencers.*

model, the 748. Remarkably the Ducatis' sleek shape remained unchanged until 2002, by which time the 998 produced 123hp from a new Testastretta or "narrow-head" V-twin engine design.

The following year Ducati finally introduced a successor to the 916 line, in the restyled and comprehensively updated 999. Powered by the same desmodromic V-twin engine as the 998, it featured more aerodynamic bodywork, a narrower frame, an adjustable riding position revised to improve comfort, advanced electronics, and a high-level silencer in the tail-piece. Reaction to the styling of the 999 and its smaller sibling the 749 was mixed. But almost everyone who rode the new models pronounced them more practical than their predecessors, and just as fast and fun.

One of the reasons for Ducati's success in the 1990s was its domination of the World Superbike Championship, in which the Italian firm benefited from rules allowing twin-cylinder bikes a capacity and weight advantage over fours. Frenchman Raymond Roche won the title in 1990, and American Doug Polen followed with successive championships. Australians Troy Corser and Troy Bayliss also won on the red V-twins. Most successful of all was Carl Fogarty, whose four titles made him the most successful Superbike rider of all.

■ ABOVE *The 749S and similar 999 began a new era for Ducati.*

■ LEFT *The naked Monster's brutal styling made it a big hit.*

ENFIELD

■ LEFT *The Indian-built Bullet, seen here in Madras, has also become an export success for Enfield.*

■ ENFIELD BULLET 500

The single-cylinder Bullet was one of the most popular models of Britain's old Royal Enfield firm, which manufactured the simple, light bike between 1949 and 1962, initially in 350cc and later in 500cc form. The Bullet was widely exported, and was used by the Indian armed forces. In 1958 production was started in Madras, using machinery from the old Royal Enfield factory. The 350cc bike sold well in India, and by the mid-1980s it was also being exported to

much-improved front brake. By modern standards the Enfield was inevitably crude, with modest acceleration, a realistic cruising speed of 65mph (104kph), considerable vibration and harsh handling. It was also cheap, economical, reliable and provided an unmistakable classic feel that some riders enjoyed.

countries including Britain.

The 500cc model followed a few years later and was also successful, despite its basic layout having remained unchanged since the mid-1950s. The pushrod-operated engine produced 22bhp, and was held in a simple tubular steel frame. For domestic use many of the details had changed little, too, but export bikes incorporated numerous refinements including a

ENFIELD BULLET 500 (1990)	
Engine	Aircooled 2-valve OHV pushrod single
Capacity	499cc (84 x 90mm)
Power	22bhp @ 5400rpm
Weight	169kg (270lb)
Top speed	80mph (128kph)

■ BELOW *The 500cc Bullet was built in 1990 but looks almost identical to its predecessor of the 1950s.*

■ RIGHT *Bullet handling is inevitably crude but can be uprated by specialists such as Fritz Egli.*

■ OPPOSITE MIDDLE *Even when tuned the pushrod Bullet engine lacks power, but it is economical and fairly reliable.*

OTHER MAKES

■ ECOMOBILE

Looking like a large, wingless glider, the Ecomobile produced by Swiss engineer Arnold Wagner was one of the most unusual machines on two wheels. The first versions, produced in 1982, held a BMW flat-twin engine in the Kevlar/fibreglass monocoque body. In 1988 the design was uprated using the four-cylinder K100 engine, giving the streamlined Ecomobile a top speed of over 150mph (241kph).

■ EGLI

Swiss engineer Fritz Egli has built chassis, invariably featuring his trademark large-diameter steel spine frame, for a huge variety of engines since starting with the Vincent V-twin on which he became Swiss racing champion in the late 1960s. In the 1970s he turned to four-cylinder Hondas and Kawasakis, and his bikes were highly successful in endurance racing. In recent years he has produced his first Harley-Davidson special. And as the Swiss and Austrian importer of Enfield Bullets, he tuned the Indian-made single's engine and

uprated its chassis to produce the considerably improved Swiss Finish Bullet.

■ ELF

The string of racebikes backed by French petrochemicals giant Elf were some of the most innovative of recent years, all using non-telescopic suspension of various designs. Radical early models such as the Honda-powered Elf E endurance racer of 1981 pioneered features including carbon fibre disc brakes. In 1985 Elf moved into Grands Prix with backing from Honda, using a more conventional forkless chassis. Despite a works V-four engine, British rider Ron Haslam could never make the Elf 3 truly competitive, and Elf pulled out after the 1988 season. Honda's involvement yielded benefits including development of the single-sided swing-arm found on many recent roadsters.

■ EMC

Austrian-born two-stroke tuning wizard Dr Joe Ehrlich came to England in the 1930s and set up his Ehrlich Motor Co in London after the War. His Model S and Model T 350s used unusual split-single engines, and were unsuccessful. In the early 1960s

■ LEFT *The amazing 170mph (273kph) Turbo Ecomobile combined superbike speed and cornering ability with sports car comfort.*

■ ABOVE *Ron Haslam lifts the Elf 3's forkless front wheel at the 1988 French Grand Prix.*

Ehrlich built a 125cc racer on which Mike Hailwood scored good results. After a successful move to F3 car racing Ehrlich returned to bikes in the early 1980s, when his 250cc Rotax-engined racers were highly competitive in Grands Prix and the TT. After another absence, the veteran Dr Joe – now in his 80s – returned with yet another EMC racebike in 1995.

■ ABOVE *Egli's 1983 Harley special, nicknamed Lucifer's Hammer, was fast, loud and powerful.*

EXCELSIOR

■ EXCELSIOR MANXMAN
Excelsior became Britain's first motorcycle manufacturer when it began selling
bikes in 1896 under the firm's original
name of Bayliss, Thomas and Co. In

1910 the company's name was changed
to Excelsior, following the demise of a
German manufacturer of the same name.
Excelsior specialized in small-capacity
bikes and produced racers, notably the

250cc Mechanical Marvel – which won
the Lightweight TT in 1933.

That result increased interest in
Excelsior and led to the firm producing
a replica racer, but a loss of nerve by the

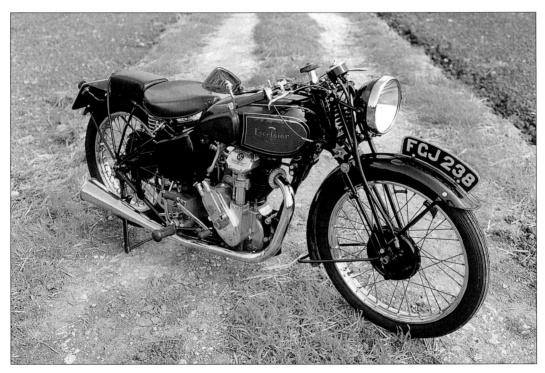

EXCELSIOR MANXMAN 250 (1936)

Engine	Aircooled 2-valve SOHC single
Capacity	246cc (63 x 79mm)
Power	25bhp approx
Weight	132kg (290lb) dry
Top speed	80mph (128kph)

OTHER MAKES

■ **EXCELSIOR**
The American motorcycles of this name were built in Chicago by the Schwinn bicycle company. The firm built its first machine in 1907. By the time Excelsior fell victim to the Depression in 1931, the factory had won many races and taken over production of the four-cylinder Henderson, becoming America's third largest marque. Excelsior's best-known model was the Super X, a 750cc (45ci) V-twin introduced in the mid-1920s. Excelsior-Henderson was reborn in 1999 with a 1386cc V-twin cruiser also called the Super X, but production was short-lived.

engineers – who thought club racers would be unable to maintain such a complicated engine – prompted a simpler motor with a single overhead camshaft. The Manxman was released in 1935 in 250cc form, and was later produced in 350 and 500cc capacities too. Its good performance and impressive strength made the single popular with road riders and club racers.

After the Second World War, Excelsior concentrated its efforts on two-stroke roadsters such as the 250cc Viking and Talisman, but sales fell and production came to an end in 1962.

■ OPPOSITE TOP
A Manxman at speed on the TT circuit from which its name is derived.

■ OPPOSITE
MIDDLE *The Excelsior's SOHC engine, seen here in 350cc form, was simple and reliable.*

■ OPPOSITE
BELOW *As well as being a competitive racer, the Manxman was a popular roadster in the late 1930s.*

■ RIGHT
Excelsior's 250cc four-valve Mechanical Marvel was ridden to TT victory by Sid Gleave in 1933.

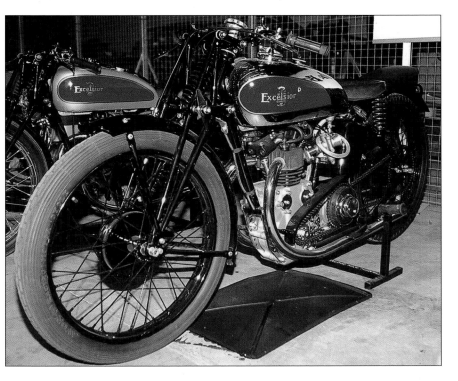

FN

■ FN FOUR

The world's first mass-produced four-cylinder motorcycle was the Belgian-built FN, which was a revelation when it was introduced in 1904. The company had been founded near Liège in 1899 to manufacture arms and ammunition, and began making single-cylinder bikes in 1902. But it is the four-cylinder bike, designed by Paul Kelecom, for which FN is remembered. The 362cc in-line engine was notable for its high tension magneto ignition and fully-enclosed shaft final drive; the chassis incorporated one of the earliest forms of telescopic forks.

Initial doubts led *France Automobile* magazine to regard it as more of a curiosity than a practical motorcycle,

despite its remarkable engine. But the FN was far more than that, and would be gradually updated over two decades of production. Engine capacity grew to 412cc and then to 491cc in 1911, by which time the FN Four produced about 4hp, had gained a clutch and two-speed gearbox, and was capable of 40mph. An

updated 748cc four was introduced just before the First World War during which the occupied factory produced bikes for the German army. The FN did not recapture its popularity after the War, although a 1923 redesign – when chain final drive replaced the shaft – kept the model going for three more years.

FN FOUR (1911)	
Engine	Aircooled 8-valve inlet-over-exhaust in-line four
Capacity	491cc
Power	4bhp
Weight	75kg (165lb) dry
Top speed	40mph (64kph)

OTHER MAKES

■ FANTIC

After starting production in the 1960s, Fantic gained a reputation for small-capacity two-strokes, particularly the range of Caballero trail bikes. The Italian firm has built many bikes for motocross and particularly trials, where it has been a leading contender for many years.

■ FATH

German racer-engineer Helmut Fath's greatest achievement came not in 1960, when he won the world sidecar championship for the first time, but eight years later, when he returned from serious injury to regain the title on a machine he had designed and built himself. The URS, named after Fath's village of Ursenbach, was a 500cc DOHC transverse four that revved to 15,000rpm and produced a reported 80bhp. The URS was also raced as a solo using chassis from Seeley and Metisse, most successfully in 1969 by veteran German Karl Hoppe. After selling his team to Friedel Münch, Fath built a powerful 500cc flat-four two-stroke engine that was raced in both solo and sidecar classes in the 1970s.

■ FRANCIS-BARNETT

Never the most glamorous of manufacturers, Francis-Barnett specialized in producing economical roadsters from its start in 1919 until its demise in 1966. The firm's most famous model was the 250 Cruiser of the 1930s, which combined its single-cylinder Villiers two-stroke engine with pressed-steel leg-shields, large mudguards and partial engine covers. In 1947, the Coventry firm was taken over by Associated Motor Cycles, after which it continued to build small-capacity roadsters, as well as trials and scrambles bikes, profitably for several years. But the rise of Italian scooters hit sales, and Francis-Barnett's attempt to design and build its own engines was unsuccessful. "Fanny-B" returned to Villiers engines for its single and twin-cylinder models, also called Cruisers, in the 1960s.

■ LEFT *Helmut Fath won the 1968 sidecar world title with his own four-cylinder URS.*

■ ABOVE *Fantic is known for trials bikes such as this 125cc, seen tackling the Scottish Six Days Trial in 1991.*

■ ABOVE *The bodywork of this 1936-model Francis-Barnett Cruiser gave its rider useful protection.*

■ RIGHT *This single-cylinder Francis-Barnett Falcon provided reasonable small-capacity performance in 1959.*

GILERA

■ GILERA SATURNO

Gilera was one of motorcycling's big
names in the 1950s, racing with great
success and building some fine roadsters. The firm was founded by a youthful Giuseppe Gilera in 1909, and
represented Italy in the International Six
Days Trial in the 1930s. Gilera's most
famous roadsters were four-stroke
singles, notably the 500cc Saturno that
was much loved for its blend of clean,
handsome styling and lively
performance.

The Saturno was designed and briefly
raced just before Italy entered the
Second World War but was first
produced in 1946, in Sport, Touring and
Competition versions. Early models had
girder forks and Gilera's own brand of
rear suspension – horizontal springs in
tubes, with friction dampers. Telescopic
forks and vertical shocks were introduced in the early 1950s. The bike
quickly became popular thanks to its

■ ABOVE *In recent years, the once-proud
Gilera name has only been used for
Piaggio-built scooters.*

GILERA SATURNO (1951)	
Engine	Aircooled 2-valve OHV pushrod single
Capacity	499cc (84 x 90mm)
Power	22bhp @ 5000rpm (Sport version)
Weight	170kg (374lb) dry
Top speed	85mph (136kph)

■ LEFT *The
Saturno racer's
look and
performance
changed little
throughout most of
the 1950s.*

■ OPPOSITE
The modern
Saturno was a
sporty roadster
with traditional red
finish and single-
cylinder engine.

■ LEFT *The*
CX125, a two-
stroke sportster
introduced in
1991, featured
single-sided
suspension at front
and rear.

excellent road-going performance and some impressive racing results, notably Carlo Bandirola's win at the new Sanremo circuit in 1947, which led to the Saturno racer being known as the Sanremo.

Saturnos were not competitive at Grand Prix level but continued to be raced successfully in Italy several years after production had ended in the late 1950s. But by then Giuseppe Gilera had lost enthusiasm following the early death, of a heart attack, of his son Feruccio in 1956.

In 1969 the company was sold to small-bike specialist and Vespa scooter producer Piaggio, who developed a range of new models in the late 1980s. These included a new Saturno, a stylish 500cc four-stroke single with half-fairing, disc brakes and single-shock rear suspension, which was produced mainly for export to Japan. Later models included the Nordwest 600 single and

the CX125, an innovative two-stroke sportster with forkless front suspension. Sales, however, were moderate, and Gilera's 250cc Grand Prix comeback in 1992 was sadly an expensive failure

that the company could ill-afford. In 1993 Piaggio announced the closure of the factory at Arcore, near Milan, although the Gilera name continued to be used for scooters.

OTHER MAKES

■ GARELLI

When Garelli began production in 1913 it was with an unusual 350cc twin-pistoned two-stroke single, which won many races. Recent production has concentrated on

■ LEFT *Angel*
Nieto cornering his
125cc works Garelli.

■ FAR LEFT
Spain's trials
superstar Jordi
Tarrés takes a rare
"dab" to steady his
factory Gas-Gas.

small-capacity two-strokes and mopeds. Garelli's most successful racing years were the 1980s, when the Italian firm's monocoque-framed 125cc parallel twins, acquired from Minarelli, won seven consecutive world titles at the hands of Fausto Gresini, Luca Cadalora and Angel Nieto.

■ GAS-GAS

Spanish specialist firm Gas-Gas has made a huge impact in trials over recent years, scoring numerous wins through their riders, including the great Jordi Tarrés who clinched his seventh world championship in 1995.

GILERA

■ LEFT *Piero Remor's 500cc powerplant set the pattern for modern transverse four-cylinder engines.*

■ BELOW *Unlike the "dustbin" fairings often used, this 1956 Gilera's fly-screen leaves the engine visible.*

■ GILERA 500cc FOUR

Gilera's 500cc four-cylinder racer made even more of an impact than its impressive haul of six world championships between 1950 and 1957 suggests. Its transverse four-engine layout provided the inspiration not only for MV Agusta, whose similar machines dominated the 500cc world championship after Gilera's withdrawal, but later also for the Japanese factories on both road and track.

The original 500 four was designed as early as 1923 by Carlo Gianini and Piero Remor, two young engineers from Rome. Initially aircooled and with a gear-driven single overhead camshaft, by 1934 the four was called the Rondine, featured twin cams and a

supercharger, and was producing an impressive 86bhp. Gilera bought the project, and the four was soon winning races and setting a world speed record of 170.15mph (273.8kph).

After the War supercharging was banned, halving the four's power output. Piero Remor, one of the original designers, produced a new aircooled, twin-cam powerplant, then in 1949 left for MV, who soon adopted a similar layout. Nevertheless Gilera's Umberto Masetti won two championships and Geoff Duke added three more between 1953 and 1955. After Libero Liberati's win in 1957 the Arcore firm joined rivals Guzzi and Mondial in pulling out of Grand Prix racing completely.

GILERA 500cc-FOUR (1956)	
Engine	Aircooled 8-valve DOHC transverse four
Capacity	499cc (52 x 58.8mm)
Power	70bhp @ 11,000rpm
Weight	150kg (330lb) dry
Top speed	145mph (233kph)

■ RIGHT *John Hartle howls his Gilera through Quarter Bridge on the way to second place in the 1963 Senior TT.*

OTHER MAKES

GNOME & RHÔNE

Between the Wars the Paris-based factory moved from aircraft engine production to build a variety of bikes with single-cylinder and flat-twin engines of up to 750cc. After 1945 Gnome & Rhône built small-capacity two-strokes, but didn't survive the 1950s.

GREEVES

Best known for its trials and motocross bikes, Essex firm Greeves also built roadsters and the Silverstone road-racer in the 1950s and 1960s. Most of the roadsters were 250 and 350cc two-strokes, with engines bought from British Anzani or Villiers, and given names such as Fleetmaster, Sportsman and Sports Twin. Off-road successes included many wins for the

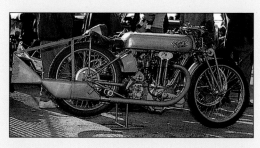

■ LEFT *The exhaust of this Grindlay-Peerless racer from the 1920s is fitted with a huge "Brooklands can" to reduce noise.*

Greeves Hawkstone scrambler, and the European 250cc championships won by Dave Bickers in 1960 and 1961. Bill Wilkinson's Scottish Six Days Trial victory on a 250cc Greeves Anglian in 1969, ahead of Sammy Miller's Bultaco, brought to an end British bikes' domination of the trials world.

GRINDLAY-PEERLESS

Bill Lacey gave Grindlay-Peerless its greatest success when he covered over 100 miles (160km) in an hour to set a world record in 1928. Roadsters ranged from big 1000cc V-twins to 150cc two-strokes, but although the bikes were regarded as stylish, production ended in 1934.

■ LEFT *Bill Wilkinson won the 1969 Scottish Six Days Trial on a 250cc, Villiers-engined works Greeves Anglian.*

■ LEFT *This 250cc Sports Twin two-stroke from 1963 was typical of Greeves' roadster production.*

HARLEY-DAVIDSON

■ BELOW *Harley's Model 9E of 1913 featured the 45-degree, V-twin engine layout that remains today.*

■ HARLEY-DAVIDSON MODEL 9E

William S Harley and Arthur Davidson were former school friends who, while working for a Milwaukee engineering firm, dreamt of producing a motorbike. In 1902 they built a 400cc (25ci) single-cylinder engine, and a year later, after being joined by Davidson's elder brothers Walter and William A, they fitted it into a bicycle frame to complete the prototype Harley-Davidson motorcycle. The motor proved reliable but underpowered, so was enlarged. The frame was too weak so it was replaced with a more substantial structure built along similar lines.

HARLEY-DAVIDSON MODEL 9E (1913)	
Engine	Aircooled 2-valve inlet-over-exhaust single V-twin
Capacity	1000cc (61ci)
Power	10bhp
Weight	150kg (330lb) dry
Top speed	60mph (96kph)

Two more bikes were produced in 1903, and another three the following year. By 1907 the Harley-Davidson's growing reputation for reliability had helped push annual production above 150. In that year Harley-Davidson raised money for expansion by becoming a corporation, with shares divided among 17 employees. The firm had by now moved across Milwaukee from its first base, a small shed in the Davidsons' yard, to bigger premises in what would become Juneau Avenue, the firm's current address.

Very early models had no lights or suspension but within a few years Harley had fitted leading-link forks, a carbide gas headlamp and magneto ignition. The Model 5 of 1909 produced about 4bhp from its 494cc (30ci) inlet-over-exhaust engine, and was good for 45mph (72kph). It had bicycle pedals to

start the engine and set the bike in motion, after which the leather drive belt was tightened using a hand lever.

Harley's first V-twin, the Model 5D, was built in 1909, but was not an immediate success. It produced about 7bhp, almost twice as much as the

■ FAR LEFT *This official photograph from 1910 shows founders William, Walter and Arthur Davidson and William Harley.*

■ LEFT *The Harley legend began in this tiny shed at the rear of the Davidsons' home in Milwaukee.*

■ BELOW *Harley launched a new 5bhp single in 1913, and a year later introduced a kickstart and rear drum brake.*

single, but was hard to start and suffered from a slipping drive belt. Two years later the 45-degree V-twin was reintroduced with revised valvegear and a new frame; soon afterwards it was fitted with chain drive and a full floating seat. The improvements made a big difference and the V-twin grew rapidly in popularity. By 1913, the Model 9E's 1000cc (61ci) powerplant was producing about 10bhp, giving a top speed of 60mph (96kph).

Harley-Davidson had initially been reluctant to get involved in racing, preferring reliability runs, but in 1914 finally entered a factory team. The Milwaukee firm's so-called "Wrecking Crew", riding powerful eight-valve V-twins, were very competitive against rivals Indian, Merkel and Excelsior both before and after the First World War. This period was one of great fluctuation for Harley-Davidson. Production rose to over 22,000 bikes and 16,000 sidecars in 1919, before halving two years later due mainly to the rise of the Model T Ford, which put most of the American motorcycle firms out of business.

HARLEY-DAVIDSON

■ HARLEY-DAVIDSON WL45

Harley is best known for large-capacity V-twins, but the smaller 45ci (750cc) Forty Five also played a vital part in the company's history. The first 45ci model, a basic machine with a total-loss oil system, was produced in 1928. Nine

HARLEY WL45 (1949)	
Engine	Aircooled sidevalve 45-degree V-twin
Capacity	742cc (70 x 97mm)
Power	25bhp @ 4000rpm
Weight	240kg (528lb) wet
Top speed	75mph (120kph)

■ BELOW *The look of this "hard-tail" 1949 WL45 is reflected in the styling of many modern Harleys.*

years later, it was restyled and updated to create the W series. Simple and strong, if not particularly fast even in its day, the Forty Five kept Harley going through the Depression of the 1930s. As the WLA model it also proved an ideal military machine, with around 80,000 being used in the Second World War.

After the War many ex-army 45s were converted for civilian use, which did much to popularize Harleys worldwide, and the Milwaukee factory recommended building the W in various forms, including the WR racer. The WL name denoted a sportier version of the basic W, with slightly raised compression increasing power to 25bhp. The three-speed gearbox was operated by a hand lever, with a foot clutch. In 1949 Harley introduced its Girdraulic damping system on the WL's springer front forks,

■ ABOVE *The K-series V-twin, introduced in 1952, featured unit construction and a four-speed gearbox.*

in place of the simple friction damper used previously. The bike had a sprung saddle and no rear suspension.

Nevertheless the ride was fairly comfortable, handling was adequate and the WL was capable of cruising steadily and reliably at 60mph (96kph). It remained in production until 1952, when it was replaced by the Model K,

featuring a unit-construction engine and four-speed gearbox, with foot change. The three-wheeled Servicar, powered by the faithful 45ci engine, was built until 1974.

In 1936, with America still suffering the effects of the Depression, Harley bravely introduced the Model 61E. The new bike's 61ci (1000cc) V-twin engine

was a major advance due to its over-head-valve design and recirculating oil system. The 61E was also neatly styled, and became a big success. Known as the Knucklehead after the shape of the engine's rocker covers, it gave Harley the technical edge over great rivals Indian and became the illustrious ancestor of all modern Harleys.

■ RIGHT *The shape of this 1946 Knucklehead's rocker covers clearly shows where it got its name from.*

■ ABOVE *Harley's wartime WLA and WLC, built for Canadian forces, proved to be rugged and reliable.*

■ ABOVE *The three-wheeled Servicar, produced for commercial use in 1931, was a long-running success.*

HARLEY-DAVIDSON

HARLEY-DAVIDSON XLCH SPORTSTER

At its peak in the early 1960s, the XLCH Sportster lived up to its name by being one of the quickest bikes on the road. It roared to a top speed of over 100mph (160kph), turned standing quarters in around 14 seconds and, in a straight line at least, was a match for lighter British 650cc twins. That was then. In recent decades the name has remained while the Sportster models, smallest machines in a range of cruisers, have become about as far from a sports motorcycle as possible.

The Sportster was launched in 1957, with an overhead valve V-twin motor

HARLEY-DAVIDSON XLCH SPORTSTER (1962)	
Engine	Aircooled 4-valve OHV pushrod 45-degree V-twin
Capacity	883cc (76.2 x 96.8mm)
Power	55bhp @ 5000rpm
Weight	220kg (485lb)
Top speed	110mph (177kph)

■ LEFT *The original XLCH's 883cc engine-capacity is also used for the smaller of the two current Sportster models.*

■ BELOW *Lean, loud, powerful and respectably light, the Sportster fully lived up to its name back in 1959.*

■ LEFT *By 1991, the Sportster's capacity had grown to 1200cc but its performance had barely changed at all.*

■ BELOW *Harley attempted to build a true sportsbike with the XLCR Café Racer of 1977, but it was not a great success.*

for mediocre suspension and brakes by plenty of others, the current XLHs are the best yet, combining age-old charm with five-speed gearboxes, belt final drive systems and reliability unheard of from Milwaukee in 1957. Its name may not ring true any more, but the Sportster looks set to stick around for many more years to come.

In contrast, one of Harley's most distinctive but least successful, and shortest-lived, models of all was the lean black XLCR Café Racer that was introduced in 1977. Consisting of the 1000cc Sportster engine in a new frame developed from that of the XR750 racebike, the Café Racer incorporated racy features such as a bikini fairing, twin front discs, matt-black siamesed exhausts and single seat. The look was attractive and by Harley standards the performance was good, but the XLCR appealed neither to traditional riders nor to the café racer crowd. Few were sold and the model was quickly dropped; ironically it has become quite highly sought-after in recent years.

whose 54ci (883cc) capacity was the same as its KH predecessor, but used a larger bore and shorter stroke to allow higher revs. The original XL model had a big gas tank and fenders, but a year later Harley produced the XLCH, complete with tuned engine, small headlamp, tiny gas tank, lower bars and loud pipes: the classical Sportster style had arrived.

The Sportster's look and performance have varied remarkably little over the years. Capacity has increased via 1000cc to 1200cc, joined in 1986 by the Evolution-engined 883cc model that has served as a popular entry-level Harley. Although frequently derided by riders of big-twin Harleys, and criticized

HARLEY-DAVIDSON

■ HARLEY-DAVIDSON ELECTRA GLIDE

For many people the Electra Glide is the quintessential Harley-Davidson: big, simple, traditional, ostentatious; a bike built by Americans, for Americans, for travelling across the vast country of its birth. More than just a comfortable, slow-revving V-twin tourer, the Electra Glide has become a rumbling, rolling symbol of two-wheeled freedom — albeit one hampered over the years by dubious reliability, handling and braking.

The Electra Glide was launched in 1965, when Harley added an electric starter to the 74ci (1200cc) V-twin that had been steadily developed since

1947. The legendary name followed a pattern; the 1949 model Hydra-Glide featured hydraulic front suspension and the Duo-Glide of 1958 had added rear

■ LEFT *Harley introduced fuel-injection with the range-topping Ultra Classic Electra Glide in 1995.*

■ BELOW *This 1978 Glide shows classic features, including big fenders, fat tyres and lots of chrome.*

suspension. With high handlebars, big gas tank and fenders, footboards, a single saddle, and fat white-wall tyres on wire-spoked wheels, the Electra

■ LEFT *The Hydra-Glide was introduced in 1949, taking its name from its new hydraulic front forks.*

to benefit from the hugely improved alloy Evolution engine introduced by a revitalized Harley in 1984 – from which point it has been success all the way. In 1995, the range-topping Ultra Classic Electra Glide debuted the fuel-injection system designed to take Harley's faithful aircooled, pushrod V-twin towards the 21st century.

The Electra Glide may have been the most famous Harley, but the Softail model introduced in 1984 was perhaps the most significant. As well as the new Evolution engine, the Softail featured clean, traditional looks and rear suspension cleverly hidden under the engine to give the illusion of a solid or "hard-tail" rear end.

The Softail marked Harley's entry into the nostalgia market that has served the company so well ever since. Its most vivid interpretation came in 1993 with the Heritage Softail Nostalgia – complete with two-tone paint, white-wall tyres and cowhide patches on both the seat and the saddlebags.

HARLEY-DAVIDSON ELECTRA GLIDE (1965)	
Engine	Aircooled 4-valve OHV pushrod 45-degree V-twin
Capacity	1198cc (87.1 x 100.6mm)
Power	60bhp @ 4000rpm
Weight	350kg (770lb)
Top speed	95mph (152kph)

■ ABOVE *Styling chief Willie G Davidson, grandson of William A, has played a big part in Harley's recent success.*

■ BELOW *The Heritage Softail Nostalgia sums up Harley's approach to design.*

Glide looked elegant. Despite plenty of engine vibration and poor suspension and braking – problems exaggerated by its massive 350kg of weight – the bike was well received.

Just a year later, in 1966, Harley changed the engine from the Panhead to the Shovelhead – named after the shape of their cylinder head covers – which added a modicum of reliability. Other changes over the years included adding a fairing and hard luggage, enlarging the V-twin lump to 80ci (1340cc) in 1978, and rubber-mounting the powerplant to combat vibration. All helped make the Glide ride better and in more comfort.

The biggest shake-up in Harley-Davidson history came in 1981 when the management, led by Vaughn Beals, raised the money to buy Harley from parent company AMF, under whose control in the 1970s Harley had seen a deterioration in quality and sales. The Electra Glide was one of the first models

HARLEY-DAVIDSON

■ **HARLEY-DAVIDSON V-ROD** Harley created a shock in 2001 with the launch of the striking and powerful VRSCA V-Rod, whose so-called "Revolution" engine featured a watercooled, 60-degree layout with twin overhead camshafts and four valves per cylinder. Based on the motor from Harley's VR1000 road-racer, and developed in partnership with Germany's Porsche Engineering, the V-Rod motor produced 115bhp, far more than any previous Harley streetbike.

The rest of the V-Rod's design was just as distinctive. The bike was long and low, with a unique shape and a striking silver finish. That gave an air of custom-bike menace in conjunction with solid disc wheels and front forks kicked out at 38 degrees. Neat details were everywhere, from the slanted headlamp and "clamshell" instrument console, via prominent steel frame tubes to the aluminium swing-arm.

At slow speed the V-Rod felt laid-back and much like a typical cruiser, but opening the throttle sent the bike rocketing forward like no other Harley, as it headed smoothly towards its 9000rpm rev limit and a top speed of

HARLEY-DAVIDSON VRSCA V-ROD (2001)	
Engine	Watercooled 8-valve DOHC 60-degree V-twin
Capacity	1130cc (100 x 72mm)
Power	115bhp @ 8500rpm
Weight	270kg (594lb) dry
Top speed	135mph (217kph)

■ LEFT *Rodney Ferris crouches low and revs his Harley XR750 towards 130mph (209kph) at the Sacramento Mile.*

■ FAR LEFT TOP *The incomparable Scott Parker won nine National titles on factory XR750s.*

■ FAR LEFT BOTTOM *Italian star Walter Villa won four 250 and 350cc world titles in the mid-1970s.*

■ BELOW *Harley's watercooled, 60-degree V-twin engine was first used in the aluminium-framed VR1000 Superbike racer.*

135mph (217kph). The exposed riding position inevitably limited high-speed riding potential, but the V-Rod was otherwise comfortable. It also had great brakes and handled well for such a long machine. By no means every Harley enthusiast was convinced, but the bike earned many plaudits for its bold and innovative design.

The V-Rod's engine owed much to that of the aluminium-framed VR1000 road-racer, which the factory built for the 1994 AMA Superbike season. Miguel Duhamel took a second place that year but the VR was never fully competitive in subsequent seasons, and Harley reluctantly abandoned the project in 2001.

That failure contrasted with the success of the XR750 V-twin, which has dominated American dirt-track racing for decades. The XR was introduced in 1970, when race-team manager Dick O'Brien put a modified Sportster engine into the chassis of Harley's outdated KR racer. The result was initially unsuccessful but in 1972 the XR's iron-barrelled engine was replaced by a new aluminium V-twin, and Mark Brelsford won the first of its many titles.

Since then the XR750 has generally ruled the US racing roost, with championships for riders including Jay Springsteen, who won three in a row from 1976-8, and Randy Goss, a double champion in the early 1980s. Most successful of all was Scott Parker, who rode factory XR750s to no fewer than nine National titles. Since 1980 Harley has not built complete XRs, instead selling engines which are then built into bikes using parts from firms such as frame specialist Champion. A modern XR750 produces over 100bhp, and reaches over 130mph (209kph) on the mile circuits. In over 30 years the XR look has barely changed, despite the appearance of upside-down forks, cast wheels, rear brakes – early XRs had none at all – and huge silencers.

■ BELOW *By 1920s' standards,
Henderson's in-line four-cylinder engine
was supremely smooth and powerful.*

■ BOTTOM *The KJ model, known as the
"Streamline", was a fast, refined and
inevitably expensive machine.*

HENDERSON

■ HENDERSON KJ

Arguably the finest and most sophisticated machines in the years up to 1930, American-built Hendersons featured four-cylinder engines mounted in-line with the bike. The firm began production in 1911, using the engine layout and long wheelbase format that would become its trademark. Six years later, founder Bill Henderson sold the firm to Schwinn, makers of bicycles and Excelsior motorbikes, and left to found Ace. The Henderson firm continued development, and its 1301cc K model of 1920 produced 28bhp to give an impressive top speed of 80mph (128kph). Among its several advanced features were electric lighting and a fully-enclosed chain.

HENDERSON KJ (1929)	
Engine	Aircooled 8-valve inlet-over-exhaust in-line four
Capacity	1301cc
Power	40bhp
Weight	225kg (495lb) approx.
Top speed	100mph (160kph)

In 1929, Henderson reached new heights of luxury with the Model KJ, known as the "Streamline", which featured improved cooling to a stronger, 40bhp engine of the familiar in-line four-cylinder layout. The Streamline was fast – capable of a genuine 100mph (160kph) – and typically advanced,

with leading-link forks and such details as an illuminated speedometer set into the fuel tank. But it failed to sell during America's Depression, and Schwinn halted production in 1931. By then Indian had bought the rights to produce Ace machines, and continued to build its own four into the 1940s.

OTHER MAKES

■ HARRIS

Brothers Steve and Lester Harris set up
their chassis firm in Hertford in the
1970s, and made their name with a series
of fine-handling café racers, known as the
Magnums. These featured Harris-made
tubular steel frames, with a range of top-
quality cycle parts. Engines were normally
Japanese fours, ranging from the Kawasaki
Z1000-engined Magnum 1 of the late
1970s to the recent Magnum 4, powered
by Suzuki's GSX-R motor.

Throughout the 1980s Harris produced
numerous chassis for racing, and
developed aluminium beam frames for
road and track. In the 1990s the firm was
heavily involved in 500cc Grands Prix
and, along with French company ROC,
worked in conjunction with Yamaha to
produce bikes powered by the Japanese
factory's V-four engines.

■ HERCULES

After building bicycles for several years,
Germany's Hercules produced its first
motorbike in 1904. After the Second
World War, Hercules concentrated on
small-capacity two-strokes with engines
from Sachs. The firm rapidly built up a
large range of bikes in the 1950s, notably
its first twin-cylinder model, the 318. This
was billed as a luxury tourer, and had a
247cc engine that produced 12 bhp. Sachs
took control of the firm in 1969. The
Hercules name survived, notably with the
W2000 of the mid-1970s – the world's
first commercially built Wankel rotary-
engined motorbike. Its 294cc – or 882cc,
depending how it was measured – motor
produced a claimed 27bhp at 6500rpm
and gave a top speed of almost 90mph
(145kph). But the rotary, which was
marketed as a DKW in Britain, did not
sell well, and recent production has been
limited to two-stroke motorcycles of below
100cc.

■ RIGHT *The Hercules/DKW W2000
rotary had lively performance but was
not a sales success.*

■ FAR RIGHT *Post-war Hercules
production concentrated on two-strokes
such as this enduro machine.*

■ ABOVE *The Harris
Magnum 4 held a
four-cylinder Suzuki
GSX-R engine in a
frame of traditional
steel tubes.*

■ LEFT *Steve
Harris and brother
Lester based their
500cc Grand Prix
chassis on Wayne
Rainey's factory
Yamaha.*

HESKETH

■ HESKETH V1000

When it was launched in 1981, the
Hesketh V1000 was billed by its creator
as being the finest machine in the world,
a two-wheeled Aston Martin which
would prove that the British could still
build motorcycles. Lord Alexander
Hesketh had money, he had run a high-
profile Formula One car-racing team,
and on paper his handsome V1000 was
very promising. Its aircooled, 992cc, 90-
degree V-twin engine, designed by four-
stroke specialist Weslake, used twin
cams and four valves per cylinder to
produce an impressive 86bhp. The
Hesketh's frame was a neat structure of
nickel-plated steel tubing, and it held
top quality motorcycle parts including
Marzocchi suspension and Brembo disc
brakes from Italy.

■ LEFT *When
cruising on an open
road, the Hesketh
felt impressively
fast, smooth and
relaxed.*

■ BELOW *The
V1000's neat
bodywork, nickel-
plated frame and
V-twin engine made
an attractive
combination.*

HESKETH V1000 (1982)	
Engine	Aircooled 8-valve DOHC 90-degree V-twin
Capacity	992cc (95 x 70mm)
Power	86bhp @ 6500rpm
Weight	230kg (506lb) dry
Top speed	120mph (193kph)

Despite an excessive weight of 230kg (506lb), the bike handled and braked very well. It was also reasonably fast and smooth, too, with a top speed of 120mph (192kph) and a pleasantly relaxed cruising feel at 90mph (145kph). But the Hesketh was plagued by problems from the start. In particular, the V-twin engine was noisy, unreliable, leaked oil and suffered from a horribly imprecise and noisy transmission. Production was delayed, faults were slow to be corrected, losses mounted, and Hesketh Motorcycles went bust in May 1982. The following year Lord Hesketh set up a new firm to build a fully-faired Vampire tourer, but most of the faults remained and few were produced.

OTHER MAKES

■ HILDERBRAND & WOLFMÜLLER

The world's first motorcycle to achieve series production was the 1488cc four-stroke built by brothers Heinrich and Wilhelm Hilderbrand, and Alois Wolfmüller. Starting in 1894, the Munich-based partnership produced about 1000 examples of the watercooled parallel twin, which developed 2.5bhp and had a top speed of 25mph (40kph). Normal braking was by a steel spoon pressed on the front tyre, supplemented if necessary by a large rear bar that could be released to dig into the road. Motor-cycling's rapid development at that time meant the twin soon became outdated, and production ended in 1897.

■ HOLDEN

Colonel Sir Henry Capel Holden was one of the great characters of motorcycling's pioneering years. He designed the world's first four-cylinder motorbike, a 1054cc watercooled, flat-four that was built in Coventry between 1899 and 1902. The four-stroke engine produced 3bhp, giving the bicycle-style Holden a top speed of about 25mph (40kph). Colonel Holden went on to design Brooklands, the world's first purpose-built race circuit, in 1906.

■ ABOVE *Hilderbrand & Wolfmüller's 1488cc twin, the world's first production bike, revved to just 240rpm.*

■ ABOVE *As well as designing the world's first four, Holden produced this stem-powered bike in 1898.*

HONDA

■ HONDA CB77

The world's largest motorcycle manufacturer was founded in October 1946,
when Soichiro Honda set up the Honda
Technical Research Institute in a small
wooden shed in Hamamatsu. Aiming to
provide cheap transport for a population
hit by defeat in the Second World War,
Honda first bolted army-surplus engines
to bicycles. A year later he built his own
50cc two-stroke engine, and in 1949
Honda and his 20 employees produced
their first complete bike: the 98cc two-
stroke Model D, or "Dream". Sales were
good, progress was rapid and by 1953
Honda had developed the more
sophisticated Model J Benly, whose

90cc four-stroke single-cylinder engine
design owed much to Germany's NSU.

The first Hondas to make an impact
in export markets were the 250cc CB72
and 305cc CB77 of the early 1960s.
Sportier versions of the four-stroke

HONDA CB77 (1963)	
Engine	Aircooled 4-valve SOHC parallel twin
Capacity	305cc (60 x 54mm)
Power	28.5bhp @ 9000rpm
Weight	159kg (350lb) dry
Top speed	95mph (152kph)

■ LEFT *Soichiro Honda built and raced cars before starting his bike firm in 1946.*

■ BELOW LEFT *Honda's first complete bike was the 98cc Model D of 1949.*

■ BELOW *Clever advertising made the C100 a success.*

■ BELOW *Much of Honda's success in the 1960s was due to simple, reliable roadsters like this 125cc Benly.*

■ BOTTOM *Although it was neither fast nor successful, the CB450 heralded Honda's big-bike challenge.*

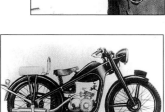

parallel twin C72 and C77 models, the Hondas differed from British twins by using a 180-degree crankshaft, with the pistons rising and falling alternately. Honda's conventional pressed-steel frame, as used on the popular 125cc CB92, was replaced by a tubular steel structure, holding telescopic forks, twin shocks and powerful front and rear drum brakes. With a top speed of 95mph (152kph) and good handling, the CB77– known as the Super Hawk in the States – was a match for many larger British bikes. It was also reliable and oil-tight, and did much for Honda's growing reputation – as did Mike Hailwood's 250cc world championship win in 1961.

Of all Honda's bikes over the years, the most important was arguably the humble C100 Super Cub that was launched in 1958. Combining scooter-style full enclosure with large wheels and an engine placed in the conventional motorbike position instead of under the seat, the Super Cub offered convenience, economy, reliability, cleanliness and even a certain style. Boosted by the famous advertising line,

"You meet the nicest people on a Honda", and by the firm's decision to sell it in American sports and leisure goods shops as well as bike dealerships, the C100 soon became the best-selling motorcycle of all time.

The bike that proved Honda was becoming a major force in motorcycling was the CB450 of 1965. Until the CB's arrival, the Japanese firm had been content to build small-capacity bikes. But with its DOHC, parallel twin engine

displacing 445cc and producing 43bhp, the bike, publicized as the "Black Bomber" or "Black Hawk", was a clear challenge to the long-dominant British twins. In fact, the CB450 turned out to be smooth, comfortable and softly tuned, with a top speed of around 100mph (160kph). Despite respectable handling it couldn't keep up with the British opposition, and was not a great success, but the CB450 signalled the start of Honda's attack on the big bike market.

HONDA

■ HONDA CB750

Modern day motorcycling arrived with
Honda's CB750, which offered a new
level of performance and sophistication
when it was released in 1969. The
CB750 was the first mass-produced
four-cylinder bike, a fact emphasized by
its impressive array of chromed
tailpipes, and it incorporated an electric
starter, disc front brake and five-speed
gearbox, all at a competitive price. The
CB750 dominated the early 1970s,
became known as the first superbike
and had a great influence on machines
that followed.

The CB750's major attraction was its
736cc, four-cylinder engine, which was

■ LEFT *The
CB750's chassis
was less impressive
than its engine, but
the Honda handled
reasonably well.*

■ OPPOSITE
*With its four-
cylinder engine
and front disc
brake, the CB750
was in a class of its
own in 1969.*

■ BELOW *As well
as being powerful,
the 736cc four was
smooth, reliable,
oil-tight and came
fitted with an
electric starter.*

■ BOTTOM *Handsome, agile and capable of 100mph (160kph), the CB400 was dubbed the "poor boy's superbike".*

■ MIDDLE *Dick Mann's 1970 Daytona-winning CB750 is seen here ridden by racer/journalist Alan Cathcart.*

HONDA CB750 (1969)	
Engine	Aircooled 8-valve SOHC transverse four
Capacity	736cc (61 x 63mm)
Power	67bhp @ 8000rpm
Weight	218kg (480lb) dry
Top speed	125mph (201kph)

smooth, reliable and produced an impressive 67bhp. Although the four-pot motor was an SOHC, two-valves-per-cylinder design, its development could be traced to Honda's racing exploits with high-revving twin-camshaft fours in the 1960s. The CB750 was a big and rather heavy bike with high handlebars, intended as an all-rounder. But it still whistled to a top speed of about 125mph (201kph), handled reasonably well and sold in huge numbers worldwide.

In the 1970s, Honda did relatively little to uprate the CB750, which meant that it lost ground to newer rivals including Kawasaki's 900cc Z1, which arrived in 1973. The Honda actually lost some performance, as its engine was detuned to reduce emissions. When it was given a facelift to produce the CB750F in 1976, the new bike's flat handlebars, racier styling, vivid yellow paintwork and four-into-one exhaust system were let down by a top speed of below 120mph (193kph). The DOHC, 16-valve CB750K of 1979 had an unreliable engine and poor handling, all of which seemed a far cry from the

brilliance of the original CB750.

Although the CB750's engine formed the basis for many specials and racebikes throughout the 1970s, the Honda made less of an impact on the track than in the showrooms. One racing highlight was veteran American star Dick Mann's victory at Daytona in 1970, which did much to boost the four's image. Some of the most successful straight-four racers were the RCB endurance bikes of the mid-1970s, which dominated long distance events in the hands of riders such as French duo Christian Léon and Jean-Claude Chemarin.

The CB750's success inspired Honda to produce several smaller fours in the 1970s, starting with the CB500 that arrived in 1971, and which was in some respects an even better bike. Its 498cc, 50bhp engine gave a top speed of just over 100mph (160kph), and the CB500's reduced size and weight gave improved handling and manoeuvrability. Honda produced another winner in 1975

with the CB400. Designed mainly for the European market with flat handlebars, sporty styling and a neat four-into-one exhaust system, the CB400 was much loved for its blend of lively performance and taut handling.

HONDA

■ HONDA GL1000 GOLD WING

Few bikes provoke such extreme reaction as Honda's Gold Wing. Much more than simply a motorcycle, the large and luxurious Wing has inspired, over two decades of production, a cult following that no other single model can match. Throughout most of that time it has offered unmatched levels of two-wheeled comfort and civility. Yet to many motorcyclists the Wing – always most popular in America, and built in Ohio since 1980 – is merely overweight, overpriced and overrated.

The original, unfaired GL1000 Gold Wing was the world's biggest and heaviest bike when it was introduced in 1975. Most notable for its unique, watercooled flat-four engine, the GL also

HONDA GL1000 GOLD WING (1975)	
Engine	Watercooled 8-valve SOHC transverse flat-four
Capacity	999cc (72 x 61.4mm)
Power	80bhp @ 7000rpm
Weight	260kg (571lb) dry
Top speed	122mph (196kph)

featured shaft drive, twin front disc brakes and an under-seat fuel tank. The Wing produced 80bhp, had a top speed of 120mph (193kph), and accelerated hard despite 260kg (571lb) of weight. Its smoothness and comfort rapidly won a large following, especially among middle-aged Americans.

Many riders fitted accessories to their Gold Wings, prompting Honda to introduce a fully-dressed model in 1980. Called the Interstate in America and the De Luxe in Europe, it combined an enlarged 1100cc engine with a fairing, luggage and crash bars. The bike was a hit, as was the Aspencade – named after a big American rally – that was launched two years later with a sound system, passenger backrest and onboard compressor for adjustment of the air suspension.

For many owners the Gold Wing provides an entry to club runs, rallies and other social events. The two main American Wing owners' clubs each have branches all over the States. Thousands of riders gather at the annual Wing Ding, for entertainment, custom contests, technical seminars and accessory stands. Similar meetings are called Trefferns in Europe.

The Gold Wing's size and sophistication reached new levels in 1988 with the GL1500, powered by an all-new flat-six engine. Fully-enclosed, complete with a big fairing, built-in luggage, cruise control and an electronic reverse gear to help when parking, the GL1500 was the heaviest and most complex Gold Wing yet. It was also the fastest, smoothest and most responsive. For such a huge bike, it also handled and braked remarkably well. And the Wing got better still in 2001, when the GL1800 arrived with a more powerful, 1832cc engine and a sportier chassis with aluminium frame and single-sided swing-arm.

■ ABOVE *Back in 1984, the Aspencade's lavish control console looked like something out of an aeroplane.*

■ RIGHT *For comfortable two-wheeled travel in your old age, nothing could beat the six-cylinder GL1500.*

HONDA

■ HONDA CBX1000

The stunning six-cylinder CBX1000 was released in 1978 to demonstrate Honda's ability to build powerful, race-developed motorbikes. At its heart was an aircooled, 1047cc motor containing twin camshafts and 24 valves. A descendant of Honda's multi-cylinder racers of the 1960s, the engine produced 105bhp to send the CBX accelerating smoothly to a top speed of 135mph (217kph), with a spine-tingling note from its exhaust. The huge powerplant, with six shiny exhaust downpipes jutting from its bank of angled-forward cylinders, was left uncovered by frame tubes for maximum visual effect.

Designed as an out-and-out sports-bike by former Grand Prix engineer Shoichiro Irimajiri, the CBX featured sleek, restrained styling and used its engine as a stressed member of the steel frame. Firm suspension helped give

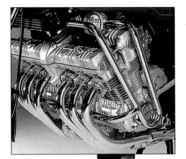

■ ABOVE *The CBX1000's steel frame was designed to leave the huge six-cylinder engine on show.*

■ BELOW *Despite its high bars, the CBX was a sportsbike by 1978 standards, complete with lean, aggressive styling.*

good handling despite the bike's considerable weight, and no rival superbike could match the Honda's blend of speed, smoothness and six-cylinder soul. Unfortunately that was not enough to make the CBX successful, particularly in the important American market. In 1981 the bike was detuned slightly and fitted with a fairing and single-shock, air-assisted suspension. The CBX-B was a competent sports-tourer, and sold well. But it had none of the raw appeal of the original six.

Arguably Honda's most singleminded roadster of the early 1980s was the CB1100R, an exotic 1062cc straight-four produced in small numbers mainly

■ BELOW *In Ron Haslam's hands, the superb CB1100R made an almost invincible production racer.*

■ BOTTOM *The CX500 Turbo was a magnificent technical achievement, but not an outstanding motorcycle.*

■ BELOW *For such a big, heavy motorcycle, the firmly suspended CBX1000 handled exceptionally well.*

HONDA CBX1000 (1978)	
Engine	Aircooled 24-valve DOHC transverse six
Capacity	1047cc (64.5 x 53.4mm)
Power	105bhp @ 9000rpm
Weight	263kg (580lb) dry
Top speed	135mph (217kph)

to win prestigious long-distance production races such as the Castrol Six-Hour in Australia. A development of the CB900, the 1100R combined a tuned, 115bhp engine – the most powerful four-cylinder unit in motorcycling – with an uprated chassis and a racy fairing. Not only was the CB1100R almost unbeatable on the track, but it also made a superb road-going Superbike too.

Among Honda's many innovative bikes of the 1980s was the CX500 Turbo, which was launched in 1981. Less of a practical motorcycle than a corporate statement of engineering expertise, the Turbo used the world's smallest turbocharger to boost the output of the CX500 V-twin – one of the least suitable engine layouts for forced induction – from 50 to 82bhp. The CX chassis was comprehensively redesigned

and given a large fairing. Although heavy, the result was a fast, stable and comfortable sports tourer. But the CX Turbo's performance did not justify its complexity and high price and few riders were tempted to buy one. After first enlarging the engine to produce the CX650 Turbo – and seeing the other three Japanese firms follow with turbo-bikes of their own – Honda abandoned the turbocharging experiment.

HONDA

■ HONDA VFR750F

In the early 1980s Honda produced a
series of roadsters powered by four-
stroke V-four engines, and the watercooled, 90-degree layout – which is
well-suited to bike use due to its narrow
width, smoothness and low centre of
gravity – looked set to challenge the
transverse four's domination. The
VF750F of 1983, in particular, was a
fast and fine-handling machine. A year
later, Honda's range included five
different VF models, from 400 to

HONDA VFR750F (1994)	
Engine	Watercooled 16-valve DOHC 90-degree V4
Capacity	748cc (70 x 48.6mm)
Power	100bhp @ 9500rpm
Weight	209kg (460lb) dry
Top speed	150mph (240kph)

1000cc. But the VF750 developed
mechanical problems that proved hugely
expensive and embarrassing to Honda,
and the V-four revolution faded.

In the circumstances the VF's
successor, the VFR750F, became one of

the most important bikes Honda has
ever produced when it was launched in
1986. Happily for Honda, it was also
one of the best. Its V-four motor
produced an improved 105bhp, was
smooth and flexible and supremely

■ BELOW *The 1994-model VFR, like its
predecessors, was arguably the best all-
round motorcycle money could buy.*

■ OPPOSITE *VFRs have traditionally handled very well, despite being designed for all-round ability rather than speed.*

■ BELOW *For both performance and race-replica style, the magnificent RC30 was in a class of its own in 1988.*

■ BELOW *Handsome, swift and agile, the VF750 was a fine bike in 1983 – until its engine self-destructed.*

■ BOTTOM *The exotic NR750 had oval pistons and great looks, but it was far too heavy and expensive.*

reliable. The VFR's chassis, based around an all-new aluminium frame, gave good handling. And the Honda's efficient bodywork and high-quality finish contributed to a uniquely well-balanced bike.

The VFR has been gradually refined in subsequent years, generally becoming sportier without losing the sophistication and all-round ability that made it unique. A significant change came in 1990 with the VFR750L, which featured sleeker styling, a stronger, twin-spar frame and a single-sided swing-arm. From 1998 the V-four was known as the VFR800FI, due to its larger, fuel-injected 781cc engine, which gained VTEC variable valve technology in 2002.

Honda had redefined the limits of sportsbike design back in 1988 with the release of the VFR750R, better known by its code-name RC30. Essentially a road-going copy of the factory RVF racebike that had dominated Formula One and endurance competition in the mid-1980s, the hand-built RC30 was powered by a tuned, 112bhp version of the standard VFR750 engine. The RC30's twin-headlamp fairing, compact layout, light weight and huge twin-beam aluminium frame – rumoured to have been cast in the same dies as the RVF's – made for a super-fast, fine-handling

bike that was virtually unbeatable on both road and track.

The most exotic V-four of all was the oval-pistoned NR750, descendant of the NR500 with which Honda had taken on the two-strokes in 1979, when returning to Grand Prix racing. In 1992, over ten years after abandoning that attempt,

came the gorgeously styled and hugely expensive NR roadster, whose 32-valve motor produced a class-leading 125bhp at 14,000rpm. Its chassis was superb, too, but despite much use of lightweight materials the NR weighed an excessive 222kg (489lb) and was no faster than 750s costing a fraction of the price.

HONDA

■ HONDA FIREBLADE

Honda's CBR900RR heralded a new
level of superbike performance when it
was launched in 1992. The CBR, known
as the FireBlade in most markets, relied
on a conventional format of 893cc,
16-valve, straight-four engine and twin-
beam aluminium frame. It gained its
edge by housing an 124bhp motor – good

HONDA CBR900RR (1992)

Engine	Watercooled 16-valve DOHC transverse four
Capacity	893cc (70 x 58mm)
Power	124bhp @ 10,500rpm
Weight	185kg (407lb) dry
Top speed	165mph (265kph)

for a top speed of 165mph (265kph) – in
a bike which, at just 185kg (407lb),
weighed less than most 600cc middleweights. The smooth motor, racy steering
geometry and taut suspension gave a
straight-line and cornering speed that no
mass-produced machine could match.

The FireBlade was refined to good
effect on several occasions during the
1990s, without quite recapturing the raw

■ BELOW *The 1992-model CBR900RR's
performance lead resulted from a
combination of power and light weight.*

■ OPPOSITE *For 2002 the Honda FireBlade gained sleeker styling, a bigger 954cc engine and an even lighter chassis than it had before.*

■ BOTTOM *The Super Blackbird's bodywork was not very stylish, but contributed to the bike's fearsome high-speed performance.*

■ RIGHT *Full bodywork kept both engine and frame hidden when the CBR600F was introduced in 1987.*

■ ABOVE *Honda's CBR1000F, seen here in original 1987 form, evolved into a fine sports tourer.*

■ BELOW *The 2003-model CBR600RR resembled Honda's MotoGP racebike, and was far sportier than previous CBR600s.*

spirit of the original model. That changed in 2000, with the arrival of an all-new Blade, known as the CBR929RR in America. Its larger, 929cc engine was fuel-injected for the first time and produced 150bhp. It was held in a lighter chassis featuring Honda's "pivotless" frame design, upside-down forks and a 17-inch front wheel. The result was searing speed, pin-sharp handling and phenomenal performance – which was further improved two years later with another capacity increase, to 954cc.

Few bikes have been able to compete with the FireBlade on a racetrack over the years, but one machine that was faster still in a straight line was Honda's CBR1100XX Super Blackbird. A descendant of the CBR1000F sports-tourer of the late 1980s and early '90s, the Blackbird was powered by an 1137cc, 16-valve engine producing a monstrous 162bhp. Equally important was the CBR's visually dull but aerodynamically efficient bodywork, which helped give a top speed of 180mph (290kph), making it the world's fastest superbike in 1996.

The Blackbird was a bigger, heavier and more comfortable bike than the FireBlade, and was successful as an ultra high-speed sports-tourer.

Honda has also produced hugely popular middleweight fours, notably the CBR600F, which sold in huge numbers in the 1990s due largely to its versatility and high performance at a reasonable price. The original CBR600F, launched in 1987, combined a top speed of

135mph (217kph) with excellent handling, comfort and impressive reliability. Regular revisions kept the CBR competitive in motorcycling's most competitive class, while retaining its all-round appeal. Honda's approach changed in 2003 with the much more aggressive CBR600RR, a true super-sports bike with a new, 115bhp 16-valve engine, plus styling and chassis layout inspired by Honda's MotoGP racer.

HONDA

■ BELOW *This immaculate RC166, owned by enthusiasts Team Obsolete, has been raced in classic events by Jim Redman.*

■ HONDA RC166 SIX

Soichiro Honda had raced cars with some success before turning to motorcycle production, and knew competition could bring both prestige and technical knowledge. Honda entered some Japanese meetings in the mid-1950s, and in 1959 made a first visit to the Isle of Man TT. The early 125cc racebikes were based on German NSU twins but proved uncompetitive against the dominant MV Agustas, but Honda learned fast. In 1961, aided by MV's retirement from the smaller classes, Honda's Tom Phillis and Mike Hailwood won the 125 and 250cc world championships.

In the next season Honda was even more successful. Swiss star Luigi Taveri won the first of his three 125cc titles, and Jim Redman of Rhodesia took both 250 and 350cc championships. Redman

HONDA RC166 (1967)	
Engine	Aircooled 24-valve DOHC transverse six
Capacity	247cc (39 x 34.5mm)
Power	60bhp @ 18,000rpm
Weight	120kg (264lb) dry
Top speed	153mph (245kph)

went on to win a total of six titles on Honda's fours. But it was the six-cylinder machine, raced to 250 and 350cc championships by Mike Hailwood in both 1966 and 1967 that was Honda's finest four-stroke racebike.

The six was designed to resist Yamaha's increasingly strong two-stroke challenge by allowing very high revs. In 250cc form its compact engine, containing 24 tiny valves, emitted an unforgettable exhaust howl and produced 60bhp at a heady 18,000rpm. The six was debuted prematurely by Redman in late 1964, and improved for both reliability and handling during the following season. In 1966 Hailwood won ten out of 12 Grands Prix on the 250cc RC166, and also took the 350 title on a bored-out 297cc version. Hailwood retained both championships on the six before Honda quit Grand Prix racing in 1968.

Despite success in the smaller classes, Honda could not win the 500cc championship in the 1960s. Mike Hailwood came agonizingly close on a four-cylinder 500 whose handling and reliability did not match its power. In 1966 a breakdown in the final round at Monza cost Hailwood the title, which Giacomo Agostini won for MV Agusta by six points. In the next season's

■ **LEFT** *Even Freddie Spencer could not make the NR500 competitive against the 500cc Grand Prix two-strokes.*

■ **BELOW** *Swiss star Luigi Taveri, here in action on a 250, won three 125cc titles for Honda in the 1960s.*

■ **ABOVE** *Mike Hailwood, riding this 250cc six, won the Junior TT on his way to the world title in 1967.*

■ **BELOW** *The oval-pistoned, monocoque-framed NR500 proved uncompetitive when it was first raced in 1979.*

penultimate race, Hailwood broke the lap record and led by half a lap – before his Honda stuck in top gear. Mike won the final race but Ago took the title – not on points or even race wins, which were equal, but on his greater number of second places.

When Honda returned to Grands Prix to take on the two-strokes in 1979, company policy dictated using a four-stroke. Thus was born the NR500: a watercooled V-four whose oval pistons – in fact shaped like running tracks, with two plugs, two conrods and eight valves to each cylinder – were intended to give the next best thing to a V-eight now that engines had been limited to four cylinders. The radical bike also used a monocoque aluminium frame and 16-inch wheels. Its engine revved to 20,000rpm, but Honda had attempted too much and the NR was slow and unreliable. Simplifying the chassis and redesigning the engine brought improvements by 1981, but Honda abandoned the NR that year without having come close to a Grand Prix win let alone the championship.

■ **ABOVE** *Honda's four Japanese riders all managed respectable placings at the firm's first Isle of Man TT in 1959.*

HONDA

■ **LEFT** *Freddie Spencer rode Honda's NS500 triple to the title in 1983.*

■ **BELOW** *Spencer used Honda's works NSR250 V-twin to complete a championship double in 1985.*

■ HONDA NSR500

Honda's first 500cc world championship was won with an unconventional two-stroke machine. Freddie Spencer beat the four-cylinder Suzukis and Yamahas in 1983 with the NS500 – a reed-valve triple whose 125bhp output was 10bhp down on the opposition's, but which had an advantage in manoeuvrability. Fast Freddie's second championship, though,

was won in 1985 on the V-four that would be Honda's weapon for almost two decades: the NSR500.

For much of its life the NSR was the most powerful of the factory Grand Prix 500cc machines, partly due to its unique single-crankshaft design (the others used twin geared-together cranks), which reduced friction but increased width. After unsuccessful experiments with the fuel tank under the engine in 1984, the NSR used a conventional chassis layout, with an aluminium twin-beam frame. In Honda tradition, the V-four's handling often failed to match its horsepower – notably in 1989, when Eddie Lawson tamed a wayward NSR to win the title.

HONDA NSR500 (1994)	
Engine	Watercooled 112-degree V-four crankcase reed-valve two-stroke
Capacity	499cc (54 x 54.5mm)
Power	187bhp @ 12,500rpm
Weight	130kg (286lb) dry
Top speed	197mph (315kph)

■ BELOW *Eddie Lawson tamed the NSR
and won the title in 1989.*

The NSR evolved and got even faster over the years while retaining its basic V-four layout. Japanese ace Shinichi Itoh was the first Grand Prix rider to be timed at 200mph (320kph), on an NSR500 at Germany's Hockenheim in 1993, by which time the Honda was producing 185bhp. In the following season Mick Doohan won the first of five consecutive titles. Spaniard Alex Criville took over to keep the NSR on top. Valentino Rossi won the final 500cc world championship in 2001, giving the NSR its tenth title in 18 years, before the two-stroke era was ended by the arrival of 990cc MotoGP four-strokes.

Honda found more success after effectively cutting the 500cc V-four motor in half to produce the NSR250 V-twin. Highlights included two titles for Sito Pons and Luca Cadalora. Perhaps the finest achievement was by Freddie Spencer, who won both 500 and 250cc titles on NSRs in 1985.

OTHER MAKES

■ HOREX

A leading German make for many years, Horex was founded in 1923 and built many sophisticated road and race bikes in the following years. The firm's most successful model was the Regina, a 350cc OHV single, produced from the late 1940s. The 400cc Imperator, a stylish and technically advanced SOHC parallel twin introduced in 1951, featured telescopic or leading-link forks, twin-shock rear suspension and an enclosed drive chain.

Horex hit problems in the mid-1950s, partly due to the disastrous 250cc Rebell scooter, and the factory closed in 1958. In the 1970s, Friedel Münch and fellow enthusiast Fritz Roth attempted to revive the name with a 1400cc turbocharged

■ FAR LEFT *Former racer Sammy Miller
on Husqvarna's 1930's V-twin in a TT
classic parade.*

four, based on Münch's Mammut, and a series of small-capacity two-strokes. More recently the Horex name was used on a Honda 650cc single-cylinder engined sportsier called the Osca, which was built and sold in Japan.

■ HRD

Howard Raymond Davies was a racer and former First World War air ace who in 1924 set up a firm to build bikes under his own name. The following year Davies won the Senior TT on an HRD, and Freddie Dixon scored a Junior win two years later. But roadster sales were disappointing, and the firm went into liquidation shortly afterwards. The HRD name was later bought by Philip Vincent, to add credibility to his own machines.

■ HUSQVARNA

Best known in recent years for motocross and enduro bikes, Swedish firm Husqvarna was an armaments firm that diversified into motorcycle production in 1903. In the 1930s the firm built innovative 350 and 500cc V-twins that were raced successfully by riders including Stanley Woods. Husqvarna continued to build successful off-road competition machines after roadster production was ended in the early 1960s. In 1986 the firm became part of the Cagiva Group, and Husqvarna production was moved to Italy.

■ ABOVE *Husqvarna rider Jan Carlsson in
the 1983 International Six Days Enduro.*

■ ABOVE *French rider Vuillemin corners
his twin-cylinder Horex in a classic event.*

INDIAN

■ INDIAN POWERPLUS

Indian was founded in 1901 by George Hendee and Oscar Hedstrom, two former bicycle racers, who teamed up to produce a 1.75bhp single in Hendee's home town of Springfield. The bike was successful, and sales increased dramatically during the next decade. In 1904, the so-called diamond framed Indian single, whose engine was built by the Aurora firm in Illinois, was made available in the deep red colour that would become Indian's trademark. By now production was up to over 500 bikes annually, and would rise to a best-ever 32,000 in 1913.

In 1907, Indian built its first V-twin, and in following years made a strong showing in racing and record-breaking. One of the firm's most famous riders was Erwin "Cannonball" Baker, who set many long-distance records. In 1914, he rode an Indian across America, from San Diego to New York, in a record 11 days,

■ ABOVE *The power and refinement of Indian's new side-valve engine earned it the name Powerplus.*

INDIAN POWERPLUS (1918)	
Engine	Aircooled 4-valve 42-degree V-twin
Capacity	998cc (79.4 x 100.8mm)
Power	18bhp
Weight	186kg (410lb) wet
Top speed	60mph (96kph)

12 hours and ten minutes. Baker's mount in subsequent years was the Powerplus, a side-valve V-twin that was introduced in 1916. Its 61ci (1000cc), 42-degree V-twin engine was more powerful and quieter than previous designs, giving a top speed of 60mph (96kph). The Powerplus was highly successful, both as a roadster and as the basis for racing bikes. It remained in production with few changes until 1924.

■ BELOW *The 1918-model Powerplus had only minor differences from the machine introduced two years earlier.*

■ LEFT *In 1904 Indian's single offered a 30mph (48kph) top speed, excellent build quality and optional red finish.*

■ BELOW *This 1913-model Indian V-twin has the earlier F-head (or inlet-over-exhaust) valve layout.*

Competition success played a big part in Indian's rapid growth, and spurred technical innovation. One of the American firm's best early results came in the Isle of Man TT in 1911, when Indian riders Godfrey, Franklin and Moorehouse finished first, second and third. Indian star Jake De Rosier set several speed records both in America and at Brooklands in England, and won an estimated 900 races, on dirt-tracks and boards. He left Indian for Excelsior and died in 1913, aged 33, of injuries sustained in a board-race crash with Charles "Fearless" Balke, who later became Indian's top rider. Work at the Indian factory was stopped while De Rosier's funeral procession passed.

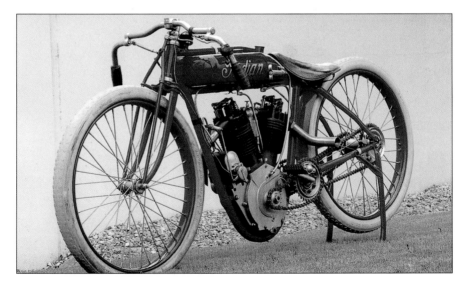

■ RIGHT *Indian's powerful eight-valve racers were very successful on the American tracks in 1916.*

INDIAN

■ INDIAN CHIEF

The Scout and Chief V-twins, introduced in the early 1920s when Indian could claim to be the world's largest motorcycle manufacturer, became the Springfield firm's most successful models. Designed by Charles B Franklin, the middleweight Scout and larger Chief shared a 42-degree V-twin engine layout.

INDIAN CHIEF (1947)	
Engine	Aircooled 4-valve sidevalve 42-degree V-twin
Capacity	1200cc (82.5 x 113mm)
Power	40bhp @ 4000rpm
Weight	245kg (539lb) dry
Top speed	85mph (136kph)

■ ABOVE *The 1200cc Big Chief was introduced in 1923, and immediately outsold Indian's smaller Scout model.*

■ RIGHT *Almost all Indian V-twin engines, including this 74ci (1200cc) unit, had a 42-degree cylinder angle.*

■ BELOW *This 1947-model Chief, with headdress mascot on its skirted front fender, epitomizes the Indian look.*

■ **ABOVE FAR RIGHT** *Scouts were raced successfully for many years, and still compete in classic events.*

■ **RIGHT** *The 500cc (30.5ci) Scout Pony, seen here in 1939 form, was aimed at the entry-level rider.*

■ **BELOW RIGHT** *Reborn Indian's traditionally styled Chief gained a new 1638cc V-twin engine in 2002.*

The first 1922 model Chief had a 1000cc (61ci) engine based on that of the Powerplus; a year later the engine was enlarged to 1200cc (73ci). Numerous improvements were made over the years, including adoption of a front brake in 1928. After Indian had been bought by E Paul DuPont in 1930, the new owner's paint industry connections resulted in no fewer than 24 colour options being offered in 1934. Models of that era featured Indian's famous headdress logo on the gas tank. Indian's huge Springfield factory was known as the Wigwam.

The Scout, initially with a 596cc (37ci) engine that was bored-out to 745cc (45ci) in 1927, rivalled the Chief as Indian's most important model. The most famous version was the 101 Scout of 1928, which featured improved handling from a new, lower frame.

In 1940 all Indian models were fitted with the large skirted fenders that became the firm's trademark, and the Chief gained a sprung frame that was superior to rival Harley's unsprung rear end. The 1940s Chiefs were handsome and comfortable machines, capable of 85mph (136kph) in standard form and 100mph (160kph) when tuned. In 1950 the V-twin engine was enlarged to 1300cc (80ci) and telescopic forks were adopted. But Indian's financial problems meant that few bikes were built, and production of the Chief ended in 1953.

Indian's history made the name valuable in the early 1990s, when Harley-Davidson's success showed there was money to be made from motorcycles. Several individuals claimed rights to the name, announced ambitious plans for new Indians, and attempted to raise millions of dollars of investment money. None produced a bike. In 1997 the dispute was settled when rights were awarded to a Canadian-based consortium.

In 1999 the newly formed Indian Motorcycle Corporation introduced a new generation Chief, a traditionally styled cruiser powered by a V-twin engine from well-known supplier S&S. Criticism that this was not a true Indian was answered in 2002, when the Chief gained a new 1638cc "Powerplus" V-twin of Indian's own design. Production numbers at the Californian factory remained relatively low but Indian faced the future with confidence.

INDIAN

INDIAN FOUR

The Indian Four is one of the most famous American motorcycles, though it was by no means one of the most successful. Indian bought the Ace firm, makers of a 1265cc in-line four, in 1927, and the first Indian Four was simply an Ace with smaller wheels and Indian badges. In subsequent years Indian improved the design with a front brake, new forks and a new frame, before introducing the Model 436 Four in 1936. Known as the "upside down" Four because its valvegear was reversed to put intake valves at the side of the engine and exhausts above, the Model 436 was unreliable and short-lived.

Indian returned to the original engine layout and added other improvements in 1938. An early 1940s Four produced 40bhp, was very smooth and had a top speed of 90mph (144kph). But the price was high, rear cylinder overheating remained a problem, and the Four tied up money that Indian might have better spent on developing an overhead-valve V-twin rival to Harley's 61E. Production of the Four eventually ended in 1943.

INDIAN FOUR (1942)	
Engine	Aircooled 8-valve sidevalve longitudinal four
Capacity	1265cc (69.9 x 82.5mm)
Power	40bhp @ 5000rpm
Weight	255kg (561lb) dry
Top speed	90mph (144kph)

■ OPPOSITE *Factory windshield was a popular accessory for both the Four and Chief in the 1940s.*

■ BELOW LEFT *The in-line four motor was handsome and smooth, but had a tendency to overheat.*

■ BELOW *This well-used Four, built in 1941, has been updated with later forks and foot gearchange.*

Indian's decision to build middleweight vertical twins in the late 1940s also contributed to its demise. The verticals were unreliable and unpopular, and production at Springfield ceased in 1953. Indian continued in business by importing British machines, notably the Royal Enfields which were sold as Indians. The firms split in 1960, after which Indian sold Matchless bikes for a few years before ceasing trading.

The Indian name was also used to sell small Italian-made bikes in the late 1960s and 1970s, before fading away and then becoming the subject of much dispute. More recently, with the Indian ownership issue resolved in the States, and production of a new generation V-twin under way, Scotland-based enthusiast Alan Forbes, who claimed the Indian name in Britain, began small-scale production of a classically styled inline four. Named the Dakota, it was powered by a car-engine-based 1845cc unit.

OTHER MAKES

■ JAMES
Starting out as a bicycle firm in the last century, Birmingham-based James built four-stroke singles and large-capacity V-twins in the 1930s. In the 1960s, production was based on two-strokes, notably the 250cc Commodore single and its twin-cylinder successor the Superswift. The firm also built a number of trials bikes, and ran a factory team for many years. James became part of AMC in 1963, and ceased production when the group collapsed three years later.

■ ABOVE *The Superswift, introduced in 1962 and powered by a 250cc Villiers two-stroke engine, was one of the last and best James roadsters.*

■ JAWA
Jawa was founded in Czechoslovakia in 1929 and built numerous road and race bikes before the Second World War. Production continued after 1945, in conjunction with CZ, most notably with simple two-stroke roadsters. Jawa also built many highly successful speedway bikes, after taking over the Eso factory in 1962.

■ ABOVE *This 350cc two-stroke from the mid-1960s is a typical Jawa – competent, cheap and strangely styled.*

■ KAHENA
Powered by a 1600cc, flat-four VW car engine producing 50bhp, the Brazilian Kahena was a huge, fully-faired tourer built for the growing South American market of the early 1990s.

KAWASAKI

■ BELOW *The H1's fierce power-band and flex-prone frame made fast cornering an exciting business.*

■ KAWASAKI 500cc H1

The motorcycle division forms a relatively small part of Kawasaki Heavy Industries, a vast firm that produces trains, boats and planes. Kawasaki's involvement with bikes began in the 1950s, when the aircraft division was looking for civilian work, and was stepped up when the industrial giant wanted to increase awareness of its name. In 1960 Kawasaki built its first complete bike, a 125cc two-stroke, and took over Meguro, Japan's oldest motorcycle manufacturer, which had been making copies of British bikes including the BSA A7 parallel twin.

Kawasaki moved into the big bike market in 1966 with the W1, a 650cc

■ LEFT *High bars and sleek styling give this American-market H1-B a deceptively docile look.*

■ OPPOSITE LEFT *The H1's two-stroke triple engine was compact, powerful and very thirsty.*

■ OPPOSITE MIDDLE *The production of triples formed just a tiny part of Kawasaki Heavy Industries' work.*

■ OPPOSITE RIGHT *Kawasaki's first big bikes were 650cc parallel twins such as this W1 SS, produced in 1968.*

■ RIGHT *The fearsome 748cc H2 triple had similar looks to the H1, plus even more power, noise and speed.*

twin, which again owed much to BSA. It sold well in Japan, but flopped against the quicker British bikes on the American market. Kawasaki's response came with lighter, smaller-capacity two-strokes, the 250cc A1 Samurai and similar 350cc A7 Avenger, which were exported more successfully. In 1969 Kawasaki released the 500cc H1, the first of the triples that would earn the firm a well-deserved reputation for outrageous high performance.

With a peak output of 60bhp at 7500rpm from its aircooled, two-stroke engine, and a weight of just 174kg (383lb), the H1 – also known as the Mach III – had an unmatched power-to-weight ratio. It looked good, scorched to

KAWASAKI 500cc H1 (1969)	
Engine	Aircooled two-stroke transverse triple
Capacity	499cc (60 x 58.8mm)
Power	60bhp @ 7500rpm
Weight	174kg (383lb)
Top speed	120mph (192km/h)

a top speed of 120mph (192kph), and had handling that made life just a little exciting. The combination of an insubstantial frame, rearwards weight distribution and an abrupt power step at 6000rpm were responsible for introducing the words "wheelie" and "tankslapper" to motorcyclists' vocabularies. Poor fuel economy completed the triple's antisocial image, but owners could live with that.

Kawasaki also built two smaller triples, the 250cc S1 and 350cc S2, and in 1972 enlarged the three-cylinder engine to 748cc to produce the H2, or Mach IV. Its 74bhp motor gave blistering acceleration and a top speed of 125mph (201kph). Handling was slightly better than the H1's, but the H2 was a wild ride and remained so until emissions regulations finally killed off the big two-strokes in the mid-1970s.

KAWASAKI

■ KAWASAKI Z1

Kawasaki's Z1 was released in 1973 and dominated superbiking for much of the decade with its combination of powerful, unburstable motor, handsome looks and competitive price. The Z1's four-cylinder, 903cc engine featured twin camshafts, unlike Honda's SOHC CB750-four, and produced a maximum of 82bhp to give the Kawasaki a top speed of 130mph (208kph). Its straight-line performance outclassed that of the

KAWASAKI Z1 (1973)	
Engine	Aircooled 8-valve DOHC transverse four
Capacity	903cc (66 x 66mm)
Power	82bhp @ 8500rpm
Weight	230kg (506lb) dry
Top speed	130mph (208kph)

■ ABOVE *The twin-cam Z1 motor was superbly strong and powerful.*

■ BELOW *Strong styling matched the Z1's awesome performance.*

Honda, whose launch in late 1968 had caused Kawasaki's engineers to delay and revise their four-cylinder project, code-named "New York Steak", which had originally been designed as a 750.

The Z1's chassis did not come close to matching the brilliance of its engine, but the Kawasaki handled reasonably well and was quite comfortable despite high handlebars. Its styling was superb, with a rounded tank, rear ducktail and four shiny silencers. Best of all, the Z1 was far cheaper than rival European

■ LEFT *Smaller aircooled Kawasaki fours included the fast and practical Z650, introduced in 1977.*

■ LEFT *Although it was prone to wobbles at high speeds, the Z1 went round slower corners quite well.*

■ BELOW *The Z1-R, with a tuned motor and uprated handling, faced fierce competition in 1978.*

superbikes. It became massively popular, acquired the nickname the "King" and earned Kawasaki a lasting reputation for horsepower and reliability.

Improvements in subsequent years included the addition of a second front disc brake in 1976, when the bike was renamed the Z900. A year later its engine was enlarged to 1015cc to produce the Z1000. In 1978 Kawasaki produced the Z1-R café racer, which featured a tuned, 90bhp engine, strengthened frame and angular styling incorporating a handlebar fairing. It was the best big "Zed" yet but faced renewed opposition from Suzuki's GS1000 and Honda's CBX1000.

The Z1's speed and reliability made it a natural for many forms of racing. In standard form the Kawasaki won Australia's prestigious Castrol Six-Hour race in 1973. In Europe the four-cylinder motor was used to power many endurance racers, notably the factory-

backed bikes on which Frenchmen Georges Godier and Alain Genoud won several 24-hour events in the 1970s.

In the late 1970s and early 1980s Kawasaki also built several smaller fours whose layout followed the Z1's pattern. Among the best was the Z650, released in 1977, which provided

typically smooth, reliable 110mph (177kph) performance with manoeuvrability and a competitive price. But although Kawasaki had billed the bike as being the 650 that would outperform any 750, they had not reckoned on Suzuki's faster GS750, which was launched at the same time.

■ ABOVE *French ace Jean-Claude Chemarin led Kawasaki's endurance team to success in the early 1980s.*

■ ABOVE *New Zealander Graeme Crosby won races and fans on a high-barred Moriwaki Kawasaki.*

KAWASAKI

KAWASAKI Z1300

The huge six-cylinder Kawasaki Z1300 was in some ways the ultimate late 1970s Superbike, the inevitable end product of the Japanese manufacturers' race towards bigger, heavier and more complex machines. Its watercooled, 1286cc engine produced a highest-yet 120bhp, and the slab-sided Z1300 weighed over 300kg (661lb) with fuel. Yet, ironically, its large radiator meant the Kawasaki had little of the visual impact of Honda's six-cylinder CBX1000, and the Z1300's performance was less startling than its specification suggested.

Despite all its weight, the Z1300 handled reasonably well, thanks to a

■ RIGHT *With an output of 100bhp, Kawasaki's six was motorcycling's most powerful engine in 1979.*

■ BELOW *The Z1300's styling and sheer bulk made the six-cylinder engine look almost ordinary.*

■ LEFT *Cornering was never going to be the Z1300's strength, but for such a big bike it handled well.*

KAWASAKI Z1300 (1979)	
Engine	Watercooled 12-valve DOHC transverse six
Capacity	1286cc (62 x 71mm)
Power	120bhp @ 8000rpm
Weight	305kg (670lb) wet
Top speed	135mph (217kph)

strong frame and good suspension, and remained stable all the way to its impressive 135mph (217kph) top speed. But the Kawasaki's exposed, upright riding position limited its high-speed cruising ability, and the six-cylinder motor had a rather busy feel. Despite its unmatched power and bulk the Z1300 offered nothing that several smaller, simpler and cheaper bikes could not provide. The expensive six marked the end of Japan's apparent belief that bigger was better.

One of the outstanding bikes of the 1980s was Kawasaki's GPZ900R, the firm's first watercooled four, which was released in 1984. The GPZ's 908cc,

16-valve engine produced 113bhp at 9500rpm, and was impressively strong in best four-cylinder Kawasaki tradition. It pulled the GPZ smoothly to a top speed of over 150mph (241kph), aided by the excellent aerodynamics of the sharply styled full fairing.

A compact, light chassis provided handling to match, making the "Ninja", as the bike was known in America, hard to beat both on the road and in production racing. Better still, the GPZ matched its speed with genuine long-distance comfort. It immediately became popular and was still being sold almost ten years later having outlasted its supposed successor, the GPZ1000RX.

KAWASAKI

■ KAWASAKI ZZ-R1100

In the ultra-competitive motorcycle world of the 1990s, it was some achievement for Kawasaki to produce a Superbike whose awesome 145bhp powerplant and 175mph (280kph) top speed simply blew away all opposition. Not only did the ZZ-R1100 make just such an impact when it was launched in 1990, but the watercooled, 1052cc

- OPPOSITE ABOVE *Handling was good, despite the ZZ-R1100's size and weight.*

- OPPOSITE BELOW *The 1993-model ZZ-R1100 had a revised chassis, but its engine remained the star attraction.*

- RIGHT *With its 176bhp engine and aluminium monocoque frame, the ZX-12R was innovative as well as very fast.*

KAWASAKI ZZ-R1100 (1990)

Engine	Watercooled 16-valve DOHC transverse four
Capacity	1052cc (76 x 58mm)
Power	145bhp @ 9500rpm
Weight	228kg (502lb) dry
Top speed	175mph (280kph)

- ABOVE *Scott Russell won the 1993 World Superbike title and three Daytonas.*

- ABOVE *High performance and bold styling made the original ZXR750 a big hit.*

Kawasaki was still the world's fastest production streetbike five years later.

Its straight-line performance came from a 16-valve engine developed from that of the 1988 model ZX-10. Big valves and lightened pistons increased power but the real boost came from the ZZ-R's ram-air system, based on Formula One car-race technology, which ducted cool air from a slot in the fairing nose to a pressurized airbox. The faster the Kawasaki went, the deeper it breathed – with thrilling result.

The ZZ-R was also a smooth and refined motorcycle that handled well thanks to a rigid aluminium frame and good suspension. It made a practical and comfortable as well as very rapid sports-tourer, and remained popular for more than a decade. Eventually, in 2002, Kawasaki replaced it with the similarly styled ZZ-R1200, featuring a larger 1164cc engine producing more midrange

power, and a slightly sportier chassis that gave more agile handling.

The new ZZ-R lined-up alongside another fearsome Kawasaki four, the ZX-12R, which had created headlines on its launch two years earlier due to its top speed of almost 190mph (307kph). The ZX-12R allegedly produced 176bhp from its 1199cc, 16-valve engine, which was held in an innovative aluminium monocoque (one-piece) frame.

Kawasaki's outstanding 750cc bike of the modern era was the ZXR750. Conventional in layout – holding a watercooled, 16-valve engine in a twin-beam aluminium frame – the ZXR provided aggressive looks and a performance of 150mph (241kph) to match. It formed the basis of Kawasaki's most notable racing success, Scott Russell's World Superbike championship win in 1993, and was followed by the similarly racy ZX-7R in 1996.

KAWASAKI

■ LEFT *The four-cylinder Z1000 matched its traditional Kawasaki name with plenty of modern style and performance.*

■ BELOW *The ZX-6R's aggressive styling was backed up by its powerful, 636cc four-cylinder engine and light, racy chassis.*

■ KAWASAKI ZX-6R

Kawasaki had lost some of its reputation for performance by the start of the new Millennium due to unspectacular racing results and the lack of high-performance roadsters in its range. That changed in 2003 with the arrival of a new ZX-6R, which in contrast to its less speed-oriented predecessor of the same name was a pure-bred sporting missile.

KAWASAKI ZX-6R (2003)	
Engine	Watercooled 16-valve DOHC transverse four
Capacity	636cc (68 x 43.8mm)
Power	116bhp @ 13,000rpm
Weight	161kg (354lb) dry
Top speed	160mph (257kph)

■ LEFT *Germany's Anton Mang won four world titles on the KR250 and 350 tandem twins in the early 1980s.*

■ LEFT *Even the fast and stylish Kork Ballington could not make the KR500 square-four a Grand Prix winner.*

The original ZX-6R, launched in 1995, was a fine bike that had been effectively revised in subsequent years, while becoming more of an all-rounder than a cutting-edge sports machine. In contrast the new ZX-6R had aggressive styling, a racy riding position, and a 636cc engine that revved to 15,500rpm and produced 116bhp even before the benefit of its ram-air system was included. Its state-of-the-art chassis featured racing style radial front brake calipers. With a top speed of 160mph (257kph), superb handling and an uncompromising personality, the glamorous ZX-6R did much to put Kawasaki back in the spotlight.

The new middleweight shared centre stage with another striking Kawasaki launched at the same time: the Z1000. This was no race-replica but a sporty roadster whose bold styling, flexible 125bhp four-cylinder engine and agile chassis made it hugely entertaining to ride, as well as very quick. Along with the ZX-6R, the Z1000 confirmed that Kawasaki president Shinichi Morita was living up to his promise to rebuild the marque's reputation for performance and excitement.

That reputation dates back to 1970s roadsters such as the Z1 and H2, and also to the racebikes that have worn Kawasaki's lime-green colours over the years. Some of the best known were the 750cc H2R triples of the 1970s, known as Green Meanies due to their paintwork and nasty handling. In 1975 Kawasaki replaced the roadster-based H2R with a purpose-built racer, the KR750. Despite its reliability problems and vicious power band, Mick Grant, Gregg Hansford and Gary Nixon had many wins on the 120bhp triple.

Arguably Kawasaki's best ever racebikes were the KR250 and KR350, watercooled two-stroke tandem twins that dominated Grand Prix racing between 1978 and '82, winning eight world championships. South African Kork Ballington began the KR's domination, winning both 250 and 350cc titles in 1978 and '79. Germany's Anton Mang added two further titles on each bike, including a double in 1981. But when Kawasaki moved up to 500cc Grand Prix racing with the four-cylinder KR500, which featured an innovative aluminium monocoque frame, even Ballington could not make it competitive.

KTM

■ **LEFT** *KTM's Adventure 950 V-twin was a true dual-purpose bike, as happy on the road as it was on rough ground.*

■ KTM ADVENTURE 950

The arrival in 2003 of the Adventure 950, KTM's first large-capacity roadster, confirmed that the Austrian firm was very serious about its stated plan to become Europe's largest motorcycle manufacturer. Powered by a sophisticated and compact 942cc V-twin engine producing 98bhp, the Adventure followed KTM tradition in being a dual-purpose machine with the emphasis on off-road ability.

Slim, light and tall, especially the Adventure S model that was identical to the silver standard model except for its orange paint and longer-travel suspension, the KTM was a more capable off-road machine than its dual-purpose rivals. It was closely based on the 950 Rally factory desert racer on which Italian ace Fabrizio Meoni had won two of the previous three Dakar Rallies; so much so that 95 per cent of parts were shared.

KTM ADVENTURE 950 (2003)

Engine	Watercooled 8-valve DOHC 75-degree V-twin
Capacity	942cc (100 x 60mm)
Power	98bhp @ 8000rpm
Weight	198kg (436lb) dry
Top speed	125mph (201kph)

■ **BELOW LEFT** *The Adventure 950's tall, slim shape was due to the V-twin's close links with KTM's Dakar desert racebike.*

■ **BELOW RIGHT** *The Duke was far from practical, but its light weight and agile handling made it fun to ride.*

The all-new LC8 engine was a DOHC, eight-valve unit with cylinder spaced at 75 degrees. A tubular steel frame held high quality suspension from Dutch firm WP. The motor was very flexible, reasonably smooth, and gave a top speed of 125mph (201kph). Handling was very good both on-road and off, helped by the bike's light weight. With further V-twin models and also a V-four MotoGP racer under development, KTM's attack on the large capacity market promised much.

The firm from Mattighofen in Austria had grown at an impressive rate since being reborn under new management in 1992, following the collapse of the original KTM company. The marque had begun production in 1953 and had earned a strong reputation, particularly in motocross and enduro racing. Early roadsters were mainly small-capacity two-strokes, powered by engines from fellow Austrian firm Rotax. Recent production has concentrated on larger four-stroke singles including the Duke, a stylish naked roadster.

LANYING

■ **BELOW** *Apart from additions such as its fairing and pillion backrest, the CJ750 was essentially a 1950s BMW.*

■ **LANYING CJ750F**

China had become the world's largest motorcycle manufacturing nation by the mid-1990s, its annual output of over three million units exceeding even that of Japan. In 1994 the Lanying factory in Hunan province employed 13,000 workers and produced 10,000 bikes per month, the majority of them simple, small-capacity machines destined for use by China's vast population. Typical of the larger bikes was the Chang Jiang or CJ750F, a flat-twin four-stroke whose design – like that of Ural and Dnepr twins from the former Soviet Union – was based on 1950s BMWs.

Lanying had made some attempts to modernize the Chang Jiang, by fitting an

LANYING CJ750F (1994)	
Engine	Aircooled 4-valve OHV pushrod flat-twin
Capacity	745cc (78 x 78mm)
Power	34bhp @ 5000rpm
Weight	230kg (506lb) dry
Top speed	70mph (112kph)

angular twin-headlamp fairing and an electric starter. But essentially the twin remained little changed. Its shaft-drive engine produced just 34bhp, good for only 70mph (112kph), its drum brakes were feeble and handling was limited. By modern standards the Lanying was a

crude device, and attempts to export it to Europe were unsuccessful. But the growing Chinese motorcycle industry is increasingly setting its sights on lucrative export markets, and looks set to become an important force in the future.

OTHER MAKES

■ **KOBAS**
Talented engineer Antonio Cobas created many innovative racebikes in the late 1970s and early 1980s. The Spaniard's Rotax-engined 250cc racer of 1983 pioneered the use of a twin-beam aluminium frame with rising-rate rear suspension, adopted in recent years as the standard format for both racing and sports road machines.

■ **KRAUSER**
Some of the most exotic café racers of the 1980s were the Krausers that combined a tuned, flat-twin BMW engine with an

intricate tubular steel spaceframe. Mike Krauser's German firm, best known for bike luggage, also built a BMW-powered road-going sidecar, the Domani, whose chassis was based on that of a Grand Prix racing "worm" outfit. Krauser's racing exploits have ranged from long-standing sidecar involvement to the championship-winning 80cc Grand Prix racers of the mid-1980s.

■ **KREIDLER**
German moped specialist Kreidler made its name with a string of 50cc world championships in the 1970s, in a team run

by Dutch importer Henk Van Veen. But the firm hit financial problems and ceased production in the early 1980s.

■ **LAMBRETTA**
Scooter specialist Lambretta was established after the Second World War and stylish, fully-enclosed machines such as the LD150 were hugely popular in the 1950s and in the UK in the 1960s when they were a symbol of the Mods. Italian production was halted in the 1970s, but Lambrettas continued to be built under licence in Spain and India.

LAVERDA

■ LAVERDA JOTA 1000

Motorcycles were just a sideline for a large agricultural machinery firm from north-eastern Italy when Francesco Laverda built his first bikes – tiny 75cc four-strokes – in the late 1940s. Small-capacity Laverdas were raced successfully in long-distance events such, as the Milano-Taranto and Giro d'Italia, in the 1950s, but the firm's later concentration on humble, economical bikes coincided with the rise of cheap cars, such as the Fiat 500, and nearly proved disastrous.

Laverda changed tack just in time in the late 1960s, releasing a 650cc four-stroke parallel twin that was quickly enlarged to produce the successful 750GT tourer and 750S sportster. Handsome, rugged and quick, especially the

■ ABOVE *The Jota's greatest asset was its powerful 981cc, three-cylinder engine.*

■ BELOW *Muscular looks and performance to match made the Jota one of the greatest superbikes of the 1970s.*

LAVERDA JOTA 1000 (1976)	
Engine	Aircooled 6-valve DOHC transverse triple
Capacity	981cc (75 x 74mm)
Power	90bhp @ 8000rpm
Weight	236kg (520lb) wet
Top speed	140mph (225kph)

later 750SF models, the twins earned Laverda a growing reputation for performance. Best and fastest of all was the exotic SFC, basically a road-going endurance racer with half-fairing, bright orange paint and tuned engine. Laverda also built an exotic V-six racebike, which was timed at 176mph (283kph) before retiring in its first and only ever

■ ABOVE *The SFC1000 of 1985, the last of the aircooled triples, could not save Laverda from financial disaster.*

■ LEFT *The exotic, half-faired SFC750 parallel twin of the 1970s was basically an endurance racer built for the road.*

■ ABOVE *In 1994, under new management, Laverda began production of the parallel twin 650 sportster.*

■ ABOVE *Laverda's legendary 1000cc V-six racer proved fast but fragile in its only ever appearance in 1978.*

■ ABOVE *After being bought by Aprilia, Laverda returned to the superbike market with the stylish SFC1000 V-twin.*

race, the Bol d'Or 24-Hours in 1978.

It was for three-cylinder sportsters, however, that the firm from Breganze became most famous. The first DOHC, 981cc triple, called the 3C, was powerful, good-looking and fairly successful when introduced in 1973. Three years later, at the request of the British Laverda importer, the factory turned the motor with hot cams, high-compression pistons and free-breathing exhausts to produce the Jota. This was a big, raw 90bhp beast that bellowed to a top speed of 140mph (225kph). In the mid-1970s it was the fastest thing on two wheels, as numerous production race victories confirmed.

The triple was modified in various ways in following years, without ever matching the success of the original Jota. The 1000cc sportster gained a fairing and a smoother-running, 120-degree crankshaft engine. A 1200cc version was also built, largely for the American market. Tightening emissions legislation prompted the quieter, less aggressive RGS and RGA triples of the 1980s. But sales were disappointing and Laverda hit financial problems that led to receivership in 1987.

Several new Laverda operations rose only to fall again in the following years until finally, in 1994, production started again at a new factory in nearby Zane, of the 650 – an aluminium-framed, 70bhp

parallel twin that had been developed several years earlier.

Other parallel twin models including the Ghost and Diamante followed, but Laverda lacked the financial resources to develop a new generation of bikes. That situation changed when the marque was bought by Aprilia. In 2002 Laverda unveiled a new SFC1000 sportster, powered by a tuned version of the 998cc V-twin engine in Aprilia's RSV Mille. After many difficult years, Laverda looked to have an exciting future.

OTHER MAKES

■ LEVIS
Between 1911 and its demise in 1940, British firm Levis built many two- and four-stroke roadsters. Racing successes included victory in the 1922 Lightweight TT, and later wins in trials and motocross.

■ ABOVE *Levis produced this attractive 500cc four-stroke roadster in 1938.*

■ **LEFT** *Matchless V-twins, including this bike raced by Charlie Collier, were successful in early TT races.*

![motorcycle icon] MATCHLESS

■ **MATCHLESS G50**

One of the great names of motorcycling's early years, Matchless was founded by the Collier family at Plumstead in south London in 1899. Brothers Charlie and Harry Collier were leading racers, Charlie winning the single-cylinder

■ **BELOW LEFT** *Good looks and comfort were not enough to make the 400cc Silver Arrow V-twin of 1930 a success.*

■ **BOTTOM** *The legendary G50 single lived up to its "winged M" badge, winning races throughout the 1960s.*

MATCHLESS G50 (1961)	
Engine	Aircooled 2-valve SOHC single
Capacity	496cc (90 x 78mm)
Power	51bhp @ 7200rpm
Weight	132kg (290lb) dry
Top speed	135mph (217kph)

event at the first ever Isle of Man TT on a Matchless in 1907, and Harry following with a victory two years later. Matchless took over the Wolverhampton-based AJS firm in 1931, and many later models of motorcycles were produced as both AJS and Matchless machines, with very few differences.

■ RIGHT *Colin Seeley bought rights to G50 production and built the Seeley G50, still a force in classic racing.*

In 1930, Matchless released the Silver Arrow, a 400cc V-twin designed by Charlie Collier, but its performance was mediocre and sales poor. Younger brother Bert took over to produce the Silver Hawk, with a more powerful 600cc V-four engine, but despite 80mph (128kph) top speed it could not compete with Ariel's Square Four and was another failure. Matchless had more success with singles, such as the 350cc G3L that was produced in huge numbers for military use in the Second World War. This was one of the first bikes to use telescopic forks, and was later adapted for civilian use in models such as the G3LS of 1959.

The most famous Matchless was the G50 single-cylinder racer, basically a 500cc version of the 350cc AJS 7R. The G50 was first seriously produced in 1959, as a rival to Norton's Manx. Although slightly less powerful, with its 50bhp engine giving a top speed of about 135mph (217kph), the Matchless was lighter and had the edge on twisty circuits. AMC, which Matchless had become part of in 1938, suffered financial problems and went bust in 1966, after which rights to G50 production were bought by Colin Seeley, who continued engine development and built his own chassis to create the Seeley G50. The four-stroke single G50 held its own against the two-strokes until the 1970s, and in recent years has been competitive in classic racing.

OTHER MAKES

■ MAICO

Best known for its highly successful two-stroke motocross and enduro machines, German firm Maico began production in 1933 and built trials and road race bikes, notably the 125cc machines on which Borge Jansson won several Grands Prix in the early 1970s. Roadsters such as the twin-cylinder 350 and 400cc Taifun models were popular in the 1950s. In later years Maico concentrated on dirt bikes, before going bust in 1987.

■ MAGNI

Arturo Magni, team manager of the all-conquering MV Augusta race team, set up in business under his own name after MV's closure in the mid-1970s. Magni

■ ABOVE *In the 1960s, Maico built some rapid small-capacity road-racers.*

produced chassis kits for MV roadsters, and then complete bikes based around Honda's CB900 four. Later Magnis have used Moto Guzzi's V-twin engine, notably the retro-styled Sfida and the sleek, fully-faired Australia sportster.

■ MARUSHO

A leading Japanese manufacturer in the 1950s and early 1960s, Marusho was best known for its Lilac range of 125, 250 and 300cc V-twins. The firm produced a series of flat-twin roadsters before going out of business in the late 1960s.

■ LEFT *Magni's Guzzi-engined Australia sportster was fast and stylish.*

MONDIAL

■ BELOW *Mike Hailwood raced a pair of ex-works 250cc Mondials with great success in 1959 and 1960.*

■ **MONDIAL 250cc RACER**
Small Italian firm FB Mondial produced some fast and beautifully engineered racebikes in the 1950s, its finest moments coming when Tarquinio Provini and Cecil Sandford won the 125 and 250cc world championships in 1957. The company's origins dated back to 1929, when the four Boselli brothers founded FB to sell other firms' bikes. The first Mondials, built at FB's Bologna workshop, were DOHC, single-cylinder 125s. They were immediately successful, winning the world title for three years after its inception in 1949.

MONDIAL 250cc (1957)	
Engine	Aircooled 2-valve DOHC single
Capacity	249cc (75 x 56.4mm)
Power	29bhp @ 10,800rpm
Weight	125kg (275lb) dry
Top speed	135mph (216kph)

■ BELOW *Cecil Sandford won the TT and the 250cc world title in 1957 on this twin-cam Mondial single.*

Mondial also produced roadsters, starting with a 125cc four-stroke that was introduced in 1950, but the firm's main interest remained in racing. After

OTHER MAKES

■ MARS

The most memorable of several manufacturers called Mars was the German firm
that produced a 959cc flat-twin roadster,
the MA20, which featured an innovative
pressed-steel frame in the 1920s. Mars
built small-capacity two-strokes until
ceasing production in the late 1950s.

■ MEGOLA

One of the strangest motorbikes of all
time, the Munich-built Megola was
powered by a radial five-cylinder engine
situated inside its front wheel. Almost as
unusual was the sheet-steel frame, which
gave an armchair riding position. The
640cc side-valve motor produced 10bhp,
and in sports form the single-speed
Megola was timed at 90mph (144kph).
Despite its unconventional design, some
2000 Megolas were built between 1922
and the firm's closure in 1925.

■ MEGURO

Founded in 1924, Meguro was one of the
earliest Japanese motorcycle
manufacturers. In the 1930s the firm's
main bike was the 500cc Z97, a copy of
the Velocette MSS. Meguro expanded to
build twins in the 1950s, such as the
500cc K1, a copy of the BSA A7. But sales
fell, and following a strike the firm was
taken over by Kawasaki in 1960.

■ MIG

Chinese firm MIG has built an
increasingly large number of bikes in
recent years, many based on earlier
Japanese designs. Most have been
mopeds, scooters and commuter bikes, but

■ ABOVE *MIG's QJ100 roadster is
typical of the many small bikes built by
Chinese firms in recent years.*

MIG did build a version of Honda's
CB500-four of the 1970s.

■ MONTESA

Spain's first major bike manufacturer was
founded in 1944 by Francisco Bulto, who

■ LEFT *The 640cc Megola engine of
1922 featured five cylinders arranged
radially inside the front wheel.*

■ BELOW *Despite its feet-forward
position, this 14bhp Megola racer won
the German championship in 1922.*

later left to form Bultaco, and Pedro Perm-
anyer. Early bikes included successful two-
stroke road racers and the Impala roadster.
In recent years the Barcelona firm has been
best known for trials, winning the world
championship in 1980 and producing the
long-running Cota model. Financial
problems in the 1980s led to an association
with Honda, whose engines have been used
by Montesa in recent years.

■ MONTGOMERY

Founded in 1902, Montgomery built a
wide variety of bikes using bought-in
engines ranging from 150cc Villiers two-
strokes to 1000cc JAPs. A typical mid-
1930s bike was the Greyhound, a 500cc
JAP-powered single capable of 75mph
(120kph). It was well-made but expensive,
and Montgomery did not resume
production after the Second World War.

---

the triumphant 1957 season Mondial,
who could not sell enough roadsters to
finance the racing team, quit the sport.
Two of the 250s were sold to Mike
Hailwood, who won many races on them
in Britain. In the 1960s Mondial made a
partially successful return to racing
using two-stroke engines. In 1992 the
Mondial name resurfaced again, in the
shape of a KTM-engined 560cc single-
cylinder racebike produced by Pierluigi
Boselli, son of the firm's former owner.

But it was ten years later that Mondial
returned to prominence, following the firm's
acquisition by businessman Roberto
Ziletti. He arranged with Honda for supply
of the 999cc V-twin engine from the SP-1,
and began production of a stylish sportster
called the Piega. Hand-built in small
numbers, the Piega was fast, handled
superbly and was very light, thanks to
much use of carbon-fibre. It was a fitting
machine for the return of one of Italian
motorcycling's legendary marques.

■ ABOVE *Finished in Mondial's traditional
silver and blue, the 140bhp Piega was a
fast and fine-handling sportster.*

MOTO GUZZI

■ BOTTOM *The Falcone Sport of the mid-1950s, with its red paint and horizontal single cylinder, was a very popular bike.*

■ MOTO GUZZI FALCONE

Italy's largest motorcycle manufacturer for much of its long history, Guzzi dates back to the closing years of the First World War when three air corps friends, Carlo Guzzi, Giorgio Parodi and Giovanni Ravelli, planned a bike firm. After Ravelli was killed in a flying crash, the other two adopted the air corps' eagle symbol in his honour. In 1920 Carlo Guzzi designed the firm's first bike, a 500cc four-stroke with a

■ ABOVE *Founding partner Carlo Guzzi designed the road and race bikes that made Guzzi a leading marque in the 1920s.*

■ LEFT *Fergus Anderson riding his works Falcone on the way to victory in the 250cc Lightweight TT in 1952.*

single, horizontal cylinder. The Normale model was released two years later and, boosted by racing success, rapidly became popular.

Guzzi retained and updated the 500cc flat-single format for many years, leaving many of its more adventurous engine layouts for racing. Landmark singles included the GT luxury tourer of 1928, with its novel sprung frame, and the Sport 15 of 1931, finished in the bright red that became a favourite

MOTO GUZZI FALCONE (1950)	
Engine	Aircooled 2-valve OHV pushrod single
Capacity	498cc (88 x 82mm)
Power	23bhp @ 4500rpm
Weight	170kg (374lb) dry
Top speed	85mph (136kph)

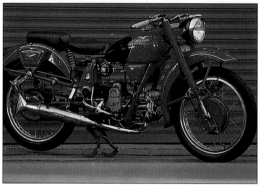

■ ABOVE *Guzzi's decision to quit racing in 1957 meant the exotic and super-fast V-eight never won a Grand Prix.*

■ LEFT *The quick and practical 250cc Airone, launched in 1939, was still popular when this bike was built in 1953.*

Sport and Touring forms. Further updates kept it in production until 1976.

Guzzi's horizontal singles were hugely successful in racing, winning three 250cc world titles between 1949 and 1952, and then being enlarged to 350cc to take five consecutive championships from 1953. The first two championships were won by Scottish ace Fergus Anderson, who then took over as Guzzi's competition manager.

The greatest machine of all was the legendary 500cc V-eight, which was designed by Giulio Carcano and first raced in 1956. The watercooled, quad-cam, 90-degree V-eight revved to 12,000rpm, produced 72bhp and was timed at a phenomenal 178mph (286kph) at the Belgian GP in 1957. Despite these feats, Guzzi unfortunately pulled out of Grand Prix racing at the end of that season, so the V-eight never really fulfilled its true potential.

Guzzi colour. The colour was also used for the famous series of production racers, which began in 1938 with the 28bhp, 100mph (160kph) Condor, and continued with the Dondolino, Gambalunga and the 250cc Albatros – all of which won at the highest level.

The best loved road-going single was the Falcone, which was introduced in 1950 showing clear links with the Normale of almost three decades earlier. Essentially a sports version of the previous year's Astore tourer, the Falcone featured flat handlebars and rearset footrests.

In standard trim its top speed was 85mph (136kph), but when tuned with Dondolino engine parts the Falcone was good for over 100mph (160kph) which, along with the lazy, low revving power delivery, helped to explain its popularity. From 1953 the Falcone was built in

OTHER MAKES

■ **MORBIDELLI**
Self-made businessman and fanatical motorcyclist Giancarlo Morbidelli used his huge woodwork machinery firm to finance production of some superb race-bikes. Morbidellis won three consecutive 125cc world titles in the mid-1970s, plus

the 250cc crown in 1977. Another 125cc title was added the following year, after the MBA firm had been created to produce replicas, and the two-stroke twins remained competitive for several more years. A four-cylinder 500cc racer proved less successful, and Giancarlo Morbidelli finally quit racing. In 1994, he developed a prototype roadster powered by a purpose-built, 850cc watercooled V-eight engine. But the strangely styled sports-tourer did not reach production.

■ LEFT *Morbidelli's V-eight prototype featured controversial styling by leading car-design studio Pininfarina.*

MOTO GUZZI

■ MOTO GUZZI
LE MANS 850

Guzzi's trademark transverse 90-degree V-twin engine design was first seen in an unusual 754cc three-wheeled mountain vehicle called the 3 x 3, built in small numbers for the Italian ministry of defence between 1960 and 1963. In 1964 Guzzi revised the engine for a military bike, and realized the machine had potential for civilian use too.

The V7 went into production in 1967, and two years later was followed by the V7 Special, whose 757cc engine produced 45bhp. With its shaft final drive, the Special was a practical machine whose smooth, 110mph (177kph) performance and stable

■ RIGHT *Fine handling combined with the Le Mans' power and smoothness to make a formidable Superbike.*

■ BELOW *The Le Mans Mk.1's tiny fly-screen added the finishing touch to the Guzzi's classically elegant profile.*

■ FAR LEFT
The protruding cylinders of Guzzi's traditional V-twin were tuned to excellent effect for the Le Mans.

■ LEFT *Guzzi's big factory at Mandello del Lario has run at well below full capacity in recent years.*

MOTO GUZZI 850 LE MANS MK.1 (1976)	
Engine	Aircooled 4-valve OHV pushrod 90-degree transverse V-twin
Capacity	844cc (83 x 78mm)
Power	71bhp @ 7300rpm
Weight	215kg (473lb) dry
Top speed	130mph (209kph)

handling did much to establish Guzzi in the large-capacity market. In 1972 Guzzi released its first genuine high-performance V-twin, the V7 Sport. It featured a reworked 748cc motor and a lower frame that gave 125mph (201kph) performance with excellent handling.

Four years later came the most famous model of all – the 850 Le Mans. This lean sportster, with its neat headlamp fairing and striking, angular seat, was powered by a tuned version of the existing 844cc motor. High-compression pistons, big valves and unfiltered 36mm Dell'Orto carburettors helped raise peak output to 71bhp, which gave a top speed of 130mph (209kph). The shaft-drive motor's long-legged power delivery, coupled with good handling and excellent braking – using Guzzi's new system, which linked the front and rear discs – made the Le Mans one of the finest superbikes of the 1970s.

Times have often been difficult at Guzzi since the firm's great days in the early 1960s, when the big, modern factory at Mandello del Lario, on Lake

Lecco, employed over 1500 people, and boasted its own hydro-electric power stations and an advanced wind-tunnel. By the mid-1960s, factors including the changing bike market, the retirement of the firm's founders and a misguided move into moped production had left Guzzi in serious financial trouble. In 1966 the company went into receivership, reopening a year later with a new owner. In 1973 Guzzi was bought by Alejandro De Tomaso, the Argentinian car baron, who maintained control for the next two decades without providing the investment that many enthusiasts had hoped for.

Guzzi's best-selling model for much of that time was the California, which was initially produced in 1971 as an American market version of the V7 Special, complete with higher bars, "buddy" seat and standard-fitment

screen and panniers. Over the years the California has seen several restyles and revisions, notably in its engine capacity which has grown to 850, 950 and finally 1100cc. In 1994 the California's aircooled, pushrod V-twin engine was fitted with optional fuel-injection, making an even more sophisticated and practical motorcycle tourer.

■ ABOVE *The 750cc V7 Special of 1969 was the basis for Guzzi's long-running range of V-twin tourers.*

■ LEFT *In 1994 the California tourer, its capacity by now 1100cc, was offered with optional fuel-injection.*

MOTO GUZZI

■ MOTO GUZZI DAYTONA 1000

Guzzi took a long time to produce a fitting successor to the original Le Mans, which was gradually developed through the 1980s while becoming decreasingly competitive. Finally, in 1992, came a new generation sportsbike, the Daytona 1000. Its design owed much to "Dr John" Wittner, an American dentist-turned-engineer who had achieved much success with Guzzi-powered racebikes in the late 1980s before coming to work at Mandello.

The Daytona's race-developed chassis held a revised 992cc version of the aircooled V-twin, with fuel-injection and four valves per cylinder. The handsome,

■ BELOW *The Breva 750 was the first new model from Guzzi's revitalized, Aprilia-owned Mandello factory.*

MOTO GUZZI DAYTONA 1000 (1992)

Engine	Aircooled 8-valve high-cam 90-degree transverse V-twin
Capacity	992cc (90 x 78mm)
Power	95bhp @ 8000rpm
Weight	205kg (451lb) dry
Top speed	150mph (241kph)

95bhp Daytona combined a 150mph (241kph) top speed with good handling plus Guzzi's traditional long-legged feel.

Along with the cheaper, carburetted 1100 Sport that followed in 1994, the Daytona proved there was still sporting life in Guzzi's V-twin format. These and other bikes including the V11 Sport kept Guzzi going through the 1990s. But it was only after Aprilia bought the company in 2000 that the Mandello firm gained the financial backing for an exciting range of more modern machines, to be built at a comprehensively modernized factory.

OTHER MAKES

■ MOTO MARTIN

Frenchman Georges Martin was one of the leading chassis specialists of the 1970s and early 1980s, producing stable-handling and beautifully styled café racers typically based on four-cylinder motors such as Kawasaki's Z1000 and Suzuki's GSX1100. Arguably the best of all was the Martin CBX1000, which was powered by a tuned version of Honda's six-cylinder engine.

■ ABOVE *The Martin CBX1000 was one of the fastest and most aggressively styled specials of the early 1980s.*

■ MOTO MORINI

Alfonso Morini began building bikes in partnership with Mario Mezzetti, under the MM name in the 1920s, and rode one himself to a class win in the 1927 Italian Grand Prix at Monza. After setting up under his own name after the War, Morini built roadsters and successful racers, most notably the superb DOHC 250 on which Tarquinio Provini was runner up in the 1963 world championship. The Bologna firm's best known roadster was the handsome and

■ ABOVE *Morini's pretty and fine-handling 3¹/₂ Sport was great fun on twisty roads, and despite the V-twin's modest power even made a useful racer.*

very quick 344cc 3¹/₂ Sport of the mid-1970s. Cagiva bought Morini in 1987, since when the name has been little used.

■ MOTOSACOCHE

Swiss brothers Henri and Armand Dufaux began by making a successful 215cc motorized bicycle in 1900, and by the 1920s had progressed to building 350 and 500cc four-stroke singles that gained many race wins and speed records. When sales fell in the 1930s, Motosacoche left bike production to concentrate on industrial engines.

■ MOTOTRANS

After being founded in 1957 to produce Ducati singles under licence, Spanish firm Mototrans became a manufacturer in its own right. Models included the Yak 410 trail bike plus some Zündapp-powered lightweights that were built in 1982, shortly before the factory was taken over and closed by Yamaha.

■ MÜNCH

The car-engined monster-bikes produced by German engineer Friedel Münch since 1966 have been some of the biggest and most expensive on two wheels. The first Münch Mammut models were powered by an aircooled, 1000cc four-cylinder NSU car engine, held in a huge chassis based on a twin-shock, tubular steel frame. By the early 1990s almost 500 had been built, later models with capacity of up to 1996cc and weight of over 350kg. The most recent Münch, the turbocharged Titan 2000, produced 150bhp and featured a hydraulic centre-stand.

■ ABOVE *The mighty Münch Mammut – or Mammoth – was one of the biggest, most powerful and most expensive superbikes of the 1970s.*

■ BELOW *MV's twin-cam four produced phenomenal performance both as a 500 and in 350cc form, as seen here.*

■ BOTTOM *John Surtees won MV's third 500cc world title on this Four in 1959.*

MV AGUSTA

■ MV AGUSTA 500cc FOUR

There is no greater name in motorcycle racing than MV Agusta, whose record of 17 consecutive world 500cc championships between 1958 and 1974 will probably never be equalled. In all, the

small factory from Gallarate won 38 riders' world titles, 37 manufacturers' championships and over 3000 international races, as well as building the mighty four-cylinder roadsters that were arguably the fastest and most glamorous superbikes of the 1970s.

The Meccanica Verghera motorcycle firm was founded in the village of Verghera towards the end of the Second World War by Count Domenico Agusta, the eldest of four brothers whose late father, a Sicilian aristocrat, had been a noted aviation pioneer. Domenico turned to bikes, and in 1945 released a 98cc two-stroke that sold well and was also raced with instant success. Pure racers as well as other roadsters followed, and

MV AGUSTA 500cc FOUR (1956)	
Engine	Aircooled 8-valve DOHC transverse four
Capacity	498cc (53 x 56.4mm)
Power	70bhp @ 10,500rpm
Weight	140kg (308lb) dry
Top speed	155mph (249kph)

■ LEFT
The Agusta firm's gear-cog logo became synonymous with success.

■ RIGHT *Count Domenico Agusta strikes a pose with team riders John Surtees, Umberto Masetti, Carlo Ubbiali, Carlo Bandirola, Angelo Copeta, Remo Venturi, Luigi Taveri and Tito Forconi in 1956.*

in 1952 Englishman Cecil Sandford won MV's first world title in the 125cc class. In the smaller Grand Prix categories the firm's star rider was Italian ace Carlo Ubbiali, who won five 125cc championships for MV between 1955 and 1960, plus three more on a 250.

But it was in the bigger classes that MV was most successful. The design of MV's first twin-cam 500cc four of 1950 owed much to Gilera, for whom both chief engineer Piero Remor and team manager Arturo Magni had worked. Early bikes featured shaft final drive and a gearlever on each side of the engine, but after poor results a more conventional layout was adopted. John Surtees won MV's first 500cc championship in 1956 and went on to take three more, often winning with ease after the rival factories' withdrawal from racing in 1957. Gary Hocking and Mike Hailwood continued the run, then Giacomo Agostini took over with seven straight championships between 1966 and 1971, using a fine-handling three-cylinder machine.

MV had little serious opposition for long periods during the 1960s, but the so-called "Gallarate fire engines" were increasingly tested by the Japanese two-stroke challenge in the early 1970s. New four-valves-per-cylinder fours were built for both the 350 and 500cc classes, the smaller bike allowing Agostini to win his sixth consecutive 350cc title in 1973. Phil Read used the new 500, which produced 102bhp at 14,000rpm, to take the championship in 1973 and 1974, averaging 130mph (209kph) in winning the Belgian Grand Prix. Ironically it was Agostini, now on a two-stroke Yamaha, who finally ended the Italian firm's domination in 1975.

■ LEFT *Giacomo Agostini, who won 14 world titles for MV, takes "Ago's leap" en route to victory in the 1970 Senior TT.*

■ BELOW *This SOHC, single-cylinder racer, built by MV in the mid-1950s, was capable of over 90mph (145kph).*

MV AGUSTA

■ MV AGUSTA 750 SPORT

Despite producing many successful small-capacity roadsters throughout the 1950s and 1960s – bikes with names like the Pullman, the Turismo Rapido and the Raid – MV was slow to capitalize on its racing success with a four-cylinder street bike. Even when a DOHC MV four did reach the road in 1966 it was not a race-replica but an

■ BELOW *With blue, white and red finish and its mighty engine on show, the 750 Sport of 1973 was a handsome bike.*

MV AGUSTA 750 SPORT (1973)	
Engine	Aircooled 8-valve DOHC transverse four
Capacity	743cc (65 x 56mm)
Power	69bhp @ 7900rpm
Weight	230kg (506lb) dry
Top speed	120mph (192kph)

ugly, hump-tanked 600cc shaft-drive tourer designed at the insistence of the firm's autocratic owner Domenico Agusta, who did not want the production bike to be raced, for fear of devaluing his factory team's hard-won reputation.

The expensive 600 Four was a flop, and in 1970 MV belatedly released a much racier and more exciting roadster called the 750 Sport. This was all that

MV's racing fans had dreamt of. The big, four-cylinder engine had gear drive to twin overhead cams and produced 69bhp. The racy chassis featured clip-on handlebars, a sculpted fuel tank, humped seat and huge Grimeca four-leading-shoe front brake. The Sport was beautiful, expensive and fast, though its 120mph (192kph) top speed did not match MV's claims. Despite too much

■ LEFT *MV's race-derived four, with gear drive to twin cams, was powerful but very expensive to produce.*

■ RIGHT *The last four-cylinder MV was the 750S America of 1975, here fitted with a handlebar fairing.*

weight and the retained shaft drive it handled reasonably well, and the howl from its four shiny megaphone exhausts was gloriously evocative of the Gallarate bikes that still dominated Grand Prix racing.

In subsequent years the Sport was updated with disc brakes, more power and a full fairing. And in 1975 came the 750S America, built for the US market with new, angular styling and a 789cc, 75bhp engine that pushed its top speed towards 130mph (209kph). Like the Sport, the America was an exotic and hugely desirable superbike, but it was no more commercially successful than its predecessor. Glamorous as the fours were, their intricate, competition-derived engine design and low-volume, hand-built construction meant that MVs were not profitable even at the huge

■ RIGHT *Its rarity has made MV's ugly 600cc tourer hugely valuable, but it was a sales disaster back in 1966.*

prices they commanded.

Far from making money for MV, the big roadsters merely added to the firm's problems. Domenico Agusta had died of a heart attack in 1971. His brother Corradino, who had taken over, could not match the passion with which Domenico had run MV's motorcycle division, by then a loss-making part of

the Agusta helicopter firm. By 1977 the Agusta family had lost control of much of the MV business, and was powerless to prevent motorcycle production being halted. Bikes remained on sale until stocks ran out, and in early 1980 MV closed. One of the most glamorous chapters in motorcycling history had come to an end.

■ RIGHT *MV's roadster production in the 1950s was based on small, sporty bikes such as the 175 CSS known as the "Disco Volante" (Flying Saucer) due to the unusual shape of its fuel tank.*

MV AGUSTA

■ MV AGUSTA 750 F4

MV made a sensational return in the late 1990s with the F4 750, a four-cylinder superbike that combined gorgeous styling and innovative engineering. The company had been bought by Cagiva boss Claudio Castiglioni, whose design chief Massimo Tamburini fashioned a remarkable bike around an all-new 749cc, 16-valve engine that had been designed with

MV AGUSTA 750 F4 SERIE ORO (1999)	
Engine	Watercooled 16-valve DOHC transverse four
Capacity	749cc (73.8 x 43.8mm)
Power	126bhp @ 12,500rpm
Weight	184kg (406lb) dry
Top speed	165mph (265kph)

initial help from Ferrari. The chassis was based on a frame that combined steel tubes with cast swing-arm pivot sections. On the initial run of exotic Serie Oro (Gold Series) F4s, these were made from lightweight magnesium, instead of the normal F4's aluminium.

Radial valves helped the motor produce 126bhp, as did an innovative exhaust system with four silencers in the tailpiece. The F4's looks, superb

handling and a top speed of 165mph (265kph) combined to make it hugely desirable. Castiglioni planned a range of bikes using the F4's basic layout, and soon unveiled a striking naked follow-up model, the Brutale. But the financial problems that had dogged Cagiva in the past returned. MV's new factory was quiet for many months before finally, with fresh investment, the famous old marque returned to production.

OTHER MAKES

■ MuZ

The original company, MZ, was founded after the Second World War at the former DKW factory at Zschopau in East Germany. The firm was successful in off-road competition in the 1960s, and also in road-racing due to the powerful two-strokes developed by engineer Walter Kaaden.

During the 1970s and '80s, MZ's roadsters were predominantly single-cylinder two-strokes of moderate performance and curious styling. Bikes such as the ES250/2 Trophy and later ETZ250 provided cheap, reliable motorcycling for large numbers of riders, mainly in Eastern Europe.

After German reunification MZ fell into financial trouble, but resurfaced in 1994 with new management, a new name – MuZ – and a stylish new roadster, the Skorpion,

■ LEFT *MZ roadsters such as the 250cc Supa Five were popular for their price and practicality, but not their looks.*

■ BELOW LEFT *Light weight and clever chassis design helped give the single-cylinder Skorpion excellent handling.*

powered by the 660cc four-stroke single engine from Yamaha's XTZ660 trail bike. The Skorpion was only moderately successful but led to further models. Production of singles including the dual-purpose Baghira continued into the new Millennium, with MuZ by this time under Malaysian ownership.

■ NER-A-CAR

The name of this unusually designed machine of the 1920s was doubly apt, because it was designed by an American called Carl Neracher with the intention of being a bike that was as near a car as possible. His long, low creation was built first in Syracuse, New York state and then in Britain, initially with a 221cc two-stroke engine and later with a 350cc four-stroke single. Although civilized and very stable, thanks partly to its innovative hub-centre steering, the Ner-a-Car was not a commercial success. Production began in 1921 at the improbably high rate of 150 per day, and lasted only until 1926.

■ NEW IMPERIAL

Birmingham firm New Imperial was notable in the early 1930s for pioneering unit construction of engine and gearbox on bikes including the Unit Minor 150 and Unit Super 250. Sporting successes included Ginger Wood's 102.2mph (164.4kph) average for an hour at Brooklands in 1934 on a 500cc V-twin, and Bob Foster's win in the 1936 Lightweight TT. The factory was bought by Jack Sangster, owner of Ariel and Triumph, and production did not restart after the Second World War.

■ ABOVE *New Imperial's fast and handsome 500cc V-twin set records and won many races in the mid-1930s.*

■ LEFT *The long and low Ner-a-Car was stable and civilized, but even in the 1920s most riders preferred sportier bikes.*

NORTON

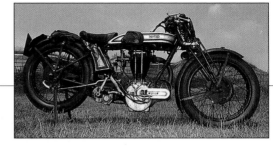

■ NORTON CS1

James Lansdowne Norton built his first motorcycle in 1902, and soon gained a reputation for rapid racing bikes and strong, reliable roadsters. In 1907 Rem Fowler used a Peugeot-engined Norton to win the twin-cylinder class of the first Isle of Man TT. A year later, Norton introduced both single and twin-cylinder engines of its own construction. Early models included the 490cc 16H, a high-performance roadster, and the 633cc long-stroke Big 4, which was named after its 4bhp rating and was popular for pulling sidecars. But James Norton was a better engineer than businessman, and the firm went into liquidation in 1913.

Norton Motors Ltd was formed shortly afterwards under joint directorship of

■ LEFT *The right of the CS1's engine shows the bevel-driven overhead cam that gave the CamShaft 1 its name.*

■ BELOW *This 1927 works CS1 is pictured at Brooklands.*

NORTON CS1 (1927)	
Engine	Aircooled 2-valve SOHC single
Capacity	490cc (79 x 100mm)
Power	20bhp approx
Weight	145kg (319lb) wet
Top speed	80mph (128kph)

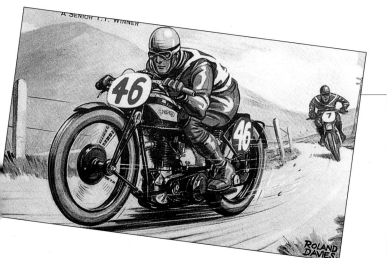

A SENIOR T.T. WINNER

ROLAND DAVIES

■ ABOVE *This scene of a victorious Norton from the early 1930s celebrates the firm's long run of wins in the Senior TT.*

■ LEFT *Norton's key figures James "Pa" Norton and tuner "Wizard" O'Donovan, pose with rider Rex Judd.*

James Norton and Bob Shelley, whose brother-in-law Dan "Wizard" O'Donovan was a top racer and tuner. Based at Brooklands, O'Donovan developed the 490cc Norton single to produce the Brooklands Special or BS, which was sold with a certificate confirming that it had exceeded 75mph (120kph) at the Surrey track. The BS was the world's first production racing bike, and was also built in Brooklands Road Special (BRS) form, timed at 70mph (112kph). The chassis that O'Donovan used to test the BS and BRS engines at Brooklands was later restored, became known as "Old Miracle", and was ridden in classic

events for many years.

In the early 1920s Norton converted the single-cylinder engine to overhead valve operation, producing the Model 18 roadster. The PHV single won the Senior TT in 1924, a year before "Pa" Norton died, aged 56, following a long-standing heart problem. In 1927 the firm from Bracebridge Street, Birmingham introduced another technical advance with the CS1, which featured an overhead camshaft. The CS1 was immediately successful in racing, being ridden to victory by the great Stanley Woods and others, and a year later was released as a super-sports roadster.

OTHER MAKES

■ NIMBUS

Throughout its existence from 1919 to closure in the late 1950s, Danish firm Nimbus concentrated solely on bikes with a 750cc, aircooled in-line four-cylinder engine and shaft final drive. Early models had inlet-over-exhaust valve operation; later bikes used a redesigned, SOHC motor producing 22bhp. Nimbus's military fours were much-used by the Danish armed forces, but the civilian models were not exported in great numbers.

■ ABOVE *The 1934 Nimbus was one of the first to use the Danish firm's new SOHC in-line-four engine, which was introduced in that year.*

■ NORMAN

In the 1950s Norman, a small firm from Kent, was as notable for its displays at London's annual bike show as for its modest range of small capacity two-strokes. Villiers-engined roadsters such as the TS Uni-Twin and the B3 were competent and reliable, but performance was only moderate and the factory was closed in 1962.

■ ABOVE *One of Norman's last and best roadsters was the B4 Sports of 1961, powered by a 250cc, twin-cylinder Villiers two-stroke engine.*

NORTON

■ BELOW *The McCandless brothers'
Featherbed frame gave the Manx, pictured
here in 1955, superb handling.*

■ BOTTOM *Classically simple, its lasting
success made the Manx the definitive
British racing single.*

■ NORTON 500cc MANX

The 1930s were great years for Norton,
who won every Senior and Junior TT
race but two between 1931 and 1938.
Led by team manager, tuner and former
rider Joe Craig, the firm more than lived
up to the "Unapproachable Norton"
slogan that had been coined years
earlier. Norton's sporting single during
the 1930s was the International. The
firm's Isle of Man success led to the
racing version of this model, produced
to individual orders at Norton's Bracebridge Street factory, being given the
name Manx.

The most famous version of the Manx
was created in 1950, when the works
racebike, which had used a twin-
camshaft engine since 1937, was

NORTON 500cc MANX (1962)	
Engine	Aircooled 4-valve DOHC single
Capacity	498cc (86 x 85.8mm)
Power	54bhp @ 7200rpm
Weight	140kg (308lb) dry
Top speed	140mph (225kph)

redesigned using an innovative tubular
steel chassis devised by Irish racing
brothers Rex and Cromie McCandless.
During testing at Silverstone, Norton
works rider Harold Daniell inadvertently
christened the frame with his comment
that the new bike felt as though he was
riding a feather bed. Geoff Duke went on
to win both 500 and 350cc world titles
on the fine-handling Featherbed Manx
in 1951, retaining the 350 championship in 1952.

Although it was eventually overcome
by the more powerful four-cylinder 500s
of Gilera and MV Agusta, the Manx took
numerous famous victories in

■ BELOW *The Dominator 99, introduced in 1956, provided 100mph (160kph) top speed and good handling.*

subsequent years, many by private riders on production bikes after Norton's factory team had been disbanded in 1955. A Manx ridden by Godfrey Nash won the Yugoslavian Grand Prix as late as 1969, and in the 1980s the single found a new lease of life with the rise in popularity of classic racing.

The success of Triumph's Speed Twin and its derivatives led Norton to introduce its own parallel twin, the 500cc Model 7 Dominator, in 1949. Designed by Bert Hopwood, the Dominator produced 29bhp, managed about 90mph (145kph), was reliable and handled well, though the initial model's brakes were poor. In 1952 Norton combined the twin-cylinder powerplant with the Featherbed frame made famous by the Manx single, to produce the Dominator 88. This was the bike that first earned the reputation for fine handling that Norton twins retained for many years.

The first Norton twin whose engine truly matched its chassis was the Dominator 650SS, which was launched in 1962 with an uprated, 49bhp motor in a Featherbed frame. With paintwork in

■ LEFT *A 600cc parallel-twin engine and Featherbed frame made the "Dommie 99" a winner.*

■ FAR LEFT *Geoff Duke won three world championships on Norton's factory singles.*

Norton's traditional silver the 650SS was a handsome bike, and it was fast, torquey and stable too. But the 650SS and later 750cc Atlas did not sell particularly well, partly due to relatively low production levels and high prices. That did not help the always difficult financial situation at Norton. In 1953 the firm had been bought by AMC, owners of AJS and Matchless, and in 1963 production was moved to AMC's factory in south London.

■ LEFT *Among the best Norton twins was the powerful and stylish 650SS, pictured here in 1966 form.*

NORTON

■ NORTON COMMANDO 750cc FASTBACK

The Norton Commando was one of the best and most famous parallel twins of them all. It was released in 1968, created massive interest – not least due to the striking styling that earned it the Fastback name – and sold well despite a backdrop of Norton's mounting financial problems. Powered by the 745cc engine from the 750 Atlas model, the Commando produced 58bhp and weighed a respectable 190kg (418lb). Its 115mph (185kph) plus performance was well-controlled by a chassis that again upheld Norton's reputation for handling and roadholding.

The Commando chassis was also notable for the way it controlled the

NORTON COMMANDO 750cc FASTBACK (1968)	
Engine	Aircooled 4-valve OHV pushrod parallel twin
Capacity	745cc (73 x 89mm)
Power	58bhp @ 6800rpm
Weight	190kg (418lb) dry
Top speed	117mph (187kph)

■ LEFT *Steve
Hislop's 1992
Senior TT win on
the rotary racer
evoked Norton's
glory years.*

■ FAR LEFT TOP
*Peter Williams won
the Formula 750
TT for Norton in
1973.*

■ FAR LEFT
BELOW *The Classic
was the first
Norton rotary to go
on sale to the
public.*

traditional big-twin vibration that had
plagued the Atlas. Norton's Isolastic
rubber-mounting system maintained a
smooth ride, even when, six years later,
the engine was bored out to produce the
850 Commando.

Despite lacking power compared to
most of its circuit rivals, the Commando
was raced with some success in the
early 1970s. Norton's Formula 750 racer
used an innovative steel monocoque
frame developed by Peter Williams, who
won the 1973 Formula 750 TT on it.
A road-going replica was also produced,
but such rearguard actions were not
enough to save Norton, which by now
was part of the Norton Villiers Triumph
group. NVT went into liquidation, and
the last Commandos were built in 1978.

Norton's name did not disappear
altogether, however, and between 1977
and 1987 the company continued low
key development of a rotary-engined
bike that was used by several British
police forces. Eventually Norton
produced a limited edition civilian
roadster called the Classic, powered by
a 588cc twin-chamber rotary engine.
The touring Commander followed, and
public interest in Norton snowballed

when enthusiastic workers built an
alloy-framed rotary racer that won two
national championships in 1989.

A race-replica sportster, the F1,
followed a year later, combining good
looks with 145mph (233kph) speed and
sure-footed handling. The F1, however,
had some rough edges, and its low-volume
production kept prices up and profits down.

The 1990s was a disastrous decade
for Norton. Several former directors were
charged with financial irregularities,
hundreds of shareholders lost money
invested in the company, and Norton's

Canadian owners abandoned the rotaries
in favour of a ludicrously optimistic
1500cc V-eight, the Nemesis, which
never reached production. But in 2003,
Norton enthusiasts' hopes were raised
when the marque was bought by Kenny
Dreer, a long-time Norton tuner and
specials builder, based in Portland,
Oregon. Dreer's Norton America firm
was well advanced with development
of a new generation parallel twin,
combining traditional styling with
modern engineering, and based on a
952cc engine producing over 80bhp.

■ LEFT *Norton
America's Commando
combined traditional
styling with a
parallel twin engine.*

NSU

■ NSU 250cc SUPERMAX
German firm NSU started off by producing knitting machines, before expanding to build bicycles and then, in 1901, its first motorbike. The first machines used a combination of a Swiss-made 1.5bhp

■ LEFT *NSU's 250cc Supermax (left) and 125cc Superfox singles shared an SOHC single-cylinder engine layout.*

■ BELOW *The Supermax was one of the most sophisticated bikes of the 1950s, but its price limited export sales.*

NSU SUPERMAX (1955)	
Engine	Aircooled 2-valve SOHC single
Capacity	247cc (69 x 66mm)
Power	18bhp @ 6500rpm
Weight	164kg (361lb) dry
Top speed	75mph (120kph)

■ BELOW *The Supermax's fuel cap celebrated NSU's Grand Prix success.*

■ BOTTOM *Werner Haas, pictured on the superb Rennmax parallel twin, won both 250 and 125cc titles in 1953.*

Zedel engine in a bicycle frame; two years later NSU produced its own single and V-twin engines. Production grew, and in 1929 Norton's designer Walter Moore was hired to create NSU's first overhead-camshaft model. In fact, the 500SS was so similar to Norton's CS1 that Norton workers claimed NSU stood for Norton Spares Used.

NSU was one of the world's leading manufacturers before the Second World War, and afterwards introduced innovative bikes including the 250cc Max. This featured an SOHC single-cylinder engine, pressed-steel frame and leading-link forks. The Max's most famous descendent was the Supermax, introduced in 1955, which provided smooth, reliable 75mph (120kph) performance, stable handling and excellent braking. It was beautifully engineered and constructed, traditional assets which led Honda to base several bikes on NSUs. But the Supermax and its 125cc stablemate the Superfox were too expensive to sell in large numbers, and in the early 1960s NSU abandoned bikes to concentrate on car production.

OTHER MAKES

■ OK-SUPREME

After beginning volume production in 1911, Birmingham-based OK concentrated on two-strokes, notably a bike called the Junior. The firm became OK-Supreme in 1927, the year before Frank Longman scored its only TT win. Its best-known bike was the early 1930s single, built in 250 and 350cc form, that was known as the Lighthouse after the glass inspection plate in its camshaft tower. The cheap and reliable 250cc Flying Cloud was popular in the late 1930s, but the firm built only a few grass track bikes after the Second World War.

■ ABOVE *Legendary rider and tuner Bill Lacey with a record-breaking OK-Supreme on the Brooklands banking.*

■ OSSA

Founded by Manuel Giro in the late 1940s, Ossa developed a reputation for trials, enduro and trail machines, mostly with two-stroke engines. The Barcelona firm built numerous small capacity roadsters and made an impact in road racing with Santiago Herrero, who won several 250cc Grands Prix on a single-cylinder two-stroke in the late 1960s. Sadly, Herrero was killed at the Isle of Man TT in 1970, after which Ossa quit Grand Prix racing. During the 1970s the

■ ABOVE *Over's Euro Twin, powered by Yamaha's TDM850 parallel twin motor, was fast, stylish and expensive.*

firm built successful enduro bikes and the rapid twin-cylinder two-stroke Yankee 500 roadster. But industrial problems and falling sales led to closure of the factory in 1984, after which some bikes were built as Ossamotos by a workers' co-operative.

■ OVER

The small firm run by Japanese engineer Kensei Sato has built several exotic and expensive specials in recent years, many using the oval-section tubular aluminium frames that have become an Over trademark. Among the best was the Euro Twin, powered by Yamaha's TDM850 engine.

■ ABOVE *Santiago Herrero cranks Ossa's rapid 250cc single through a bend at Brands Hatch in 1969.*

NSU's 250cc Rennmax made a brief but memorable impact on Grand Prix racing in the early 1950s. The powerful Rennmax, a DOHC parallel twin with a large-diameter steel spine frame, was in a class of its own when winning the world championship for Werner Haas in 1953 and 1954. NSU retired from Grand Prix racing after that season but continued to sell single-cylinder Sportmax racers, based on the road-going Max. Hermann-Peter Müller used one to win NSU's third consecutive 250cc championship in 1955.

PANTHER

■ PANTHER MODEL 100S

A big single-cylinder Panther was the definitive bike for pulling a sidecar in the 1940s and 1950s, when an "outfit" was often the main means of transport for a family unable to afford a car. Although not particularly powerful, the long-stroke Panther motor produced plenty of useful low-down torque that

■ BELOW
A Model 100S was typically fitted with a sidecar such as this 1957 bike's Watsonian Avon single-seater.

PANTHER MODEL 100S (1957)	
Engine	Aircooled 2-valve OHV pushrod single
Capacity	598cc (87 x 100mm)
Power	23bhp @ 5300rpm
Weight	193kg (425lb) dry
Top speed	68mph (109kph)

made it ideal for sidecar use. The Yorkshire firm, originally known as Phelon and Moore (P&M), had been building "slopers", named after their single, angled-forward cylinder, since 1904. Panther also built Villiers-engined two-strokes until the 1930s, and recommended two-stroke production in the 1950s with models including the 324cc Model 45 Sports.

The firm's most famous sloper was the Model 100, which was strong, slow-revving and reliable. The original 598cc

overhead-valve motor, with its twin exhaust ports, was introduced in 1928, and was relatively little changed by 1957 when the Model 100S Deluxe was produced. When fitted with a Watsonian sidecar it gave undramatic but efficient and fairly smooth performance. In 1960 the firm estimated that 90 per cent of Model 100s were attached to sidecars. That left Panther vulnerable when the attraction of three wheels faded, and production ended in the late 1960s.

OTHER MAKES

■ PARILLA

Italian engineer Giovanni Parrilla built his first bike in 1946, and became well known for fast and stylish roadsters and racers, mostly single-cylinder four-strokes with capacities of between 125 and 250cc. Parillas – the spelling was changed for simplicity – were raced with fair success in the 1950s, but Giovanni later turned to go-kart engines, and the factory closed in 1967.

■ ABOVE *A neat 250cc single-cylinder Parilla, built in 1961, being ridden on the Isle of Man circuit in 1992.*

■ PATON

Giuseppe Pattoni was a former sidecar racer and Grand Prix mechanic until Mondial's retirement in 1957. The remarkable Italian engineer then began designing and building bikes to compete in racing's most glamorous class. From four-stroke parallel twins of the 1960s to two-stroke V-fours in the 1990s, green-finished Patons were a familiar sight in 500cc Grands Prix for over 30 years.

■ PEUGEOT

A leading marque during France's great era of motorcycle production around the beginning of the 20th century, Peugeot was successful in racing and powered the Norton on which Rem Fowler won the first Isle of Man TT in 1907. As early as 1913 Peugeot built a 500cc parallel twin racebike with double overhead cams and four-valve cylinder heads. Production in recent years has concentrated on scooters, including the luxurious Elyséo and the hugely successful Speedfight models.

■ PGO

Founded in 1964, Taiwanese firm PGO is a large-volume manufacturer of scooters.

■ ABOVE *PGO's 1600cc V-twin prototype sportsbike caused plenty of interest at the Milan Show in 1991.*

In 1991, PGO unveiled the V2 1600, a prototype sportsbike powered by a 1596cc V-twin engine. But the rumoured move into the large-capacity market did not take place.

■ PIAGGIO

Best known for scooters and mopeds, Italian giant Piaggio is the largest motorcycle manufacturer in Europe and the third biggest in the world. As well as producing a large range of own-brand scooters, Piaggio also owns Vespa and once-mighty Gilera.

■ ABOVE *Piaggio's Hexagon 125cc scooter provided comfort and weather-protection with a fair turn of speed.*

■ ABOVE *In 1911, the Pierce Arrow was one of several American bikes with an in-line four-cylinder engine.*

■ PIERCE

In 1909, American car manufacturer Pierce introduced an in-line four owing much to the design of the Belgian-made FN, but production of the Pierce Arrow lasted only a few years.

■ PÜCH

Austria's oldest bike manufacturer began production in 1903. In 1923 the firm introduced a 220cc two-stroke with a split-single engine layout that was still being built well into the 1960s. Later bikes have included trials and motocross machines, some with 500cc Rotax engines, but recent production has concentrated wholly on mopeds.

■ ABOVE *In the early 1960s, Püch built some competent roadsters such as this 125cc machine from 1962.*

■ QUANTEL-COSWORTH

Perhaps the ultimate British twin, the unique Quantel-Cosworth on which Roger Marshall won at Daytona in 1988 was powered by an 823cc, watercooled, DOHC parallel twin engine that formed a stressed member of an innovative alloy chassis.

■ QUASAR

The radical Quasar, with its feet-first riding position and distinctive bodywork that incorporated a roof, was first built in 1976 by British engineer Malcolm Newell. The original Quasar was powered by a 40bhp Reliant car engine, and despite being long and heavy it combined effortless 100mph (160kph) cruising ability with very good handling. Newell's numerous later developments included the 160mph (257kph) Phasar which was powered by Kawasaki's six-cylinder Z1300 unit, but this machine was built in only tiny numbers.

ROYAL ENFIELD

■ ROYAL ENFIELD 750cc INTERCEPTOR

Throughout most of its long existence Royal Enfield was one of Britain's larger manufacturers, without matching either the production levels or the glamour of giants such as BSA and Triumph. The firm from Redditch, near Birmingham, began, like many others, as a bicycle

■ ABOVE *Royal Enfield's name, little heard of in more recent years, was a very familiar sight in the 1950s and 1960s.*

■ LEFT *The Interceptor went round corners well, despite being a tall bike with rather soft front forks.*

ROYAL ENFIELD INTERCEPTOR (1965)	
Engine	Aircooled 4-valve OHV pushrod parallel twin
Capacity	736cc (71 x 93mm)
Power	53bhp @ 6000rpm
Weight	193kg (425lb) wet
Top speed	105mph (168kph)

manufacturer before producing its first motorcycles in 1901. By the 1930s Enfield had adopted the Bullet name for a range of 250, 350 and 500cc four-stroke singles. After the Second World

War the company introduced a redesigned Bullet single that was successful on the road and in trials, and is now built in India.

Royal Enfield followed the trend for parallel twins in 1948, with a softly-tuned 500cc roadster. Five years later the engine was enlarged to 692cc to power the Meteor, the biggest parallel twin on the market. The sportier Super Meteor led in 1958 to the Constellation, which was later sold with Royal Enfield's innovative Airflow full fairing.

Biggest and best of the twins was the Interceptor, which was released in 1962 with a 736cc engine producing 53bhp. Created partly to supply the American export market's demand for cubic inches, the Interceptor combined impressive mid-range torque and reasonable smoothness with various failings one of which was a feeble front brake. In the mid-1960s Royal Enfield suffered severe financial problems. Interceptor production moved briefly to the West Country before ending in 1968.

■ LEFT *This high-handlebarred Interceptor, built for the US market in 1965, was a handsome and powerful bike.*

OTHER MAKES

■ **RALEIGH**

Nottingham-based Raleigh started as, and remains, a bicycle manufacturer, but between 1899 and 1933 the firm tried its hand at building some high-quality motorcycles. Raleigh's four-stroke single was popular in the early 1920s. It came in 350cc sports or touring form, or bored out to 400cc for sidecar use.

■ **RICKMAN**

After making a name with chassis, Don and Derek Rickman moved into road racing using Triumph Bonneville engines. The early 1970s Rickman Interceptor combined Royal Enfield's engine with a frame of nickel-plated Reynolds 531 tubing. Rickman's later fully-faired Café Racer housed a four-cylinder motor from Honda or Kawasaki, after which the firm concentrated on bike accessories.

■ ABOVE *When it produced this 350cc single in 1926 Raleigh was a well-known manufacturer of motorcycles.*

■ ABOVE *Rickman's Interceptor of 1970 was a fine-handling special, powered by Royal Enfield's 736 parallel-twin.*

■ **RENÉ GILLET**

In the 1930s, René Gillet was well known for its sturdy sidevalve V-twins of 750 and 1000cc capacity, which were well-suited to sidecar use and became popular with French armed forces and police. After the Second World War the firm concentrated on small two-strokes, and ceased production in the late 1950s.

■ **ROC**

Serge Rosset's small ROC firm, based at Annemasse in France, established itself as one of the world's leading racing chassis specialists in the 1990s. Rosset, a former ELF and Yamaha France Grand Prix team manager, was, with Britain's Harris, chosen by Yamaha to build privateer chassis for the YZR500 V-four engine. Even world champion Wayne Rainey's works YZR used a ROC frame at times during the following season. But ROC's later attempt to build a complete Grand Prix V-four, the Moto Française GP1, proved unsuccessful.

■ LEFT *Niall Mackenzie was the leading 500cc privateer riding a ROC Yamaha in 1992.*

RUDGE

■ **RUDGE 500cc ULSTER**
Two bicycle firms, Rudge and Whitworth, merged to form Rudge Whitworth and produced a 3.5bhp single-cylinder motorbike in 1909. Early innovations included a spring-up stand and a hinged rear mudguard to aid wheel removal, but it was a gearing system that led to the firm's first famous model – the Rudge Multi. This used an ingenious system of

RUDGE ULSTER (1930)	
Engine	Aircooled 4-valve OHV pushrod single
Capacity	499cc (85 x 88mm)
Power	30bhp approx
Weight	131kg (290lb) dry
Top speed	100mph (160kph)

■ ABOVE *Graham Walker's 1928 Ulster Grand Prix win led to Rudge's 500cc four-valve single being called the Ulster.*

■ BELOW *The Ulster had further success with Wal Handley's Senior TT win in 1930.*

pulleys to maintain the tension of the final drive belt, while allowing the rider to select from no fewer than 21 gear ratios. The Multi was a big success, winning the 1914 Senior TT and remaining in production for nine more years.

Rudge was a leading exponent of four-valve cylinder heads in the mid-1920s, producing the 500cc single on which Graham Walker – the firm's sales manager – sped to victory in the 1928 Ulster Grand Prix.

The sportiest of Rudge's three models was renamed the Ulster in recognition. It used the firm's celebrated linked braking system, whereby the foot-pedal operated both front and rear drums, with the hand lever also working the front brake. Rudge had more racing success in the 1930s, but hit financial trouble and ceased production in 1939.

■ RIGHT *The Rudge Multi, with its long vertical gearlever on the left of the tank, gave a wide choice of ratios.*

OTHER MAKES

■ RUKUO

Japanese firm Rukuo built copies of Harley-Davidson sidevalve V-twins under licence in the 1930s and 1940s, but was one of the many firms that did not survive the sharp contraction of the Japanese industry that followed.

■ RUMI

The Bergamo-based Rumi family has been prominent in the motorcycle world since the early 1950s, when their firm built a rapid 125cc two-stroke twin that was raced with some success. In recent years the Rumi family has been involved in various projects including running a factory-backed Honda team in the World Superbike series, and producing a fine-handling aluminium-framed sportsbike, the RMS650, powered by Honda's single-cylinder NX650 engine.

■ ABOVE *Rumi's RMS650 sportster held a 650cc single-cylinder Honda engine in an aluminium twin-spar frame.*

SCOTT

■ LEFT *This 596cc Flying Squirrel was built in 1950, shortly before production ceased.*

■ SCOTT SQUIRREL

Alfred Scott built some of the most advanced and distinctive bikes of motorcycling's early years. In 1909 he created a 333cc two-stroke parallel twin featuring the novelties of a kick start, foot-change two-speed gearbox and telescopic front forks. Shortly afterwards Scott adopted full watercooling and enlarged the engine to 486 and 534cc, adding performance that was put to good use in 1912 and 1913, when the

SCOTT SQUIRREL (1925)	
Engine	Watercooled two-stroke parallel twin
Capacity	596cc (74.6 x 68.25mm)
Power	25bhp @ 5000rpm
Weight	115kg (253lb) wet
Top speed	70mph (112kph)

two-strokes won consecutive Senior TTs. The following year saw the start of the legendary Scott Trial, held in the Yorkshire dales near the factory.

Alfred Scott left the company after the First World War to build the three-wheeled Scott Sociable car. He died in 1923, only a year after the firm introduced the Squirrel range, and expanded with a variety of capacities, and names such as Super Squirrel, Sports Squirrel and Flying Squirrel. A typical mid-1920s Squirrel was powered by a 596cc engine with a three-speed,

■ BELOW *Scott's greatest days were already over when this distinctive three-speed, 596cc twin was built in 1928.*

. hand-change gearbox. With a top speed of about 70mph (112kph), good handling and unique looks and sound, the Scotts won many followers.

The Squirrels could be temperamental, however, and prices were quite high. Later models, with conventionally shaped tanks, were heavier and less competitive, and production declined in the 1930s. In 1950 the firm was bought by Birmingham-based Scott fanatic Matt Holder, who continued developing and selling Squirrel motorcycles in small numbers right up until 1978.

OTHER MAKES

■ SANGLAS

Founded in Barcelona in 1942, Sanglas differed from other Spanish firms by ignoring racing in favour of simple, low-revving four-stroke singles, which were popular with civilians and police for many years. In the 1960s, the firm also built two-strokes, known as Rovenas, using engines from Villiers and Zündapp. In the late 1970s Sanglas became involved with Yamaha, initially by using the XS400 twin engine in a roadster called the 400Y. The bike was reasonably successful but in 1981 the Spanish firm was taken over by Yamaha, and shortly afterwards the Sanglas name was dropped altogether.

■ SEELEY

Former sidecar Grand Prix racer Colin Seeley acquired rights to the Matchless G50 and AJS 7R singles in the late 1960s, and developed both the engine and a new chassis, producing the Seeley G50 racer – highly successful in classic racing in recent years – and the Condor roadster. He also developed many other frame kits and specials, including a stylish café racer based on Honda's CB750 four.

■ SEGALE

Italian chassis specialist Luigi Segale has built many high quality specials over the last two decades, around engines ranging from Kawasaki Z1000 fours to Honda 650cc singles, many using his trademark frame layout of narrow-gauge steel tubes and aluminium side-plates. In 1993, Segale produced the rapid and ultra-light SR900R, powered by Honda's four-cylinder CBR900RR motor.

■ SILK

In the early 1970s George Silk, a former Scott apprentice, developed a roadster based on the familiar watercooled, two-stroke parallel twin format. The Silk 700S used a 653cc engine that produced 47bhp, housed in a tubular steel frame made by Spondon Engineering. Although top speed was only 110mph (177kph), the Silk was smooth, light and handled well. Small production levels led to high prices and problems with suppliers, however, and the last bikes were built in 1979.

■ LEFT *A typical Sanglas roadster of the 1970s was a sturdy, efficient but unglamorous 500cc single.*

■ LEFT *The Seeley G50, powered by a single-cylinder Matchless engine, has starred in 500cc classic racing.*

■ LEFT *The Segale SR900R weighed even less than the standard CBR900RR, but cost a great deal more.*

■ LEFT *The stylish 700S owed its two-stroke parallel twin engine layout to its creator George Silk's love of Scotts.*

SUNBEAM

■ LEFT *The S7 was comfortable, but had too much weight, poor brakes and only mediocre handling.*

■ SUNBEAM S8

Quality and attention to detail were characteristics for which Sunbeam's early motorcycles became known, following the Wolverhampton firm's introduction of its first model, a 350cc single, in 1912. Like Sunbeam's earlier bicycles, the single had a fully-enclosed drive chain that earned it the nickname

■ BELOW *The S8 was lighter and faster than the S7, but it was still not successful enough to save Sunbeam.*

SUNBEAM S8 (1949)	
Engine	Aircooled 4-valve SOHC tandem twin
Capacity	487cc (70 x 63.5mm)
Power	26bhp @ 5800rpm
Weight	182kg (400lb) dry
Top speed	85mph (136kph)

"Little Oil Bath". The 3.5bhp single, introduced a year later, sold well, was raced successfully and established Sunbeam's colours of black with gold lining. Development engineer George Dance set several records on Sunbeams, and the single scored two Senior TT wins in the early 1920s.

Sales declined in the 1930s, and Sunbeam was sold first to AMC and then, in 1943, to BSA. After the Second World War, BSA attempted to capitalize on Sunbeam's reputation as the gentleman's motor bicycle by building a sophisticated roadster. The S7, released in 1947, was powered by a 487cc four-stroke tandem twin engine with shaft final drive. It had a big, heavy chassis which incorporated fat balloon tyres. The S7 was underpowered, initially vibrated terribly and handled poorly. It was also one of the most expensive bikes on the market, and unsurprisingly, was not a commercial success.

■ LEFT
Alec Bennet won two TTs on black-and-gold Sunbeams similar to this 350cc model 2 from 1924.

In 1949 Sunbeam introduced the uprated S7 De Luxe, and also produced a sportier version of the twin, the S8. This featured new styling, a louder exhaust system, less weight, front forks similar to those of BSA's A10, and conventional wheels and tyres. With a top speed of about 85mph (136kph) the S8 was faster, and handled better than its predecessor. But further development was minimal, sales remained low and Sunbeam production finally ground to a halt in 1956.

OTHER MAKES

■ SINGER
The most notable design from early British firm Singer was a 222cc four-stroke single-cylinder engine which, together with its fuel tank and carburettor, was housed within a wheel. Singer bought the design in 1900 and used it, both as the rear wheel of a solo and the front wheel of a tricycle, for the next few years. The company also produced more conventional bikes before giving up to concentrate on building cars after the First World War.

■ SPONDON
Named after the Derbyshire town in which it is based, chassis specialist firm Spondon Engineering was founded by Bob Stevenson and Stuart Tiller in 1969. Several early Spondons used Yamaha two-stroke racing engines such as the 125cc AS1, TZ250 and 750cc OW31. Spondon has built frames for roadsters including the Silk and Norton's F1, and produced

numerous specials powered by Japanese fours, from Suzuki's GS1000 to Kawasaki's ZZ-R1100.

■ ABOVE *Many Sun roadsters were simple, single-cylinder two-strokes such as this 197cc model from 1956.*

■ RIGHT *Norton's rotary racebike, like the later F1 roadster, featured a Spondon twin-spar aluminium frame.*

■ SUN
Typical of the numerous British firms producing modest Villiers-engined two-strokes in the 1950s, Birmingham-based company Sun had a history that included the production of a rotary disc-valve two-stroke racer in the 1920s. Later roadsters such as the 250cc Overlander twin of 1957 were remarkable for the generous weather protection they offered. That wasn't enough to make them popular though, and Sun ceased motorcycle production a few years later.

SUZUKI

■ **SUZUKI T20 SUPER SIX**
Michio Suzuki set up a business manu-facturing silk looms in 1909, and ran it until the Second World War. In 1952, problems in the silk loom industry led Suzuki to develop and sell a 36cc two-stroke engine, named the Power Free, which clipped to a bicycle frame. An im-proved, 60cc version called the Diamond Free followed one year later, and in May 1954 the revived Suzuki firm launched its first complete bike, a 90cc four-stroke single named the Colleda. Entered in that year's Mount Fuji hill-climb, it triumphed over 85 rivals.

Through the late 1950s and early 60s, Suzuki concentrated on small-capacity

SUZUKI T20 SUPER SIX (1966)	
Engine	Aircooled two-stroke parallel twin
Capacity	247cc (54 x 54mm)
Power	29bhp @ 7500rpm
Weight	138kg (304lb) dry
Top speed	95mph (152kph)

■ ABOVE *The Super Six got its name from the two-stroke parallel twin engine's six-speed gearbox.*

■ LEFT *Attractive styling combined with performance and good handling to make the Super Six popular.*

■ OPPOSITE RIGHT *The GT500 parallel twin of the early 1970s combined 110mph (177kph) top speed with only mediocre handling.*

■ OPPOSITE LEFT *Suzuki's first complete bikes were the 90 and 125cc Colleda two-strokes of the mid-1950s.*

■ RIGHT *Although it was too big and heavy to handle really well, the GT750 proved a good sports-tourer.*

■ BELOW *The GT750's rather bulbous styling made little attempt to disguise its weight.*

two-strokes, in particular on the firm's first purpose-built competition machine, the 125cc Colleda RB of 1959. They included numerous cheap commuter bikes and the sportier, 250cc T10 of 1963 – the company's first export success. But it was a new generation 250 twin, the T20 Super Six – the X6 in America – that put Suzuki on the map when it was launched in 1966.

The name referred to the two-stroke's six-speed gearbox; an even more impressive – but slightly optimistic – number was the claimed top speed of 100mph (160kph). The Super Six's all-new engine produced 29bhp and incorporated a sophisticated Posi-Force lubrication system. Other classy features included Suzuki's first twin-cradle frame, which gave good handling in conjunction with light weight. True top speed was somewhere between 90 and 100mph (144-160kph) – enough anyway to make the Super Six a big hit.

In 1967, Suzuki entered the big bike market with an enlarged two-stroke parallel twin, the T500, which was known as the Titan in America and the Cobra in Britain. Although it was simple and handled rather poorly, the 46bhp T500 was reliable, economical and fast, with a top speed of 110mph (177kph). The twin remained in production for the

next ten years, gaining a disc front brake, electronic ignition, fresh styling and the name GT500 along the way.

Suzuki's first true superbike was the GT750, the big, watercooled three-cylinder two-stroke that became known as the Kettle in Britain and the Water Buffalo in America, following its introduction in 1971. The softly-tuned 738cc engine produced 67bhp, giving the triple a top speed of 115mph (185kph) to go with its generous mid-range torque. Although smooth, quiet and comfortable, the Suzuki was also big and ponderous. It couldn't match the acceleration or excitement of rivals such as Kawasaki's 750cc H1, but its all-round ability kept the GT750 popular for most of the 1970s.

SUZUKI

■ LEFT *The GS1000 combined raw power with the best handling yet from a Japanese Superbike.*

■ SUZUKI GS1000

The GS1000 was a landmark motorcycle not just for Suzuki but for the whole Japanese industry. When it was launched in 1978, the GS outperformed Kawasaki's legendary Z1, its direct rival, in almost every area. More importantly, here at last was a big four-cylinder machine whose chassis was a match for its motor. Japan had been building great powerplants for years, but the GS was the first open-class super-bike that handled really well.

The GS1000's format was conventional, closely based on that of the GS750 introduced a year earlier. The

■ BELOW *Suzuki based the GS1000's four-cylinder motor on Kawasaki's proven DOHC, eight-valve format.*

SUZUKI GS1000 (1978)	
Engine	Aircooled 8-valve DOHC transverse four
Capacity	997cc (70 x 64.8mm)
Power	87bhp @ 8000rpm
Weight	242kg (532lb) dry
Top speed	135mph (216kph)

■ RIGHT *The GS1000's rather ordinary styling disguised the fact that this was an exceptional motorcycle.*

■ BELOW *Wes Cooley won the US Superbike championship for Suzuki in 1980 on a Yoshimura-tuned GS1000S.*

■ BOTTOM *The stunning Katana 1100 of 1982, styled by Anglo-German firm Target Design, was as fast as it looked.*

■ BELOW *Suzuki's first big four-stroke roadster was the fast and sophisticated GS750 four, introduced in 1977.*

aircooled, 997cc engine used twin cams and eight valves to produce 87bhp. The chassis incorporated a rigid tubular steel frame, sophisticated, adjustable suspension parts, wide tyres and twin front disc brakes. Styling was clean and pleasant, if a bit bland.

There was certainly nothing ordinary about the Suzuki's performance, which combined fearsome acceleration with a top speed of 135mph (216 kph). Mid-range power delivery was equally strong, and the GS was comfortable and reliable too. Better still, the bike was rock-steady in a straight line, remaining stable even at cornering speeds that left most rivals wallowing in its wake. The GS1000's only failing was a certain lack of charisma. It was a hugely impressive machine that emphasized Suzuki's arrival as a leading superbike producer.

In 1977, just a year before unleashing the GS1000, Suzuki had released its first big four-cylinder bike in the shape of the GS750 – and scored an immediate success. With a maximum output of 68bhp on tap, the twin-cam GS750 whirred smoothly to over 120mph (193kph), cruised at 90mph (144kph) and outperformed rivals such as Honda's CB750 and Yamaha's XS750. It handled acceptably, establishing a reputation that would be enhanced by future models. Fast, refined and reliable, the GS750 four represented the start of great things for Suzuki.

The 16-valve GSX1100 that replaced the 8-valve GS1000 in 1980 was an even faster and more competent bike marred by ugly, angular looks. Two years later Suzuki revamped it to produce the stunning GSX1100S Katana, whose radical combination of nose fairing, low handlebars, humped fuel tank and combined seat/sidepanels gave a superbly raw, aggressive image. The aircooled four-cylinder engine was tuned to produce 111bhp, giving the Katana – named after a Samurai warrior's ceremonial sword – a top speed of more than 140mph (225kph). Handling was excellent despite 250kg (551lb) of weight, and the Suzuki's style and speed combined with a reasonable price to make it a big success.

SUZUKI

SUZUKI GSX-R750

The arrival of Suzuki's GSX-R750 in 1985 had a huge impact on the design of supersports motorcycles. This was the first true Japanese race-replica, startlingly close to being simply Suzuki's works endurance bike in road-legal form. The GSX-R was searingly fast, outrageously light and utterly singleminded. No other mass-produced four came close to matching its uniquely aggressive, race-bred image.

Every component of the GSX-R was designed for high performance and low weight. That included the 16-valve, four-cylinder engine, which was oil-cooled, had a cam cover made from lightweight magnesium, and produced 100bhp at 10,500rpm. The Suzuki's aluminium frame weighed half as much as the steel frame of the previous GSX750, and held stout 41mm diameter front forks. A racy twin-headlamp fairing, foam-backed clocks, clip-on bars and rearset footrests completed the package.

■ LEFT *The original GSX-R750's ultra-light chassis gave superb cornering but occasional high-speed instability.*

■ OPPOSITE *Early GSX-Rs held an oilcooled 16-valve motor in an aluminium frame.*

■ BELOW *Heavily based on Suzuki's works endurance motorcycles, the first GSX-R750 was a genuine race-replica.*

■ LEFT *Suzuki's repeated chassis refinements gave the GSX-R750 better handling over the years.*

■ BELOW LEFT *Later GSX-R1100 models did not match the impact of the excellent original motorcycle of 1986.*

SUZUKI GSX-R750 (1985)	
Engine	Oilcooled 16-valve DOHC transverse four
Capacity	749cc (70 x 48.7mm)
Power	100bhp @ 10,500rpm
Weight	176kg (387lb) dry
Top speed	145mph (233kph)

Performance lived up to all expectations. Acceleration was flat below 7000rpm, after which the GSX-R raced towards 145mph (233kph) with a muted scream from its four-into-one exhaust system. Handling and braking were exceptional, aided by the remarkably low weight of 176kg (387lb). The GSX-R750 was instantly successful both on the racetrack and in the showrooms, and its format was hastily followed by other manufacturers.

A year after triggering the sportsbike revolution with the GSX-R750, Suzuki produced a bigger version that brought a new dimension to two-wheeled performance. The GSX-R1100 of 1986 added mid-range power and even more outright speed to the smaller model's assets of light weight, handling and racetrack style. Its 125bhp oilcooled engine provided a 155mph (249kph) top speed, plus instant acceleration at the twist of the throttle; its lightweight aluminium-framed chassis gave unmatched open-class handling. Unfortunately for Suzuki, a 1989 redesign, the 1100K, combined fresh styling with a modified chassis that ruined the big GSX-R's handling.

■ ABOVE *Hervé Moineau led Suzuki's works endurance team to many wins.*

■ BELOW *The 1996-model GSX-R750T adopted the twin-beam frame layout.*

Frequent further revamps through the 1990s restored some poise and added even more power, but the GSX-R1100 never regained its performance lead.

Suzuki did however update the GSX-R750 successfully in subsequent years. The first major revision was the GSX-R750J of 1988, which was heavier but featured new styling, uprated chassis parts and a more powerful engine. The 1992-model 750W gained a new watercooled motor with a peak output of 116bhp, the highest yet. The most significant update came in 1996 with the GSX-R750T. This held a much revised, 126bhp engine in a new twin-spar alloy frame that replaced the taller and less rigid traditional GSX-R design. Four years later the Suzuki was updated again for the new Millennium, with power up to 139bhp and weight reduced to just 166kg (365lb). This was a very different and much faster bike than the original 1985 model, but in spirit the GSX-R750 had not changed at all.

SUZUKI

■ SUZUKI GSX1300R HAYABUSA

Suzuki had just one aim when developing the bike they called the Hayabusa: to create the world's fastest production motorcycle. The result was a 1298cc four that used fuel-injection and a ram-air system to produce 173bhp. And whose rather ugly but supremely aerodynamically efficient bodywork also played a big part in producing a top speed of 190mph (307kph), enough to displace Honda's Super Blackbird as motorcycling's fastest. The bike's model name was GSX1300R, and Suzuki named it the Hayabusa after a Japanese Peregrine Falcon, a bird whose prey included blackbirds.

Apart from its styling, the Suzuki's layout was conventional. Its 16-valve engine was an enlarged and tuned

SUZUKI GSX1300R HAYABUSA (1999)	
Engine	Watercooled 16-valve DOHC transverse four
Capacity	1298cc (81 x 63mm)
Power	173bhp @ 9800rpm
Weight	215kg (473lb) dry
Top speed	190mph (307kph)

version of the old GSX-R1100 unit; its chassis used a typical twin-spar aluminium frame, upside-down forks and six-piston front brake calipers. The Hayabusa's performance, however, was out of this world. Not only was the engine phenomenally flexible, smooth and powerful, with strong acceleration available even at 150mph (240kph), but the chassis was also very capable, combining a light steering feel with excellent stability even at outrageous speeds.

Suzuki produced another stunningly fast superbike in 2001, though this time the emphasis was on pure racetrack performance, rather than straight-line speed. The GSX-R1000 not only lived up to its GSX-R label, it exceeded all expectations by outperforming its super-sports rivals with a stunning

■ RIGHT *Kevin*
Schwantz won the 1993
title on the RGV500.

■ RIGHT AND
BELOW *Barry*
Sheene's glamour
and showmanship
were as important
to Suzuki as his
riding ability.

■ BELOW RIGHT *Texan star Kevin*
Schwantz, seen here on a GSX-R1000, won
the 500cc world title for Suzuki in 1993.

classes, with world championship wins
for Germany's Ernst Degner and Hans-
Georg Anscheidt, and New Zealander
Hugh Anderson. Britain's charismatic
Cockney ace Barry Sheene was Suzuki's
star of the 1970s, winning the 500cc
title on the square-four RG500 in 1976
and 1977. Italians Marco Lucchinelli
and Franco Uncini added further
championships in 1981 and '82. In
1987 the square-four was replaced by
the V-four RGV500, on which talented
Texan Kevin Schwantz came close
several times before eventually winning
the championship in 1993.

blend of 161bhp engine and light weight
of just 170kg (374lb). Once again,
the technical specification was
unremarkable, as the GSX-R's 998cc,
161bhp engine was essentially an
enlarged GSX-R750 unit, and its chassis
also owed much to the smaller machine,
albeit incorporating thicker frame spars,
uprated front forks, and six-piston brake
calipers. The result was devastating.
Fearsome acceleration to a top speed of
185mph (298kph), wonderfully agile
handling, and powerful brakes gave
racetrack performance that no production
bike could match. Even so, Suzuki fine-
tuned the GSX-R two years later, with
fresh styling, crisper midrange response
and even sharper steering.
   Suzuki's first Grand Prix success
came in the 1960s in the 50 and 125cc

TRIUMPH

■ LEFT *By 1950*
the Speed Twin
had telescopic
forks, headlamp
nacelle and a
maroon finish.

■ BELOW *Edward*
Turner (second
left) often provided
inspired
leadership.

■ BOTTOM
The original late
1930s Speed Twin
was fast and light.

■ **TRIUMPH SPEED TWIN**
Triumph, one of Britain's oldest and
most famous manufacturers, was
founded by two Germans. Siegfried
Bettmann sold bicycles under his own
name in the 1880s before changing his
firm's name to Triumph. In 1902, in
partnership with Mauritz Schulte,
Bettmann fitted a Belgian 2.25bhp
Minerva engine into a bicycle to
produce the first Triumph motorcycle.

TRIUMPH SPEED TWIN (1937)	
Engine	Aircooled 4-valve OHV pushrod parallel twin
Capacity	498cc (63 x 80mm)
Power	29bhp @ 6000rpm
Weight	166kg (365lb) dry
Top speed	90mph (145kph)

Three years later the Coventry firm had
designed and built its own 3bhp engine,
and soon manufactured a range of bikes
whose reliability earned the nickname
"Trusty Triumph".

Triumph enhanced its reputation with
the 500cc four-stroke single Model H,
which was built in large numbers before,
during and after the First World War.
More innovative was the Model R,
whose four-valve cylinder head layout,
designed by Harry Ricardo, would be
perfected by Honda 40 years later.
Triumph's most popular bike of the
1920s was the 500cc sidevalve Model P,

which was produced at the impressive
rate of 1000 per week. But the company
hit financial problems and in 1936 was
sold to Ariel owner Jack Sangster, who

■ LEFT *Triumph's logo was a familiar sight in the 1950s.*

■ RIGHT *Early models, like this 1912 single, inspired the nickname "Trusty Triumph".*

■ BELOW *The 650cc Thunderbird, seen here in 1956 form, was another big hit for Triumph.*

appointed 35-year-old Edward Turner as chief designer and general manager.

Turner quickly showed an inspired touch, revamping Triumph's slow-selling line of 250, 350 and 500cc singles with better finish, extra performance and new names – Tiger 70, 80 and 90. They were immediately successful, and were followed in 1937 by Turner's master-piece, the 500cc Speed Twin. This was an all-new parallel twin, a brave move considering that singles had dominated the market for several decades, and that Triumph's own 650cc Model 6/1 of four years earlier had sold poorly.

The Speed Twin produced 29bhp, had lively acceleration and a respectable top speed of 90mph (145kph), and was far smoother than most comparable singles. It was also neatly styled and compact, as the motor slotted into the familiar Tiger 90 frame. At 166kg (365lb) it was slightly lighter than the single, and was only slightly more expensive. The Speed Twin was an immediate success, marking a turning point in Triumph's fortunes and inspiring the rival manufacturers to build parallel twins of their own.

A year after the Speed Twin, in 1938, Triumph released the Tiger 100 – a sportier, 33bhp version that on a good day really was capable of touching the magic 100mph (160kph). Both models were revised slightly and continued to sell well after the Second World War. In 1950, largely to satisfy the important American export market, Triumph enlarged the engine to 650cc to produce the 6T Thunderbird. The "T-bird" was another success, its handling and acceleration more than satisfying the demands of a speed-hungry motor-cycling fraternity.

■ LEFT *Despite marginal high-speed handling, the T120R Bonneville was one of the fastest bikes on the road in 1961.*

TRIUMPH

■ TRIUMPH T120 BONNEVILLE

The most famous Triumph of all was the Bonneville, which was released as a sporty 650cc twin in 1959. The original T120 Bonneville was basically the existing Tiger 110, fitted with optional splayed inlet ports and twin Amal carburettors. Its name came from the Bonneville salt flats in Utah, where a

■ BOTTOM *This neat 650cc Bonnie was built in 1970, the year before the oil-in-frame chassis was introduced.*

TRIUMPH T120 BONNEVILLE (1961)	
Engine	Aircooled 4-valve OHV pushrod parallel twin
Capacity	649cc (71 x 82mm)
Power	46bhp @ 6500rpm
Weight	183kg (403lb) dry
Top speed	110mph (177kph)

streamlined Triumph ridden by Johnny Allen had been timed at 214mph (344kph) in 1956. Although the FIM refused to ratify the speed as a world record, on a technicality, the ensuing row gave Triumph valuable publicity.

Initially the Bonneville was styled like the Tiger with a headlamp nacelle, swept-back touring handlebars and heavy mudguards. Peak output was 46bhp at 6500rpm, which was too much for the wobble-prone original chassis. In 1960 the T120 was revamped with a

new twin-cradle frame and forks, a separate headlamp, a new seat and sportier mudguards. Combining genuine 110mph (177kph) performance with mid-range punch, reasonable smoothness, adequate handling and good looks, the resultant "Bonnie" was a popular roadburner.

The Bonneville was regularly updated over the next decade, notably with the adoption of a unit-construction engine and gearbox in 1963. In 1971 the twin gained a new oil-in-frame chassis, which was much criticized until lowered a year

■ BELOW *Its 649cc, pushrod-operated parallel twin engine kept the Bonneville on top throughout the 1960s.*

■ ABOVE *The tuned Thruxton Bonneville was named after the British circuit where the T120 scored many production wins.*

■ LEFT *In 1977 Triumph produced the limited edition Silver Jubilee Bonneville.*

later. By 1972, it was estimated that 250,000 Bonnevilles had been built. Many were raced with success. In the Isle of Man, John Hartle won the production TT in 1967, and Malcolm Uphill set the first production 100mph (160kph) lap two years later.

In 1973 Triumph increased capacity to 744cc to produce the T140 Bonneville, which was more flexible, if no faster and less smooth. But parent company Norton Villiers Triumph was losing money, and rumours of imminent closure of the Meriden factory led to an 18-month sit-in, after which production was restarted by a workers' co-operative. Triumph struggled on, and fortunes improved enough to allow introduction of electric-start and eight-valve variations of the twin in the early 1980s. But low sales and rising debts finally led to the company going into liquidation in 1983, after which it was bought by current owner John Bloor. The Bonneville's final fling came when it was built under licence in Devon, by parts specialist Racing Spares, between 1985 and 1988.

OTHER MAKES

■ TRITON

The archetypal special of the 1960s was the Triton, the blend of parallel twin Triumph engine and Norton Featherbed frame that was loved by rockers and café racers. The man who did most to make the model famous was Dave Degens, the London-based racer/engineer

who won the Barcelona 24-hour endurance race on one in 1970. Degens' firm, Dresda Engineering, built numerous Tritons in the 1960s, and was still producing near-identical machines 30 years later. A less common Triumph derivative was the Tribsa, which combined a similar powerplant with a BSA frame.

■ LEFT *A Dresda Triton built by racer/engineer Dave Degens was one of the ultimate café racers of the 1960s.*

TRIUMPH

■ TRIUMPH T150 TRIDENT

Triumph's T150 Trident was arguably the world's finest roadster when it was released in 1969. The new 740cc, pushrod-operated three-cylinder engine produced a healthy 58bhp, sending the Trident racing to a top speed of 125mph (201kph) with a pleasant howl from its distinctively shaped ray-gun tailpipes. The Trident's unusual, angular styling was by no means to every rider's taste in 1969. But the triple was smooth, allowing relaxed 90mph (145kph) cruising for as long as the upright riding position and poor fuel economy would allow. Handling was good, too, thanks to

a modified version of the chassis used by Triumph's twins.

BSA had owned Triumph since 1951, and also built a version of the triple, the Rocket 3. This had similar styling, with the motor tilted forward in a single-downtube frame. But the struggling firm had taken too long to produce the

triples, which had been under development for several years. Only a few months later, Honda released the four-cylinder CB750, with the added sophistication of an overhead-cam engine, electric starter and superior reliability. Neither Trident nor Rocket 3 came close to matching the CB750's impact.

TRIUMPH T150 TRIDENT (1969)	
Engine	Aircooled 6-valve OHV pushrod transverse triple
Capacity	740cc (67 x 70mm)
Power	58bhp @ 7250rpm
Weight	213kg (468lb) dry
Top speed	125mph (201kph)

Triples were successful on the race circuit though, in particular "Slippery Sam", the Trident that won consecutive Production TTs between 1971 and 1975. Some of the best results came in America, where Gary Nixon had been AMA Grand National champion on Triumph twins in 1967 and 1968. The road-race triples used frames made by Rob North, with blue-and-white fairings for Triumph, and red-and-white for BSA. At Daytona in 1971, the triples took the first three places, Dick Mann winning on a BSA ahead of Triumph's Gene Romero, the reigning Grand National champion. Shortly afterwards, the triples were outpaced by Yamaha's two-strokes.

The most distinctive version of the triple was the Triumph X-75 Hurricane, a special built in limited numbers from 1972. The Hurricane was commissioned by Triumph's American distributor and designed by fairing and luggage specialist Craig Vetter. It combined a lower-geared version of the standard 740cc engine with longer front forks, a stylish tank/seat unit, and a bold new three-silencer exhaust system, and was a predecessor of the modern Japanese factory customs.

In 1975, the basic triple was restyled and overhauled to produce the T160 Trident, which featured its engine angled forward in a new and improved frame. Numerous other modifications included an electric starter, rear disc brake and left-foot gearchange. Handsome styling, smooth power and excellent handling made the new Trident arguably the best British roadster so far, but it was not enough to save struggling Triumph, and production was short-lived.

■ TOP *The T160 Trident introduced in 1975 was both fast and stylish, but came too late to save Triumph.*

■ ABOVE LEFT *Triumph's works triples took riders including Paul Smart to many wins in the 1970s.*

■ ABOVE RIGHT *Meriden development rider and racer Percy Tait raced triples including the famous "Slippery Sam".*

■ LEFT *The lean looks of the X-75 Hurricane gained the American-designed factory special many admirers.*

TRIUMPH

■ TRIUMPH SPEED TRIPLE

The British motorcycle industry's decline seemed almost complete in 1983, when Triumph finally went into liquidation. But the name was bought by building multi-millionaire John Bloor, who spent the next eight years secretly developing a range of modern bikes in a purpose-built factory at Hinckley, near the old Meriden site. In 1991 Triumph released a range of six roadsters, powered by watercooled, DOHC three- and four-cylinder engines. Their unique modular design employed many identical components, reducing cost. Ironically, a series of modular designs

produced by BSA-Triumph's engineers in 1973 had not been adopted.

Base model was the unfaired Trident, which had a 749 or 885cc three-cylinder engine. The larger unit produced 98bhp with plenty of mid-range torque, giving lively acceleration towards a top speed of 130mph (209kph). Like the other bikes the Trident had a large-diameter steel spine frame, with Japanese suspension and brakes. Top of the range

TRIUMPH SPEED TRIPLE (1994)	
Engine	Watercooled 12-valve DOHC transverse triple
Capacity	885cc (76 x 65mm)
Power	97bhp @ 9000rpm
Weight	209kg (460lb) dry
Top speed	130mph (209kph)

■ OPPOSITE TOP *The 1991 model Daytona 1000 sportster (left) and Trophy 1200 shared many parts.*

■ OPPOSITE BOTTOM *The popular Speed Triple of 1994 combined a three-cylinder engine with aggressive, naked styling.*

■ LEFT *Designed largely for the American market, the Thunderbird retro-bike was a hit worldwide in 1995.*

■ FAR LEFT *The basic Triumph model has been the unfaired Trident triple.*

■ BELOW LEFT *The Daytona 1200 gave 146bhp performance in 1993.*

was the 1200 Trophy, whose 123bhp four-cylinder engine was effectively the triple with an extra pot. Smooth, well built and capable of over 150mph (241kph), the Trophy was a match for the best Japanese sports tourers.

Triumph was rapidly successful in Britain. Exports also took off, after a slow start in the important German market. Triumph soon learnt to concentrate on its traditional triples, and in 1994 produced its most inspired model yet. The Speed Triple retained the original 885cc engine and spine frame, gaining upmarket cycle parts including multi-adjustable suspension, bigger brakes and fat radial tyres. The Speed Triple was quick, responsive and agile; and its name, lean styling and low, clip-on handlebars brought to mind the 1960s' days of

burn-ups and twin-cylinder Triumphs.

Nostalgia played an even greater part in the model that Triumph developed to spearhead its delayed return to America in 1995. The Thunderbird incorporated traditional styling features such as a rounded fuel tank with mouth-organ badges, and peashooter silencers. Exaggerated cooling fins gave a new look to the 885cc triple engine, which was detuned to a modest 69bhp. Other features, including raised bars, wire wheels and a lower seat, also moved away from the modular concept.

The T-bird's style and smooth, torquey engine made it a hit. With the expanding Hinckley factory's annual production due to exceed 10,000 for the first time, John Bloor's huge investment seemed to be paying off.

OTHER MAKES

■ URAL

From a big factory in the Ural mountains, the firm of the same name has long produced 650cc flat-twins based on BMW designs of the early 1940s. Inevitably crude by modern standards, most of the 250,000 bikes built annually were sold in the former Soviet Union. British importer Neval produced custom versions including the Soviet Knight, which combined the original 32bhp pushrod motor and simple

steel-framed chassis with high handlebars, running lights and added chrome. Handling was heavy and sophistication lacking, but the Soviet Knight was cheap and cruised smoothly at 60mph (96kph) with a certain old-fashioned charm.

■ RIGHT *High bars and added chrome gave the Soviet Knight a touch of Harley-style glamour, without the expense.*

TRIUMPH

■ LEFT *The Daytona 600's handling was even better than that of its agile predecessor, the TT600.*

■ **TRIUMPH DAYTONA 600**

The Daytona 600, launched in 2003, proved that Triumph could successfully take on the Japanese giants in the competitive middleweight sportsbike market. The British bike's format of full fairing, watercooled 16-valve engine and twin-beam aluminium frame was identical to that of rivals from all four Japanese firms. Yet unlike its TT600 predecessor of three years earlier, which had been slightly but significantly lacking in both looks and performance, the Daytona was stylish and fast enough to make a big impact. With a peak output of 110bhp, the Daytona was close

■ BELOW *Distinctive angular styling helped the Daytona 600 stand out in the middle-weight market.*

TRIUMPH DAYTONA 600 (2003)	
Engine	Watercooled 16-valve DOHC transverse four
Capacity	599cc (68 x 41.3mm)
Power	110bhp @ 12,750rpm
Weight	165kg (363lb) dry
Top speed	160mph (257kph)

to the best opposition in straight-line speed; and its chassis, based on that of the fine-handling TT600, was outstanding. Sharp and distinctive styling added to the appeal of a bike that raced to 160mph (257kph), handled superbly, and even made a reasonably practical all-rounder. Twelve years after Triumph's return, the Daytona 600 proved the British firm had learned

■ RIGHT *The Daytona T595 triple,
later renamed the 955i, was a stylish,
fine-handling and very fast superbike.*

■ BELOW *The T509 Speed Triple, with its
aggressive twin-headlamp look, led a new
generation of naked sportsbikes.*

much along the way. Triumph's first purpose-built sportsbike had been another Daytona model, the T595 triple that had been launched in 1997. Initially named after its factory code-name, in Triumph tradition, the bike was later renamed the Daytona 955i to avoid confusion. The 955cc, 12-valve triple featured a tubular aluminium frame and a single-sided swing-arm, and was the first new Triumph created without the restrictions of the modular engineering concept with which the marque had been relaunched.

Although more of an all-rounder than a cutting-edge super-sports machine, the 128bhp Daytona had plenty of style and performance. It combined 165mph (265kph) top speed and flexible power delivery with stable handling and

powerful brakes. The triple was a hit for Triumph, and was uprated in 2000, with new bodywork, a revamped 147bhp engine, and lighter chassis. The Hinckley firm also produced successful sports-touring derivatives, the Sprint ST and RS, featuring detuned engines and more comfort-oriented chassis.

Daytona was an old Triumph model name that John Bloor's firm had used ever since 1991, but it took another decade before the reappearance of the most famous name of all: Bonneville. Bloor had been keen to establish Triumph's engineering credentials before launching a retro-styled parallel twin. Finally the new Bonneville appeared, designed to resemble its 650cc namesake from 1968, and powered by a new 790cc, DOHC aircooled engine producing 61bhp.

Unlike its famous forebear, this Bonnie was no high-performance machine, instead offering gentle power delivery with a top speed of 115mph (185kph), close to that of the 1960s model. Handling from the twin-shock chassis was stable; overall performance efficient rather than exciting. But the Bonneville was competitively priced and sold well, helping to establish Triumph in the American market. So did the Bonneville America and the Speedmaster twins, cruiser-styled follow-up models that were launched in subsequent years.

■ BELOW LEFT *Triumph's new generation
Bonneville had a very similar look to its
650cc predecessor from 1968.*

■ BELOW *Triumph's Speedmaster cruiser
was aimed mainly at the American market.*

VELOCETTE

■ BELOW *The sporty Clubman Venom of the early 1960s(left) was uprated to produce the Thruxton in 1965.*

■ BOTTOM *Thruxton features included tuned motor, uprated front brake, silver paint finish and humped seat.*

■ VELOCETTE VENOM THRUXTON

From the 1930s until its demise in 1971, Velocette was best known for its large-capacity four-stroke singles, most of them with traditional black-and-gold finish and a distinctive fishtail silencer. The firm was founded in 1904 by German-born Johannes Gütgemann, who later changed his name to John

VELOCETTE VENOM THRUXTON (1965)	
Engine	Aircooled 2-valve OHV pushrod single
Capacity	499cc (86 x 86mm)
Power	40bhp @ 6200rpm
Weight	177kg (390lb) dry
Top speed	105mph (168kph)

Goodman, and was later run by his sons and grandson. Initially called Veloce Ltd, the company began by producing four-strokes. The first two-stroke, built in 1913, was called Velocette, after which the name was used for all of their subsequent models.

Velocette's racing involvement boosted development and prestige, although the expense was considerable. The Birmingham firm's first great bike was the overhead-cam 350cc single, designed by Percy Goodman, which won the 1926 Junior TT. Velocette's

■ BELOW LEFT
The 350cc MAC of the mid-1930s was a hugely successful machine.

■ BELOW RIGHT
Stanley Woods powers his Velo to Junior TT victory in 1939.

■ BOTTOM RIGHT
Neglecting singles to build the LE, pictured in Mk.2 form from 1955, proved disastrous for Velocette.

■ LEFT *The rapid 500cc parallel twin Roarer of 1939 was halted by the War and subsequent ban on supercharging.*

production version, the KTT, was the ultimate privateer racebike throughout the 1930s. The single was also popular in supersports form as the KSS, although it was sales of humbler pushrod singles such as the 350cc MAC and 500cc MSS that kept Velocette profitable.

After the Second World War, Velocette's racing success continued, notably with 350cc world championships for Freddie Frith and Bob Foster in 1949 and 1950. Best known roadsters were the 500cc Venom and 350cc Viper singles, which from 1960 were available in Clubmans trim with tuned engines and stiffer suspension. Fastest of all was the Venom Thruxton, released in 1965. Its tuned engine put out 40bhp and the chassis specification included alloy rims and a powerful twin-leading-shoe front brake. Typically hard to start, and rough at low speeds, the Thruxton – named after the Hampshire track used for long-distance production races – was a rapid street racer that could cruise at a respectable 90mph (145kph).

Velocette was also keen to produce less sporty bikes, and by 1949 almost all the singles had been dropped to make way for the revolutionary LE. This strange looking bike had legshields, a pressed-steel frame and a watercooled, flat-twin sidevalve engine, initially of 150cc. Although well built and reliable, the LE was also expensive. Even when uprated with a 192cc engine in 1951 the LE was popular only with the police, earning it the nickname "Noddy bike". The later Viceroy, a large 250cc scooter, proved even more disastrous, and Velocette went into liquidation in 1971.

OTHER MAKES

■ **VAN VEEN**
Dutchman Henk van Veen's most ambitious project was the Van Veen OCR1000, a luxurious rotary-engined superbike. Although fast and smooth, the OCR was more remarkable for being the world's most expensive roadster in the late 1970s, and production was short-lived.

■ **VICTORIA**
German firm Victoria built flat-twins in the 1920s. Later bikes included the revolutionary 197cc Swing of 1956, which featured push-button gearchanging. In 1958 Victoria joined DKW and Express to form the Zweirad Union, but sales were poor and production came to an end in 1966.

■ **VICTORY**
American snowmobile and ATV giant Polaris set up Victory, its motorcycle division, in the mid-1990s. Victory's first model was the V92C, a 1507cc V-twin cruiser launched in 1998. Sales were disappointing but in 2003 Victory hit back with the Vegas, featuring much improved styling plus a more refined version of the eight-valve V-twin engine.

■ ABOVE *The long, low look of Victory's Vegas was influenced by legendary custom builder Arlen Ness, a consultant on the project.*

VINCENT

■ VINCENT RAPIDE SERIES C

Fast, rugged and comfortable, Vincent's big V-twins were the ultimate high performance roadsters of their day. The firm was founded in 1928 by visionary engineer Philip Vincent, who as a schoolboy had designed the cantilever rear suspension system that all his bikes would use. Backed by his father, Vincent bought the defunct company HRD in an attempt to overcome market resistance to his first bikes, which used JAP single engines.

Vincent and Australian designer Phil Irving produced the Stevenage firm's first engine, a high camshaft 500cc single, in 1934. The resultant Meteor tourer and Comet sports singles were a success, the latter capable of an impressive 90mph (145kph). In 1936 Irving combined two Comet cylinders at 47 degrees to produce a 998cc, 45bhp V-twin. The Series A Rapide's 110mph (177kph) top speed

VINCENT RAPIDE SERIES C (1949)	
Engine	Aircooled 4-valve pushrod 50-degree V-twin
Capacity	998cc (84 x 90mm)
Power	45bhp @ 5200rpm
Weight	208kg (458lb) dry
Top speed	110mph (177kph)

made it the fastest production vehicle on the road, but the power led to transmission problems, and external oil lines led to the bike being nicknamed "the plumber's nightmare".

After the Second World War, Vincent introduced the Series B Rapide. This featured a redesigned 50-degree, unit-construction V-twin engine that was an integral part of the chassis, taking the place of the previous tubular frame. As

■ RIGHT *The Series A Rapide's 110mph (177kph) top speed made it the world's fastest roadster in the late 1930s.*

■ BELOW RIGHT *Only about 200 of the dramatic, fully enclosed Series D models were built, before production ended in 1955.*

OTHER MAKES

■ WANDERER

German firm Wanderer was founded in 1902 and built numerous singles and twins, some of which were used by the Germans in the First World War. Janecek of Prague built the Wanderer under licence, and in 1929 became the sole manufacturer as Janecek-Wanderer, later shortening the name to Jawa.

■ ABOVE *Wanderer produced this attractive little belt-drive V-twin, rated at 3.25bhp, in 1911.*

■ WASP

Chassis specialist Wasp began building off-road competition frames in 1968. The Wiltshire, England, firm's successful involvement in sidecar motocross led to production of its own 1000cc parallel twin engine in the early 1980s.

■ WERNER

The Russian-born, Paris-based Werner brothers, Michel and Eugene, were among motorcycling's greatest pioneers. Their first 217cc single, produced from 1898 onwards, was light and practical, and sold well. But the Werners are chiefly remembered for the innovative 1901-model New Werner whose layout, with the engine set low in a diamond-style bicycle frame, greatly improved handling and set the pattern for years to come.

well as reaching an effortless 100mph (160kph) at just 4600rpm, the mighty Rapide handled well and braked hard, thanks to twin drums on each wheel. In 1949 Vincent introduced the Series C Rapide, with Girdraulic forks replacing the previous Brampton girders.

The ultimate V-twin was the Black Shadow, introduced a year earlier, which was powered by a tuned, 55bhp black-finished engine. Top speed was a remarkable 120mph (193kph) plus, recorded on a speedometer calibrated to 150mph (241kph). That speed was achieved in the same year at Bonneville when Rollie Free, riding a tuned V-twin, stripped to swimming trunks and shoes to set a world record for unsupercharged bikes at 150.313mph (241.898kph). Other legendary Vincents were Gunga Din, Nero and the supercharged Super Nero, on which George Brown set speed records and won many races.

In 1955 Vincent introduced the Series D models, the Black Knight and tuned Black Prince. Despite Vincent's traditional high prices, the motorcycles were by then being sold at a loss, and production ceased at the end of the year. Hopes that the name would be revived came 40 years later, when American Bernard Li revealed plans for a traditionally styled but modern 1500cc V-twin roadster to be called the Vincent Black Eagle.

■ ABOVE *Rollie Free stripped to just a pair of bathing trunks to top 150mph (241kph) at Bonneville in 1948.*

■ ABOVE *The less sporty of Vincent's early 500cc singles was the Meteor, seen here in 1938 form.*

YAMAHA

■ YAMAHA 350cc YR5

Torakusu Yamaha trained as a clock-maker before, in 1897, founding Nippon Gakki, which grew into one of the world's largest musical instrument manufacturers. In 1955, Nippon Gakki established the Yamaha company to build motorbikes, using machinery that had made aircraft propellers in the Second World War. The first bike was a 125cc two-stroke single called the YA-1 or Red Dragonfly, based on a German DKW. The twin-cylinder YD-1 followed in 1957 and Yamaha began establishing a reputation for quick, light and reliable two-strokes, many of which featured the company's tuning fork logo on the tank.

■ ABOVE LEFT
Good handling combined with brisk acceleration and competitive price to ensure the YR5's success.

■ MIDDLE LEFT
Victory in the 1955 Asama road race helped the YA-1's reputation.

■ BELOW *The shape of the YR5, and the RD350, was echoed in many smaller Yamahas.*

■ LEFT *Phil Read heads for victory in the 250cc TT in 1971, the year he won his fourth world title for Yamaha.*

■ RIGHT *Future Grand Prix star Niall Mackenzie heads a typically frenzied battle in a RD350 Pro-Am race in 1983.*

YAMAHA 350cc YR5 (1970)	
Engine	Aircooled reed-valve two-stroke parallel twin
Capacity	347cc (64 x 54mm)
Power	36bhp @ 7000rpm
Weight	150kg (330lb) wet
Top speed	95mph (152kph)

■ ABOVE *Yamaha's first four-stroke roadster, the XS-1 of 1969, copied British bikes with its 650cc parallel twin engine.*

In the 1960s, Yamaha's successful series of 250cc YDS models led to the first 350cc twin, the YR1. In 1970, the firm released the neatly styled YR5, its aircooled parallel twin engine producing a maximum of 36bhp, which was enough to send the lightweight Yamaha screaming to 95mph (152kph). Handling and braking were good, reliability was excellent, price was competitive and the YR5 became hugely popular. Notable successors included the six-speed RD350 of 1974; the angular, 100mph (160kph) RD400 of 1976; the watercooled, single-shock RD350LC of 1981; and the legendary 1983 model YPVS or Power Valve, whose exhaust power valve improved mid-range performance and helped produce a claimed 53bhp, over 50 per cent up on the YR5's output. The fully-faired RD350LC F2 that followed was still being built, in Brazil, in the mid-1990s.

Yamaha's first period of Grand Prix success came in the 1960s, in the smaller classes. Phil Read won the 250cc title in 1964 on the parallel twin RD56 – the first time it had been won by a two-stroke – and retained it the following season. For 1967, Yamaha built a 35bhp, 16,000rpm V-four on which Bill Ivy won that year's 125cc title. Following Honda's retirement from racing, Yamaha intended to share the 1968 championships between team-mates Read and Ivy. But Read, with the 125cc crown safe, controversially refused to play that game and went on to take the 250cc title too.

Yamaha's first four-stroke roadster was the 650cc XS-1 of 1969, a British-style parallel twin that was capable of 105mph (168kph). In America the twin was competitively priced and was a success, particularly when updated to produce a series of XS650 models. The last of these, the US-market Heritage Special cruiser, brought the XS into the early 1980s, by which time production had soared well into six figures.

■ RIGHT *The fast and popular RD350LC Power Valve was available with or without a fairing in the late 1980s.*

YAMAHA

■ YAMAHA FZR1000

The bike that brought Yamaha to the forefront of superbike design was the four-cylinder FZR1000, which many riders regarded as the best Japanese sportster in the years following its launch in 1987. Its powerplant was a watercooled, 989cc engine whose angled-forward cylinder layout and DOHC, 20-valve cylinder head format had been introduced on the FZ750 two years earlier. The FZR's peak output of 125bhp matched that of Suzuki's GSX-R1100, class leader at the time.

Yamaha's Genesis factory racebike provided inspiration for the FZR's chassis, which centred on a rigid aluminium twin-spar Deltabox frame. Cycle parts included stout 41mm forks, a 17-inch front wheel and low-profile radial tyres. The motor was more than impressive, pulling smoothly from low revs until the FZR was hurtling towards its top speed of 160mph (257kph), with its rider crouching behind an efficient twin-headlamp fairing. Handling and braking were also excellent, and the Yamaha rapidly became hugely popular.

Numerous updates in subsequent years succeeded in retaining the FZR's cutting edge – notably in 1989 when Yamaha enlarged the motor to 1002cc and added an electronically operated exhaust valve whose acronym led to the bike being universally known as the EXUP. The system added useful mid-range performance; peak power was also increased, to 140bhp. A comprehensively revamped chassis provided improved handling to match, making the EXUP the pick of the Japanese Superbikes. Two years later the package was further improved with the FZR1000RU, featuring sharper styling and upside-down front forks.

In marked contrast to the light and agile FZR1000, Yamaha's first big four, the 1978 model XS1100, was a Japanese Superbike of the old school – a large, powerful, aircooled engine in a heavy chassis that was barely capable of keeping it under control. The 1101cc twin-cam motor produced a maximum of 95bhp and was particularly memorable for its huge reserves of mid-range

YAMAHA FZR1000RU (1991)	
Engine	Watercooled 20-valve DOHC transverse four
Capacity	1002cc (75.5 x 56mm)
Power	140bhp @ 10,000rpm
Weight	209kg (461lb) dry
Top speed	168mph (269kph)

■ BELOW *By the early 1990s the FZR1000 had been overtaken by faster sportsbikes, but still remained a fine machine.*

■ LEFT *The FZR1000's torquey, 140bhp engine meant that wheelies were only a twist of the throttle away.*

torque, which gave effortless acceleration to a top speed of 135mph (217kph). The XS was also smooth, comfortable and well-equipped. But the shaft-drive Yamaha's bulk and 270kg (595lb) of weight made for ponderous handling and instability at high speed, which severely limited its appeal.

Although Yamaha's FJ1100 was billed as a pure sportsbike when it was launched in 1984, the aircooled four quickly found its niche as a smooth, comfortable and effortlessly fast sports-tourer. It looked good, handled well, had a protective fairing and a 150mph (241kph) top speed, and most of all its broad powerband gave instant acceleration from almost any engine speed. That was even truer of the FJ1200, created in 1986 by enlarging the 16-valve engine to 1188cc. In the 1990s Yamaha introduced further refinements, including a rubber-mounted engine and anti-lock brakes, that kept the FJ popular after over ten years in production.

■ RIGHT *The powerful and fine-handling FZ750 of 1985 did not attract the sales that it deserved.*

■ RIGHT *Few rival sports-tourers have approached the FJ1200's blend of speed and long-distance comfort.*

YAMAHA

■ YAMAHA YZF-R1

Few bikes have made the impact that Yamaha's YZF-R1 did in 1998, when it burst on to the scene with a blend of aggressive styling and all-conquering performance. The R1's 998cc 20-valve four-cylinder engine produced 150bhp and was very compact, contributing to the bike's short wheelbase. As well as being short the Yamaha was very light at just 177kg (389lb), and had excellent suspension and brakes. Its handling was wonderfully precise, and the motor combined low-rev flexibility with enough top-end power for a top speed of 170mph (274kph).

The fast and focused R1 quickly became a huge hit. It remained popular

■ BELOW *As well as stunning the superbike world with its speed, the R1 made an impact with its sharp, aggressive styling.*

YAMAHA YZF-R1 (1998)	
Engine	Watercooled 20-valve DOHC transverse four
Capacity	998cc (74 x 58mm)
Power	160bhp @ 10,000rpm
Weight	177kg (389lb) dry
Top speed	170mph (274kph)

in subsequent years as Yamaha revised it with uprated suspension, fuel-injection instead of carbs, and reshaped bodywork, while retaining the bike's essential style and feel. The R1 also became the head of a family of Yamahas, beginning in 1999 with the YZF-R6, a

■ LEFT *Wayne Rainey (17) took over from Eddie Lawson (3) to win a hat-trick of titles for Yamaha.*

■ LEFT *The steel-framed Fazer 1000 was very fast for a semi-naked bike, thanks to its barely detuned YZF-R1 engine.*

■ BELOW AND INSET BELOW *Kenny Roberts won world titles with Yamaha as a rider and, more recently, as a manager.*

OTHER MAKES

■ ZENITH
A leading marque in the early years of the century, Zenith was best known for the popular Gradua with its adjustable gearing, operated by a long, so-called coffee grinder hand lever. Zenith built Villiers and JAP-engined singles in the 1930s, but production effectively ended at the start of the Second World War.

■ ZÜNDAPP
One of the major German firms for many years, Zündapp was founded in 1917 initially to make gun parts. Successful bikes included numerous flat-twins such as the KS750, much used by German troops in the Second World War, and the sporty 1951 model KS601, known as the Green Elephant. Zündapp thrived in the 1960s and 1970s, producing successful off-road competition bikes and two-stroke roadsters. But sales fell dramatically in the early 1980s. Stefan Dörflinger won the 80cc world title for Zündapp in 1984, but the firm went into liquidation the following year.

similarly raw sportster with a 120bhp, 599cc engine and a top speed of 160mph (257kph). Two years later the range was broadened with the FZS1000 Fazer, an entertaining semi-naked roadster with a slightly detuned 143bhp R1 engine in a tubular steel frame, and plenty of musclebike attitude.

Yamaha has produced many great Grand Prix racing bikes over the years, not least the TZ range, from 250cc twins to 750cc fours, that won many races in the 1970s and '80s. Giacomo Agostini won Yamaha's first 500cc world championship in 1975, before Kenny Roberts arrived to take a hat-trick of titles between 1978 and 1980, also riding inline four-cylinder two-strokes. Roberts' fellow Americans Eddie Lawson and Wayne Rainey were equally successful, each winning three championships on Yamaha's YZR500 V-four between 1984 and 1993. When

racing's top class became MotoGP in 2002, Yamaha introduced the YZR-M1, an R1-style 20-valve transverse four. Despite an output of over 200bhp the M1 was initially less competitive than Yamaha had hoped, but Max Biaggi managed two wins in its debut season.

THE WORLD OF
HARLEY-DAVIDSON

"If you have to ask..." said the Harley-Davidson slogan, "...you wouldn't understand." Just what is it that makes Harley-Davidson so special? The company makes motorcycles, true, but it is much more than a mere motorcycle manufacturer – Milwaukee makes legends. The company that has become an American icon crafts heavy metal into love affairs, forges lifestyles and fulfils dreams. As much myth as motorcycle – often imitated, never copied – there is simply nothing quite like a Harley-Davidson.

Today, Harleys are as recognizable around the world as the Stars and Stripes, as ubiquitous as McDonald's and as prized for their rugged honesty as Zippo lighters and Levi's. They appear in movies and advertising; they're the wheels of choice for celebrities and stars. Elvis owned one and, according to the T-shirt at least, God rides one too. Men have raced them almost as soon as the first one came out of the shop. They have been a unique facet of American life through two world wars and a crippling Depression.

Harley-Davidson's is the longest history in motorcycling, almost the story of motorcycling itself, and *The World of Harley-Davidson* is the epic tale of the making of an American legend.

The Evolution of Harley-Davidson

From uncertain beginnings in a Milwaukee basement in 1903, Harley-Davidson has witnessed and withstood everything a turbulent century could throw at it. Once the world's largest producer of motorcycles, Harley's sales shrank to a mere 10,000 per year during the 1950s. Increasing competition – first from Europe, then from Japan – brought the once-proud giant to the brink of ruin. By the 1970s, changes of ownership, confusion about its markets and a moribund model range made Harley-Davidson almost a joke to all but its most devoted fans. As recently as the mid-1980s this vibrant dream factory was effectively broke.

Today, the company is booming. Inspired styling and brilliant marketing, combined with modern manufacturing techniques, see Milwaukee's finest thundering confidently into the future.

EARLY YEARS

In the early days of the 20th century, young men in dingy workshops across the industrialized world tinkered with an endless array of new-fangled mechanical contraptions. There may have been hundreds of such enthusiastic amateurs in Wisconsin alone, but it was the relatively untutored tinkering of two young Milwaukee men in particular that would give rise to an American legend.

The story begins in 1900 – 15 years after Gottlieb Daimler created the world's first powered two-wheeler and only six years after the first production machine – when William Sylvester Harley and Arthur Davidson got together in a Milwaukee basement with motorcycling in mind.

Information from these early years is sketchy, so the inspiration for their enthusiasm is unclear. A primitive motorcycle was demonstrated by its creator, Edward Joel

Pennington, on nearby Wisconsin Avenue as early as 1895, though it's not clear whether the duo actually witnessed the event. They are known to have been impressed by a variety act five years later, however, in which comedienne Anna Held rode a French-built motorcycle across the stage of Milwaukee's Bijou theatre.

Harley was just 20 at the time, Davidson a year younger. The pair had been friends since their school days and, by accident or fate, had already accumulated some of the skills their

■ ABOVE *The founders, from left: Arthur Davidson, Walter Davidson, William Harley and William Davidson.*

■ BELOW *What is believed to be the very first production Harley-Davidson, now fully restored, enjoys pride of place in the Juneau Avenue lobby.*

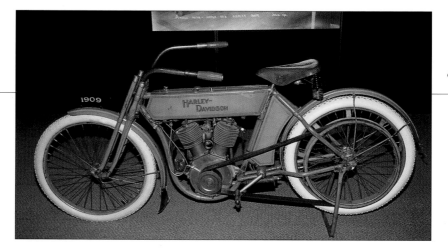

■ RIGHT AND BELOW
*The Model 5D twin from
1909 was essentially
two singles on a
common crankcase.
Valve gear problems
meant that only 27
were built. Production
of an improved version
began for 1911 with
the Model 7D.*

■ RIGHT *America's
early road network was
primitive, but
motorcycles proved
easier to manhandle
than cars.*

dreams required by the time they began
working together in that Milwaukee basement.
Harley worked as a draughtsman and had six
years of experience in bicycle manufacturing;
Davidson was a pattern maker with the same
company as Harley, working on small petrol
(gas) engines. They were also fortunate enough
to have working alongside them a German
colleague familiar with pioneering European
motorcycles. Work on the first Harley-Davidson
engine began in 1900 or 1901 and was
probably based on one of the do-it-yourself kits
then available, itself roughly based on the
French De Dion-Bouton design. A drawing
dated 20 July 1901 shows a 7.07cu in
(115.8cc) engine with a bore and stroke of
2 x 2.25in (50 x 55mm). When installed in a
bicycle, power proved deeply disappointing.

At least one more prototype followed,
including a machine capable of "thrilling
speeds up to 25mph" and measuring 10.2cu in
(167cc). It soon became clear that their
venture required more expertise if it was
ever going to get up to speed – beginning
with the need for a skilled mechanic.
Fortunately, Arthur's brother, Walter
Davidson, was just such a man.

Walter was working as a railroad machinist
in Parsons, Kansas, at the time, but was due in
Milwaukee for the wedding of a third Davidson

brother, William A. (Bill). Arthur wrote to
Walter, offering him a ride on their new
motorcycle. It was only later that he discovered
("imagine my chagrin") that he would have to
help build it first. He must have liked the idea
though –, enough to find work in Milwaukee
and join the team. The founders became four
when William, the eldest Davidson brother and
a foreman railway toolmaker, jumped on board
– and the four began the ride of their lives.

The machine recognized as the first true
Harley-Davidson engine was built during
1902-3, by which time locally built Merkel and
Mitchell motorcycles were already a familiar
feature of Milwaukee life. Bore and stroke were
3 x 3.5in (76.2 x 88.9mm) for a displacement
of 24.74cu in (405cc) but the Harley-Davidson
engine incorporated many technical
refinements. The new engine was of F-head
layout, with much larger cooling fins than
before, as well as much larger flywheels –
almost 10in (250mm) across. Some of the
machining was done on a lathe belonging to a
friend, Henry Melk, while other parts were
crafted illicitly as parts for foreign sales in the
toolrooms of William A. Davidson's employers,
the Chicago, Milwaukee and St Paul Railroad.
Legend has it that the first carburettor was
made from a discarded tomato can (although
this could as easily refer to the 1901 engine),
and Bill Harley later described its spark plug,
which had cost the princely sum of $3.00, as
being "as big as a doorknob".

■ ABOVE *By 1913 all
Harley twins enjoyed all-
chain drive, although the
basic Model 9A single
(right) continued with
leather belt drive.*

■ BELOW *A well-to-do
couple with a Model 9A,
pictured in 1913.*

Assistance with the design came from
Arthur's childhood friend, Ole Evinrude, who
was already making liquid-cooled engines of
his own and would later find fame with his
outboard motors. Evinrude is credited with
setting up the carburettor, but other
components – notably the roller tappets still
used on Harleys today – may have been his
idea as well. Scaling 49lbs (22kg), this engine
was installed in a loop frame similar to the
existing Merkel design, in the Davidson
family's back yard at 315 37th Street. The site,
known as 38th Street today, is now owned by
the giant Miller Brewery and is little more than
a stone's throw from Juneau Avenue.

■ THE HARLEY-DAVIDSON MOTOR CO.

So it was that in 1903 – the same year the Wright brothers took to the air – the Harley-Davidson team created its first motorcycle and readied itself to produce similar machines for public consumption. This handsome machine was gloss black with gold pinstriping, a single-loop tubular steel frame, unsprung forks and leather belt final drive directly from the crankshaft. Additional power was offered by pedals, which also provided the only braking force. It is unclear how many machines were built during 1904 – sources suggest figures anywhere from one to eight, although anything over three seems unlikely. However many there were, each was assembled in a 15 x 10ft shed erected in the Davidson back yard by the boys' father, a cabinet-maker. Modest though it was, the shed bore the legend "Harley-Davidson

■ BELOW *This celebratory restoration of a 1913 single shows an image of the first factory (which was located on Juneau Avenue, Milwaukee) on the tank.*

Motor Co." on its front (and only) door with typical understated pride.

The first production Harley has a tale to tell all its own. It carried its first owner, a Mr Mayer, for almost 6,000 miles before passing to George Lyon, who covered another 15,000 miles. It was sold in turn to a Dr Webster, followed by Louis Fluke and Stephen Sparrow, who between them clocked up almost another 62,000 relatively untroubled miles (a total of 134,000 km). By 1913, the company decided to advertise the bike's exploits, promoting an image of dependable travel:

■ ABOVE *The inlet-over-exhaust valve layout is clearly seen on this early "Renault Gray" single.*

■ LEFT *William S. Harley on the left and Walter Davidson on the right getting a motorcycle over the rocks of a creek, 1912.*

"100,000 miles on its original bearings and no major components replaced". Harley-Davidson engines were also produced for use in "buckboards" (four-wheel wagons) and the company's earliest advertisements also proposed their use in boats.

Motorcycle production soared to seven in 1905 as the company took on its first outside employee and attracted its first dealer, C.H. Lang of Chicago, who would become the largest motorcycle dealer in the country within a dozen years. A year later, in 1906, "Renault gray with red pinstriping" joined black as a colour option, and the model became known as "the Silent Gray Fellow", a name that reflected its quietness and dependability.

Engine capacity had by now increased to 26.84cu in (440cc) and the list price for the latest models was $200.

■ BELOW RIGHT AND LEFT *An unrestored and original 1915 61-inch F-head twin. Note that pedal assistance is still retained.*

Production had soared to 50 units by 1906, prompting a move from the company's original hut on 37th Street and Highway Boulevard into its first proper building on the present Juneau Avenue site. The new factory turned out to be sitting partially on land belonging to the railroad. Fortunately, the "factory" was a wooden structure, and at 28 x 80ft (9 x 25 metres) eight or ten people were able to carry it the few feet to its proper location.

Finance for expansion came from a relative, James McLay, known as "the honey uncle" due to his generosity and hobby of beekeeping. This affectionate tribute was more appropriate than anyone could imagine, for Juneau Avenue was to become a veritable hive of activity, seven days a week, 365 days a year.

■ **FORGING AHEAD**
By 1907, the company was getting serious: it became Harley-Davidson Inc. Walter was the largest stockholder, followed by Arthur, with the two Williams a joint third. A Davidson sister, Elizabeth, also had the good sense to buy Harley-Davidson shares early in the firm's

■ ABOVE *A rare 1914 Model 10C single with hugely complex two-speed rear hub.*

■ BELOW *Harley-Davidson motorcycles and sidecars were used by the rural postal service.*

life. (By 1916, Davidson family stockholders would outnumber Harleys seventeen to three.) It was a heady time. The company had already taken on extra staff; William Harley had begun an engineering degree at the University of Wisconsin in Madison; Walter was exploring the mysteries of heat treatment on metals; and the enterprise, and Arthur, as company secretary and sales manager, was taking a more

professional approach to production and training. The company may have begun as four young men with more enthusiasm than talent, but they had ambitions for the company they had created. That year, they produced no fewer than 150 machines and within 12 months had sold the first of many thousands for police duty.

Even so, it was clear that further progress demanded a more ambitious new motorcycle than the existing single, which in 1909 expanded to 30.17cu in (495cc). By 1908, William Harley had graduated and continued work on a more potent engine. This bore fruit a year later with the launch of the company's first production V-twin, the Model D, essentially a doubled-up single with strengthened bottom-end.

The first such model became officially available on 15 February 1909, although the first working prototype appears to have been built as early as 1906. A press report from the time clearly mentions a 53in (869cc) Harley twin in April 1908, while a privately-owned Harley-Davidson twin won a hill climb event at Algonquin, Illinois, in July that same year.

Whatever its exact development history, the Model D twin was an inlet-over-exhaust valve design with a capacity of 53.7cu in (880cc), developing around six horsepower and capable

■ LEFT *By 1917 Olive Green had replaced Renault Gray as the factory colour, here on a Model J twin three-speed.*

The factory resisted official racing for several years despite widespread success in competitions. The factory's reluctance continued even when a private owner took the new 61in (989cc) X8E twin (the first Harley with a clutch) to victory in the 1912 San José road race by no less than 17 miles (27km): Bill Harley established a works race department two years later.

of a top speed close to 62mph (100 kph). The cylinders were splayed apart at the trademark 45 degree angle.

The strength of the Model D twin was amply proven in June 1908 when Walter drove one of his bikes to its first "official" competition success, a two-day endurance run in New York's Catskill Mountains. The sole Harley scored a "perfect" 1,000 points, outstripping all the more fancied runners in a field of 61 machines. Surprisingly – and embarrassingly – the first production twins were beset by valve-gear problems, with production being suspended during 1910.

■ BELOW LEFT *Since opening in 1919, this Juneau Avenue factory has been the home of Harley-Davidson.*

■ BELOW RIGHT *William Ottaway, who was Harley's first race boss, sits astride a 1924 Model JDCA.*

■ **A DEPENDABLE TWIN**
When the V-engine reappeared as the "50-inch" (810cc) Model 7D of 1911, no expense had been spared and every effort made to produce a machine worthy of Harley-Davidson's reputation. Not only had proper mechanical valves replaced the hit-and-miss automatic inlets, an adjustable tensioner had been added to the slippage-prone belt final drive.

Another notable improvement to this model saw the revised powerplant housed in a new, much sturdier frame.

■ RIGHT *Gordon, Walter Jnr. and Allan Davidson (sitting on bikes) in San Francisco after a cross-country ride in 1929.*

A year later, a 61cu in (989cc) version, the chain-drive Model X8E, reinforced these developments. With its second attempt, Harley hit the nail on the head, and the V-twin took its rightful place in Milwaukee history.

Production in the rapidly expanding company soared to 450 machines in 1908, housed in a new, brick-built factory of

■ RIGHT *Harley-Davidson's first V-Twin engine, introduced in 1909. It displaced 49.5cu in (811cc).*

2,380sq ft (221sq metres) and employing 18 people. New machinery arrived almost weekly and was set to work, according to legend, "as soon as the cement was dry", and in what must have seemed like an instant, became obsolete. Two years later, 149 staff were engaged in another new factory – a reinforced concrete structure of 9,520sq ft (885sq metres).

By the time the new 5hp, 35cu in single model (565cc 5–35) appeared in 1913, the company had established a reputation for producing machines that were dependable in both domestic and competitive use. The factory was hurtling ahead as well in this changing age and included a separate Parts and Accessories Department. More than 1,500 employees worked for a company whose manufacturing floor area had grown from nothing to almost 300,000sq ft (28,000sq metres) within a decade. Production rocketed from eight machines in 1905 to 1,149 in 1911 and 17,439 in 1916, the year prior to the United States' entry into the First World War.

Though not yet dominant in the industry, in 1913 Harley produced around 18 per cent of the 70,000 American-built motorcycles.

Very soon, however, all this would change, and much of this energy would be called to the service of Uncle Sam.

WAR AND PEACE

On 6 April 1917, the United States declared war on Germany. Harley's successful peace-time formula suddenly faced an entirely new set of demands for which, five years earlier, the company may have been ill-prepared. By 1917, however, this bullish, expanding company was ready to go to war for real.

Harley-Davidson supplied the best part of 20,000 motorcycles to the American military in total, the majority being 61-inch twins. Indeed, the war did little but good for the company's prospects. Rival European motorcycle manufacturers were preoccupied by hostilities for a much longer period (1914–18) than those in the United States. Consequently, Milwaukee was able to extend its markets and reputation overseas. By 1918, aided by a $3 million loan from the M&I bank, Harley-Davidson had

become the world's largest manufacturer of motorcycles. Within a year, "Hap" Scherer had been appointed Harley-Davidson's first publicity manager. By 1921, machines were being sold through 2,000 dealers in 67 countries, with product catalogues printed in seven languages. As the dust settled on the carnage of the war, one-sixth of Milwaukee's production was destined for export.

■ ABOVE *Harley was quick to develop its bikes for war, including mounting them with machine guns.*

■ BELOW *Milwaukee-built sidecars proved to be extremely popular for both military and civilian use.*

■ RIGHT *Board racers were Harleys in their leanest form, stripped of even any semblance of brakes...*

The aftermath of war had other, less predictable side-effects. One of these was the retention of army green as the company colour in place of the pre-war pale grey. Another more enduring effect concerned training. To help military personnel keep Milwaukee's wares reliable, the Harley-Davidson Service School was established in 1917. Initially intended as a military measure and as concerned with riding instruction as mechanics, the Service School soon developed into a crucial arm of the factory's civilian service.

By the eve of the "Roaring Twenties", the Juneau Avenue factory had become a colossus. In 1919, close to 1,800 employees toiled on a floor area exceeding 400,000sq ft (37,000sq metres) to produce 22,685 motorcycles and

■ RIGHT *...or silencing, as can clearly be seen on this handsome 1916 F-head twin.*

■ BELOW *Front brakes finally arrived in the late 1920s, as on this Model J Big Twin.*

over 16,000 sidecars. The Model J Sport Twin, unveiled that same year, was unique among Harleys, if not American motorcycles in general. Instead of the "V" layout, the 35.6cu in (584cc) twin adopted a horizontally opposed design, akin to today's BMWs. Instead of lying across the frame, the cylinders were orientated fore-and-aft. Although long and unwieldy, the layout offered a very low centre of gravity and a compact width, ideally suited to America's then-primitive road network.

There were other innovations, most of which would stand the test of time better than the model itself. The final drive was sensibly protected from dust in a metal enclosure, not unlike more recent MZ machines, lubricated by oil mist from the engine breather. It was also the first model to feature a full electrical

■ LEFT *Before 1927,
only a rear brake
was fitted onto bikes.*

system produced by the Harley factory.
Although the Sport set many records – Canada
to Mexico in less than 75 hours, no easy task
even today – its six horsepower engine lacked
the bottomless big-inch power America
demanded, and was discontinued after 1922.

The 1920s didn't so much roar as whimper
where motorcycles were concerned. Much of
the blame for the Sport Twin's relative failure
lay far beyond Milwaukee's control – 1920

■ BELOW *Inventiveness
is apparent in this 1919
twin, fitted with
stabilising skis for
use in icy conditions.*

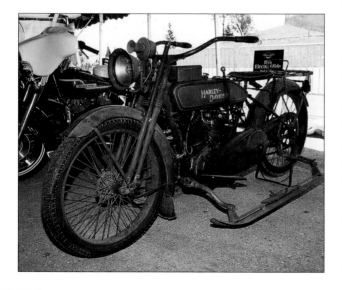

witnessed a major trade recession with a
massive over-supply of manufactured goods as
global economies struggled to adjust to peace-
time trade. One of the consequences was
Henry Ford's slashing the price of his Model T
car to $395, the same as the biggest Harley
twin. The effects on motorcycle sales were
inevitable. The trade slump was brief, but
America's love affair with the car was not, and
neither Harley nor any other bike manufacturer
fully recovered their previous momentum.

Milwaukee's sales collapsed from over
28,000 in 1920 to 10,202 in 1921, with sales
so poor during that spring that the factory,
which had expanded 12 months before, shut
down for a month. Sales would not return to
1920s levels for a further 21 years. Most of the
machines that were sold during that time were
61-inch V-twins.

Although the Sport failed to make the impact
Harley hoped, one of the next models quickly
became a Milwaukee legend. In 1921, the V-
twin was replaced by the JD and FD, the first
74-inch (actually 74.2cu in/1,216cc) models,
with F-head, inlet-over-exhaust (ioe) valve
layout. Each example was dubbed a
"Superpowered Twin" in tribute to its 18-hp
engine and both underwent rigorous pre-
delivery testing: yet another Harley innovation.

■ RIGHT *The 1920s was marked mostly by F-head machines like this 1922 61-inch twin. Flatheads began to appear from 1926, the same year as the first overhead valve engines.*

As for the rest of the range, the 30-inch single had been dropped after 1918. In 1926, a new single – the 21in (344cc) Model A – was introduced, joined four years later by a 30.5in (492cc) sister. In a radical move, Harley-Davidson pioneered the front brake in 1928, just as the company had pioneered kick-starts and three-speed transmissions more than a decade earlier. All models were sold in varied specifications of transmission, valve-gear and power, so that in 1928, for instance, three basic

engine types accounted for no less than a dozen models. By this time, Harley's only surviving domestic competitors were Indian, Henderson, Cleveland and Super-X.

The last year of the decade introduced the machine that would become Milwaukee's bread and butter. The new WL was a 45in (742cc) side-valve V-twin which supposedly combined the single's agility with the power of the bigger twins. Capped by rakish twin "bullet" headlights, the new model was an instant success and constituted the lowest rung on a V-twin ladder made up of 45-, 61- and 74-inchers). Star billing in the 1929 Harley-Davidson catalogue went to the JDH Two-Cam, which housed a specially-prepared variant of the 74-inch engine that had been developed for the factory's all-conquering board racers.

Billed as "the fastest road model that Harley-Davidson has ever offered to the public", it could probably out-run any other two-wheeler on the American highway.

The WL may have been humbler but it proved its worth by keeping Milwaukee's head above water in the years ahead.

■ RIGHT *This stylish ohv "Peashooter" speedway machine dates from 1927.*

THE 1930s

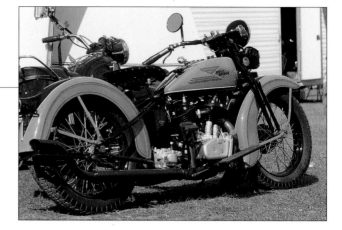

The 1930s began in high spirits with arguably the most mouth-watering range to come out of Milwaukee for years. All models now had bigger brakes and tyres, improved ground clearance, lower saddles and – best of all – removable cylinder heads. These "Ricardo" heads were far more practical and efficient than the one-piece iron cylinders previously employed. Although plagued by early problems, the new high-compression 74.2cu in (1,216cc) VL offered fully 15 per cent more power than any previous Harley roadster. A nation-wide "open house" attracted customers by the thousands and, with sales quickly up 30 per cent on the previous year, the new decade appeared rich in promise.

There was one cloud on the horizon, however. In October 1929, a few weeks after the 1930 range was unveiled, the Wall Street stock market crashed, sending tremors throughout the American economy and the rest of the world. President Herbert Hoover's initial rapid intervention seemed to stem the tide but economic confidence continued to wilt. In 1930, 1,300 banks went to the wall. Manufacturers in every industry offered incentives to stimulate business, but to no avail. Within 12 months, the mighty Juneau Avenue factory was running at a mere 10 per cent of production capacity and would report a loss of more than $320,000 the following year. By 1933, one quarter of the United States workforce was unemployed. Few people had

■ ABOVE *By the 1930s all Harleys were flatheads, such as this imposing 74-inch VL from 1933.*

■ LEFT *1932 saw the introduction of the enduring Servi-Car, which would continue in production for 40 years.*

■ ABOVE *The troubles of the Depression encouraged novel art-deco styling, such as the tank badge on this mammoth 80-inch VLH from 1936. The same motifs can be seen even on modern Harleys.*

money to spend on motorcycles. Of hundreds of American bike manufacturers, only Harley and Indian had the financial strength and acumen to survive. Industry-wide production fell from 32,000 to 6,000 units per year by 1933, by which time fewer than 100,000 motorcycles were registered in the whole of the United States. Of these new sales, Milwaukee's share was just 3,703 – its lowest in 23 years.

Desperately, Juneau Avenue wracked its brains for innovative sales ideas, ranging from savings plans to a medal scheme intended to turn every Harley owner into a salesman. One enduring response was the sale of branded clothing and accessories – a sideline now worth millions of dollars per year. A superficial but significant measure was the abandonment of dull green paint in 1933, in favour of more vivid colours and art-deco graphics which continue to brighten Harley-Davidsons today.

An altogether grittier response was the three-wheeled Servi-Car, a cheap delivery and police

vehicle powered by the 45-inch (742cc) Model D engine. Surprisingly, given the fraught circumstances of the time, this three-wheeler was both a sound design and a solid piece of engineering – so tough and enduring, indeed, that it survived in production from late 1931 until 1974. The true hero of the Depression years was the side-valve twin: cheap to produce, economic to run and maintain, and easily repairable.

Almost on their own, the D and V models saw Harley through the Depression, along with the 30.5in (492cc) single-cylinder machine of 1929. As the financial vice tightened, no other significant new models were developed during those six years.

In many ways, the worst of the Depression also brought out the best in the company. By reducing the length of the working week, as many staff were kept on as possible, although this was less generous than it might appear, since it was partially mandated by the

government's National Recovery Administration, and every skilled hand would be needed when the slump finally abated. Prudent financial controls, police and military contracts, novel sales strategies and energetic pursuit of exports kept the company afloat, and by 1934, the books were back in the black.

■ KNUCKLING DOWN

Painfully slowly, President Roosevelt's "New Deal" began to take effect and, by 1936, the

■ ABOVE LEFT *A WLA in desert camouflage stands out against civilian chrome.*

ABOVE RIGHT AND BELOW *Drab green was more common. Almost 90,000 of these 45-inch (742cc) flathead twins were built for the military during the Second World War, and thousands served with the Soviet forces.*

crippling Depression came to a close. New machines began to emerge from Milwaukee, whose 1935 model range had comprised a mere two basic models. These were the 45-inch (742cc) Model R (essentially the D model with light alloy pistons, soon to become the heroic W) and the 74-inch (1,216cc) Model V and its derivatives, now cured of its original and varied ills. Both were side-valve designs, slow and steady, whereas the American public increasingly craved more advanced machines.

The biggest newcomer was the V-twin Model UL. Although still side-valve and visually similar to the proven DL45, it displaced a stupendous 78.9cu in (1,293cc), making it ideal for heavy sidecar use. It was to continue in production until 1945. Most important of all was a new generation of 61-inch (898cc) twin with overhead valves and twice the power of its predecessor. The legendary Model E – the Knucklehead – had arrived.

The 1936 Knuckle could have appeared in 1934 but for government restrictions aimed at reducing employment. For company and public alike, this was frustrating but certainly worth the wait. The Knuckle was a Juneau Avenue first in many respects – the first four (forward)

■ ABOVE LEFT AND RIGHT *The "A" in WLA stood for army, so naturally military rules came with the machines. Soldiers were warned not to exceed 65mph.*

■ RIGHT AND BELOW *Even soldiers could be customizers: note the "Uncle Sam" on the fuel tank (right) and grenade-box lettering (below).*

speeder; the first overhead valve roadster twin; the first hemispherical heads. The engine was heavily influenced by the competition experience of the legendary Joe Petrali, Harley development rider and near-unbeatable racer. It announced its arrival by 136.183mph (219.16kph) on the sands of Daytona Beach, Florida. The rider, naturally, was Joe. His waterside speed record stands to this day.

With the new model as its flagship, Harley's fortunes rapidly improved. In 1937, sales exceeded 11,000 for the first time since 1930. The same year brought significant improvements elsewhere in the range: full roller bearing engines, chromolly fork tubes and interchangeable wheels.

As well as these technical advances, the lessons of the Depression had instilled in the company a faith in styling and cosmetics which

stands them in good stead even today. The
aftermarket and art-deco innovations of 1932
were continued. Balloon tyres appeared in
1940 (more striking, if less functional, than
new aluminium alloy heads for the flathead
side-valve models). In 1941, four-speed
transmissions became standard across the big
twin range. Eleven models were now on the
books in four basic engine configurations: side-
valves of 45-, 74- and 80-inch (742, 1,216 and
1,293cc), and Knuckleheads of 61-inch Model
E (989cc) and 74-inch Model F (1,207cc).

■ **LEFT** *Civilian
versions of the humble
WL45 could be
surprisingly handsome.*

■ BACK TO WAR
Motorcycle production in Milwaukee rose from
a low of 3,703 in 1933 to more than 18,000 in
1941. Harley made it through the Depression
by the narrowest of squeaks, emerging stronger
than ever before. However, not long after this
rocky period in Harley-Davidson's history, a
catastrophe of an altogether more terrible kind
occurred: the world once again went to war.

The United States entered the conflict after the
bombing of Pearl Harbor on 7 December 1941.

As the country's largest motorcycle producer,
it fell to Harley-Davidson to underpin the
bulk of the country's two-wheeled war effort.
Throughout the years of America's involvement
in the war (1942–45), practically the entire
output of the Milwaukee factory was turned
over to military production – some 90,000
machines in total.

As with the First World War, the Second was
fairly good to Milwaukee. In 1940, sales

■ **LEFT** *Astonishingly,
the WL45 engine
survived until the
1970s in the Servi-Car.*

■ LEFT *During the Second World War almost no machines were made for civilian use. This is one of the first post-war WL45 twins, in vibrant red.*

totalled less than 11,000. These soared to 18,000 as the military build-up began in 1941, reaching more than 29,000 in each of the two years that followed before tailing off again as peace approached. However, since the military favoured Harley Davidson's robust side-valve plodders over the new Model E and Model F, this meant that Knucklehead production was practically zero during the same period.

■ RIGHT *The noble Knucklehead, Milwaukee's first overhead valve roadster twin.*

HARLEY JAPAN

One little-known, highly ironic consequence of Milwaukee's quest for export markets in the 1920s and the economic slump of the 1930s was the creation of a Japanese big twin. During the 1920s, Arthur Davidson had pursued new sales openings with vigour, including the establishment of the Harley-Davidson Sales Company of Japan with a comprehensive network of dealers, agencies and spares distributors. Milwaukee's stock stood so high that Harleys soon became Japan's official police motorcycle.

Less worthily, in 1924 the Murata Iron Works began building copies of the 1922 Model J, but the quality was appalling. Murata would later build the Meguro, a distant precursor of modern Kawasakis. Harley exports to Japan all but ceased in

the wake of the 1929 Wall Street crash, as the global economic slump crippled the yen. The story might have stopped there but for Alfred Childs, head of Harley's Japanese operation, who asked: "Why not build Harleys there?"

Juneau Avenue was sceptical at first, but such was Childs' persistence that Harley's first overseas factory soon began production at Shinagawa, near Tokyo. Built with tooling, plans, blueprints and expertise borrowed from Milwaukee, the factory was considered the most modern in the world. By 1935 Shinagawa was manufacturing complete motorcycles, mainly 74-inch V-series flathead twins. In 1930, these had become the official motorcycle of the Japanese Imperial Army. Later, when the army became the effective civil power, it declined the chance to

convert production to the new ohv Knucklehead, preferring the proven durability of the side-valve twin. It was at this point that the Sankyo corporation took over control of the factory and began selling Japanese Harleys under the Rikuo name. The "74" twin became the Rikuo Model 97.

As an increasingly truculent Japan readied for war, Harley cut its losses and sold out. As military demand increased (especially after the invasion of China in 1937), Rikuo sub-licensed the product to Nihon Jidosha ("Japan Combustion Equipment Co."). Its "Harleys" were variants of the model 97s, entitled Kuro Hagane ("Black Iron").

Ominously, the factory had only a few more years to run. Nihon Jidosha was located in Hiroshima.

BACK TO PEACE

Although the Second World War ended on 15 August 1945 following the Japanese surrender, it would be more than a year before the unveiling of any new revisions from Milwaukee. Even these – theoretically 1947 models – were no more than cosmetic updates of Harley's pre-war machines. Of all the changes, perhaps the best remembered is Brook Steven's design for new "streamlined" H-D tank badges. A revamped clothing and accessories catalogue appeared in the same model year, a harbinger of the direction the company would take three decades later.

For the time being, however, motorcycles were scarce as the industry readjusted to civilian production and the loss of military demand. In the aftermath of the War Department's cancellation of orders for over 11,000 machines in 1944, more than 500 Harley-Davidson workers were let go. The rest, limited to a shortened working week, went on strike in late 1945. Paradoxically, limits on civilian production remained in force, and

■ BELOW *But by 1948 the Knucklehead was history as the era of the Panhead had begun, as with this HydraGlide.*

things went from bad to worse when 15,000 war surplus WLs were offered for public sale. It would be two more years before motorcycle production regained its pre-war level.

There was only one thing that had not changed in the forced interlude of war – Harley-Davidson's winning ways. In 1947, among other successes, seven of the first ten Daytona finishers rode Harleys. Over the next two years, 36 of 47 AMA championship events went to the Milwaukee marque.

Harley-Davidson took up residence in a second factory on Capitol Drive, Wauwatosa, in 1947. By 1948, production was at an all-time high and, more important to America's highways, the replacement for the noble Knucklehead made its first public appearance that same year. The Panhead as it became known, was a development of the Knuckle rather than an all-new concept. As well as a revised (and much more oil-tight) lubrication

■ LEFT *Before the appearance of the HydraGlide's telescopic forks, the first Panheads ran with the old girder-fork chassis, as with this magnificently restored 1948 example.*

front forks. It was also, of course, the first model granted one of the most evocative titles in motorcycling: "Glide". The Panhead engine would do much to get the species on its famous way, propelling not only the DuoGlide of 1958 but the first of the ElectraGlides as well.

Though no-one knew it at the time, this first Glide was to set the visual cues for the "Retro-Tech" Harleys which would appear four decades later. From its deeply-valanced mudguards and its chromed fork shrouds to its stylized rear end, the style of modern Softails owes much to the HydraGlide.

■ **INTO THE 1950S**

Harley-Davidson styles of the 1950s were in many ways a contradiction of those with which the company is now synonymous. True, 1950s imagery rates high in current Harley design but the decade began under the cloud of the Hollister "riots" of 1947, which tarnished the

system, the Pan featured aluminium alloy cylinder heads in place of the Knuckle's iron and hydraulic "lifters" rather than solid push-rods. The Pan, so named because its chrome-plated rocker covers resembled inverted baking pans, was built in both 74cu in (1,200cc) and 61cu in (1,000cc) sizes; the latter was discontinued in 1953. The larger version retained the "traditional" bore and stroke dimensions of 3$\frac{7}{16}$ x 4in (87 x 101mm).

The first all-new model powered by the Panhead engine was the HydraGlide of 1949, so-called because it was the first Harley to incorporate hydraulically-damped, telescopic

■ RIGHT *Another perfectly restored example of a 1948 Panhead.*

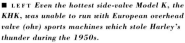

■ LEFT *Even the hottest side-valve Model K, the KHK, was unable to run with European overhead valve (ohv) sports machines which stole Harley's thunder during the 1950s.*

Even if the typical Harley owner of the day could handle the tarnished image of the motorcycle he loved, he may have been less sanguine about another development: in 1947, the world's foremost manufacturer of big V-twins began the manufacture of two strokes.

image of motorcycling and alarmed motorcycle manufacturers. The true creator of the riots, however, was the media (including *Life* magazine) which represented the gathering in Hollister as a major assault on small-town America. The world was just getting over the shock when the Hollister-inspired film *The Wild One* was released in 1953, reopening old wounds. Although the film's star, Marlon Brando, rode a Triumph Thunderbird on screen, many people still swear it was a Harley.

■ RIGHT AND BELOW *The Model K-derived KRTT fared better on the track, whilst on the street, their slowness made them popular with the insurers of Hollywood stars.*

This seemingly radical departure was an attempt to bring Milwaukee's appeal to a wider market, a move that was applauded at the time by many observers.

The line began with the 125cc Model S, a 1.7 horsepower machine based on the same German DKW RT125 design as the BSA Bantam, the rights to which both companies acquired as part of Germany's war reparations. More than 10,000 were built in the model's debut year, based on the expensive misconception that war veterans would buy almost anything with wheels, before production slipped to a more realistic 4,000 or so per annum. The engine grew to 165cc in 1954, powering the Models ST and Super Ten before increasing to 175cc for the Ranger/Pacer/Scat series in 1962. Perhaps Harley's best-known lightweights were the 125cc Model B Hummer, produced from 1955–59, and the 165cc Topper Scooter of the early 1960s.

■ ABOVE *The HydraGlide was special, but something was missing...*

■ BELOW *...this came with the DuoGlide, the first Harley big twin to feature real suspension at both ends.*

Unfortunately, other manufacturers were also intent on broadening their markets. Harley-Davidson had by now introduced dealer demonstrator models and was to lose one competitor with the demise of Indian in 1953, but Triumph's creation of a vibrant new American import network in 1951 was a major alarm.

Isolated by war and supported by military production, Harley had enjoyed easy pickings for too long. Triumph – along with other British marques such as BSA, Norton and Royal Enfield – had a range of cheaper yet much more exciting and technically sophisticated models than Harley-Davidson (whose flagship model persisted with hand-gear-change until 1952).

Harley's response was heavy-handed and ultimately counter-productive as they attempted to bully dealers into having no business with the British pretenders.

Milwaukee also went so far as to apply for federal trade protection in 1952, alleging that the British machines were being subsidized and "dumped" on the American market. They asked for a 40 per cent import tax and quotas on the number of machines that Triumph (and parent company BSA) could import.

Thirty years later, Harley would get the protection that it had wanted, this time against the Japanese. The first time around, however, the Government's Tariff Commission found that Triumph had no case to answer. Worse still, they told Harley to quit its restrictive trading practices – a ruling that was to have devastating echoes for the company in the decades ahead.

■ OLD, SLOW AND OBSOLETE

No model summed up Harley's problem more than the Model K, introduced in 1952 to replace the WL. The K was a heavy 45.3cu in (742cc) side-valve design compared to the overhead valves, lightweight construction and good suspension offered by British twins (and, in the case of Norton, arguably the finest handling motorcycle in the world). Granted, the K included proper suspension at both ends – a first for Milwaukee – but in virtually every other respect it was woefully outclassed by the British-made bikes.

Harley claimed 30 horsepower for the Model K, which was only a little less than the contemporary Triumph Thunderbird. Whether or not this was true, the 85mph (137kph) V-twin was no match for the 103mph (166 kph) British model, although the KK version, which had hotter cams, was better. Early Model Ks also had serious mechanical problems, although quality and power was improved by a capacity increase to 883cc for the 55-inch KH model in 1954.

■ ABOVE *Not quite King of the Road: a Milwaukee two-stroke.*

■ BELOW *The Shovelhead would replace the Panhead for the 1966 model year, as with this ElectraGlide.*

Remarkably, Paul Goldsmith took a K-based KR racer to victory by more than two miles (3km) in the Daytona 200 road race of 1953, a victory Harley-Davidsons were to repeat for the remainder of the decade. In 1954, the legendary Joe Leonard became first American national champion on KR and KR-TT racers. Although superficially impressive, these exploits owed much to the now familiar ploy of persuading the authorities to handicap the opposition. In this case, foreign ohv engines competing against 750cc Harley flatheads were limited to 500cc.

The K sold moderately well but overall sales figures show the full extent of Milwaukee's problem. In wheel-hungry 1948, Harley-Davidson produced more than 31,000 machines, the largest figure in its history. Yet by 1955, sales had plummeted to a low of less than 12,000. The problem could not be blamed on public disaffection with motorcycling, either – during the same period sales of imported machines went from strength to strength.

The machine which superseded the Model K in 1957 – the XL Sportster – was better in every way, eventually. The original Sportster's performance was lacklustre but by 1958 it benefited to the tune of 12 horsepower, due to lighter valve-gear, higher compression, larger ports and valves, and a legend was born.

■ RIGHT *What Harleys are best at: cruising the vastness of the good ol' US of A.*

Displacing 53.9cu in (883cc), as today, the XL boasted unit construction for the engine and gearbox. Swing-arm rear suspension with car-type dampers allowed early Sportsters to be sold for either on- or off-road use. The XL was an instant hit, accounting for almost 20 per cent of Harley's 1957 production of more than 13,000 machines. In 1958, the stock XL was joined by one of the most legendary Harleys ever produced, the XLCH – "Competition Hot". Other variations have included the low-riding Hugger (1979) and the limited-edition XR1000 (1983). The Sportster is also father to the remarkable XR750 dirt oval racer.

■ RIGHT *The Topper scooter was another of
Milwaukee's attempts to diversify. At best, these
achieved very limited success.*

■ GLIDING INTO THE 1960S

As the 1950s drew to a close, the HydraGlide
finally got the rear suspension it deserved and
the Model F DuoGlide was born in 1958. The
Duo featured a hydraulic rear brake as well as
handsome two-tone styling and a swinging-fork
rear end. However, this was something of an
indulgence as both wheels contained puny six-
inch drum brakes which struggled to slow down
the Glide's substantial bulk, whatever their
means of operation. The Duo is perhaps better
remembered for film stardom – Dennis Hopper
rode one in the cult movie *Easy Rider*.

With a new heavyweight on the block and
the Sportster selling moderately well, Harley-
Davidson renewed its attention to expanding its

market base. One of the more successful
measures was a move into glass-fibre moulding
– initially boats, but later golf carts and
motorcycle accessories. The main goal was still
a foothold in the global boom in motorcycle
sales. At the time, this meant lightweight
machines, a demand to which the existing two-
strokes were proving unequal. Sales of the ST

■ BELOW *Harley would
surely have done better
to concentrate on its
core business, big
V-twins, than on
other models.*

were roughly similar to those of the Sportster, yet profit margins were much lower. Juneau Avenue's Development Committee, responsible for future planning, decided that collaboration with an overseas company might be the most effective way forward.

Consequently, Harley became half-owner of the motorcycle division of Aermacchi, or Aeronautica Macchi SpA, for just under $250,000. Harley anticipated the partnership would generate sales of 6,000 lightweight bikes per year, to be produced in Varese, Italy.

The first Harley-Aermacchi appeared in September 1960, quickly announcing its pedigree with a 1-2-3 result at the Santa Fe AMA short track championship races. The 250 Sprint was based on a spine-framed, horizontal, single-cylinder, four-stroke design similar to that of the famous Aermacchi racers, although most subsequent "joint venture" models would be small two-strokes. The 250 was light, powerful (the company claimed 21 horsepower, growing to 25 by 1964), handled well and spawned a line of superb racing machines.

Yet the Sprint and its fellow Macchis – and indeed Milwaukee's home-grown lightweights – all failed to live up to Harley's commercial expectations, for a variety of reasons. Communications between the company's headquarters in the United States and Varese were often poor, causing continuous supply problems with bought-in components and

■ BELOW *ElectraGlide, possibly the most evocative badge in motorcycling.*

incompatibility with American parts. Later, after the AMF take-over of Harley-Davidson in 1969, specifications were often changed erratically, without appropriate consultation or repricing. Most of all, the products were not wanted by a public being offered Japanese machines of ever-more sophisticated specification at lower prices (Honda had entered the American market in 1959). Nor were they wanted by dealers who had to carry new parts stock, retrain staff and relearn their business – all for a much smaller profit margin.

There were high-points, though – not least Walter Villa's consecutive world 250cc road-race titles in 1974 and 1975. The four-strokes got into the act: Roger Reiman took a Sprint-powered streamliner to a new world 250cc speed record of 156mph (251.05kph) in 1964, improved to 177mph (284.85kph) in 1965.

It was an unrewarding marriage and divorce came too late.

In June 1978, Harley closed its Italian factory. Juneau Avenue would never again aspire to a true mass market.

THE AMF YEARS

In 1964, Harley-Davidson not only unveiled its first new corporate logo in almost 60 years but also the model bearing possibly the most evocative name in the company's long history: ElectraGlide. Yet it was the following year that would be remembered as the more momentous. According to Harley lore, 1965 represented two climactic events. The first was the unveiling of a new generation of Shovelhead engines, replacing the venerable Panheads. Second, and ultimately more far-reaching, was the decision to list the company on the New York Stock Exchange – after more than 60 years as a family firm, its founding families were now to lose complete control.

More than 1.3 million Harley shares were sold in the four years that followed the original listing. They performed well and investors – and straightforward enthusiasts – felt good. Optimism was short-lived once again, however, as imported Japanese motorcycles made ever-

increasing inroads in the American market. Initially, these machines were middleweights – light, fast, affordable and refined – but soon Honda would begin a full-frontal assault with the seminal four-cylinder CB750. The age of the high-performance "superbike" had arrived.

As Harley's fortunes ebbed and its shares dipped, it came under threat of takeover from an industrial conglomerate, Bangor Punta, which was busily accumulating Harley-Davidson stock. In 1968, fearful of the

■ ABOVE *Under AMF's ownership, sales improved but quality reputedly suffered, yet the Shovelhead soldiered on.*

■ LEFT *80-inch (1,340cc) versions of the Shovelhead first appeared in 1978, as with this FLH.*

sweeping changes proposed, company president William H. Davidson resumed talks with American Machine and Foundry (AMF).

AMF was another industrial giant with designs on Harley but with less of a predatory reputation (chairman Rodney C. Gott was a keen motorcyclist). Harley recommended AMF's offer to shareholders, most of whom did well out of the subsequent $21 million deal. So it was that on 18 December 1968, Harley-Davidson voted to merge with AMF, a move ratified by shareholders on 7 January 1969. Thus the American icon became AMF property, with Gott as chairman, although it wasn't until 1971 that the new owner's logo would be seen on Harley-Davidson machines.

Today, it is fashionable to believe that AMF starved and milked Milwaukee's finest, that it didn't understand motorcycles or motorcyclists, that quality went to the dogs and that Harley/AMF never built a decent bike. Some of this is probably true, but AMF did sink millions of dollars into its new project. During its first three years in control, total sales more than doubled and, during its 12 years at the helm, sales of American-made machines more than tripled. In addition, the company diversified into such unlikely fields as snowmobiles and desert racers. Sales were reasonably strong but profits, unfortunately, were not.

Difficult labour relations at Capitol Drive were another concern. As a consequence of the

■ **RIGHT** *The look was still there, as with this flathead, but quality was declining as Harley struggled to keep pace with a changing market.*

tension, the bulk of production was moved to a
vacant AMF plant in York, Pennsylvania
(where it remains to this day, although
Milwaukee has always made engines).

More exciting developments were afoot.
1970 brought a whole new kind of iron, the
FX1200 SuperGlide. This was the first of a
string of startling cosmetic innovations from the
fertile mind of William G. Davidson. Just as
crucial was AMF's marketing and promotion
expertise, which certainly rubbed off on the
future, independent Harley-Davidson company.

■ EXCITING IRON

If the 1970s was a commercially disastrous
decade for Harley-Davidson, the hardware it
produced at least paved the way for better
times to come. Nowhere was this more evident
than with the SuperGlide, the first major new
twin launched by Harley after the takeover by

■ ABOVE *"AMF" on
the tank was not well
received by many, but
others still considered
the ElectraGlide the
king of the road.*

■ LEFT *The King of
the Road title actually
referred to optional
touring accessories.
Bolt-on parts and other
"goodies" would
become huge business
in later years.*

■ ABOVE *A 1972 ElectraGlide: no other motorcycle could get away with a white leather seat.*

AMF. The SuperGlide's hybrid philosophy – a little bit from one model, some from another and more parts from a third – became the essence of all the most memorable Harleys produced since. Despite the splash it made at the time – most road tests praised the Super-Glide expansively – early examples were

distinctly under-specified for the new "superbike" age. Disc brakes arrived in 1973 and an electric start option, the FXE, in 1974.

By 1977, Willie G. launched another classic derivative: the FXS Low Rider, complete with standard highway pegs, Fat Bob two-piece petrol tank and a seat just 27in (685mm) above the ground. Later the same year, the XLCR Café Racer was launched. This sinister all-black device was too radical a statement to enjoy much sales success at the time, but is a highly-prized collector's piece today.

The range of options increased further with the introduction of the 80-inch (1,340cc) Shovelhead engine, initially on the Electra-Glide in 1978. This led to the FLH one year later, offered as standard with a complete set of touring extras, later to become the long-haul norm: saddlebags, luggage rack, fairing, running boards and additional lights. This in turn led to the FLT TourGlide of 1980, similar to the full-dress Glide but with better brakes and a larger, twin headlamp touring fairing. More significantly, the FLT featured Harley-Davidsons' first five-speed transmission and, not least, its first use of rubber-mounting to protect the rider from engine vibration.

■ RIGHT *Twin filler caps, tank-top speedometer and lashings of chrome: all Harley hallmarks.*

■ OPPOSITE *Willie G. Davidson (second left) pictured at Daytona with the Japanese-built Sundance racer.*

In fact, 1980 can be viewed as a vintage year all round. The Super Glide cruiser became the FXB Sturgis, named after the famous rally held annually in North Dakota. The "B" represented the first toothed-rubber belt drive – a clean, smooth and trouble-free system now standard across the range. For good measure, there was the FXWG Wide Glide and FXEF Fat Bob.

■ ABOVE *Willie G. Davidson's immortal "factory custom": the trend-setting SuperGlide.*

■ CHALLENGE FROM JAPAN

Nostalgia tells us that the 1970s produced a stream of classic Harley-Davidson models but, hardware aside, it was all an illusion. Even after shedding its Italian operation, the unpalatable truth was that, at the start of the 1980s, few people gave AMF Harley-Davidson very much chance of survival.

Who was to blame? It is tempting to point the finger at AMF, but whatever the company's shortcomings as custodians of the Milwaukee legend, Harley's biggest problem lay in a quite different direction. After all, it was scarcely AMF's fault that this period coincided so precisely with the rise to global domination of the Japanese motorcycle industry.

It is also a myth that Japan hijacked the American motorcycle market, either from Harley-Davidson or from the Europeans. Even after the British invasion of the mid-1950s, sales of new motorcycles in the United States stood at a paltry 60,000 units per year. By 1973, annual sales had soared to more than

■ BELOW *Another SuperGlide, this time fitted with optional pillion backrest.*

two million. This staggering increase was almost solely due to the inventiveness and enterprise of the Japanese, who produced reliable, fast and exciting machines far more advanced than any Harley, at a far lower price. Whatever "image" Harleys possessed was undersold, with few buyers prepared to pay the premium. The AMF years had seen turnover grow from $49 million to over $300 million but profits were going into reverse.

Milwaukee's response was to allege cut-price "dumping" of Japanese models, as with Triumph 20 years earlier. The American International Trade Commission agreed that dumping had taken place but that the effective subsidy was almost negligible. It concluded that the practice had not significantly harmed Milwaukee's sales and that the principal cause of Harley's difficulties was self-imposed: its model range was obsolete.

More than a decade earlier, William H. Davidson had remarked that AMF "thought Harley-Davidson could become another

■ BELOW *The American – or is it Harley? – Eagle, proudly displayed in the Visitor Center lobby at Wauwatosa.*

Honda. That's ridiculous... we were never meant to be a high production company."

AMF had to some extent attempted to compete head-on with Japan rather than concentrating on the more specialized market that Harley suited best. Production figures for 1982 offer some measure of the hopelessness of such a strategy: Honda built more than 3.5 million bikes in the year; Harley built less than 50 thousand.

The situation was desperate. Just six short years after 1973, Harley's share of the rapidly growing American big-bike market had plunged from almost 100 per cent to less than 40 per cent.

Production in the United States plummeted from 75,000 motorcycles in 1975 to 41,000 in 1981. Dire labour relations had brought a 101-day strike in 1974 over cost-of-living wage increases. Some in the company saw this coming, despite an artificial

■ BELOW *Another symphony in metal from Willie G., the XLCR Café Racer.*

boost in 1978 due to the company's 75th birthday celebrations. Vaughn Beals, company president since 1977, and chief engineer Jeff Bleustein alerted top managers to the unpalatable realities. Beals set up a quality control and inspection programme that began to eliminate the worst of the problems, but all these measures were at a prodigious cost.

New initiatives slowly began to put Harley-Davidson back on track. But what would be the first to give: the problem or the company?

"THE EAGLE FLIES ALONE"

The year 1981 brought what was probably the most momentous – and certainly the most audacious – episode in the long history of Harley-Davidson. With AMF losing interest and patience, chairman Vaughn Beals persuaded 12 other Harley executives to join him in an $81.5 million leveraged buyout from AMF control. The group included Charlie Thompson, appointed president the previous year, and Willie G. Davidson. A letter of intent was signed on 26 February and the bid went public five days later at Daytona Beach. The group found a willing lead lender in Citicorp Bank and after several months of tough bargaining with AMF, the newly-independent Harley-Davidson Motor Co. began business on 16 June 1981. The event, not surprisingly, was accompanied by widespread rejoicing and fanfares, under the slogan "The Eagle Flies

Alone" – including a symbolic ride-out by the new owners, from Milwaukee to York, as well as a solid gold dipstick for the first bike built under the new regime. Harley-Davidson was

■ ABOVE *There's no mistaking the American roots of this early Evo FLH model.*

■ LEFT *One of the very first Evo engines in one of the very first Softail models, pictured here.*

finally owned and run by real motorcyclists, men who loved the big V-twins, men who really cared. They were heady days, but the euphoria counted for nothing on its own. The American market, and Harley-Davidson's part in particular, was about to cave in even further. The buy-out did not enhance the buyers' fortunes as much as had been hoped – the newly-independent company's share of the shrinking American big-bike cake had dropped to a mere 23 per cent by 1983.

Ownership may have changed but one fundamental truth had not: Harley-Davidson's competitors were still producing better bikes at lower cost.

Over-staffing was part of the problem, and almost 200 clerical jobs went almost at once, but there was much more to it. Put bluntly, Harley's – indeed, much of America's – manufacturing culture was antique. Beals and other managers had toured Japanese plants in 1980 but it wasn't until after the buyout, when they were given the opportunity to inspect the Honda assembly plant in Marysville, Ohio, that they began to understand fully.

■ ABOVE *As quality suffered, many US police forces spurned Milwaukee machines.*

■ BELOW LEFT *To confirmed Harley aficionados, nothing beat customizing, whether of an old Panhead...*

■ BELOW RIGHT *...or perhaps something more recent... a Shovelhead.*

As chairman Vaughn Beals remarked: "We found it hard to believe we could be that bad – but we were. We were being wiped out by the Japanese because they were better managers. It wasn't robotics, or culture, or morning callisthenics and company songs – it was professional managers who understood their business and paid attention to detail."

Beal's message wasn't lost on the new team. With help from industrial fixers Andersen Consulting, within four months pilot programmes for "just-in-time" statistical process control (Harley called this "MAN" – Materials As Needed) and other up-to-date production systems were initiated and staff levels were slashed from 3,800 to 2,200. Tom

Gelb, in charge of production, explained the situation to Harley-Davidson staff as directly as possible: "We have to play the game the way the Japanese play it or we're dead."

Quality and efficiency was one thing, getting the message across to potential customers quite another. The company shifted its marketing focus, stopped trying to compete against Japanese mainstream motorcycles and threw all of its resources into developing what we now take for granted as its uniquely American big-bike niche. (Along the way, a little-known project inherited from AMF for an overhead camshaft V-four was quietly dropped after several working prototypes were produced.) Was it too little, too late? Despite new models such as the five-speed FXR SuperGlide II and a new Sportster, the lone-flying eagle reported a loss of $25 million in 1982. It was going to be a close-run thing.

■ **THE PRESIDENT STEPS IN**
In August 1982, another Harley delegation made the trip to Washington, again alleging illegal trading practices by Japanese motorcycle companies. Yet again, the ITC was told that cheap motorcycles were being illegally dumped on the market and that the Japanese were "virtually copying" Harley models, all of which was seriously undermining their sales. This time Harley had a case, as

■ ABOVE LEFT *AMF did not realise how lucrative Harley lifestyle and hardware were to be in the future.*

■ ABOVE RIGHT *The Evolution engine, as in this 95th Anniversary 'Glide transformed Harley's fortunes.*

■ BELOW *Meanwhile, loading the heavyweights with goodies opened up a whole new field of Harley machines.*

massive over-supply in declining markets meant that many machines were sold at a loss. As Vaughn Beals put it, "We simply want the US government to restore order to a motorcycle market under siege by Japanese manufacturers who increased production in the face of sharp market decline."

As if to highlight the problem, the local Wisconsin police force bought Kawasaki motorcycles rather than Harleys, prompting a mass ride-out in protest from Capitol Drive.

The Commission duly found in Milwaukee's favour and recommended as much to President Ronald Reagan. On All Fools Day 1983, the White House confirmed that import tariffs were to be imposed on Japanese machines. The tariffs would apply to all imported models of

more than 700cc, at the hefty rate of 45 per cent (in addition to the existing 4.4 per cent duty), decreasing year-by-year to 35, 20, 15 and 10 per cent until April 1988.

Although Japanese machines built in the United States, such as Honda Gold Wings, were exempt, the levy was inevitably a major asset to Harley-Davidson's regeneration. In the meantime, they had to continue to improve quality and efficiency. Perhaps most crucial of all, a credible replacement for the aged Shovelhead was long overdue. Short-term fixes such as the digital ignition introduced on the new FXRT in 1983 were no longer enough.

Harley threw $3 million into a "Super Ride" demonstration programme in 1984, to show that the company had solved its notorious quality-control problems. TV commercials invited bikers to visit any of its 600-plus dealers to road test a new Harley. Over three weekends, the company gave 90,000 rides to 40,000 people, half of whom owned other brands. At first, the venture didn't sell enough bikes to cover its cost, but it made the point.

Then there was HOG – the Harley Owners' Group. This was a major corporate effort to bring customers together in the Harley-Davidson lifestyle. Nothing so ambitious had ever been attempted by any motorcycle manufacturer, yet HOG proved uniquely suited to the Harley image. A runaway success, HOG now boasts almost half a million committed members worldwide and is a model for similar schemes by other motorcycle manufacturers.

The company also began to defend its name, copyrights and trademarks for the first time,

■ LEFT *The "CowGlide", Heritage Softail Nostalgia, coolest of all the Softails...*

■ ABOVE RIGHT *...although even this wasn't radical enough for some owners, as shown by this Springer Softail.*

■ BELOW *Meanwhile, out on the open highway, Milwaukee's long-legged punch counts for more than mere paint.*

and vigorously. In future, if anyone wanted a Harley-Davidson logo, Milwaukee would demand its rightful royalties. Over half a century after pioneering the sale of branded accessories, Harley was at last determined to cash in on the image it had taken eight decades to create. Slowly, Vaughn Beals and his team began to turn the near-disaster around. Thanks to improvements in quality and efficiency, and more aggressive marketing, Harley began steadily to catch up with mighty Honda in the heavyweight division.

At last, this very American company was beginning to make the most of its uniquely American image. 1982's loss became a small surplus in 1983.

A year later, in 1984, Harley reported a profit of $2.9 million on sales of $294 million. Even though there was still a very long way to go, the eagle was on its way.

EVOLUTION

The anxiously-awaited replacement for the Shovelhead finally arrived in 1984 – and Harley-Davidson's future balanced precariously on a knife's edge. The V2 Evolution engine certainly looked like the answer to everyone's prayers. Despite a bottom-end with origins dating back to the 61E of 1936, it was an altogether better powerplant than the Shovelhead it replaced.

As the name suggests, the "Evo" is a development of the Shovel rather than a totally new design, yet almost every component was different and improved. Its cylinders, splayed at the "classic" 45 degrees, displace 81.8cu in or 1,340cc (although badges round this down to 80in). Scaling 20lbs (9kgs) less but producing 15 per cent more torque than its predecessor, the Evo would prove to be all it was cracked up to be.

In 1983, Harley-Davidson made sure its new baby created an impact with a publicity stunt to mark the company's 80th birthday celebrations: 8,000 miles (12,875

km) at an average of 80mph (128.7kph) with none of the routine servicing a customer's machine would receive on standard FLT Tour Glides. At Talladega Speedway in July 1983, the Evolution-engined TourGlides thundered through the designated 8,000 miles, but slightly off the scheduled pace: allowing for mishaps that never occurred, they averaged 85mph (136.8kph).

A brand-new engine was cause enough for celebration (helped perhaps by the new H-D brand beer), but the first model powered by the Evo engine was a landmark in its own right. This was the 1984 FXST Softail, and with it came a whole new concept in motorcycle style and design. With its fake "hardtail" rear end, gleaming chrome and low, rounded lines, the Softail was a

■ ABOVE *Cruisin' through town can just look so cool.*

■ BELOW *Retro-Tech: the hardtail look of this Heritage Softail is clear. The system uses twin shock absorbers hidden beneath the engine.*

■ BELOW *The Springer Softail adopts a girder-style front end.*

strident echo of motorcycles of the 1950s: the age of Retro-Tech had dawned. Sportsters still cut a dash, especially with the launching of the new XR750-inspired XR1000. A year later, the Heritage Softail followed the basic FXST.

Almost overnight – or so it seemed – Harley-Davidson had a credible range and, after the gremlins of the Shovelhead years, a reputation for the dependability that had once been its hallmark. Again it had a product capable of meeting the demands of the California Highway Patrol (CHiPs) who, after a decade mounted on Kawasakis and Moto Guzzis, in 1984 ordered 155 FXRP Police Specials.

To Harley insiders, however, the "Evo year" was probably far more memorable for the financial strife which continued to undermine them. In 1984, Citicorp Bank, underwriter of the original buy-out, was becoming concerned that Harley's future might not be so rosy once the tariff on foreign competitors ended in 1988. Reasoning that the best time to get a good price for the company was when sales were still on the rise, they moved quickly, hitting Harley's directors with the bombshell: all credit facilities would be severely restricted from the following year.

This was a major blow to Harley's ambitious plans and the survival of the entire buy-out. Harley-Davidson was broke.

■ ABOVE *"Basic" Softails retain telescopic front forks.*

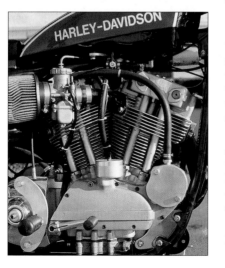

■ RIGHT *At the opposite extreme is this road-registered XR750 racer, as used in US dirt-track competition.*

■ LEFT *ElectraGlides and TourGlides evolved ever-more luxury features such as cruise control, CB radio and intercoms.*

■ **TURNING BACK THE TIDE**
"Hawking begging bowls around Wall Street" was how Vaughn Beals described his desperate response. Over the summer of 1985, Beals and chief financial officer Richard Teerlink (later to succeed Beals as H-D's head), chased in vain after new lenders. Then, with the situation looking hopeless and lawyers drafting bankruptcy plans, Dean Witter Reynolds put Beals and Teerlink in touch with the Heller Financial Corporation. Luckily for Beals, Heller's second-in-command, Bob Koe, was a long-time Harley buff and willing to listen. He was impressed by what he heard, and on 23 December 1985 a financial package was agreed – the best Christmas present for which Harley could have wished.

The rescue package turned out to be a good deal for everyone but Citicorp, who had badly underestimated the outlook for this vibrant new Harley-D. Including credits, the bank received $49 million for the deal, $2 million less than it had poured in. Harley received $49.5 million of working capital. In a supreme irony, Harley recovered the Number One spot from Honda a year after being abandoned by Citicorp, with 33 per cent of the over-850cc American market. The long struggle to improve production

■ LEFT *Detail of the striking Ultra Classic ElectraGlide.*

■ BELOW *In stark contrast was the Sportster series, of which this 1984 XR-1000 is surely the best looking and most prized.*

■ ABOVE *In Europe, as well as the United States, Evo Harley sales began to boom. This Heritage Softail Classic thunders across the Belgian Ardennes.*

and marketing, and regenerate the model range was beginning to pay dividends. 1986 profits were $4.3 million on sales of $295 million.

Harley's financial base was secured in June 1987 by floating the company on the New York Stock Exchange. The offer raised more than £30 million, allowing the company to reschedule its debts and buy the Holiday Rambler Corporation, a leading manufacturer of recreational vehicles. In October, the manufacturing rights to the military MT500 motorcycle were acquired from the British

Armstrong company. Less comforting was the closure of the competition department, though it made sound financial sense. Production of XR750 dirt-track engines was unaffected, and racing continued in the famous livery through independent dealer teams.

The most impressive news of all came on 17 March. In what turned out to be a public-relations triumph, Harley had taken the unprecedented step of asking that trade protection be removed a year ahead of schedule. As Vaughn Beals explained at the time, Harley-Davidson "no longer need tariff relief to compete with the Japanese". The chairman highlighted "the strong message… to the international community: US workers… can become competitive in world markets." Harley was again "the pride of America".

This was brought home best of all by President Ronald Reagan. After touring the York factory in Pennsylvania in May 1987, he

■ RIGHT *In places such as Florida's Daytona Beach, Harleys inspire crowds of fans of American iron. Fittingly, this is the famous Iron Horse Saloon.*

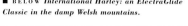

hailed the turnaround in Harley-Davidson's fortunes as "an American success story". And how right he was.

A major contribution to future success was tied up with the XLH 883 Sportster. With a price tag of just under $4,000 when introduced, the 883 was the type of entry-level machine so conspicuously absent from the Milwaukee stable in the past. In 1987, 883 owners got an even better deal with the announcement of Harley's innovative buy-back scheme: "Trade in your XLH against an FX or FL within two years and we'll guarantee $3,995 on your old machine."

Major new models included the stunning Heritage Softail Classic, ElectraGlide Sport and Low Rider Custom. By the end of 1987, Harley had 47 per cent of the American "super-heavyweight" market, a figure which would rise to 54 per cent just one year later. At last, Harley-Davidson was on its way.

■ SPRINGING AHEAD

1988 saw the debut of the largest-capacity Sportster ever – the 1100 grew to the full 1200cc of the XLH 1200. 1988 also brought a revamped FXRS Low Rider with improved forks and twin-cap Fat Bob fuel tank. Most striking of all was the model chosen to mark

H-D's 85th birthday, the FXTS Springer Softail. The Springer was a radical step both forward and back. Looking like a 1950 classic, it dispensed with the telescopic front end in favour of gleaming, chromed, lookalike girders. For the first time, a Harley had Retro-Tech at both ends and, almost overnight, became the style king of the Milwaukee range.

Within a year, the Springer and new Low Rider were joined by "Ultra Classic" versions of the all-conquering TourGlide and Electra-Glide models. These luxurious machines came equipped with a host of extras as standard, including cruise control, cigar lighter, intercom, CB radio and a sophisticated stereo hi-fi system. These were, and remain, the best-equipped and most expensive models in the Harley-Davidson range.

Ironically, as standard equipment became even more comprehensive, there was counter demand for a model more like the stripped-down Glides of the 1970s, such as the handsome FLHS ElectraGlide Sport introduced two years earlier. The FLHR Road King of today is in much the same mould as its handsome predecessor.

In 1989, a revamped clothing division – "MotorClothes" – was launched. MotorClothes, allied with Harley-Davidson's flourishing aftermarket hardware accessories, accounts for a substantial portion of overall annual profits. It is now possible to buy anything from bowie knives to toiletries bearing the celebrated H-D motif. Since the early 1990s there have been "Harley" shops that sell no motorcycles at all. The company's image had been transformed from a sick joke to the height of fashion.

With this priceless image came a turnaround in overall fortunes, from near-broke leviathan to glorious sales success. The foundations were varied: much-improved manufacturing of a broader, better model range allied to shrewd financial management, as well as inspired marketing. Production methods had witnessed a revolution, with each worker both a vital part

■ BELOW *During the 1990s' DynaGlides evolved from Low Riders to become one of the core elements of the Milwaukee line-up.*

of the quality-control process and a partner in Harley-Davidson's affairs. The Evolution engine earned a deserved reputation for rugged durability, oil-tightness and general user-friendliness.

Not least was Harley-Davidson's good fortune in being located in the world's largest market for big-inch touring machines.

■ ABOVE *The moody Road King was a stylish attempt to return to the leaner, cleaner lines of the earliest ElectraGlides.*

■ INTO THE 1990S

By the early 1990s, the tide had well and truly turned – indeed the boot was on the other foot. Annual production had reached more than 62,000 units, with 20 models accounting for 61 per cent of the American heavyweight market and more than 30 per cent of output exported to Milwaukee fans worldwide, double the figure of four years earlier. At the same time, sales of Japanese motorcycles were in steep decline, their dealers cutting margins or going out of business altogether.

New hardware continued to stream out of York. Many Harley fans rate the star of the 1990 catalogue as one of the most beautiful Harley-Davidsons ever created. "Fat Boy" was its unprepossessing title, yet the original FLSTF was an understated symphony in silver-grey. Later versions, in less restrained colours, never quite had the same class. The FXDB DynaGlide Sturgis, a mean and moody all-black cruiser unveiled for 1991, was the first of a new generation, and classy to boot.

If Milwaukee had any problems during the 1990s, one was encroaching noise and emissions regulations; the other the sheer difficulty of meeting soaring demand as

■ BELOW *By the mid-1990s, top of the range Glides had added fuel injection to their extensive repertoire of "goodies".*

customers waited up to a year for their new dream machines. A major victory for environmental concerns was the first fuel-injected Harley roadster, the FLHTC-I Ultra Classic ElectraGlide, in 1985. Injection made the twin smoother, cleaner and more powerful than any previous Harley-Davidson.

Then came the Twin Cam 88 powerplant for 1999, which promised to take the same qualities even further. After four years and more than 2.5 million test miles (4 million km) under development, Harley-Davidson's new Twin Cam offers new levels of performance, reliability and durability.

Solving the supply problem involved a whirlwind programme of capital investment, culminating in the opening in 1998 of an $85 million Sportster plant at Kansas City. The spending began with the opening of a huge new automated paint plant at York in 1992. This $23 million facility finally broke York's crippling production bottleneck, taking manufacturing capacity beyond 110,000 machines per year.

■ RIGHT For 1999, 15 years after the arrival of the redoubtable Evo, a new generation of Twin Cam 88 big twins hit the Harley scene.

■ BELOW The Deuce, introduced for the year 2000, sports the latest balance-shafted Twin Cam 88B engine.

Accompanying this has been a hard-nosed commercial edge which began with the defence of trademarks – even including attempts to copyright the "Harley sound". To many die-hard fans, Harley's corporate clout sits uneasily alongside the image of easy-going, down-home virtues the company is at pains to present. Some might even prefer the mom-and-pop-corner-shop image of decades before – the one that almost went bust.

New Harleys might be objects of desire, but they are conceived and developed in an environment as implacably space-age as the bikes themselves are defiantly old-fashioned. The Willie G. Davidson Product Development Center was completed in 1997, at a cost of $40 million. Standing just a stone's throw from the existing Capitol Drive engine factory, it boasts a floor area of 213,000sq ft (20,000sq metres) under a graceful arc of concrete and glass, a structure befitting 21st-century ambitions. A new Big Twin powerline plant was also opened in 1997, located at nearby Menomonee Falls. Buell, now half-owned by Harley, assembles motorcycles in nearby East Troy, Wisconsin.

Harley-Davidson hasn't witnessed expansion like this since the years either side of the First World War. In fact, 1998 marked the thirteenth consecutive year in which Harley-Davidson had achieved record earnings. Sales topped $2,000 million for the first time, with output totalling 150,818 machines.

Thanks largely to the impetus provided by Kansas, production capacity is planned to reach 200,000 units.

For Harley-Davidson, the future of motorcycling at Milwaukee is looking good.

Faces and Places

Harley-Davidson was founded on friendships, family and youthful enthusiasm. The single Harley (William S.) and the three Davidson brothers (Arthur, Walter and William) were practical men who would transform some garden shed engineering into an enduring motorcycle legend.

Although it is now more than 30 years since Harley-Davidson ceased to be a family company, it's a matter of pride to both the company itself and to its followers that at least one founder's name remains on the payroll. Willie G. Davidson is, of course, the man. As much as any other individual, his flair for expressing Harley-Davidson traditions in new and dramatic ways has been at the root of the success of the company his grandfather helped found.

The factories in which Harley dream-machines are now designed and built are a long way from the little wooden shed that was used in the early years. However, even though the Harley factories of today may in no way resemble the Harley factories of yesterday, the company has remained true to the ideal of building the ultimate motorcycle.

THE FOUNDERS

■ WILLIAM S. HARLEY

"Young Bill" began work at the age of 15 in a Milwaukee bicycle factory, and even as an enthusiastic dabbler soon showed engineering skills. As able in the saddle as he was in the workshop, he later became Harley-Davidson's chief engineer and treasurer, positions he held until his death from heart failure on 18 September 1943.

On graduating from university in 1908, he had set about designing Harley's first successful V-twin, which appeared the following year, although it was 1911 before the design became as dependable as earlier singles.

Bill was later responsible for a host of classic Harleys, not to mention the first clutch, kick start and many other developments. In 1914, he established the factory's race shop, which scored 26 major wins in its first season. During both world wars, his contacts with the military were vital to the company's (and the nation's) success. Active in the governing body of American bike racing, the American Motorcycle Association (AMA), he was also a keen wildlife photographer in private life.

■ ARTHUR DAVIDSON

A pattern-maker by trade, Arthur had the reputation of being the most outgoing of the founders, his energetic temperament making him particularly suited to sales. Arthur became the company's secretary and general sales manager, roles he discharged with distinction until his death in a car accident on 30 December 1950, at the age of 69. His own son, James, and James' wife, were also to die in a road accident 16 years later.

Perhaps Arthur's most lasting legacy was the establishment of Harley-Davidson's nationwide and international dealer networks. Beginning

in 1910, he had no fewer than 200 American outlets by 1912, later expanding to include official Harley-Davidson dealerships as far away as Australia and New Zealand. In the early years he practically ran the AMA "because there was no-one else around". After the Second World War, he spent an increasing amount of time at his farm in Waukesha County where he raised prize-winning Guernsey cattle.

■ WALTER S. DAVIDSON

Trained as a mechanic and machinist, Walter was a naturally gifted rider who brought the emergent Harley-Davidson company its first competition success. In June 1908, he entered a Harley-Davidson single in a two-day endurance run in New York's Catskill Mountains. The sole Harley in a field of 61, he scored a "perfect" 1,000 points, outstripping all of the preferred bikes. One month later, Walter was at it again, winning a Long Island economy run at no less than 188mpg (66km/litre) over 50 miles (80.5 kilometres).

Walter is best remembered, however, as Harley-Davidson's first president. Generous and scrupulously honest, he also became a

■ ABOVE *The founders, left to right: William A. Davidson, Walter Davidson, Arthur Davidson and William S. Harley.*

■ RIGHT *Harley-Davidson's first "factory", a 15 x 10ft wooden shed.*

■ RIGHT *Harley-Davidson's first "factory", a 15 x 10ft wooden shed.*

director of First Wisconsin, the state's biggest bank. Walter died on 7 February 1942, still in charge at Juneau Avenue.

■ WILLIAM A. DAVIDSON

If Walter was the head of the company, "Old Bill" Davidson was regarded as its heart and driving force. Perhaps the least able rider of the foursome, Bill quickly found his niche as works manager, a vital position in a company expanding as quickly as Harley-Davidson. A big, burly character equally at home hunting and fishing as on the factory floor, he had a generous but paternalistic attitude to Harley's employees. Despite his bitter opposition, the factory first became unionized in April 1937. Within two years, Old Bill was gone, the victim of diabetic complications and the first of the founders to die. His son, William H., believed the stress of losing the battle to the unions hastened his father's death.

■ SECOND GENERATION

In the late 1920s, the founders' sons began to join the company. William H. Davidson joined in 1928, although he had worked on the shop floor while a student at the University of Wisconsin. A year later, he was joined by Gordon and Walter C. (both sons of Walter S.)

■ RIGHT *The famous Juneau Road factory, which was a large step up from the wooden shed.*

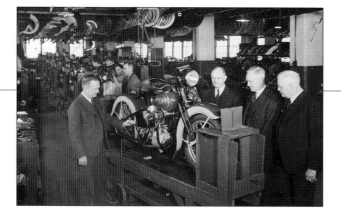

Davidson, William J. Harley and, later, John E.
Harley. Of the other sons, Allan Davidson, son
of William A., worked only briefly for the
company and died young; Arthur Davidson Jr.
made a successful business career in his own
right. Four of these "first generation founders"
were to make major contributions to the
American icon the company would become.

William J. Harley succeeded his father as
the company's chief engineer. He became vice
president in charge of engineering in 1957, a
position he held until his death in 1971. A
connoisseur of fine wines and cheeses, he
evidently needed little encouragement to visit
the Harley-Davidson factory in Varese, Italy,
after the take-over of Aermacchi.

John E. Harley, younger brother to
William J., was elected to the board in 1949
and ran the Harley parts and accessories
business, today one of Milwaukee's major profit
centres. He rose to the rank of major during the
Second World War, including a spell
instructing army motorcyclists.

Walter C. Davidson ultimately followed his
uncle Arthur as vice president of sales, earning
a reputation during the Second World War as
the man who could somehow get materials
other companies could not. After the war, he
fought Harley's increasingly rebellious dealer
network, as Triumph and BSA in particular
began offering cheaper and faster products in
the American market. Harley's efforts to hold

■ ABOVE *The Founders
inspect the first
Knucklehead to roll off
the Juneau Avenue
production line for the
1936 model year.*

the fort not only backfired at the time but were
to lead to legislation which would later open
the door for the Japanese. When AMF took
over the company in 1968, Walter saw the
writing on the wall and took early retirement.

William H. Davidson, the son of William
A., made the most lasting mark of all. A skilled
rider (he won the prestigious Jack Pine Enduro
in 1930 riding a Model 30DLD), he was later
described as "the mortar that cemented the
company". He joined Harley-Davidson full-
time in 1928, was elected to the board in 1931
and became vice president six years later. For
the next five years, he was the driving force
behind Harley-Davidson's vital government
contract work. When Walter S. died, William
H. was the obvious candidate to lead the
company, becoming president "by common
consent" 16 days later, on 23 February 1942.

William H. had no doubts about where the
company's future lay: "We tried for a long time
to convince people that motorcycles had some

■ RIGHT *During the
Second World War John
E. Harley, younger
brother of William J.,
was responsible for
training army
motorcyclists on
bikes such as the
one pictured.*

■ LEFT *The famous "Silent Gray Fellow" of 1914.*

■ RIGHT *The 2000 Harley model: the Deuce.*

utility value," he once presciently observed, "[but they] have never been anything but pleasure." In 1971, three years after the AMF takeover, he was appointed chairman of Harley-Davidson, but felt that the new company had "pulled my teeth" and soon resigned. Nor did he fully share AMF's ambitions, observing with typical foresight that AMF "thought Harley-Davidson could become another Honda. That's ridiculous... we were never meant to be a high production company."

■ WILLIE G. DAVIDSON

Willie G. is a remarkable man from a family of remarkable men. Yet it's perhaps surprising that he began his working life not with Harley-Davidson, but cutting his teeth with Ford and Excalibur cars. By the time he joined his grandpa's company in 1963, he had a broad schooling in industrial design – although he had also found time to design a new Harley-Davidson tank logo in 1957. He has spent most of the intervening years as vice president of styling – arguably the single most important role in such an image-conscious company. In another quirk of fate in which Harley seems to specialize, the model that made Willie G.'s name, the FX Super Glide of 1971, was the first major new model produced by the much-maligned AMF. A decade later, he was one of the prime movers of the buy-out from AMF orchestrated by chairman Vaughn Beals.

AMF's hold on Harley-Davidson may not have lasted but Willie G.'s has. During the week, his domain is the Willie G. Davidson Product Development Center, a space-age structure of steel and glass tucked behind the Sportster Engine Plant on Wauwatosa's Capitol Drive. Yet to the biking world he's the man in the trade-mark black beret at gatherings such as Sturgis and Daytona Bike Week, ogling hardware just like any other Harley fan.

Willie G. has an uncommonly successful stylist's touch, yet he also has the common touch. To many he *is* Harley Davidson, and when he finally hangs up his leathers, there are two Davidsons waiting in the wings. Son Bill, who joined the firm in 1984, runs HOG, while daughter Karen runs the MotorClothes division. Harley-Davidson is truly a family affair.

■ BELOW *Willie G. Davidson, grandson of the founder, and a great guiding spirit of Harley.*

HARLEY-DAVIDSON FACTORIES

William S. Harley and the Davidson brothers first went into production in 1904 in a shed hastily thrown up in the Davidson backyard, bearing the grand legend "Harley Davidson Motor Co." on its humble wooden door. These days, the location of the famous shed, 38th and Highland Boulevard, is owned by a company producing something else for which Milwaukee is famous – the huge Miller Brewing Company.

■ JUNEAU AVENUE

The founders took on their first employee in 1905, and moved into their first building on the present Juneau Avenue site twelve months later (although the road was then called Chestnut Street). In that year another five workers joined the Harley bandwagon as production soared to 50 motorcycles. Progress was relentless – and punishing. Walter Davidson later described how "we worked

■ ABOVE *3700 Juneau Avenue, possibly the most famous address in motorcycling.*

■ LEFT *Like it says, "motorcycles only".*

■ ABOVE *On Juneau Avenue, even the water is branded Harley-Davidson.*

■ LEFT *Now more than 80 years old, the former main factory is a protected historical site.*

■ LEFT AND BELOW *The Juneau Avenue factory now houses only management and administrative personnel, but echoes to almost a century of Harley's history.*

every day Sunday included, until at least 10:00. I remember it was an event when we quit work on Christmas night at 8:00 to attend a family reunion."

So it continued: 1907 – around 150 machines built, including the first police Harleys; 1908 – 18 employees and production tripled again to 450 units. By this time, manufacturing was in Harley-Davidson's first brick building, with a floor area of 2,380sq ft (220sq metres).

Such was the pressure to grow and get new bikes through the door that workers recall "putting machinery in place and starting production before the cement was dry". From 1907 to 1914, the Harley facility at least doubled in size every single year. At the outbreak of war in Europe, 1,574 employees built more than 16,000 machines in a factory of almost 300,000sq ft (28,000sq metres). With no exaggeration, the Milwaukee Journal described the company's breakneck progress as a "modern miracle".

Wartime pressure for space became so intense that the company once threw up a 2,400sq ft (220sq metre) brick building, only to tear it down and build something even bigger six months later. Buildings were leased on a temporary basis all over Milwaukee. Even Prohibition came to the company's aid, in a

manner far more benign than Al Capone's. When breweries became idle, Harley-Davidson stepped in to rent the Pabst Brewing Company as storage space for Harley parts.

The post-war boom helped Harley-Davidson become, briefly at least, the largest motorcycle manufacturer in the world, pumping machines out of its huge, six-storey plant on Juneau Avenue, offering more than half a million square feet (50,000sq metres) of floor space on its completion in April 1919. The distinction

■ BELOW *The Harley "bar and shield" is as recognizable in Morocco as here in Milwaukee.*

■ LEFT AND RIGHT
*High-tech computerized
machining is now part
of the Harley way (left),
but testing (right) is still
hands-on. And could
this man work for
anyone else?*

been no manufacturing at Harley's most
evocative address: 3700 West Juneau Avenue,
Milwaukee. Instead, the old site – and the
grand old building – houses H-D's corporate
headquarters and training departments.

lasted only until the Depression of 1920, when
annual sales collapsed from more than 28,000
to just 10,202. America's economy recovered
from this slump but motorcycle sales somehow
did not. It was 1942 before Harley sales again
exceeded 1920 levels. Under these
circumstances, the last thing Milwaukee
needed was more plant. Since its conversion to
offices and warehousing in 1973, there has

■ BELOW LEFT
*Sportster engines
awaiting shipment from
Capitol Drive to Kansas.*

■ BELOW RIGHT
*Heavyweight engines are
now made at Pilgrim
Road before shipment
to York for their
final assembly.*

■ CAPITOL DRIVE
No sooner had Harley sales begun to recover
from the Depression of the 1930s (sales slid to
a pitiful 3,703 bikes in 1933) than Pearl
Harbor was bombed and the United States
entered the war. Towards the end of the 1940s,
the company was looking to expand again as
markets recovered. At the end of 1948, Harley
moved into its first new address for 42 years, in
the Milwaukee suburb of Wauwatosa.

■ RIGHT *For finishing
items such as
mudguards, no machine
can match a craftsman,
as here at the factory in
York, Pennsylvania.*

Thus, Capitol Drive, a single-story building
of more than 260,000sq ft (24,000sq metres)
which had previously housed the A. O. Smith
propeller plant, became Harley-Davidson's
second manufacturing centre. In anticipation of
a boom in post-war demand for motorcycles
(and the opposite for aircraft propellers), the
factory had been bought for $1.5 million two
years earlier. Harley dealers – introduced to

the new facility in a night-time "mystery tour"
– weren't the only ones impressed.

Within a year, production was at an all-time
high, although tougher times lay ahead. Also,
less auspiciously (for V-twin die-hards, at
least), November 1947 marked the debut of the
1.7 horsepower Model S 125cc single – a two-
stroke Harley, heaven forbid. This was based
on the same German DKW RT125 design as
the BSA Bantam (and later Yamaha's very first
model, the YA1 "Red Dragonfly") – and not
least on the expectation that demobbed GI's
would buy almost anything with wheels.

It was to be decades before the potential of
Capitol Drive was fully realized, however. From
today's viewpoint, it's difficult to envisage the
trials cash-starved Harley-Davidson faced after
that first burst of post-war optimism. During
the 1950s, Harley sales were totally
outstripped by British imports. From 31,000
units in 1948, sales never exceeded 17,250

■ RIGHT *Capitol Drive,
home of Sportster
engines and the official
Harley Visitor Center.*

■ ABOVE *"Heavy powertrains" – Evo engines – awaiting shipment to York.*

again until 1965 – and for most of that time they were nearer 12,000. Paradoxically, matters only began to improve when the mass arrival of Japanese motorcycles stimulated wider interest in two-wheelers. Sales averaged around 30,000 for the remainder of the 1960s, rising to 70,000 by the mid-1970s.

This latter upturn in sales was due largely to AMF's heavy investment in manufacturing space, much of which is still in use today. The biggest single purchase was a $4.5 million

monster for machining five-speed cases. Prior to this, Juneau Avenue had been a model of inefficiency, with part-assembled machines wheeled about and moved from shop to shop in lifts. Engine assembly moved from Juneau Avenue to Capitol Drive in 1971, although Harley-Davidson headquarters continued to undertake engine painting and the assembly of XR race engines for some years, the last actual manufacturing at the original site.

The addition of a modern facade means the Capitol Drive site no longer looks like a war-time propeller plant, but behind the facade the old factory now makes "small powertrains" for final assembly at Buell and the new Sportster plant in Kansas City. The facility also houses Harley's official Visitor Center, as well as a new customer engine reconditioning plant which is quite unique among volume motorcycle manufacturers.

■ RIGHT *Chrome and glass: a Springer guards The Willie G. Davidson Product Development Center (PDC), where the dreams of the future are generated.*

■ RIGHT *The PDC is located to the rear of the "small powertrains" plant on Capitol Drive.*

■ VARESE

With the exception of the original wooden sheds, Harley-Davidson has never abandoned one of its permanent sites on American soil. Overseas, however, it is a different story.

Milwaukee's Italian connection arose out of a desire to diversify into smaller, cheaper models, in order to hoist itself out of the financial mire of the 1950s. In 1960, Harley bought half of Aermacchi's two-wheeler division, based in Varese, Italy. The purchase was seen as a more sensible means of expanding the Harley-Davidson range than actually trying to develop new, cheaper models

from scratch. In September 1960, the first Italian Harley emerged. This was the 250cc four-stroke Sprint, although two-strokes later predominated. (Although a stinkwheel Harley may sound like an offence against nature, lightweight two-strokes were produced in Milwaukee from 1947 until 1965.)

The joint venture didn't quite work out as hoped, but it did give Milwaukee its first and only world road race titles, with Walter Villa taking three 250cc and one 350cc crowns between 1974 and 1976, all on two-stroke twins. Roadster production was dogged by such absurdities as fitting American-made cables and controls to bikes built in Italy (where they made such things quite well).

Fundamentally, however, Varese couldn't compete with Japan. In June 1978, John A Davidson announced the closure of the project. The factory was bought by Cagiva which was producing 40,000 machines per year within less than three years.

■ YORK

In 1972, AMF's massive plant in York, Pennsylvania, lay almost idle. This coincided, after two decades in the doldrums, with Harley-Davidson's dire need for more manufacturing capacity and, not least, with one of

■ BELOW *Many Harley employees favour motorcycles, but winter in Milwaukee is no place to be riding them.*

■ RIGHT *"The Tool",
a 70 year-old monster
which presses fuel
tanks at York.*

Milwaukee's periodic upsurges in union
militancy. York was refurbished and motorcycle
final assembly took over. The first "York"
Harley rolled off the lines in February 1973.
Capitol Drive would now build only engines
and transmissions. York remains Harley's
largest production facility, although production
is less diverse than it once was. After buy-out,
York continued to manufacture military

■ BELOW *Capitol Drive
now reconditions
customer engines.*

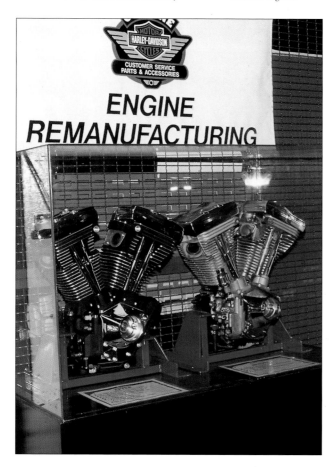

hardware – the casings on some of the bombs
dropped over Iraq during the Gulf War were
made at York – as well as IBM circuit boards.
These peripheral activities have now ceased.

In common with the rest of the company, the
plant at York has received massive investment
in recent years – not the least of which was a
new paint shop to unplug what was once the
biggest production bottleneck.

With the transfer of Sportster production to
Kansas, York now concentrates on building Big
Twins on four lines – three for customs and one
for heavyweight tourers

■ **TOMAHAWK, WISCONSIN**
About 250 miles (402 km) north-west
of Milwaukee lies the old Tomahawk boat
company plant, of which Harley-Davidson
bought a 60 per cent share in 1962. The
35,000sq ft (3,250sq metre) plant was
purchased principally to make Servi-Car
three-wheeler and golf-cart bodies (for which
Harley-Davidson once controlled a third of the
American market). It has since specialized
in the manufacture of fairings, saddlebags,
windshields and sidecars.

Like pretty much everywhere else in the
Harley-Davidson empire, Tomahawk was

■ RIGHT *This plant on Pilgrim Road, Menomonee Falls was once the home of Briggs and Stratton engines, but has produced Harley "heavy powertrains" since 1997.*

recently expanded after an extension of 14,250sq ft (1,300sq metres) was completed in 1997.

■ KANSAS CITY, MISSOURI

The brand-new $85 million plant in Kansas City is the jewel in Harley's manufacturing crown. The first machines rolled off the line at the 330,000sq ft (30,000sq metre) factory in 1998. Kansas builds all Sportster models.

Kansas is the nearest Hog-building comes to state-of-the art. Expressions like "evolutionary turning point" and "ergonomically-friendly production lines" roll off corporate tongues as easily as "unique labour-management joint leadership philosophy".

■ MILWAUKEE

There was a time when "Milwaukee" meant just one thing – Juneau Avenue. Capitol Drive then opened to confuse the issue. Now there are six facilities in the Milwaukee area.

The Product Development Center (PDC) is where future H-D models are created. It is immediately behind the Capitol Drive engine

■ BELOW *Pilgrim Road is where the latest Twin Cam 88 and 88B engines are built.*

factory measuring 213,000sq ft (20,000sq metres), was completed in 1997 at a cost of $40 million.

In 1997, a new Big Twin powerline plant was opened in nearby Menomonee Falls, and a new P&A Distribution Centre at Franklin, outside Milwaukee.

Pilgrim Road now produces all Evo and Twin Cam engines, before final assembly at York. Buells are built a half-hour's drive to the south-west, in East Troy, Wisconsin.

Harley-Davidson hasn't witnessed such expansion since the First World War. Production for 1998 totalled 148,000 machines compared to just 62,000 at the start of the 1990s. Thanks to the impetus provided by Kansas, production is planned to increase even further in the near future.

All of this is a very long way away from that little wooden shed where it all began.

The Hardware

Wild innovation has never been the Milwaukee way. Neither young Bill Harley nor the Davidsons had a taste for the radical or the extreme. Almost from the outset, their target was dependability. That's not to say that Juneau Avenue was opposed to progress. In the pre-First World War years, Harley maintained a steady stream of technical novelties. By 1912, Harley-Davidson offered a choice of all-chain drive and a primitive clutch on the X8E model. The 1914 models boasted carburettor chokes, internally-expanding rear drum brakes and two-speed transmission. The first three-speed Harley appeared the following year, with a proper engine clutch.

Bill Harley was quick to understand the importance of heat-treatment and metallurgy, and quick to employ this new, unseen technology in his designs. Exotic alloy steels appeared inside even the first Milwaukee V-twins; similar developments occurred with frame construction and lubrication.

This tradition of rugged simplicity and steady improvement can be traced to the present day, through seven generations of classic V-twin engine. First came the inlet-over-exhaust and side-valve designs, followed by the revered Knucklehead, Panhead, Shovelhead and Evolution motors. By 1998, the latest in 90 years of big-inch V-twins, the Twin Cam, had graced the Milwaukee stage.

F-Heads & Flatheads

■ F-HEADS

A halfway house between flathead and overhead valve design was the inlet-over-exhaust (ioe) layout. Also called the "F-head", as the name suggests, this configuration combined an overhead inlet valve with a side exhaust valve.

All early Harleys followed this design, with one important additional characteristic. For reasons of simplicity, the inlet valve was of the "automatic" or induction type, in which the descending piston simply "sucks" the valve open only for it to be returned to its seat by a conventional spring. This spring was of necessity light, which precluded high engine revs. One major advantage of the system was that by removing the inlet valve housing, both valves could be removed easily for servicing – a considerable advantage on these relatively primitive engines. It was also found that since the valves directly faced each other, the incoming fuel charge helped cool the exhaust valve, extending its life. As well as the early singles, the first V-engines adopted the same

■ LEFT *The F-head. The long push-rods to the overhead inlet valves and the "under head" exhaust valves are clear on the 1915 twin shown here.*

layout – to their cost, for it proved an untimely failure with the twin cylinder design.

Both the revised twin and the 5–35 series singles of 1913–18 moved to a far more positive ioe arrangement with a conventional, mechanically-operated overhead inlet valve. The same design was grafted on to the 74-inch Model J of 1922, also known as the "Super-powered Twin". This 18 horsepower engine was also the first Milwaukee twin to feature lightweight aluminium pistons. When Model J

■ LEFT *Inlet-over-exhaust layout was the norm on singles, such as this 1914 example.*

production ended in 1929, Harley twins remained exclusively side-valvers for the next six years.

◼ FLATHEADS

"Flathead" was the unflattering generic title given to any side-valve engine, whether made by Harley-Davidson or not. The reason for the nickname is obvious: with all the valve gear, including the valves themselves, located below the level of the piston at the top of its stroke, the heads were flat. The first side-valve Harleys were the Series A and B singles of 1926. All roadster twins from the end of the 1920s until the arrival of the Knucklehead in 1936 were flatheads as well. Milwaukee's catalogues continued to feature side-valve models until 1951 and even into the 1970s.

Side-valve engines were popular because they were relatively cheap to make and maintain, as well as much more compact than F-head and overhead valve designs. Although valve control was usually quite good – the camshaft and valves were in close proximity – the side-valve layout inevitably produced an elongated combustion chamber with tortuous gas-flow characteristics and poor valve cooling. This placed a severe limitation on the power such designs could produce. Side-valvers were renowned as dependable plodders, such as the seemingly unstoppable WL45.

◼ ABOVE LEFT *By the late 1920s, side-valve engines were the norm.*

◼ ABOVE RIGHT *Sidevalve engines formed the backbone of the Harley range into the 1950s, as with this WL45.*

◼ BELOW *This angle clearly shows the utter simplicity of the basic side-valve V-twin.*

Harley's side-valve years threw up one notable exception, however – the overhead valve 21-inch (346cc) single, produced from 1926 until the eve of the Knuckle in 1935. Designed with the help of Harry Ricardo, this single was not only successful in its own right but gave rise to the celebrated "Peashooter" racer. Five years earlier, Ricardo created the Model R, Triumph's first four-valve engine. His company contributed to the development of the latest Triumph triples and Aprilia's new V-twin, the RSV Mille.

KNUCKLEHEAD, 1936–47

The Knucklehead's chunky looks make it the quintessential Harley-Davidson. To many motorcyclists its debut in 1936 announced the end of years of crippling economic depression survived by only two American motorcycle manufacturers – Harley and Indian. Sales were so poor that, only one year earlier, Harley's entire range comprised just two models. With the new model – formally designated the Model E – as its flagship, Harley's fortunes rapidly improved. Sales in 1937 exceeded 11,000 for the first time in the decade.

Development of what would become the Knuckle effectively began in the late 1920s, first with specials comprising single-cylinder Peashooter top-ends grafted on to existing V-twin JDH crankcases, then with the factory DAH racers. Although substantially new, the DAH utilized heads derived from the Peashooter's. Board approval for the "official" Knuckle project was granted in 1931 – a bold move at a time when the factory was running at just ten per cent capacity. The engine would probably have been in production by 1934 but for government

■ ABOVE *The Knucklehead, Harley's first production overhead valve twin.*

■ BELOW *Developed from the ohv Peashooter single, the Knuckle was a direct ancestor to the Evo engine of 1984.*

restrictions intended to reduce unemployment which effectively barred overtime in the engine development shop. It was a long haul but certainly worth the wait.

The Knuckle was a Juneau Avenue "first" in many respects – the first four (forward) speeder, the first engine with hemispherical (hemi) heads and the first overhead valve roadster twin. The engine was heavily influenced by the competition experience of the legendary Joe Petrali, Harley-Davidson development rider and near-unbeatable racer. The Knuckle announced its arrival with a resounding flourish by posting 136.183mph on the sands of Daytona Beach, Florida. This speed record still stands.

The 61-inch – actually 60.32cu in (989cc) – Knuckle was initially available in three specifications: E (standard), ES (sidecar) and EL (high compression sport, with 6.5:1 pistons). Petrali's influence was clear. With more than 40 horsepower at 4,800rpm, the EL

in particular offered a huge increase in performance over the sluggish side-valvers. Despite its leisurely route to production – and not for the first time – there were initial reliability problems.

The worst of these concerned its new dry-sump lubrication. Some parts got too little oil while others – including the road underneath – got too much. A partial fix came in 1937 but the problem was not solved fully until the arrival of the 73.7cu in (1,207cc) Model F Knuckle in 1941, with its centrifugally-controlled oil pump by-pass. Although notorious for oil leaks through its many external seals and separate primary drive oiling, in very hot conditions many riders would prefer the big Knuckle's oil system to that of the later, "improved" Panhead.

■ ABOVE *But for the Depression, the Knucklehead would almost certainly have reached production before 1937.*

■ BELOW LEFT AND RIGHT *The numbers of Knucklehead models built were severely curtailed by the Second World War, three years after which it was succeeded by the Panhead.*

The bigger Knucklehead had come about largely in response to competition from large-capacity Indian V-twins. The larger engine's extra torque demanded a new seven-plate clutch in place of the old five-plate device, giving 65 per cent greater friction area. In addition, there was a bigger rear brake, an "airplane-style" speedometer and a larger, more efficient air-cleaner.

For a variety of reasons, the Knuckle never quite made the impact it deserved. It would certainly have reached production earlier, but for the Depression. No sooner had the Model F reached the street than the Japanese attacked Pearl Harbor in December 1941. The outbreak of war obliged the factory to divert most of its attention to military production.

Milwaukee lore has it that the best of the big Knuckles were those built in that final pre-war year, but hostilities meant that relatively few 74-inch (1,207cc) Knuckles reached the road until 1947.

By 1948, a new boss at Harley meant that the Knuckle was consigned to the annals of company history.

PANHEAD, 1948–65

In 1945, Harley resumed civilian motorcycle production, although sales would not return to pre-war levels (partly due to industrial action) until 1947. In 1948, the replacement for the noble Knucklehead made its first public appearance.

In the Milwaukee tradition of steady evolution, the "Panhead", as it was dubbed, was a development of the Knuckle rather than an all-new concept. So-named because its chromed steel rocker covers (stainless steel from 1949) resembled inverted baking pans, the Pan was built in both 74-inch – actually 73.66cu in or 1,207cc – and 61-inch (989cc) sizes, although the latter was discontinued in 1953. The larger version retained the "traditional" bore and stroke dimensions of 3⁷⁄₁₆ x 3³¹⁄₃₂in (or 87.3 x 100.8mm).

The Pan featured aluminium alloy cylinder heads in place of the Knuckle's cast iron ones, new rocker gear and hydraulic tappets (or "lifters" as they're known in the United States)

RIGHT The Panhead powered Harley-Davidson's big twins from 1948 until 1965.

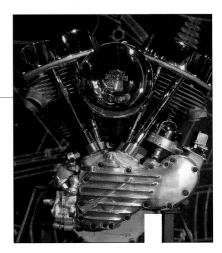

BELOW LEFT Since 1948 Pans have powered everything from the first Glide, the HydraGlide...

BELOW RIGHT ...to crazy dirt racers, as pictured here.

rather than noisier solid push-rods, as well as a revised and less leaky lubrication system. The camshaft was also new. Although the bottom-end was substantially like the Knuckle's, the oil system benefited from a larger capacity oil pump and the main oil feeds were now internal rather than untidy external lines.

The new aluminium heads not only improved engine cooling but contributed to an engine weight 8lbs (3.6kg) lighter than before. To ensure durability, the spark plugs and cylinder bolts threaded into steel inserts rather than the

■ BELOW *One of the first Panhead Harleys, a 1948 girder-forked Model F.*

relatively soft aluminium of the head itself. Despite these improvements, the power output of early Pans was about the same as the Knuckle's – around 50bhp at 4,800rpm for the 74-inch motor. The valve lifters were relocated from the top of the push-rods in 1953, to lie between cam lobe and push-rod in the timing case. At the same time, both crankcase halves were heavily modified, with particular emphasis on oil control. In 1956, Harley-Davidson introduced even more of the same. By now, a freer-breathing air cleaner and high-

lift "Victory" camshaft had brought a gain of around 5bhp on the Pan's original power output. Near the end of its life in 1963, the Panhead reverted to the Knucklehead's external top-end oil feeds to prevent overheating, a particular problem in the scorching deserts of the American south-west.

At least as enduring as the Panhead itself was the name given to the first new model to bear such an engine.

The HydraGlide of 1949 was the first Harley-Davidson to employ hydraulically-damped telescopic front forks.
It was also the first model granted one of the enduring names in motorcycling: "Glide".

The Panhead engine would do much to get the famous species on its way, propelling not only the DuoGlide of 1958 but the very first of the ElectraGlides as well.

SHOVELHEAD, 1966–84

■ LEFT *Early Shovelheads used an all-new light alloy top end on what were essentially Panhead crankcases.*

According to Harley lore, 1965 is notable for two things. The first was the unveiling of a new generation of Shovelhead engines, replacing the venerable Pans. Second and ultimately far more momentous was the decision to list the company on the stock market. What no doubt seemed a good idea at the time would ultimately lead to takeover by American Machine and Foundry (AMF).

Popular opinion now says that AMF neglected the company, that it didn't understand motorcycles and that quality went rapidly downhill. Much of this criticism has an element of truth to it but AMF actually sank millions of dollars into its new project and actually tripled annual sales.

If Harley had a problem it was probably as much to do with being part of America as being part of AMF for, like many other sectors of American industry, it was overwhelmed by the

tidal wave of sophisticated new products pouring in from Japan. As the British motorcycle industry learned to even greater cost, the 1960s and 1970s were no place for leisurely updates of a 1930s design. Put simply, the Shovelhead never had a chance.

First seen on the 1966 ElectraGlide, the Shovelhead followed the usual Harley practice of bolting a new top-end on to the tried-and-tested crankcases developed during the course of the previous generation of engines. There were minor revisions to the right crankcase half and a fin-less timing cover, but the bottom-end was essentially that of a 1965 Panhead, including the external oil feeds reintroduced in 1964.

An all-new top-end included aluminium alloy cylinder heads and iron cylinder barrels. Light alloy was also used for the rocker boxes in place of the Panhead's pressed steel. These were derived from the XL Sportster engine and enclosed redesigned rockers and exhaust valves. Although this rendered the Shovel top-end slightly reminiscent of the Sportster range, the latter was a quite separate family of unit-construction engines. Equally striking was the Shovel's "Ham-can" air cleaner cover, mated to a constant velocity Tillotson diaphragm carb from late 1966 onwards. The "Power Pac" head

■ FAR LEFT *This is a "generator" Shovelhead, produced up to 1970.*

and one reverse). The Shovel received its new bottom-end in 1970, in which a crankshaft-mounted alternator replaced the previous generator (and made the engine even wider) – hence "generator" and "alternator" Shovels. The later type, also called "cone motors", are recognized by their cone-shaped, right-side engine cover. The ignition points assembly was moved from its original external position inside the timing case and the timing gears simplified.

Originally produced in 74cu in (1,207cc) form, Shovels grew to 80cu in (1,340cc) with the FLH-80 of 1978, when electronic ignition was added. Two years later, the first five-speed gearbox appeared, firstly on the FLT Tour-Glide, and was also the first of Harley's rubber-mounted engines.

design gave around 60bhp in FLH specification, 5bhp more than an equivalent Panhead. The standard FL developed 54bhp. Observers described the new heads as resembling the backs of coal shovels, hence the nickname.

Like all Harley Vs, the ohv engine runs forked con-rods with both cylinders in the same plane to eliminate rocking couple. Primary drive is via chain to a four-speed box (with a sidecar option up to 1980, of three forward

■ BELOW *"Alternator" Shovelheads are recognizable by the conical housing on the end of the crankshaft, here marked with AMF's Number One logo.*

V2 EVOLUTION, 1984–PRESENT

Perhaps the biggest fault of the next in Milwaukee's noble line of big twins is the lack of an attractive nickname. Its official title is "V2 Evolution" which, in common with most Milwaukee monikers, is a registered trademark. It is also profoundly fitting, since like the Shovel and Panhead before, it evolved from its predecessor rather than representing an all-new design.

Appropriate as the name might be, it is not evocative at all. After decades of Flatheads, Knuckles, Pans and Shovels, it has to be said that "Evo" lacks the same gritty authentic ring. Happily for its creators, an unkind early suggestion of "Blockhead" failed to stick.

It's a curious Milwaukee fact that all major Harley-Davidson ohv engines have been born in the midst of strife. The Knuckle was a child of the Depression, the Pan arrived surrounded by strikes and post-war rebuilding, and the Shovel heralded years of decline. As the long-

■ LEFT *The Evolution engine was developed from the Shovelhead twin, but soon proved itself stronger, cleaner and more dependable. It saved Harley's fortunes just in time.*

awaited replacement for the Shovel arrived in 1984, Harley-Davidson was effectively broke. The story of how the company got out of perhaps the biggest crisis in its history is

■ LEFT *By 1985, Evolution engines powered the entire big twin range, with Sportsters getting similar treatment one year later. It eventually gave way to the Twin Cam.*

related elsewhere, but never was Milwaukee in greater need of an engine that would deliver the goods for them.

Fortunately for Harley-Davidson fans everywhere, the Evo was – and remains – everything they and Milwaukee had hoped for. Compared to the venerable Shovel which began life 18 years before, the Evo is 20lbs (9kgs) lighter and generates 10 per cent more horsepower and 15 per cent more torque. Its cylinders retain the "classic" dimensions of 3⁷⁄₁₆ x 4¼in (88.8 x 108mm), giving an actual displacement of 81.8cu in or 1,340cc (not 80in as it is nominally called). As with the evolution of Pan to Shovel, the Evo uses a bottom-end derived from its (alternator-type) predecessor but with improved con-rods and a new all-alloy top end. Efforts were made to improve oil-tightness and reliability, and decrease maintenance chores, with great success.

The extra power (around 70bhp at 5,000rpm) comes mainly from steeper, straighter ports feeding into redesigned combustion chambers, a new ignition, revised valve timing and higher compression ratios. During the seven years of the new engine's

development, much effort also went into redesigning the lubrication system to prevent the Shovel's notoriously leaky nature. All but a handful of Evos sport five-speed transmission and, from later 1984, a much-improved diaphragm clutch. By 1986, the 1340 Evo had been joined by V2 Sportster cousins offering 883cc and 1100cc, the latter growing to become the first 1200cc Sportster two years later. Unlike the 1340s, Sportster Evos are of unit construction in which the crankcases and gearbox form a single unit.

So much for metal. As far as the vibrant, imaginative management team running the newly-independent company was concerned, the Evo had one other priceless asset the much-derided Shovelhead lacked. Milwaukee now seemed to have its finger on the pulse of motorcycle culture, and most importantly, seemed to understand its market.

Those at the helm now reached out to their customers in a way that the remote, faceless AMF never could, in stark contrast to the Shovelhead era. They sold their new product as if Harley's life depended on it – which, make no mistake, it did.

ᗯ TWIN CAM 88

The Twin Cam was unveiled in 1998 and billed as "the biggest change in engine design since the Knuckle". First seen on the 1999 SuperGlides, DynaGlides, Road Kings, RoadGlide and ElectraGlide, the Twin Cam offers more power and torque in a smoother, more refined package. Yet despite the name, this is still an overhead valve engine – the cams in question are downstairs. Unlike the gear-driven camshafts of previous big twins, these are chain-driven and far less costly to produce. Considerable savings are also made in crankcase machining, which required 37 distinct operations on the Evo but only three on the Twin Cam.

One area which received particular attention was the oil circulation. Surprising though it may seem, as they set out to create the Twin Cam, Milwaukee's engineers had very little idea what the lubricating oil in the Evo engine actually did – except that it didn't always go where it ought and that pressure could fall dangerously under very hot conditions. After 18 months of painstaking work on engines littered with Plexiglass "windows", the engineers believed they had the new engine figured out at last. In fact, the actual hardware

■ RIGHT *Known as plain P22 during development, the Twin Cam has yet to attract a pet name, despite unkind suggestions that "Fat head" might fit the bill.*

■ BELOW *The Twin Cam brought a new dimension of power and refinement, first to heavyweight Glides, then the Softail range.*

– a high-capacity "gerotor" pump and two distinct scavenge systems – is less crucial than the engine's internal detailing. This was simple compared to the project's biggest problem, which had nothing to do with hardware, but with people. After the lay-offs of the 1980s, Harley simply didn't have a team capable of developing a new engine. One had to be created almost from scratch before work on the Twin Cam could begin.

■ ABOVE *Faster, cleaner, easier to service–any Harley rider's delight.*

Depending on the state of tune, Harley claims a 14–22 per cent power increase (to 87bhp on the DynaGlides) compared to the previous Evolution design. This is achieved partly through higher compression ratios, improved combustion-chamber shape and induction plumbing, as well as a new ignition pack.

Last but not least is a ten per cent increase in capacity to 88.4cu in (1,449cc), making this the largest stock engine Milwaukee has ever built. To achieve the extra volume, the stroke has decreased from 4¼ to 4in (108 to 101.6mm) while the bore has risen substantially from 3⁷⁄₁₆ to 3¹³⁄₁₆ (88.8 to 95.3mm). Traditionalists

may bemoan the departure from the hallowed 88.8 x 108mm (3⁷⁄₁₆ x 4¼in) dimensions which have endured since the Shovel.

They will certainly not bemoan, however, the Twin Cam's prodigious peak torque: 86lb/ft (116Nm) at a mere 3,500rpm. Riders needing more can take heart: the Twin Cam was designed to allow an increase in displacement as high as 1550cc, adding another six to eight horsepower.

Compared to the bolted-up crankshafts of previous ohv twins, the Twin Cam has a pressed-up crankshaft. With its shorter stroke, it is capable of higher revs. Although the 5,500rpm redline is only 300rpm higher than before, development engines have been safely tested at up to 7,000rpm.

Harley surprised everyone by dropping the Evo and unveiling the Twin Cam 88B for the year 2000, a unit-construction engine specifically tailored for the Softail range.

It represents another Harley first – twin balance-shafts to smooth out engine vibrations. Softails will no longer be able to lay claim to being the "judderers" of the range.

■ RIGHT *Twin Cam power reached the Softail range with the balance-shafted Twin Cam 88B for year-2000 models.*

RETRO - TECH

Harley-Davidson, like any ambitious pioneer motorcycle company in its early years, introduced scores of new ideas and technologies as its motorized bicycles evolved into true motorcycles. With running gear, as with engines, change was based on a trial-and-error philosophy, in which good practice prospered and bad quickly failed and fell into disuse. It was soon clear to Harley-Davidson's founders, however, that their interests lay foremost in making things that worked – and dependably. Unfamiliar ground was broached only in response to some specific need or shortcoming, and then with a thoroughness that often escaped their rivals. To this extent, the company has changed little.

It's perhaps surprising, then, that Juneau Avenue occasionally lapsed into dubious claims of motorcycling "firsts". The "step-start" and front brake, introduced in 1914 and

1927 respectively, are cases in point. British Scotts had kick-starts much earlier and front brakes were already commonplace on European machines by the 1920s. In 1923, for instance, Douglas racers were sporting quite modern-looking front-disc brakes. When Harley-Davidson claimed a "first", what it really meant was an American first.

Milwaukee makes little pretence at space-age technological innovation these days, although it might claim its machines are state-

■ ABOVE *Even today, all Harleys use variations of twin-loop steel frames, as on this one on the York assembly line.*

■ FAR LEFT AND LEFT *Two of Milwaukee's major innovations: belt final drive, as on this five-speed 883 Sportster (far left) and the "Retro-Tech" Springer front end (left).*

of-the-art – with the emphasis very much on "art". In sheer performance terms, novel engineering is usually introduced slowly: its first five-speed gearbox in 1980; fuel injection in 1995 (to clean up emissions more than to enhance power); and the long-awaited and still anticipated overhead cams (other than on the high-tech VR1000 Superbike racer). The two fields in which Harley-Davidson has taken a lead are in toothed-belt final drive – a relatively simple but truly wonderful development first seen on the 1980 FXB Sturgis – and, most strikingly, the concept of "Retro-Tech".

Retro-Tech grew out of the imaginations of Willie G. Davidson and his colleagues at the Product Development Center as well as the ingenuity of Harley's engineers. It is the means by which modern engineering receives a post-modern styling twist which is uniquely Harley-Davidson, which can contrive to make a 1999 model look for all the world like a 1949 HydraGlide but function far better. Willie G. coined the phrase, the "New Nostalgia".

Its chief elements are the Springer and Softail front and rear ends, respectively. The Softail system, designed by consulting engineer Bill Davis and much imitated by

■ ABOVE *Another view of the Springer front forks, inspired by the girder forks of Harleys of the 1940s.*

■ BELOW *Detail of the revolutionary Sturgis of 1991.*

■ LEFT *This deceptively simple-looking rubberized mounting transformed the ride of the 1993 WideGlide and subsequent Dyna-Glide models.*

competitors, comprises a cantilever suspension system using two underslung shock absorbers cunningly persuaded to look like the rigid rear end of bygone days. Hence the name – Softail, a play on the "hard tail" nickname of custom machines whose rear suspension has been removed in favour of lines that are cleaner, if distinctly less comfortable.

Springer front forks are highly-stylized facsimiles of the girder forks used on Harleys prior to the HydraGlide. Despite the 1940s looks created by their exposed springs and brilliant chrome blades, Springer forks benefited from more computer-aided design than any previous piece of Harley-Davidson hardware had done.

Almost any other make of motorcycle you can mention boasts "more" than any Harley-Davidson – more cylinders, valves and camshafts, more gears, more revs, more power – but with Milwaukee's finest, as the cognoscenti well understand, less is more.

If a Harley is about anything, it's about getting back to motorcycling's roots. As styling vice president Willie G. himself observed a few years ago, owners "rank the Harley look right up there with motherhood and God and they don't want us to screw around with it." Like that other American icon, the Zippo cigarette lighter, "It Works".

And, as the saying goes, "if it ain't broke, don't try to fix it."

🏍 ODDBALLS

■ LEFT *The TourGlide certainly wasn't strange, but for a while motorcycles towing trailers were. Now they are commonplace.*

Harley-Davidson began as a company with lofty aspirations, but some developments must have surprised even the founders. In 1924, a Harley-engined (18hp) plane built by Harvey Mummert won the speed and efficiency contest at an air race at Dayton, Ohio.

Four years later, Flying and Glider Manual published plans for crafting a propeller for a 74-inch Harley twin. By the mid-1930s, several hundred light planes were powered by Harlequin engines, using Harley-Davidson cylinders on special, horizontally-opposed crankcases. The resulting boxer twin produced 30 horsepower and could be built for less than $100. At the opposite end of the spectrum was the bicycle built for Harley by the Davis Sewing Machine Co. from 1918–24 – a "Hog" with no engine at all.

Milwaukee twins have also been used in boats and as all manner of stationary engines. Contrary to popular belief, it has not been a single, seamless tide of thundering big twins from almost the dawn of the 20th century into the 21st. Other than the early singles, perhaps

■ ABOVE *Harley-Davidson golf clubs?*

■ LEFT *Well, Milwaukee did make golf carts for a while.*

■ ABOVE *Another variation on Harley wheels, this time used as paddock transport by the factory race squad.*

■ LEFT *One American icon mutates into another: the Harley hamburger.*

the best-known variation from the V-twin theme was the Sport Twin of 1919–22, using a 37in (584cc) horizontally-opposed engine, similar to contemporary Douglas motorcycles. A generation later, the military XA appeared during the Second World War, powered by a transverse, horizontally-opposed, flathead twin.

Even the oddball XA might not have made it had other military prototypes reached production. These included a three-wheeler for use over rough ground, an armoured machine-gun carrier and a small tank powerplant consisting of a linked pair of Shovelheads. By then, one Milwaukee three-wheeler was an everyday part of American civilian life.

They called it "Servi-Car" when introduced in 1932. Although the front end – "borrowed" from the Model D side-valve V-twin – was fairly conventional, what lay behind caused surprise. Above a two-wheel rear axle sat a metal-framed "boot" (trunk): this ungainly-looking device was a cheap delivery vehicle which found a ready market in Depression-torn America. For many Harley fans worse was to come, beginning with the 1947 Model S and ending with the Topper Scooter.

■ LEFT *Odd, but the Servi-Car worked, from 1932 until the 1970s.*

■ ABOVE RIGHT *Harley was one of the world's biggest sidecar manufacturers, as with this WL45 outfit.*

■ BELOW LEFT *This Evo-engined prototype of a Servi-Car successor failed to reach production.*

■ BELOW *The little-known XA was a boxer twin.*

One of the strangest ventures was a Harley two-stroke actually manufactured in the United States – without wheels. The Harley Snowmobile, powered by either 400 or 430cc engines, was built for four years until 1975.

Another quest for diversity saw the company branching out to build military bomb casings, computer circuit boards and "Holiday Rambler" recreational vehicles.

If nothing else, this demonstrates just how far the company had strayed from what it now regards as its essential roots.

Legislation permitting, in the future, all Harley-Davidsons will be air-cooled, 45-degree V-twins with both cylinders precisely in line. You can bet your house on it.

Work and War

Almost as soon as the first model rolled off the Milwaukee production lines,
Harley-Davidsons have been involved in all kinds of work.

In 1909, Harley provided motorcycles for the fledgling Rural Mail Carriers of
America, but it is their association with police forces across the United States that
is most well-known. 1908 was the year when the first Harley became involved with
law enforcement; since then they have gone on to be an integral part of police
forces' transportation worldwide.

Fire engines, delivery vans, golf carts: Milwaukee-built engines have driven them
all. And if they were indispensable as civilian workhorses, as a tool for the military
they were unsurpassed. The First World War was the first time a Harley had been
used in a major conflict and, having established themselves as "Uncle Sam's
choice", they went on to be even more invaluable during the Second World War.

Whether with a side-valve V-twin Model D for the police, a Servi-Car for
deliveries or military 45-inch WLA, Harley-Davidson has always been able
to come up with the goods.

WORK AND WAR

■ WORK

Throughout the 1920s and 1930s, the words "Harley-Davidson" and "workhorse" were almost synonymous. Surprising though it may seem now, much of America's road network scarcely existed until President Roosevelt's job-creation programmes of the Depression years. Even the celebrated Route 66 dates from only 1926 (and was almost obliterated by Interstate 40 after 1985). Any affordable, rugged machine able to cope with rough terrain had something going for it, and Milwaukee's finest certainly met that bill. Harleys have offered mobility in every walk of American life, from painters to policemen. The company saw this potential early – Arthur Davidson attended the annual meeting of the Rural Mail Carriers of America as early as 1909, coming away with a pocketful of sales. It is with the police, however, especially the Highway Patrol, that Milwaukee twins are best associated.

Literally thousands of Harleys have joined America's police forces since they first went into uniform in 1908. Until recently, it was believed that the first police Harley went to Pittsburgh in 1909, although the distinction

actually goes to Detroit one year earlier. Indeed, Harley-Davidsons have been popular across the globe, and Milwaukee twins have often been prominent in newsreel footage of presidential cavalcades in countries as far-flung as Burma and Guatemala. By 1915, Juneau Avenue was also producing "rapid response" sidecar outfits equipped with fire extinguishers and first-aid kits. A decade later, Harley motorcycles were in use by more than 2,500 American police forces, some of which quickly saw the public-relations benefits of organizing their riders into display teams. By the 1930s, police-model special equipment

■ ABOVE *Police officers on 1944 UL models patrol Minneapolis, Minnesota. Harleys have been involved in law enforcement since 1908.*

■ BELOW LEFT *The Servi-Car three-wheeler did much to allow Harley to endure the Depression.*

■ BELOW RIGHT *A police Panhead, one of thousands of machines to have served US law-enforcement.*

■ ABOVE *An impressive line-up of police Harleys outside the Juneau Avenue factory.*

included radios (initially only one-way; two-way arrived 1948), although some squads made riders buy their own police lights and sirens.

The same period also welcomed two definitive Harley-Davidson workhorses. The archetypal side-valve V-twin Model D, introduced in 1929, became the Model W in

■ RIGHT AND BELOW *This immaculately restored Flathead served with the Daytona Beach Fire Department.*

1937 and continued in production until 1951. Although crude and slow – its 22-or-so-bhp, 45-inch engine generated around 65mph (105kph) – it was rugged, dependable and easy to fix – ideal for cash-strapped Depression America. The American military version, known as the WLA – the "A" stood for "Army" – represented the bulk of Milwaukee's contribution to the Second World War. Though the majority of WL production during the war years was earmarked for military use, some also went to police forces and other strategic or security operations.

The Servi-Car, introduced for 1932, was the Model D's three-wheeled sister ship, and enjoyed an even longer production run – until 1974. The model's capacious boot (trunk) made it as popular with trade and delivery men as it was with local police forces. This unique three-wheeler remained in service, even in metropolitan San Francisco, into the 1990s. One clever and user-friendly Servi-Car touch

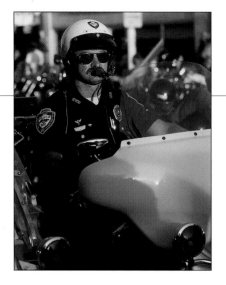

was the adoption of the same 42in (1,070mm) wheelbase as the typical car – so inexperienced riders would not need to forge their own ruts in mud and snow.

So enduring was the Servi-Car's appeal that for a period during the late 1970s and early 1980s it was the only Milwaukee machine serving many American police forces.

The later Shovelhead years were not happy ones for Harley-Davidson's law-enforcing pretensions. Quality-control problems and general performance issues caused many forces to look elsewhere. For around a decade, even the California Highway Patrol (CHiPs) found itself powered by Italian Moto Guzzi V-twin and Japanese Kawasaki four-cylinder machines. It was not until the arrival of the Evolution engine in 1984 that Harley could again supply machinery that met CHiPs' requirements. Since then, Harley's principal police models have been the FLHT-P Electra-Glide and FXRP PursuitGlide.

■ **THE FIRST WORLD WAR**

By the time the United States entered the First World War in 1917, H-D machines had already seen action in skirmishes against the forces of Pancho Villa, the Mexican revolutionary. Under

General "Black Jack" Pershing, machine-gun-toting Harley-Davidsons proved themselves ideal for border patrols in rough terrain.

In the process, Juneau Avenue proved itself adept at meeting military demands. An order for additional machines was placed by a War Department telegraph on 16 March 1916. A

■ ABOVE LEFT *Fancy being paid to ride a Harley at Sturgis: a local cop.*

■ ABOVE RIGHT *Busted for good taste? Harley catches Harley.*

■ LEFT *An Evo serving with Volusia County Police, one of several forces in the Daytona Beach area.*

■ LEFT *Since the first police Harley of 1908 there have been literally thousands, most of which have travelled further than this.*

dozen motorcycles equipped with William Harley's design for a sidecar gun carriage duly arrived at the border – more than 1,000 miles (1,610km) distant – two days later. Nine days later still, a second order for six machines reached Milwaukee. This one was filled in just 33 hours. Needless to say, the factory was not slow to advertise its efficiency in meeting "Uncle Sam's Choice".

Harley was just as quick to recognize the contribution it might make to the war in Europe. Within four months of the United States' entry into the war, Arthur Davidson was telling a sales meeting where the country's – and perhaps the company's – destiny lay:

"The time is coming when no man can be in the middle of the road. He must be either for America or against America, and the sooner we get together on this question, the better able we will be to win the war."

During the first year of America's war, roughly half of all motorcycle production went to military service. By the end of the conflict, every motorcycle Milwaukee made was built for Uncle Sam. Along the way, William Harley, a member of the Motorcycle War Service Board, was instrumental in giving motorcycles a "B-4" classification, which gave them essential production status with priority for raw materials. Some 312 Harley-Davidson employees also enlisted, of whom all but three survived the experience.

As to hardware, in all some 20,000 motorcycles became American "conscripts" in the First World War, the vast majority of which were Harley-Davidsons. This success finally

■ ABOVE *Daytona: Sun, sea and Harleys.*

■ RIGHT *William Harley oversees the testing of specially equipped Harley twins during the early years of the First World War.*

leap-frogged Harley ahead of its main rival, Indian, a position it was never to relinquish. Military Harleys were mainly 61-inch (989cc) twins of conventional F-head design, producing almost nine horsepower. They were employed mainly for dispatch and scout duty. One became a cause célèbre.

Its rider was Corporal Roy Holtz of Chippewa Falls, Wisconsin, little more than 200 miles (320 km) from downtown Milwaukee. On 8 November 1918, with the German army in chaotic retreat, Holtz was assigned to take his company captain on a reconnaissance mission. At night and in foul weather, the captain became disorientated and, over Holtz's objections, directed him across enemy lines where the duo eventually stumbled across a German field headquarters at which Holtz was instructed to ask directions. They were taken prisoner but released with the Armistice three days later. Holtz – and his Harley V-twin – thus became the first American serviceman on German soil.

■ THE SECOND WORLD WAR

No sooner had Harley sales begun to recover from the Depression of the 1930s than Pearl Harbor was bombed and the United States entered the Second World War. Milwaukee had begun planning in anticipation of military needs as early as the autumn of 1939, shortly

■ ABOVE *A Second World War WLA45 assigned to the US military police.*

after the outbreak of war in Europe. Early work, in competition with Indian and Delco, focused on a flat twin Servi-Car to meet army proposals for a three-wheeler for rough terrain. Other unfinished projects were even stranger, including an armoured machine-gun carrier and a prototype powerplant for a small tank comprising paired overhead valve engines.

With civilian motorcycle production suspended, by far the bulk of Harley-Davidson's war effort was the production of military versions of the WL side-valve V-twins, the WLA. The equivalent 74-inch (1,207cc) military UA and USA (sidecar) models were built in much smaller numbers. Of almost 90,000 military Harley-Davidsons, around 88,000 were 45-inch WLAs, of which one third served with Soviet forces. The same attributes of rugged simplicity that had brought the side-valve twin such a dependable peacetime reputation made it ideally suited to the harsher demands of war.

With very few Knuckleheads "enlisting" (although a special ELC model was built for the Canadian army), Milwaukee's other major contribution was the oddball Model XA, powered by a horizontally-opposed flathead twin displacing 45cu in (739cc). The XA was

■ RIGHT *A particularly war-torn WLA, but they were remarkably sturdy machines.*

■ RIGHT *The
horizontally-opposed XA
twin looked more like a
German BMW or
Zundapp, but served in
small numbers during
the Second World War.*

expressly designed for use in the North African
desert, with its shaft final drive and plunger
rear suspension. There was also an XS variant,
with sidecar. Less well known was a mission for
American intelligence, the stripping and
assessment of a Russian motorcycle.

Harley-Davidson's contribution was not
confined to hardware. John E. Harley, later in
charge of the parts and accessories division,
rose to the rank of major in the Second World
War. Among his various tasks, and one to which

he was eminently suited, was the training of
army motorcyclists at Fort Knox, Kentucky.
WLAs in the hands of raw recruits must have
tested Harley's talents to the limit. Even
setting off on such a machine was a knack,
thanks to its hand gear-change and foot-
operated "suicide" clutch.

From late 1941 until the armistice in 1945,
Juneau Avenue burned the midnight oil to meet
the escalating demands of the forces as almost
the whole of American industry was turned
over to the war effort. Fittingly, Harley-
Davidson's special contribution was recognized
by the award of three coveted Army-Navy "E"
awards for excellence in wartime production.
Milwaukee's factory workers couldn't
necessarily go to war with the enemy but they
could certainly help those who did.

Some might believe Harley's military career
ended with the Second World War but there are
two surprising post-scripts.

The first was the 1987 purchase of the rights
to the military MT500 motorcycle from the
British Armstrong company.

The second was a legacy of the AMF
takeover: one "sideline" at the former AMF
plant in York, Pennsylvania – where Harleys
are still assembled – was the manufacture of
bomb casings, a practice which continued well
into the 1990s. It is likely that some of these
found their way into the Gulf War.

■ RIGHT *Although
intended primarily for
service in the North
African desert – hence
this colour scheme – the
XA suffered badly from
all the sand which
would collect in its
wheel bearings.*

Live to Ride... Ride to Live

To aficionados, a Harley-Davidson is as much an emotion as a lump of metal, and certainly much more than a mere motorcycle. Precisely what the "more" constitutes isn't easy to explain, except that Milwaukee iron can be almost anything you want it to be: wheels, plaything, lifestyle accessory, fashion statement, membership card or any of a hundred other things. To many owners, their Hog is almost as crucial as life itself. Transport is often the last thing on a Harley owner's mind.

STYLE

The image forged from steel in the American Midwest travels across frontiers and media. It's as instantly recognizable in Bangkok as it is in Brooklyn, as rich with associations in Clackmannanshire as it is in Cincinnati. Advertisers know this and use it as shorthand for youth, freedom, rebellion and freewheeling affluence. It is almost impossible to watch a commercial for anything from cars and pensions to jeans and toiletries without a Harley-Davidson cropping up sooner or later in a mood-setting role. In other words, Harleys may be motorcycles – but they're also stars.

Some of this rubs off on the people who ride them. Owning a Harley isn't about speed or performance, or about imitating your favourite racer or impressing friends. It's about individuality but also brotherhood, retro-cool and happening places, latter-day cowboys or folk who just want to get away from it all.

When they move, Harley-Davidsons cruise. To the ear, they also thunder rather than rev.

■ ABOVE *Poster of Peter Fonda and Dennis Hopper cruising to New Orleans in* Easy Rider.

■ LEFT *Christian Slater and Harley in* Heathers.

You can cruise around the block, along the beach or down to the bar; equally you can cruise from New York to San Francisco if that's your thing. They work equally well on the long-haul because of where they evolved – in a land of empty spaces and almost no corners at all.

■ BELOW LEFT *"Captain America" and helmet, as ridden by Peter Fonda.*

■ BELOW *"Harley-Davidstones" – one Stones fan wears his heart on his Harley.*

■ ABOVE *You will find Hogs everywhere!*

■ ABOVE *"Made in the USA" – and long before Springsteen sang it.*

■ RIGHT *Nothing else out there: just you, your Harley and the open road.*

■ LEFT *Mickey Rourke cuts loose on a Harley in* The Marlboro Man.

■ BEAUTIFUL PEOPLE

"God rides a Harley", according to some. The King certainly rode one. As well as Elvis Presley, celebrity hoggers have included Muhammad Ali, Bob Dylan, Clint Eastwood, Sly Stallone, Mickey Rourke, Dan Ackroyd, Malcolm Forbes, Cher, Whoopie Goldberg and dozens more. You're as likely to see a film star in Hollywood riding a Harley-Davidson today as lounging in a stretch limousine. Often, the stars want something out of the ordinary. Custom builders can easily charge $40,000 for bespoke machines and, in the process, become minor celebrities themselves.

The phenomenon is far from new, especially in Tinseltown. Photographs from Hollywood's golden years show everyone from *Gone with the Wind*'s Clark Gable to Marlene Dietrich astride Milwaukee machines. In some cases, the pictures were pure publicity stunts, but even Roy Rogers rode a Harley when he wasn't riding Trigger. Hollywood even had its own Harley group once – the Three Point Motorcycle Club.

Harleys themselves have become film stars, notably Robert Blake's mount in *Electra Glide in Blue* and, of course, in the hugely successful *Easy Rider* starring Dennis Hopper. Hopper's co-star in the film, Peter Fonda, remains a committed Harley-Davidson fan to this day.

RALLIES: STURGIS

Sturgis is an unremarkable little farming community in South Dakota. For most of the year very little happens until, in mid-August, this sleepy little hamlet goes motorcycle crazy as the famous Sturgis Rally lets rip.

The monster that Sturgis has become was born way back in 1938 when the Jackpine Gypsies Motorcycle Club organized the first Black Hills Rally and Races, with a $300 purse to the winner. Almost every year since, bikers by the thousand have cruised in along Interstates 85 and 90 to renew old friendships or make new ones. Being conveniently located in middle America – if 900 miles (1,450 km) from Chicago and 1,500 miles (2,410 km) from San Francisco can be considered convenient – attendance tends to be huge. Any old Sturgis Rally attracts 50,000 of the faithful. For the 50th anniversary in 1990, somewhere between 250,000 and 300,000 turned up.

Sturgis is not specifically a Harley rally – not that you'd notice if you were there for all the Harley bikes on site. It lasts for a week – a week of swap meets, hog roasts (pigs, not bikes), drag-bike racing at the Sturgis Dragway, tours, gawking at fancy Harley hardware and generally having a good time. Bikers hang out at joints like the Bear Butte Café. Main Street is air-cleaner to wheel-spindle full of Hogs. If you need a break, there are tours to the nearby Dakota Badlands, Devil's Tower (featured in the movie *Close Encounters of the Third Kind*) or Mount Rushmore.

There's strangeness, as well. One year, a guy rode a buffalo into town, moseyed down Main Street and hung a left on to Junction Avenue. Another year, the nearby US Air Force base

■ ABOVE *At Sturgis, you don't necessarily need a lot of clothes, but they have to be the right ones.*

■ BELOW LEFT *Usually the action lasts right through the night.*

■ BELOW RIGHT *And some people say all Harley owners are alike.*

■ RIGHT *Ladies are welcome, too.*

■ BELOW *Main Street in Sturgis, as can be seen, is a car-free zone.*

reputedly laid on a rather special kind of fire-works display when a couple of their jets dipped low over town, hit their afterburners and drowned out even the noise of a thousand V-twins.

The whole town joins in (Sturgis is usually quite lucrative, although the town is so outnumbered by bikers it has little choice)

from the women of the United Presbyterian to the Grace Lutherans. There have been occasional troubles with biker gangs, notably in 1982, but on the whole Sturgis is comparatively peaceful (if far from tranquil). These gangs are actively encouraged by the Sturgis city fathers, who clearly know a good deal when they see one.

According to Jackpine founder, former Indian dealer J.C. "Pappy" Hoel, there's never been a serious problem with outlaw biker groups: "We have their co-operation as long as we don't hassle them."

Mainly, it's a week-long party. Behaviour has been known to be on the excessive side, but it's usually harmless and only takes place once a year. Besides, it's legendary.

RALLIES: DAYTONA CYCLE WEEK

■ BELOW *Like it says: "Daytona Beach Welcomes Bikers".*

Outside the Rat's Hole custom shop, Main Street reverberates to the rumble of big-bore Vs on open pipes. Heavy-looking bikers in wraparound shades stand beergut-to-beergut, shoulder-to-tattooed-shoulder on every inch of sidewalk. It's March and almost 200,000 bikers have Daytona Beach under siege.

Like Sturgis, this is a week-long party. For the most part, the siege is friendly. As the barmaid at La Playa Hotel put it, "Bike Week's the best because they're all really nice. You don't see manners like this any other time. Wannanother beer?"

■ BADASS BIKERS?

Like Sturgis, Daytona's Cycle Week is one of those mammoth events that didn't begin as a celebration of all that is Harley-Davidson but somehow became one. Cycle Week takes place each year during March's Spring Break in the Florida coastal city of Daytona Beach. Its focal point is ostensibly the races at nearby Daytona International Speedway, a spectacular banked oval which also hosts the famous Daytona Nascar races.

■ ABOVE LEFT *At Daytona you can cruise or watch others cruising...*

■ ABOVE RIGHT *...or you can just chill and chew the fat.*

It's yet another of those Harley enigmas that, as the factory's twins' interest in the races has declined, its profile in Cycle Week as a whole has risen dramatically. Milwaukee's official XR750 road racer last competed there in 1973 (although the VR1000 has competed in recent years) and hasn't had a win since Cal Rayborn's in 1969, but this hasn't spoiled the party one bit. Quite the reverse – not having to ride the few miles out to the Speedway seems to leave more time for downtown fun. Daytona has become pure festival.

Sturgis, a small town, is understandably overwhelmed by bikes. Daytona Beach is big, yet the effect is much the same. The scene centres on the junction of Atlantic and Main Street, where bikes and bodies are crammed sidewalk to sidewalk. Harley-Davidson – wise

to the public relations coup Daytona has handed them – takes over the city's Hilton Hotel to strut its corporate stuff and show the latest models. However most Daytona life goes on in the street, in the bars, on the beach and in nearby campgrounds.

Cycle Week has custom shows and impromptu drag races. During the day, bikes cruise along Daytona's beaches. There's official racing at the local quarter-mile dirt track and the main event at the International Speedway. There are swap meets in which enthusiasts sell or search for bike parts, notably at the Volusia County Fairgrounds.

Mainly it's lots of partyin', posin' and cruisin', and if you can't wait 12 months for your next Daytona fix, you can show up at the HOG "Biketoberfest" in October.

■ OPPOSITE BELOW LEFT *Spot the Honda.*

■ OPPOSITE BELOW RIGHT *If you can find a standard bike, you can keep it.*

■ RIGHT *If you can't paint your Hog, paint your clothes...*

■ FAR RIGHT *...if there's anything left to paint, that is.*

BAD BOYS

Mention Harley-Davidson to anyone in the street and they'll probably mutter back something about "Hell's Angels". The original Angels were a California bike gang of Second World War veterans sensationalized by magazines such as Life and author Hunter S. Thompson in his book *The Hell's Angels: A Strange and Terrible Saga of the Outlaw Motor Cycle Gangs*. Almost overnight, the Angels became a role model for "outlaw" groups across the globe.

According to many observers, such groups revelled in their new-found celebrity status and, in living up to their reputation, became even more shocking and antisocial than before. Inevitably, bikers in general and Harley-Davidson riders in particular were tarred with the same unsavoury brush. Some stereotypes persist, but the bad old days of

negative biker images have largely passed. In the United States, Harley owners have been growing older, wealthier and better educated. In 1984, the average age of a Harley buyer was 34; today it is almost 40, around one third of whom enjoyed a college education. Indeed, the modern stereotype is more of the well-off professional cruising any city's more fashionable streets rather than the grime-ridden outlaw of the past.

These days Harleys are the weekend wheels of lawyers, mayors and bankers: respectability, with an edge. This is all in motorcycle manufacturers' interests, for minority groups,

■ ABOVE *The original Hell's Angels were a group of Californian war veterans. Note Willie G., standing, facing the camera, third from the left.*

■ FAR LEFT *Imitators of the original Angels have since evolved as far apart as New Zealand...*

■ LEFT *...and Germany.*

■ RIGHT *Although "Hell's Angels" has become a cliche, Satan's Slaves is another well-known group of affiliated biker gangs.*

apart from tarring the rest, inevitably buy in minority numbers. One of the secondary purposes of HOG – the factory-sponsored Harley Owners' Group – was to broaden both the marque's appeal and its respectability, a service from which all bike producers benefit.

Hell's Angels and other so-called "outlaw" groups survive, and occasionally their activities hit the headlines. Perhaps the most notorious was a wave of knifings, bombings and shootings between rival Canadian gangs in the early 1990s, which left around 40 dead yet only attracted serious police attention when an

innocent bystander became a victim. In the late 1970s, Australia was the scene of a shoot-out in a supermarket parking lot between rival gangs. More recently, Denmark witnessed a spate of murders and even anti-tank missile attacks arising from a long-standing feud between the Angels and Bandidos for control of drugs interests. Crime – particularly the sale of stolen goods – and later the manufacture and dealing of hard drugs has long been a source of income for some outlaw bands which, in Europe in particular, are also associated with neo-Nazi activities. Even the FBI has shown an

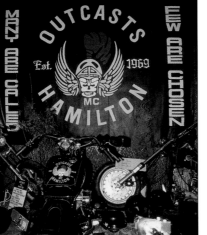

■ RIGHT *"Many are called... few are chosen" and even fewer care.*

■ FAR RIGHT *Sometimes known as "One Per Centers", although this veteran Angel begs to differ.*

351

A DAY OF INFAMY

One of the most notorious episodes in American motorcycling history concerned the so-called Hollister riots of 1947. Events unfolded around the first Hollister Memorial Day races to be held since the Second World War, a focal point for recently demobbed biking GIs. As with the Isle of Man Tourist Trophy ("TT") today, the races were welcomed by residents of the little Californian town for the business and prosperity they brought.

Thousands arrived for the races, including bike clubs such as the "Booze Fighters" from Los Angeles and San Francisco. Main Street was crowded "like sardines" and undoubtedly rowdy. The press loved it: "Riots... Cyclists Take Over Town" and "Havoc in Hollister" cried the *San Francisco Chronicle*. Other papers and magazines quickly jumped on to exploit the bandwagon. Six years later, the "riots" would be commemorated on celluloid in

the film *The Wild One*, starring Marlon Brando and Lee Marvin. In the film, Johnny – angrily and effectively played by Brando – is asked what it is he's rebelling against. "Whaddya got?" he replies, one of Hollywood's most memorable lines. Although Harley-Davidsons feature heavily in the film, Brando is actually portrayed riding a Triumph. Nonetheless, the American Motorcycle Association saw fit to picket the movie on its release.

It was one thing for the movie to portray fiction, quite another for the contemporary press to do the same. For the truth was that the Hollister riots were largely fabricated. Some people were arrested for drunkenness but this was certainly nothing resembling a riot. As local hotelier Catherine Dabo later recalled to journalist Mark Gardiner, "I didn't even know anything had happened until I read the San Francisco papers."

Other Hollister residents were equally baffled: "It was a mess but there was no real evidence of physical damage," said Harry Hill, of the American Air Force.

"I brought my two daughters along... it never occurred to me to be worried about their safety," remembered local pharmacist Marylou Williams.

Finally and perhaps more to the point was the observation made by car mechanic Bert Lanning: "Some people don't like motorcycles, I guess."

According to one witness, cinema projectionist Gus Deserpa, a famous *Life* magazine photograph of a drunken biker sitting on his Harley surrounded by bottles, was faked. The drunk was real but it wasn't even his bike and the bottles had been gathered expressly to "improve" the picture.

Yes, Hollister was a weekend of infamy: for the media.

avid interest in them and certainly not because the G-men have an innate love of motorcycling. These self-styled "One Percenters" mostly exist on the fringes of Harley-Davidson culture and of motorcycling in general. Ironically, much of HOG's paraphernalia – its insignia, colours and organisation into "chapters" –

echoes the ways of the outlaw gangs. Beards, badges and leather are part of many everyday Harley riders' uniforms but the trappings don't always say much about the person underneath. Sometimes the individual in the street must be hard-pressed to tell the difference. Perhaps Milwaukee likes it that way.

■ LEFT *These guys are probably discussing needlework.*

HARLEY AND ITS PUBLIC

Harley-Davidson has a long and imaginative tradition of embracing the interests of its customers. As early as 1916, Juneau Avenue was producing its own magazine, *The Enthusiast*, to encourage pride of ownership and fellowship among Harley owners – and to do no harm to sales. Within three years, sales of the nickel magazine had reached 50,000. A trade equivalent, *Dealer News*, began in 1912 and a Spanish-language manual and catalogue, *Los Entusiastas Latinos*, appeared briefly the following year. *The Enthusiast* carried tales of racing, travels and other daring Harley deeds.

In the dark days of the 1930s Depression, the Harley "medal system" was born in which bonuses were offered to owners generating a motorcycle sale. January 1951 brought the Harley-Davidson Mileage Club which offered recognition for riding achievements. Harley riders could earn a pin badge and membership card for clocking up 25,000, 50,000 and 100,000 miles. By the end of 1954, no fewer than 73 Mileage Club members had logged 100,000 miles (160,930 kilometres).

The same concept of customer involvement – and a certain degree of desperation – lay behind the creation of the Harley Owners' Group (HOG). It was founded in 1983 (a year after Carl Wick's less phonetic HDOA – the Harley-Davidson Owners' Association).

Today, HOG is run by its own vice president (Bill, son of Willie G. Davidson). Under the factory's guidance and auspices, many Harley dealerships worldwide now run HOG groups, arranging everything from hog roasts to ride-aways, dances and charity events.

With the creation of HOG it was no longer enough to sell a customer a motorcycle – dealers had to be able to offer the lifestyle to go with it. A shrewd and prescient move, it

■ ABOVE *Years of effort and imagination have made HOG the envy of other manufacturers.*

■ BELOW *You need long sleeves to be a lifetime HOG devotee.*

anticipated the way motorcycling was going before any other manufacturer really took note. HOG now boasts more than 450,000 members in over 1,000 local chapters world-wide and has its own website, www.hog.com. On almost any summer weekend, it offers a choice of half a dozen rallies in the United States – plus others as far flung as Tunis, Darwin or Argentina. Like the motorcycles themselves, it is often imitated but never equalled.

If this portrays the company as only interested in the bottom line, it is also true that many of Harley's employees – at every level – are also committed motorcyclists. Harley-Davidson is fiercely protective of its interests, but also seeks to understand its customers. As the official company policy statement suggests: "It's one thing to have people buy your products. It's another for them to tattoo your name on their bodies." Sentiments such as that have brought Harley-Davidson a very long way.

CRUISING

Harley-Davidsons may be sold, cherished and owned in every corner of the globe but there isn't a hogger alive who doesn't fantasize about cruising a Hog across the good ol' US of A. Epic American journeys are the stuff of Milwaukee dreams: thundering across the wide-open Midwest prairies or the baking deserts of Utah and the south-west; soaring over the Rocky Mountains or gliding down California's coast-hugging Highway 1. There is simply nowhere else where Harleys feel so resolutely, resoundingly right.

Harleys suit the United States perfectly because they're part of the cultural landscape you find yourself riding through. In the United States, Harleys open doors, start conversations and bring smiles to passing faces, but best of all is the way they glide over the staggering panoply of scenery that is the American West.

■ CRUISING

From the saddle of an ElectraGlide or Low Rider, America passes by at a pace your senses can get a hook on; horizons rise in waves, roll

■ ABOVE *The author heading north on Route 95 in Utah, with the Colorado River in the background.*

■ LEFT *Dream come true: a group on a Harley package tour cruises through Baja, Mexico.*

■ OPPOSITE LEFT *What Hogs do best: thundering towards distant horizons in the American south-west.*

■ OPPOSITE RIGHT *A Fat Boy swings through the bends under the towering cliffs of Zion National Park, Utah, USA.*

■ LEFT *A group of German riders on hired Harleys near Monument Valley on the Arizona/Utah border.*

different: Arches, Canyonlands, Bryce, Capitol Reef and glorious Zion, to name but a few. Next door to Utah are Arizona and the Grand Canyon, Colorado and the Rockies, Nevada's sweeping high desert basins and the red rocks and white sands of New Mexico.

From magical, mystical Moab, it's just a short ride up Highway 191 to Canyonlands. Hang a left and let the Harley thunder up the

in like a gentle swell and gently recede under your wheels. It demands a different sort of tempo – more relaxed, less preoccupied with destinations – than riding in Europe. As it thumps over hills and plains, the big, lazy V-twin engine seems attuned to the environment in a way that other machines never could be. Then, with a jolt, you encounter somewhere like Utah – scenic America at its most extraordinary.

Utah is Mother Nature under hallucinogenic influence. Utah has National Parks in profusion, all with something spectacular and

■ LEFT *Hoggers on a traditional ride-out from the Sturgis Rally to Dakota's Devil's Tower.*

■ BELOW *Baja California, the sea of Cortez beyond, and what better way to enjoy them?*

endless grades until suddenly the road stops and the world simply disappears. Gone. In its place, space – a void as big as the Alps. Half a mile (800 metres) below, the Colorado River surges noiselessly, framed by a rocky never-never-land that might be awe-inspiring if it were real. It takes a while to get your head around the fact that it is.

There's more. There always is in Utah. Shafer Canyon, Grand View Point, and then the daddy of them all, the Green River Overlook on the "Island in the Sky". From here, the western horizon is 100 miles (160km) away, about the distance from London to Bristol. Around where Berkshire ought to be is the baking wilderness of the Soda Springs Basin, through which Stillwater Canyon carves a distant trench which looks tiny but is fully 1,000ft (300 metres) deep. But for the shadows of passing clouds,

■ BELOW *108°F (42°C) in the shade, and there is no shade. Must be time for a cold beer.*

creeping as though in awe of the landscape, it could be the dark side of the Moon.

If the landscape is dramatic, the sheer scale is extraordinary. Take Route 41 – cresting a rise north of Montezuma Creek,

■ LEFT *Dead Horse Point, near Moab, just one of the scenic jewels of dazzling Utah.*

a view 200 miles (320km) wide leaps into sight. Seventy-five miles (120km) away in Arizona, the orange spires of Monument Valley guard the western horizon; to the east, the snow-capped Colorado Rockies are fully 125 miles (200 km) distant. This a scene that is far larger than many countries in Europe, and yet

it's a single, sweeping view – or a panoramic day's ride on a Harley-Davidson. For the great, mythic emptiness of the United States, nothing else comes close to experiencing it all – and more – as from the seat of a Harley-Davidson V-twin that has been made in Milwaukee.

■ BELOW *This man emigrated to the United States just to be able to do this.*

The Custom Scene

The identity of the first Harley-Davidson custom isn't recorded but it's surely almost as old as the company itself. It's in the nature of motorcycles that owners seek to "improve" them – not because there's necessarily anything wrong with the way they came out of the crate, but to add that extra touch of individuality.

Over the years, this "extra touch" turned from a trend into a craze and finally into a phenomenon. Today you'd be hard-pressed to find a Harley that has not been altered in some manner from the original that Milwaukee intended. Indeed, to judge by the amount of customizing that goes on, a Harley certainly isn't finished when it leaves the factory, if ever. Far from being discouraged by this slight on its judgement, the company actively encourages it. It's no coincidence that Harley-Davidson produces three catalogues crammed full of official "goodies", while the bikes themselves warrant only one. Custom Hogs are booming.

CUSTOM HARLEYS

■ BELOW *Bob Lowe's custom creation "Evil Twin".*

A customized Harley today can be anything from a Sportster pared down to the barest essentials to a Glide decked out with almost anything you'd expect to find in a deluxe motorhome. Perhaps in the very early days, changes were functional: one carburettor worked better than another, this mudguard kept you cleaner than that. And, since America fell in love with horsepower almost as soon as there was such a thing, engine tuning quickly became a growth industry: in almost every state of the union, someone was willing to sell you high-lift camshafts, high-compression pistons or any of the other goodies that make an engine even stronger. In the racing field in particular, many tuners became legends for their prowess at extracting more power.

Extravagant cosmetic "tuning" came later. More than with any other make of motorcycle, Harley-Davidson customizing is an oddly circular process. First came Harley-Davidsons, which owners either lived with as they stood or adjusted to their tastes. Many of these creations were attractive in the extreme, a fact that was not lost on the people back at base in Milwaukee. Styling ideas which had first

■ ABOVE *Not surprisingly, this one goes by the name of "Full Metal Jacket".*

■ LEFT *This level of detail can take months to achieve.*

appeared as owners' one-offs fed back into the melting pot of Juneau Avenue design. Eventually, the wheel came full circle as the echoes reverberated through standard "factory custom" machines, beginning in 1970 with the FX1200 SuperGlide – although, at the time, the FX was resented by many in the custom scene for doing their job for them. Let's not forget that Buells – now an integral part of the Milwaukee range – began life as specials.

As far as graphics and paint are concerned, the inspiration reaches back farther still, to the art-deco designs with which the company

■ ABOVE *Custom can be three wheels...*

■ ABOVE RIGHT *...or designer grunge!*

attempted to sell bikes during the hardships of the 1930s. At the time, Harley was already marketing aftermarket parts such as mirrors and racks, but most were more functional than decorative. The true custom scene arrived in the California of the 1950s, with men such as Von Dutch and Ed Roth prominent. Often, 1930s art-deco was their inspiration in creating "blend" bikes – machines built from parts of several different models, as well as one-off components. Today, stylistic cues sometimes come from the Harley-Davidsons of the past, as demonstrated by the whole concept of "Retro-

Tech". Harley brochures today speak about machines of the 1950s inspiring several of their Softail models, although the Springer looks more like a child of the 1940s.

The 1960s and 1970s, of course, were the heyday of the chopper, with its radically extended forks, limited lock and lousy handling. These days, customizers and riders alike look for either something more functional or something that is very much more art than motorcycle – such as the creations of the doyen of customizers, Arlen Ness. Other celebrated custom artists include Dave Perewitz, Ricki

■ RIGHT *Presence, yes, but if you want ground clearance and rear suspension, look elsewhere.*

■ RIGHT
Sometimes
practicality
comes a very
poor second
to effect.

Battistini and Donnie Smith, but almost anyone with a Hog can join the scene in their own small way.

Mechanically as well as cosmetically, Harley-Davidson gladly promotes change, chiefly through its range of "Screaming Eagle" accessories, and they tacitly acknowledge that, even at 1450cc, the new Twin Cam engine can be further enhanced with a factory kit, increasing displacement to a mammoth 1550cc. Other suppliers, such as California's Custom Chrome, feed the fertile ground of Harley customs.

■ ARLEN NESS

The most revered of all Harley special builders is Arlen Ness, a slight, grey-haired Californian who doesn't so much customize Harleys as transform them into works of rolling art. Like so many others in the custom field, Arlen Ness' interest started as a hobby, growing and growing as people took note of his creations and begged him to craft something equally extraordinary for them.

Beginning with a 1937 Knucklehead bought for $300 in 1967, he now designs and manufactures everything from the tiniest, most exquisite chrome-plated detail to his own overhead-cam "Harley" twin, the engine that powers the gleaming Light-Ness machine. "I started out painting motorcycles in my

garage," he explains, "but it got so busy with people coming and going that I couldn't get any work done, so I ended up renting a little store. This meant people would go there instead so I could work at home in the daytime and kept the shop open at night."

From paint jobs and custom handlebars, he now runs a huge mail-order business from a 70,000sq ft (6,500sq metre) building in San Francisco's Bay area. He actually builds just a handful of specials each year, at prices ranging from $25,000 to $50,000, but turns away far more customers than that. Sometimes the problem is sheer pressure of work (would "Busy-Ness" make a good project?), sometimes it's aesthetic.

■ ABOVE *"Choppers"*
like this are now passé
in the US, but live on in
parts of Europe.

■ BELOW *Sometimes,*
Milwaukee must wonder
why it bothers at all.

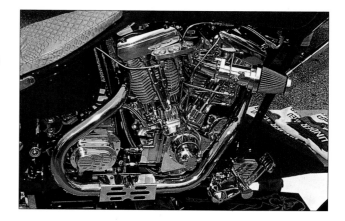

■ **LEFT** *Light-Ness (closest), Antique-Ness and Smooth-Ness, three of Arlen Ness' most famous creations.*

■ **BELOW** *Arlen Ness (left) with Hank, president of the Chopper Club.*

"We turn away quite a few people if we don't like a style they want or if we don't think they would be real happy… and others can't seem to make up their mind," he explains.

"There isn't a lot of money in building bikes. I just do it for fun." Or maybe Arlen just hates the one he hasn't built yet: Idle-Ness.

■ **THE BIKES**
The silver machine – "Light-Ness" – is powered by Ness' 100-inch (1,639cc) ohc "lightweight" motor housed in a special aluminium frame. Following the same theme, tank, fenders, mufflers and most other components are also highly-polished aluminium. Arlen values the bike at some $40,000.

The yellow bike is "Antique-Ness", Ness' first sidecar outfit. Based around a 1200cc Harley Sportster engine, it was created over a period of nine months by Arlen and fellow American customizers, Mun and Jimmy Rose. Built for Ness' wife, Bev, it was styled along the lines (if not the colour) of Harleys of the

■ **BELOW** *An earlier and slightly less radical Ness special.*

1920s. Similar machines can be bought in kit form for around $27,000.

Although to some eyes it resembles half of a 1959 Cadillac, "Smooth-Ness" was inspired by the sleek, flowing lines of a classic Bugatti motor car. The all-aluminium body houses a rubber-mounted Harley "Evo" V-twin in a prototype Softail-type chassis. It took a year to build and is valued at $100,000.

Competition

Although Harley-Davidson is not always automatically associated with the white heat of competition, it is part of the deep-seated American tradition of racing pretty much anything on wheels. The first mention of a Harley racing dates from 1904. Perry Mack (possibly the company's first employee) set a speed record on a local Milwaukee track as early as 1905. The first recorded "factory" win in actual competition came in 1908, with Walter Davidson at the controls.

Company presidents don't figure among the results any more, but Harley-Davidson has won since on tarmac, dirt, boards, ice, grass and just about any other medium possible. Much of this success has been in the spectacular field of American dirt-track racing, 130mph (210kph) speedway, with huge fields of 16 riders competing like fury for millimetres of space. On the grand prix front, Harley's Italian connection Aermacchi brought Walter Villa four world crowns between 1974 and 1976. The factory has recently been striving towards a competitive presence in world superbike action with the VR1000 twin ridden by former AMA Number Ones Chris Carr and Thomas Wilson, and more recently by former World Superbike champion Scott Russell.

☙ RACING

Harley-Davidson's early years were marked by racing successes too numerous to mention. The earliest of note came in 1908 when one of the first V-twins, ridden by company president Walter Davidson claimed victory in the FAM (Federation of American Motorcyclists) seventh annual endurance event in New York's Catskill Mountains. The 365-mile (587km) course was dauntingly rugged, yet "so strong was my confidence," Davidson later said, "that I carried with me no additional parts." This was in marked contrast to several other manufacturers, whose machines were followed by car-loads of spares.

In July of the same year, the Chicago Motorcycle Club sponsored a hill climb in nearby Algonquin, Illinois. Fastest time of the day went to Harvey Bernard riding a Harley-Davidson. Mysteriously, contemporary photographs clearly show Bernard aboard a V-twin machine, yet the model did not officially appear until early the following year.

The succeeding years were distinguished by numerous, similar Harley-Davidson successes, yet they almost exclusively involved machines which were privately owned and run. A company advertisement from September 1911 bragged, "We don't believe in racing and we don't make a practice of it, but when Harley-Davidson owners with their own stock machines win hundreds of miles from the factory, we can't help crowing about it."

This boast was nowhere more graphically demonstrated than in the San José road race of 1912, in which a 61-inch Model X8E triumphed by the small matter of 17 miles

■ ABOVE *Harley-Davidsons board racing in Los Angeles, 1912.*

■ LEFT *Harley had major success in racing from the outset.*

(27 kilometres). That same year, Harley-Davidson twins won at Bakersfield and the following year took first, second and third place in a 225-mile (362km) dash from Harrisburg to Pennsylvania and back, but these were private machines contesting relatively obscure races.

In 1914 – four years after Indian had won the prestigious Isle of Man TT – Milwaukee bowed to the inevitable when Bill Harley established a works race department which was to continue its winning ways into the 1970s. Some reports refer to instant success in taking that year's Dodge City 300-mile (480km) race, when in fact only two Harleys finished, well off the pace, in a race dominated by Indian. Clearly, the battle-hardened Springfield eight-valve twin was a formidable foe, but under the direction of the Bills Harley and Ottaway, Harley's progress was rapid. By 1915, Milwaukee twins were the bikes to beat.

■ ABOVE *One of the legendary "Peashooter" racers of the 1920s, in this case prepared for hill-climbing.*

■ BELOW RIGHT *From 1920, a board-track racer.*

The step from factory racers to racer production was a short and logical one. By 1916, $250 would buy any aspiring racer a special stripped-down competition version of the Harley twin, producing 11 horsepower and capable of around 75mph (120kph).

As well as speed, Harley iron chased many endurance records during the same period. In 1917, a Harley-Davidson ridden by Alan Bedell covered 1,000 miles (1,610km) non-stop at Ascot Park, taking almost 21 hours and averaging a remarkable 48.3mph (77.7kph).

In the same year, another Harley set a similar mark fitted with a sidecar.

RACE BOSSES

It's a remarkable fact that, once it finally got around to racing officially, Harley-Davidson needed a mere three race-team managers in all its many decades of competition – Bill Ottaway, Hank Syvertson and Dick O'Brien. They, too, became legends.

The factory crew's early successes were overseen by the cool gaze of Bill Ottaway. Described as "a wizard" by William Davidson, Ottaway began his career at Thor, manufacturer of proprietary motorcycle engines, leaving for Juneau Avenue in 1913. A talented engineer and a shrewd manager, he saw the factory squad through its formative years and into the glory days of the 1920s before

Hank Syvertson took over as director of racing.

Dick O'Brien began a lifetime of working on Harley engines at Puckett's in Orlando, Florida. Apart from a period of military service as a senior aircraft mechanic during the Second World War, he continued as a Harley service-shop manager, with a special talent for tuning racing machines – Daytona Speedway was, after all, only a couple of hours distant. In June 1957, he joined the factory race squad as Syvertson's assistant. Three months later Syvertson retired and O'Brien took the helm, a position he held until his retirement in 1983.

■ LEFT *Wrecking Crew at Dodge City in 1920. From left: race boss Bill Ottaway, Maldwyn Jones, Ralph Hepburn, Fred Ludlow, Otto Walker, Ray Weishaar, Jim Davis and mechanic Hank Syvertsen.*

■ **THE WRECKING CREW**

During the buoyant 1920s, Harley-Davidson's competitive exploits were even more remarkable than the salvos of new models roaring out of Milwaukee. In 1920, a Harley became the first powered vehicle to top California's 10,000ft (3,050 metre) "Old Baldy" hill-climb. In February 1921, at Fresno, a Harley became the first bike to win a race at an average of more than 100mph (160kph).

Many of the factory's innumerable successes came courtesy of the legendary Harley-Davidson "Wrecking Crew". The Crew was almost unbeatable on the dirt and boards of America from the days before the First World War until the factory briefly pulled out of racing following the 1920 slump. Board racing, on banked ovals of raw wood, was uniquely – and spectacularly – American.

The Crew included barnstorming individuals: Eddie Brinck, Otto Walker, Jim Davis, Leslie "Red" Parkhurst and many more. Walker marked the factory's withdrawal by taking a 61cu in, eight-valve machine to victory in a 50-mile (80km) race at San Joaquin, California, at the sensational average

speed of 101.43mph (163.23kph). The crew began 1920 by taking the first four places in the Ascot 100-miler (160.93km) race on America's fastest track. In February, Harleys set 23 records, including four by Parker at the kilometre, mile – both at more than 103mph (165kph) – two mile and five mile marks.

■ LEFT *Scott Parker, the most successful dirt-track rider in AMA history.*

These men, riding in little more than cloth caps, sweatshirts and jodhpurs, were tough little heroes in the same mould that was later to produce stars such as Cal Rayborn, Jay Springsteen and Scott Parker. The racing life was hard and cruel. Eddie Brinck himself was killed when a tyre blew out in a race at Springfield, Massachusetts.

As America's road system developed, it was only natural that men would create some form of contest on it. As early as 1920, Hap Sherer took a Sport Twin (584cc boxer) from Denver to Chicago in 48 hours – no easy feat even today. Meanwhile, Walter Hadfield made a habit of lowering the "Three Flags Run" record from Vancouver (Canada) to Tijuana (Mexico), a route on which Fred Deeley later averaged more than 104mpg (36km/litre). Perhaps most impressive of all was the remarkable Earl Hadfield, who covered more than 3,000-plus miles (4,800-plus km) between New York and Los Angeles in less than 78 hours. At around the same time, the immortal Windy Lindstrom was king of America's booming hill-climb scene, on specially-modified Milwaukee iron.

Harley victories were by no means confined to the United States. Harley-Davidson found willing, winning pilots as far apart as Scandinavia and Australia, notching up successes in fields as diverse as ice speedway and grass track. At the legendary banked

■ ABOVE *The legendary Cal Rayborn on the XR750, Brands Hatch, 1972.*

■ BELOW *Jay Springsteen is one in a long line of champions that stem from the legacy of the Wrecking Crew of the early part of the 20th century.*

Brooklands track in Surrey, England, Doug Davidson (no relation) took a factory 1000cc ioe twin to a record-breaking average of 100.76mph (162.15kph) over a flying kilometre. Within a few months, a similar machine ridden by Claude Temple had taken records in the hour, five mile, flying mile and kilometre.

Yet even these efforts paled when compared to those of the mercurial Englishman, Freddy Dixon, riding a special twin with four pipes and eight overhead valves. Dixon was nearly unbeatable in all forms of competition from hill-climbs to long-distance events around the daunting Brooklands circuit. On 9 September 1923 at Arpajon, near Paris, Dixon set a new world speed mark of 106.8mph/171.8kph (a record Harley-Davidson would not hold again until 1970). Ten months later he was at it again, flying through the half-mile at the Clipstone Speed Trials at 103.44mph (166.47kph). In 1925 he averaged 100.1mph (161kph) winning the Brooklands 1000cc championship – possibly the noisiest victory ever, for the machine had no exhaust pipes.

■ LEFT *The
Knucklehead
streamliner on which
Joe Petrali set record
speeds at Florida's
Daytona Beach.*

■ JOE PETRALI

If Freddy Dixon had a counterpart on Harley's
home turf, it was surely the legendary
Joe Petrali. More than perhaps any other man,
Petrali single-handedly made Harley-Davidson
an unbeatable force during the late 1920s and
throughout the 1930s. Born in Sacramento,
California in 1904, he owned his first bike at
13 years of age and was racing – and winning –
on boards by the time he was 16. Petrali first
hit the big time when he showed up bike-less
at Altoona, Pennsylvania, in 1925. Luckily for
him, former Wrecking Crew man Ralph
Hepburn had broken a hand. Petrali took over
the factory Harley-Davidson instead. He was
practically unknown at the time.

Less than an hour later (59 minutes and 47.2
seconds later to be exact), Petrali was a legend.
He left the entire field of hardened pros in a
cloud of dust, averaging 100.32mph
(161.45kph) in the 100-mile (160.93-km) race
over Altoona's lightning-fast boards. Earlier
that same day, Jim Davis won the five-mile
"sprint" at over 110mph (177kph) – at a time
when the Indianapolis car race was being won
at less than 101mph (163kph). From then on,
there was no stopping Joe Petrali. He became
so dominant that, for more than a decade, the
rest were effectively riding for second place. In
1935, he won every single event of the
National season, including five wins in a single

day at Syracuse, New York. In 1937, he took a
Knucklehead streamliner through the timing
strip on the sands of Daytona Beach at
136.183mph (219.159kph), a record that
still stands.

■ THE MICHIGAN MEN

Flint, Michigan, must be a remarkable place.
Jay Springsteen is from Flint, where they build
Chevrolets out of the same hard stuff. So is
Scott Parker. So, too, is "Black" Bart Markel.

■ BELOW *Scott Parker
rockets the XR750
around the Del Mar
track.*

refused to slow down for the turns," according to Harley-Davidson race boss Dick O'Brien. Instead, he just threw the bike sideways and slid round the turn – or slid off.

During a dirt-track career that began in 1957 and spanned 23 years, Markel was the original Michigan hard man. He won three national titles (in 1962, 1965 and 1966) but it was his style that caught the eye. Old boys still whistle in awe at the memory of Markel bouncing off guard rails, bales and other bikes – whatever it would take him to get to the finish line first.

Like the rest, he had to race on tarmac as well as dirt to take those titles. He crashed an awful lot, for the simple reason that "he

■ ABOVE LEFT *Scott Parker (left) and Jay Springsteen (right), both chips off the same Flint block.*

■ ABOVE RIGHT *During the 1950s, the flathead KRTT needed a capacity edge to compete with European ohv twins.*

■ BELOW *As well as his prowess on dirt, Springsteen was an able road racer, as here with the Sundance twin.*

For the past decade and perhaps for all time, Parker has been "The Man" on the ovals, picking up titles most years and smashing every record in the books. Like his buddy Jay Springsteen (who was champion from 1976 to 1978), he's also from Flint, Michigan.

Born in 1962, Parker started riding at the age of six and racing at 13. He picked up his first Number One plate in 1988, posting four consecutive titles before Harley-Davidson team-mate Chris Carr took the crown in 1992. Ricky Graham won in 1993, but Parker struck back with five consecutive crowns since. His nine titles make him far and away the most successful rider in AMA dirt-track history.

THE HOLE IN THE WALL GANG

In the Depression years of the 1930s, people would try almost anything to turn a buck. If Evel Knievel enlivened the 1970s, the 1930s shone for an assorted bunch of desperadoes who might be called the "Hole in the Wall Gang". These weren't Butch and Sundance but a fellowship of maniacs who believed that if you hurtled a bike fast enough at a solid timber wall, you could punch clean through it. The first recorded case of a Harley-Davidson attempting the stunt came in Texas in 1932 when Daisy May Hendrich thudded repeatedly through inch-thick boards. (Daisy May, incidentally, was a man.) J.R. Bruce of Wooster, Ohio, went one better by setting the wall ablaze before the stunt. Wall stunts, burning or not, were a common feature of American county fairs in the 1930s.

■ RIGHT *Quarter-mile action at Daytona. The bikes are Rotax-engined single-cylinder "Harleys".*

■ DIRT TRACK

Dirt track "oval" racing spans the decades and is the essence of American motorcycle sport. This is the craziest and meanest of them all – chasing the prized "Number One" plate of the AMA champion. Although superficially similar to speedway, oval racing is held on tracks a mile or half-mile long where 750cc machines reach speeds in excess of 130mph(210kph).

Dirt track grew up on the county fairgrounds of middle America, a sort of rodeo on two wheels. In the early years, it was barely organized and, even during times when it was, it often wasn't: an "outlaw" series flourished in the 1940s. In 1946, the AMA founded the national championship which has been keenly contested ever since.

■ LEFT *Scott Parker leads the field into turn one during the Sacramento Mile.*

■ BELOW *The start of the "Dash for Cash" race at Daytona. Winner takes all.*

The pre-eminence of Americans in 500 road-racing grands prix has been ascribed to the special skills honed by dirt-track experience. Champion riders, including the likes of Kenny Roberts, Wayne Rainey, Eddie Lawson and most of the rest cut their teeth learning how to control bucking, sliding motorcycles on dirt.

The early Harley-Davidson heroes were men like Jimmy Chann, Joe Leonard and Carroll Resweber, who took ten titles between them from 1947 to 1961. In those days and until 1986, the champion's cherished "Number One" was decided in a series which included

■ ABOVE *What it's all about: the coveted Number One plate.*

■ BELOW *The all-conquering XR750, brutal and elegant at the same time.*

quarter-, half- and mile flat-track racing, TT Steeplechase (a cross between dirt track and motocross) and European-style road-racing. These days, there's a separate road-race series, and the days of the great all-rounders are over – Bubba Shobert was the last, with three consecutive AMA titles. Shobert held the record for mile wins with 25, until eclipsed by current champ Scott Parker in 1991. The famed Harley-Davidson "Number One" logo, incidentally, was designed in 1970 to celebrate Mert Lawwill's AMA Grand National title.

Done well – and the top exponents do it very well – dirt track is oddly balletic, almost poetry on wheels. But it can go wrong with sickening suddenness, ending in a maelstrom of muck, blood and machinery. Catch the motorcycle film *On Any Sunday* and you'll see men thrown through four-inch fence posts, clamber to their feet, dust off the dirt and the straw and climb right back on their bikes. You'll see men who can't walk drifting both wheels at three figure speeds. You'll see Dick Mann saw off a plaster cast – "I'm a fast healer" – just to chase that Number One plate.

■ ABOVE *Springsteen's XR750, sponsored by Bartels of California.*

DRAG RACING

If all Harley-Davidsons thunder, none thunder with quite such a clap as fire-breathing drag machines. Like so much else in motorcycle sport, drag racing lies deep in the soul of America. Naturally, Harley-Davidsons have always been there when the lights go out at the start of the quarter mile. Men like Marion Owens, Leo Payne and Danny Johnson, with his celebrated double-engine Harley, continued to show that big-twin power was a force to be reckoned with long after multi-cylinder machines and two-strokes had dominated in other fields.

■ ABOVE, LEFT AND RIGHT *The idea is to expend as much money and effort in the shortest possible time. Strange, but thousands are addicted to this power-mad sport.*

■ CAL RAYBORN

The great Cal Rayborn never won the coveted Number One plate but that didn't stop him being the best. Rayborn was the consummate road racer, a true natural and arguably the man who opened the door to Kenny Roberts, Wayne Rainey and other Americans who have since made their mark in grand prix competition. From Spring Valley, California, Rayborn won Daytona twice, as well as nine other major AMA road-race wins. Yet his career almost never began at all – in 1958, at only 18 years of age, he broke his back at California's Riverside circuit.

Never truly at home on dirt, Rayborn compensated with absolute mastery on tarmac. In 1968, he became the first man to average 100mph (160.93kph) winning the then world-renowned Daytona 200-miler (321.86km) – and comfortably: he recorded 101.29mph (163kph). In the process, his XR750 Harley-Davidson lapped the entire field. He won again

in 1969, in what would prove to be the last Daytona triumph for Milwaukee. British fans will remember him for trouncing the field in the Easter Match Races in 1972, also on a factory XR750. The big V-twin had almost

■ BELOW *The late, great Cal Rayborn pictured at Oulton Park, England, at the Easter Match Races, 1972.*

EVEL KNIEVEL

If Harley-Davidson's earlier successes had been in racing, Evel Knievel had a better idea: he'd make them fly. A pure showman, Knievel chased women and long-jump records in roughly equal measure. Beginning in 1970, his crazy schemes ran on Harley-Davidson power, mainly with a succession of XR750 machines.

Knievel's bikes had to be tough – if not quite as tough as the man himself. He jumped cars (21 at Ontario Speedway on 28 February 1971), trucks, buses and even the fountain at Caesar's Palace in Las Vegas. Evel's problem was that he was effectively on piece-rate – his fees rose with the number of obstacles cleared. And he liked money: the jumps got bigger and the litany of crashes grew longer. In the process, he broke most of his important bones and a lot of smaller ones. When you went to watch Evel Knievel, you knew that you were in for a show. The Las Vegas leap resulted in one of his more spectacular crashes when he

■ ABOVE *Evel Knievel, the ultimate showman – especially for Milwaukee. The tank says "Harley-Davidson" but the engine's a Triumph twin.*

been dismissed in favour of factory Triumphs, Nortons and Japanese machines, but Rayborn made them eat their words.

Rayborn also found time for a succession of speed record attempts, in his case on Utah's Bonneville salt flats. In 1970, he took a pencil-thin, 19ft (6-metre), streamlined 1480cc Sportster to a staggering 254.84mph (410.11kph), a figure he later improved to 265.49mph (427.25kph).

Rayborn was killed tragically in 1973 while riding in Australia, ironically on a two-stroke which seized and threw him into a trackside barrier.

■ RIGHT *The Sport-engined streamliner which took the 250cc land speed record in 1965, driven by George Roeder, pictured here.*

■ FAR RIGHT *Here the Knievel flying machine is pictured astride the genuine Harley article.*

bounced off cars, cartwheeling through the
Caesar's Palace parking lot.

By 1978, Knievel had run out of
conventional things to jump and crash into, and
announced he would leap the Grand Canyon
instead. The Canyon is over a mile wide and
almost as deep, so the local Native American
tribe probably did him a favour when they
vetoed the plan. Undeterred, Knievel turned
his sights to the Snake River Canyon,
abandoning his beloved Harley-Davidson for a
rocket-powered projectile. However, the rocket
only fizzed, and the attempt was a failure.

In 1999, Knievel's son put the record
straight when he, finally and triumphantly,
leapt over the Grand Canyon.

■ GRANDS PRIX

Whatever disappointments the arrangement
brought in terms of sales, Harley's ties to
Aermacchi produced resounding success on
the world stage during the mid-1970s. Factory
RR-250 and RR-350 twins ridden by Italy's
Walter Villa won three consecutive 250cc
world titles and one 350cc title between
1974 and 1976.

Producing 58bhp at 12,000rpm and 70bhp
at 11,400rpm respectively, these were unlike
traditional Harley-Davidson twins.

The engines were two-stroke, initially aircooled but later with full liquid cooling. The
gearboxes housed six ratios, due to the RR's
narrow, peaky powerband. These two-stroke

■ ABOVE LEFT *Based
on the XR1000 roadster
engine, Lucifer's
Hammer surprised many
onlookers by its speed
in Battle of the Twins
competition during
the 1980s.*

■ ABOVE RIGHT
*Walter Villa contesting
the 250cc Belgian
grand prix at Spa-
Francorchamps in 1977
on an RR250. Despite
carrying the number 10,
he was world champion
at the time.*

■ LEFT *An Aermacchi
350 charges round the
Brands Hatch circuit.*

twins were also raced with some success in the United States by championship-winning riders such as Cal Rayborn and Gary Scott.

■ LUCIFER'S HAMMER

Perhaps the single most celebrated Harley racer of recent times, Lucifer's Hammer began its racing life with a win at Daytona in 1983 with the great Jay Springsteen on the saddle. The same bike went on to dominate American Battle of the Twins racing (under Harley Owners' Group sponsorship) during much of the 1980s, taking Gene Church to three consecutive American titles.

Powered by a highly-tuned XR1000 engine generating 104bhp at 7,000rpm, the Hammer was timed at no less than 158mph (254kph) at Daytona. The XR750 road race frame, albeit heavily reworked, had debuted at Daytona fully ten years before Springsteen's epic win, showing that at Milwaukee, they build 'em to last.

■ 883 SPORT TWINS SERIES

The Sport Twins series, launched in the United States in 1989, quickly became a worldwide phenomenon. A "one-make" competition for modified 883cc Harley twins, the series' instant success saw it exported to race tracks

■ ABOVE *A Harley superbike – the factory VR1000.*

■ ABOVE RIGHT *Harley's inspired 883 Sportster series even attracted stars such as Jay Springsteen.*

■ BELOW *Using double overhead cams in each head, four valves per cylinder and fuel injection, the VR1000 is unlike any Harley ever seen on the street.*

all around the world, where spectators would flock to hear the thunder of a grid-full of Milwaukee twins. When Harley created the series, it probably expected it to be an all-American affair. If so, they were mistaken. That very first American Sports Twins series title was won by an Englishman, Nigel Gale.

■ VR1000

The factory has recently been striving towards a competitive presence in world superbike action. This has been achieved with the VR1000 twin ridden by former AMA Number Ones Chris Carr and Thomas Wilson and, latterly, by the former World Superbike champion, Scott Russell.

HARLEY-DAVIDSON
MODELS

The section that follows is a guide to the major models produced by Harley-Davidson, from the first primitive single of 1903 to the style kings and lavishly-equipped cruisers of today. It is not an attempt to cover every Harley-Davidson model, but all the most important and significant examples are included.

In reviewing machines spanning Harley-Davidson's history, the reader might become aware of one overriding enigma. The company is certainly the most enduring of all the world's motorcycle marques and is currently enjoying an almost unparalleled period of success. Yet, while other motorcycle manufacturers leap headlong into increased technical complexity, Harley-Davidson is as dedicated as ever to its original convictions of sound design and solid simplicity, remaining faithful to its dependable, thoroughbred V-twins.

What Harley-Davidson has in abundance is that indefinable quality called "character" – an attribute no specification panel can reveal. Harley-Davidsons are visceral. They have guts and charisma. Only by riding one can you really begin to understand.

The Singles

Harley-Davidson's future was forged not out of the rumble of V-twins, but with the thump of simple, single-cylinder engines. The very first examples differed little from the 1903 prototype, and the engines conformed to the same basic "F-head" design housed in a primitive chassis only slightly removed from bicycle practice.

It was inevitably plain and basic, but this humble single showed a ruggedness that was to become a Milwaukee hallmark. Only ten years after the debut of the first Harley-Davidson model, the company was advertising that one of its machines had travelled 100,000 miles (160,930km) on its original bearings. In those days of dirt roads, mud, dust and potholes, bikes had to be tough.

These attributes of durability, simplicity and economy ensured that singles figured somewhere in the Harley-Davidson range well into the 1930s. It was during the era of the singles that Harley's credo was first expressed: "Experience has shown that it is preferable to use a comparatively large motor running at moderate speed in preference to a small motor running at high speed." Those words appeared in a publicity brochure printed in 1905 but could almost have been written today.

FIRST SINGLE, 1903–11

■ BELOW AND BOTTOM *One of the first De Dion-Bouton-inspired singles. Pedal assistance was essential on hills. The belt final drive with its crude de-clutching mechanism is clearly seen in the lower photograph. The 1910 "Silent Gray Fellow" is altogether more sophisticated but retains pedals and belt final drive.*

Harley-Davidson's first motorcycle, though nominally a single-cylinder model, evolved with the company over a production span of eight years. During that time, annual production figures soared from fewer than a handful to over 4,000 as demand – and know-how – grew in leaps and bounds. One thing that changed relatively little was the price: $200 in 1904, yet only $25 more by the time production ceased in 1911.

The heart of the engine was a bolted-up crankshaft running car-type, plain, big-end bearings in cast aluminium crankcases. Above this sat a one-piece iron cylinder head and cylinder barrel housing an iron piston. To allow for differential expansion – its top generated far more heat than its bottom – each piston was tapered, a considerable machining achievement for the time. Valve layout was inlet-over-

exhaust, the "automatic" or "vacuum" inlet valve controlled – crudely – via pressure created by the rise and fall of the piston. Removable housing permitted the extrication of both valves for servicing: no method of valve-lash adjustment was available until 1908.

The initial cylinder dimensions of 3 x 3½in (76.2 x 88.9mm) gave a displacement of 24.74cu in (405cc). In 1905, the bore increased to 3⅛in (79.4mm), giving 26.84cu in (440cc). At the same time, the single loop frame was redesigned, as all previous examples

SPECIFICATIONS (1909)	
Engine	single cylinder ioe with automatic inlet valve
Capacity	30.16cu in (495cc)
Transmission	single speed, leather belt drive
Power	around 3.5bhp
Weight	185lb (84kg)
Wheelbase	51in
Top speed	around 45mph (72kph)

showed a tendency to crack at the headstock. Capacity was further increased to 30.16cu in (495cc) in 1909 by a ⅟₁₆in (1.6mm) increase in bore, by which time the exhaust port had also migrated from the side towards the front of the cylinder. Until 1910, all the motors had used horizontal "beehive" finning for both barrel and head; in 1911 this changed to distinctive vertical cylinder head finning.

Lubrication, like almost all engines of the time, was "total-loss" – a gravity feed dripping oil into the engine from a half-gallon (1.9 litre) tank, good for around 750 miles (1,200km). Transmission was of the simplest possible type with a 1¼in-wide (32mm), two-ply leather belt driving the rear wheel directly. There was no gearbox or clutch, although belt tension could be adjusted on the move by 1911.

The starting technique was straightforward, if energetic – run alongside then jump on board and pedal like mad until the motor fired.

A hand-crank starter became available in 1906 for an additional cost, and was standardized the following year, although neither method of starting was notably elegant.

Like modern motorcycles, power was governed by a twist-grip on the right-hand handlebar and a simple "coaster" brake in the rear hub slowed things down. Lighting of any kind was only

made available with the introduction of acetylene lights in the final year of production. Initially, suspension consisted entirely of springs under the leather saddle – and whatever the rider could suffer – but, in 1907, a crude but remarkably effective Sager front fork was added to ease the pain.

As well as standard, conservative "piano" black, by 1906 the single was also available – at an extra cost – in "Renault" pale grey with red pin-striping. This model thus became known from then on as "The Silent Gray Fellow", partly in tribute to its unusually effective silencing. Unpainted metal parts were nickel-plated and the aluminium engine covers were brightly polished to a high shine.

■ ABOVE LEFT *By 1907, the single had grown to 26.84cu in (440cc), was looking more sophisticated and had changed hue: "The Silent Gray Fellow".*

■ ABOVE RIGHT *A 1905 24.74cu in (405cc) single, which cost $200 when new.*

■ ABOVE *A very original 1907 single undergoing restoration work.*

HIDDEN TREASURE

The very first production Harley-Davidson may currently enjoy pride of place behind a bullet-proof glass screen in the Juneau Avenue lobby, but it hasn't always been quite so treasured.

The bike was originally retained by the company and sent to the Pan American Exposition in California in 1915 (since which time Harley has kept at least one example from each year of production). Upon its return, however, the company somehow "forgot" this bike was Number One. During the 1970s, it was damaged in transit to the Rodney C. Gott

Museum in York, but its true identity remained unrealized, even while it was being repaired.

It was only when it underwent a recent comprehensive restoration at the hands of Harley Archives craftsman, Ray Schlee, that the machine's true pedigree was disclosed – by internal parts bearing the legend "Number 1." It is believed to have been raced in 1904 but is now housed in a 1905 frame, as all the earlier examples broke at the headstock.

This unique machine has now been insured for $2 million.

MODEL 5-35 SINGLES, 1913–18

The second-generation single-cylinder machine, produced from 1913 to 1918, housed a refinement of the earlier engine rather than an all-new design. Although the bore remained unchanged at 3⅜in (84.1mm), the stroke increased from 3½ to 4in (88.9 to 101.6mm), giving a capacity of 34.47cu in (565cc). The new engine was known generically as the 5-35, signifying 5 horsepower and 35 cu in.

Many lessons learned during the troubled development of the first twin were incorporated in the new single's design. Valve layout was still inlet-over-exhaust, although now the inlet valve followed the revised V-twin practice of mechanical operation via a long push rod on the motor's right-hand side. The camshafts – one exhaust, one inlet – were driven by a chain of gears, ending with the Bosch magneto (replaced by a Remy instrument from 1915) which provided the sparks.

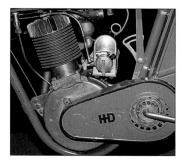

SPECIFICATIONS	
Engine	ioe single
Capacity	34.47cu in (565cc)
Transmission	1-, 2- and 3-speed
Wheelbase	55in (1,400mm)
Top speed	around 54mph (87kph) (side-valve) or 65mph (105kph) (ohv)

■ ABOVE AND BELOW *By the time this Model 9-B was built in 1913, chain drive was a factory option on single-cylinder machines and twins. Both the chain-drive and belt-drive singles cost the same: $290, $60 less than the twin.*

As before, the iron cylinder head and barrel were one-piece, accommodating a steel three-ring piston. The crankcases were of aluminium, in which a high-grade steel crankshaft ran on phosphor-bronze main bearings, with the whole crank assembly balanced. Lubrication was still total-loss, engine oil being metered by hand from its own compartment in the tank slung beneath the frame's top rail. A sight-glass below the tank gave the rider some idea how frequently to deliver drops of oil. As well as manipulating this, the rider was required to adjust the degree of ignition advance (in other words, the precise point at which the spark plug ignited the mixture), by means of yet another control lever. In those days, getting the best out of an engine was not a simple business. It demanded considerable awareness from the operator.

Perhaps the most obvious difference between these early singles was the replacement of belt with chain as the drive medium, eliminating the wet-weather slip that plagued all leather belt drives. On early examples, the drive was taken direct, via roller chain, from a sprocket on the left-hand end of the crankshaft to another on the rear hub. The same hub also contained a type of rudimentary clutch operated by a long lever on the left side of the machine. Starting involved placing the machine on its stand, which lifted the rear wheel off the ground, then vigorously rotating the bicycle-type pedals. These same

pedals, when rotated backwards, engaged the "coaster-type" rear brake via a chain on the right-hand side. Lever-operated brakes did not appear until 1918.

A "step-starter" and Harley's first two-speed rear hub arrived in 1914 (also in the V-twin), offering increased flexibility with maximum speeds of around 54 and 65mph (87 and 105kph) in the two ratios. Within a year, this deceptively intricate device had given way to three-speed transmission with a true sliding-pinion gearbox on better-specified models. Nonetheless, single-speed and even belt-drive models continued to be built for some years.

Chassis refinements included a more robust front suspension offering around 2in (50mm) of travel. The rear, of course, would remain rigid for many years. However, a degree of consolation was provided by Harley's patented "Full Floteing" seat.

As well as the paired springs common on other motorcycles, this seat featured a hinge at the front and a coil spring inside the seat post to cushion the rider from the worst of the bumps.

MODELS A & B SINGLE, 1926–34

Although single-cylinder machines were as much a hallmark of Harley-Davidson's formative years as the big V-twins with which they are now associated, Juneau Avenue produced almost no such models from 1919 until 1926. The sole exception was the Model CD, a 37.1cu in (608cc) machine created by the simple expedient of removing one pot from the 74-inch twin. It was built in very small numbers from 1921 to 1922 and was intended for commercial use only. When singles did reappear, they were considerably smaller than before, displacing just 21.1cu in (346cc) compared to the earlier 30-inchers.

Somewhat confusingly, the single was known simultaneously as both Model A and Model B. The former denoted a magneto version, the latter that the

machine was fitted with a generator and coil ignition. This was further refined into Models AA and BA Sport Solos, where the second letter indicated that the engine had overhead valves. The

SPECIFICATIONS	
Engine	side-valve or overhead valve single
Capacity	21.1cu in (346cc)
Transmission	3-speed
Power	8bhp (side-valve) or 12bhp (ohv)
Wheelbase	55in (1,400mm)
Top speed	around 50mph (80kph) (side-valve) or 60mph (96kph) (ohv)

more basic model, designated by a simple A or B was of straightforward "flathead" design, with valves side-by-side and operated by short push-rods.

The overhead-valve model was an altogether more potent piece of machinery that would achieve considerable competition success as the legendary Peashooter racer. It was inevitably less aggressive in roadster trim, yet still capable of what was then a giddy 4,800rpm and close to 65mph (105kph). Its side-valve sibling, on the other hand, struggled to exceed 50mph (80kph). Despite this marked difference, both engines were rated at 3.31 horsepower. At the time, quoted power figures were not a measure of actual output, merely a function of piston displacement and thus quite meaningless as a reflection of performance. Modern power figures, of course, describe actual output. Strangely, Harley chose to promote the flathead at the expense of the more advanced engine, probably because side-valves would soon comprise the vast bulk of the Milwaukee range.

Mechanically, the engine featured a lightweight aluminium alloy piston

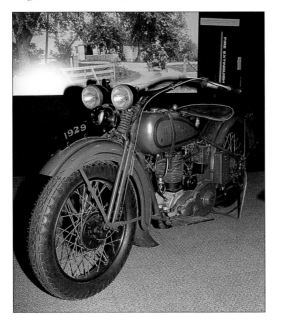

■ ABOVE *The ohv "Peashooter" engine. The push-rods, rocker arms and exposed valves are clearly visible.*

■ LEFT *Dual "bullet" headlights first appeared on this 1929 500cc single, derived from the Models A and B. Note the front brake – another novelty introduced the previous year.*

■ LEFT *Stripped-down racing version of the ohv "Peashooter". Note low, pulled-back handlebars and spartan saddle.*

(initially iron for the side-valve machines) running in a cast-iron cylinder. Typically for the time, the overhead's valve gear was exposed, although the 21.1 cu in (344cc) single was the first Milwaukee engine lubricated by a proper mechanical pump. Nonetheless, a hand pump was retained for supplementary oiling when the engine was under extreme loads. Transmission was by the now-familiar three-speed sliding gear, driven by a foot-operated single-plate dry clutch.

By the time of the new single's debut in 1926, electrical equipment had leaped forward in specification and dependability. Although full electrical equipment was optional (Models A and AA came as standard with just a magneto to generate sparks), it was also comprehensive. Generator models featured a coil and distributor (to power and time the ignition), battery, horn, two-bulb headlight and tail-light, all controlled from a switch on the steering

head – everything you might expect to find on a modern motorcycle, except stop-light and indicators. Less can be said for the cycle parts. True, the single wore the new type of teardrop petrol (gas) tank, which wrapped over the top frame tube rather than hung from it, as

before. At the front, Harley's familiar sprung forks gave some comfort and control, but the rear end was rigid and would remain so for more than 20 further years. The rear hub did contain a brake – a 5¾in (146mm) drum – but the front wheel contributed nothing to retardation. It would be another two years before Milwaukee installed their first front brake. During the early 1930s, "21"'s sales were hit, partly by the relative success of the Series C single, but mainly by the Depression. Domestic supplies were halted during 1931 when just three examples were exported. The ohv model never reappeared, although flathead sales rallied slightly before the model was axed at the end of 1934.

■ ABOVE RIGHT *Note the gear lever (left) and fillers for oil and fuel. The switch console is a later addition.*

■ RIGHT *Although only $40 cheaper, flatheads such as this Model 26-B solo comfortably outsold the more exotic ohv singles.*

MODEL C SINGLE, 1929–34

In 1929, the Model A and B singles got a bigger brother with the introduction of the Model C. Displacing 30.1cu in (493cc), the newcomer's top end was essentially half of the old 61-inch Model F/J twin, mated to the 21-inch single's bottom end. This was clearly a more sound solution than the trick many American racers had been pulling for years – they had simply removed one top end and connecting rod from the J, blanked off the hole and let rip on the track. Road riders demanded something slightly more elegant.

Unlike the "21" however, this time no overhead-valve variant was offered; the model was resolutely side-valve, although the greater pulling power of the 30-inch motor meant that, for the modest uses for which most singles were destined, no overhead valves were required. Power was sufficient for a top speed approaching 60mph (96kph).

Compared to the smaller single, the "30" was both bored and stroked with even more undersquare dimensions of 3 1⁄16 x 4in (78.6 x 101.6mm). Since it

SPECIFICATIONS	
Engine	side-valve single
Capacity	30.1cu in (493cc)
Transmission	3-speed
Power	10bhp
Wheelbase	57½in (1,460mm)
Top speed	around 56mph (90kph)

was also slower revving than the "21", a 42 per cent increase in capacity realised only a 25 per cent increase in power, from eight to ten horsepower. Both machines shared a similar three-speed transmission. An overhead-valve competition derivative, the Model CA (later CAC) was produced in very limited numbers. By the time of the Model C's debut in 1929, Harleys had begun to develop front brakes (they also

■ ABOVE *This Series C 500cc 3-speed single shows the low-line frame introduced in 1930.*

■ LEFT *A 1929 500cc single. At the time, the vibrant paint job was optional only on twins.*

featured on the 45-inch twin that
appeared in the same year). Like the
rear brake, this was a simple, single-
leading shoe drum, but activated by a
lever on the right handlebar, as is the
practice today.

Early examples shared the same
frame and running gear as contemporary
21-inch singles, but during the second
year of production the larger engine was
installed in a chassis "borrowed" from
the twin. This turned the robust little
single into a "full-size" motorcycle –
ironically with a lower seat height but
increased ground clearance.

More ironically still, in 1933 it was
joined by the Model CB, essentially a
30-inch engine in 21-inch running gear

– a choice perhaps prompted by excess
stock of the latter.

Worthy as the Model C was, the
majority of American motorcycle buyers
still hankered after twin-cylinder
pulling power even during the depths
of the Depression.

A measure of the singles' problem at
home was that, during 1929, sales of the
21- and 30-inch singles combined were
little more than half of those of the
Series D twin – 3,789 units compared
to 6,856.

Nonetheless, though comparatively
unheralded in their own country, the
sturdy little singles proved popular
overseas as Harley-Davidson continued
to develop its international markets,

■ ABOVE *This mammoth modern
ElectraGlide might look a far cry from
the early singles, but they are very much
its ancestors.*

where the sheer weight and size of the
big twins often posed problems to
potential buyers. Not surprisingly, the
larger single had soon became the
dominant seller.

Initially priced at just $20 more
than the $235 price-tag of the "21", the
Model C comfortably outsold the
smaller machine from 1930 onwards.
More than 5,000 units of the popular
Series C were produced in total over
the life span of the model, which was to
be six years in all.

Lightweights

When the Second World War ended, Harley-Davidson was a purveyor of large-capacity, four-stroke V-twins, precisely the type of machines on which their recent success has been built. Yet it somehow became corporate policy to diversify, entering any other niche market they might find. During the next 30 years, Milwaukee's catalogues would reverberate with the sounds of two-stroke commuters, scooters, middleweight four-strokes, trail bikes, minibikes and whatever else an increasingly desperate company believed might sell – even snowmobiles.

Although some of these lightweight models were half-baked and ill-conceived, others were fine machines – but they never could be "proper" Harley-Davidsons. It took Harley many years to realise that it was not a volume manufacturer. The process involved the ultimately abortive purchase of Italian subsidiary Aermacchi, a takeover by AMF and a slow decline into crippling financial difficulties. Worst of all, the core big twin models were neglected to a degree that almost proved fatal.

STATESIDE
STROKERS

■ LEFT AND BELOW LEFT *Two variants of the Milwaukee two-stroke derived from the German DKW. Note rigid rear end, "Tele-Glide" front forks and the fuel tank shape which would become the inspiration for the Sportsters.*

■ MODEL S-125, 1948–52
MODEL ST-165, 1953–9
MODEL B HUMMER,
1955–9

Harley-Davidson's first venture into the world of two-strokes owed much to the end of the Second World War. On the one hand, it was assumed that thousands of demobbed GIs would crave almost any motorcycle they could lay their hands on, and the 125cc single was considered the ideal low-cost candidate. Second, the design was basically that of the pre-war DKW RT125.

When partition placed the factory in the new East Germany, the design passed to the Allies as war reparations. British BSA's hugely successful Bantam was also a DKW copy, as was the very first Yamaha, the YA1 "Red Dragonfly".

Producing just three horsepower from its simple piston-ported, air-cooled engine, the S-125 must have been a profound disappointment to any American biker raised on big four-stroke power.

Juneau Avenue was evidently hopeful about selling these machines in huge

SPECIFICATIONS: S-125

Engine	2-stroke single-cylinder
Capacity	125cc
Transmission	3-speed
Power	3bhp
Wheelbase	50in (1,270mm)
Top speed	around 40mph (64kph)

numbers, producing more than 10,000 in the model's first year, but sales proved poor, settling to around 4,000 per annum even after the introduction of a "Tele-Glide" version with telescopic forks in 1951.

A bore increase in 1953, from 52 to 60mm, resulted in the slightly zippier 165cc Model ST. A restricted version, the STU, was also available.

Two years later, the Model B Hummer – using essentially the same 125cc engine and transmission as the first Model S – appeared in the Harley-Davidson catalogue.

From 1960 to 1961, an updated 165cc range continued as the 6bhp BT and BTU (restricted to 5bhp) Super Ten. Harley-Davidson's slogan for this model went: "keen wheeling for teen wheeling".

■ ABOVE *The ST-165: the striking quartered tank emblem dates from 1957.*

■ LEFT *The first two-stroke was this Model S of 1948. Note the girder front forks.*

■ BELOW *The Pacer was the pure street version of the Model BT range of 165 and 175cc two-strokes.*

■ BOTTOM *A Topper in conventional livery. Although quite advanced, the $450 machine failed to cash in on the scooter boom.*

■ BELOW *A Topper Scooter, now used as Harley's corporate paddock transport.*

■ RANGER, PACER, SCAT, BOBCAT, 1962–6

This quartet was another attempt to broaden the Harley range and allow Milwaukee to compete as a mass-market player. In hindsight, the strategy was clearly misguided, but Milwaukee believed there was a niche market of buyers not quite ready for the new 250cc Sprint (nor for the big twins). The Ranger and its siblings were the result.

All four machines, designated Model BT, shared a two-stroke engine derived from the Super 10, but with increased stroke from 60 to 61mm for a capacity of 175cc on all but the 1962 Pacer and Ranger. As with the Topper, "full power" and 5bhp versions were built.

Models that year were the street-only BT Pacer, the dual-purpose BTH Scat and the BTF Ranger, a stripped-down, off-road variant without lights. The first examples had rigid rear ends, but

models that had swinging-fork suspension appeared for 1963.

The Ranger was dropped for 1963 while the Pacer and Scat gave way to the BTH Bobcat in 1966.

Available in road and optional off-road guises, this lasted for one year, proving to be the last of the American-built Harley lightweights.

■ TOPPER SCOOTER, 1960–5

The Model A Topper – which was Milwaukee's obvious attempt to cash in on the scooter boom which swept the Western world during the late 1950s – employed a 165cc two-stroke with identical bore and stroke to the old ST but with the cylinder laid down horizontally to reduce engine height.

Power was claimed to be 9bhp from the 1961-on high-compression engine (Model AH), with a "restricted" five-horsepower version (Model AU) sold in those American states which permitted the use of low output two-wheelers without a driver's licence.

Unlike earlier three-speed Harley strokers, this time the "Scootaway" transmission was automatic, using belt drive and variable flanged wheels to change ratios.

The system was unusual but by no means new – the Rudge Multi and

American-built NeraCar had featured similar drives decades before – yet it did anticipate today's fully automatic commuter machines.

Other Topper novelties included a rubber-mounted engine with reed-valve induction, a parking brake, under-seat stowage space and lawnmower-style hand-starting.

By all accounts, the boxy Topper was a quirky but competent device which might have fared better had it not arrived just as the scooter market went into decline.

Sales of the $430 machine went from almost 4,000 to just 500 during its six years on the books.

Ironically – given that Harley-Davidson by then had an Italian factory – being "Made in Milwaukee" was no substitute for the true Latin style of other more genuinely Italian scooters, such as those that were made by Vespa or Lambretta.

SPECIFICATIONS: BOBCAT	
Engine	2-stroke single-cylinder
Capacity	175cc
Transmission	3-speed
Power	8bhp
Wheelbase	52in (1,320mm)
Top speed	around 60mph (96kph)

SPECIFICATIONS: TOPPER	
Engine	2-stroke single-cylinder
Capacity	165cc
Transmission	variable belt
Power	5bhp or 9bhp
Wheelbase	51.5in (1,310mm)
Top speed	around 50mph (80kph)

FORZA HARLEY

■ LEFT *Stripped-down Sprints proved surprisingly adept at dirt-track racing.*

■ SPRINT, 1961–74

The Sprint family of four-stroke singles, unveiled in September 1960, was the first tangible result of Harley-Davidson's purchase of the Aermacchi concern in Varese, Italy. Compared to much contemporary Milwaukee hardware, this was a technically advanced machine derived from the existing 250cc Ala Verde model, with an in-unit overhead-valve engine and superb handling from its spine frame, telescopic forks and swinging-fork rear end. With its unmistakable horizontal cylinder, variants of the same engine went on to innumerable race wins, including the famous Isle of Man TT, and remain hugely popular (and competitive) in classic racing today.

American buyers – despite the invitation to "thrill to the dynamic, virile note of its Hi-Flo tuned exhaust" – never quite warmed to the Sprint's lack of cubes and relatively revvy nature, yet the bike was as capable a standard production machine as its siblings were racers. The stock street version, the

■ BELOW *Note the carburettor's steep downdraught angle, which is a hallmark of Aermacchi design.*

SPECIFICATIONS: SPRINT C (SS-350)	
Engine	ohv horizontal single
Capacity	246cc (344cc)
Transmission	4-speed (5-speed)
Power	18bhp @ 7,500rpm (27bhp @ 7,000rpm)
Weight	unknown (355lb/161kg)
Wheelbase	52in/1,320mm (56in/1,420mm)
Top speed	around 75mph/120kph (85mph/136kph)

■ BELOW *This early Sprint enjoys pride of place in the Harley Museum.*

Model C, claimed a potent (if slightly ambitious) 18bhp at 7,500rpm from its eager, free-breathing engine. This was joined by the Model H, an off-road variant, one year later, with high-compression pistons and an additional 1.5bhp. The "H" quickly became the more popular model and was used in a wide range of American competitions, from flat track to motocross as well as for purely recreational use.

The Sprint Model H later became known as the Scrambler, producing as much as 25bhp at a relatively giddy 8,700rpm.

In 1967, the original long-stroke configuration changed to short stroke – "The Sprint holds two land speed world records, so we improved it", went the ad. Two years later, the first 350 Sprints appeared, the ERS dirt racer and road-going 350cc SS. The SS was joined by the dual-purpose SX-350 in 1971 and given an electric starter two years later as the "Sprint" title was dropped from the range.

Pure road racing examples of the same 344cc single produced as much as 38bhp, good for 130mph (210kph) with

■ BELOW RIGHT AND LEFT *The M-50,
one of Milwaukee's strange two-stroke minibike range. Left is a 1965 example. By
1966 (right) it looked rather more like a
motorcycle. Such lightweights never truly
caught on in the USA.*

racing streamlining. Road riders,
with maybe 25bhp, had to be content
with top speeds in the low nineties.
Although a simple spine frame was
always good enough for the racers, the
final SS-350 inexplicably included a
heavy and wholly unnecessary twin-
downtube chassis.

With a career spanning 14 years, the
Sprint can rightly be regarded as one of
Harley's more successful forays away
from its core big twin-activities.

The Sprint's arrival coincided with
the appearance of advanced, lightweight
machines from Japan and, to some
extent, it profited from their success.

For the first time since the 1920s,
motorcycling in the United States was
developing a broad appeal, and the
market was soaring.

In 1971 it would peak at 2.1 million
new machines sold – a 40-fold increase
in less than 20 years.

The Sprint's weakness was not the
way it went (when the typically feeble
Italian electrical system was not
playing up), but in the way its price
kept rising when Japanese machines
seemed, year after year, to be offering
much more for much less.

SPECIFICATIONS: M-50	
Engine	2-stroke single-cylinder
Capacity	50cc
Transmission	3-speed
Wheelbase	44in (1,120mm)
Top speed	around 40mph (64kph)

■ BELOW *Trying hard to look like a "real"
bike, this 1967 M-50 sports saddlebags and
screen, despite a top speed of only around
40mph (64kph).*

■ **M-50, M-65, 1965–71**
In the mid 1960s Harley-Davidson's
quest for wider markets led it into the
50cc domain, a move which was
ultimately no more successful than its
other oddballs of the time. Ironically
those other V-twin warlords, the British
Vincent company, had dabbled
unsuccessfully with lightweights a
decade earlier.

The range began with the M-50 in
1965 and a racer-looking Sport version
12 months later. Both were built in
huge numbers – more than 25,000 in
the first two years – causing massive
oversupply and a sharp fall in price.
1967 brought an increase in capacity for
the M-65 and Sport, and more realistic
production figures.

For 1967, the original 50cc version
developed much-needed extra power
with the 65cc M-65, by which time
some 4,000 unsold M-50s were flooding
the market at knock-down prices.

Both models were available in
standard and "Sport" guise, the latter
with a racy fuel tank and seat.

A 65cc Leggero (which in Italian
means "light") version was also built
for the years 1970–1.

STRIVING FOR SALES

■ RAPIDO, TX, SX, STX, 1968–77

The Rapido family of machines was yet another attempt to find a profitable niche at the lightweight end of the market, this time with mainly off-road machines (although the first batch to be built were street bikes). Powered by a simple 123cc two-stroke single with four-speed transmission, the Rapido ultimately gave way to the five-speed, oil-injected TX, SS and SX models. Although often overlooked – not least by traditional big-twin dealers – the range established its pedigree in 1969 when three Rapidos completed an epic, 2,000-mile (3,2000km) ride across the Sahara, from Morocco to Nigeria. A smaller version of the TX, the 90cc Z-90, was produced.

■ SS AND SX SERIES, 1974–8

By the start of the 1970s, off-road machines were huge business in the American motorcycle scene. Inevitably, this market was hugely competitive, with prices pared to the bone – so much so that even the super-efficient Japanese factories would soon find themselves with massive amounts of unsold stock.

SPECIFICATIONS:
SX-175 (SX-250)

Engine	2-stroke single-cylinder
Capacity	174cc (243cc)
Transmission	5-speed
Wheelbase	56in (1,420mm)
Top speed	around 70mph/112kph (80mph/128kph)

At the same time, environmental concerns were targeting the high hydrocarbon emissions of the two-stroke engine. It was into this unpromising scene that the off-road SX range was launched for 1974. The SX was joined by the street-only SS-250 in 1975 plus its larger dirt sibling, the SX-250, with

■ TOP *Models such as this 1970 Rapido attempted to cash in on the Stateside boom in lightweight off-road machines.*

■ LEFT *An SX-250, one of the Italian two-stroke singles which tried to cash in on the trail-bike boom.*

the road-going SS-175 introduced for 1976. It was the off-roaders, however, that dominated production and sales. More than 25,000 machines were built in 1975, of which all but 3,000 were SX models. In the face of declining demand and over-supply, production slumped to 12,000 for 1976, then 1,400 in 1977 before disappearing almost completely as Harley-Davidson disentangled itself from its Italian partner in 1978.

These were actually quite competent motorcycles despite being very much copies of Yamaha's DT-series engines. The SX-250 in particular achieved quite striking competition success. More successful still was the MX250, derived from what was substantially the same engine. Both failed to survive the closure of Harley-Davidson's Italian operation in 1978.

SPECIFICATIONS:
SX-175 (SX-250)

Engine	2-stroke single-cylinder
Capacity	174cc (243cc)
Transmission	5-speed
Wheelbase	56in (1,420mm)
Top speed	around 70mph/112kph (80mph/128kph)

■ RIGHT *Outlandishly racy, maybe, but such dual-purpose lightweights were too far from Harley's heritage to succeed.*

SPECIFICATIONS: BAJA SR-100	
Engine	2-stroke single-cylinder
Capacity	98cc
Transmission	5-speed
Wheelbase	52in (1,320mm)
Top speed	around 60mph (96kph)

■ **BAJA, SR-100, 1970–4**
Named after the notorious desert race down Mexico's Baja peninsula, this 98cc off-roader used a high-performance engine derived from the Rapido's (with the bore reduced from 56 to 50mm) but now with five-speed transmission. The little machine was surprisingly potent and almost 7,500 were built during its five year span. It was ultimately unable to overcome both environmental concerns and the increasingly sophisticated Japanese competition, despite the introduction of an improved, oil-injected SR-100 version for 1973.

■ **MINIBIKES: SHORTSTER, X-90, Z-90, 1972–5**
Anything further removed from big-inch cruisers would be hard to imagine, but that's exactly what Harley unveiled with

the MC-65 Shortster of 1972. An obvious word play on "Sportster", the minibike used the M-65 engine and tiny 10in (254mm) wheels. Only 800 Shortsters were made before it grew to 90cc and became the X-90, which was built from 1973 to 1975. The Z-90 used the same engine, but in a quasi off-road chassis with larger wheels. "The Great American Freedom Machine" was how Harley billed the Italian-built two-

SPECIFICATIONS: X-90	
Engine	2-stroke single-cylinder
Capacity	90cc
Transmission	4-speed
Wheelbase	40.75in (1,035mm)
Top speed	around 55mph (88kph)

strokes, intended mainly for hitching on the back of a camper van rather than as serious commuter machines. Almost 17,000 of these minibikes were made, plus a similar number of Z-90s.

■ **SNOWMOBILE, 1970–5**
Like the Topper Scooter, Harley's Snowmobile was a tardy response to a passing craze. The fad initiated by the Canadian Bombardier company in the mid-1960s produced many similar machines, most with the same mechanical layout. Milwaukee's version, released in 1970, was steered by paired skis linked to motorcycle-type handle-bars at the front and driven by a broad belt at the rear. It was powered by a twin-cylinder two-stroke engine and the all-chain drive featured automatic transmission. There were two capacities (398 or 433cc) and electric or manual start. The Snowmobile was dropped from 1975, the victim of three consecutive mild winters.

■ LEFT *The X-90. Dismissed as "a menace" at the time, the minibike range is now considered cute and even collectible.*

■ RIGHT *Harley's snowmobile sold poorly. Maybe if they'd called it a SnowGlide...*

The First Twins

From a modern perspective, the expressions "Harley-Davidson" and "V-twin" are practically synonymous, yet it was not always so. Expanding the Harley range from singles to twins was a logical progression as Harley attempted to broaden its share in the rapidly expanding American market. The first American V-twin was the 695cc Curtiss of 1903 and Harley's first prototype was built three years later, making its first public appearance at the Chicago motorcycle show in 1907.

Exactly two years later, the Model 5-D twin was offered for sale, with the 45-degree configuration that is now a Harley hallmark. In almost every other respect, however, the engine was entirely different. As with the contemporary singles on which it was based, the F-head valve layout was inlet-over-exhaust, with the inlets of the "automatic" type, in which the valve was simply "sucked" open by the falling piston rather than being moved mechanically by a cam. After almost two decades of painstaking evolution, the F-head layout culminated in the legendary JH and JDH twin-cam models, the "superbike" race replica machines of their day.

As the 1920s drew to a close, side-valve engines became the Milwaukee norm, heralding an era dominated by flatheads such as the enduring "45" and the mammoth 80-inch VL – machines that put the muscle into Milwaukee.

EARLY TWINS

With the single having amply demonstrated its ruggedness, the twin that evolved from it ought to have been the same – only more so. Like the singles, the twin was single-speed with belt final drive, one-piece heads and barrels with horizontal "beehive" finning. Capacity was 53.7cu in (880cc), although several development engines of varying capacity had been built and even raced during the previous two years.

Yet the Model D proved remarkably troublesome, with a mere 29 built in 1909 and just one in 1910. Harley-Davidson appears to have blamed its shortcomings on its automatic inlet valves, although other sources suggest slippage of the belt drive was at fault. Either way, when the re-engineered twin returned in 1911, it had both mechanical inlet valves and a simple but sturdy belt tensioning device which could be operated on the move by the rider's left hand.

Although still designated the Model D, other changes included a slightly reduced capacity of 49.5cu in (811cc), from a bore and stroke of 76.2 and 88.9mm respectively, the same as the

SPECIFICATIONS: 1911 MODEL D	
Engine	F-head V-twin
Capacity	49.48cu in (811cc)
Transmission	single speed, leather belt drive with freewheel "clutch"
Power	around 7bhp
Wheelbase	56½in (1,435mm)
Top speed	around 60mph (96kph)

■ ABOVE RIGHT AND BELOW *Two views of another 1913 twin. Note the long push-rods to the inlet valves, far more dependable than the earlier "automatic" mechanism. The colour is "Renault Gray".*

1904 single. Beehive finning had also given way to vertical cylinder-head finning. At $250, the asking price was the same as the twin of 1908.

By all accounts, the revised twin proved far more dependable than its troublesome predecessor. Although little faster on the flat than the 30-inch single, it climbed hills far better – not least because the belt tensioner allowed the rider to maintain drive. Even so, a welter of improvements followed year on year. 1912 brought a new frame and a free-wheel clutch assembly in the rear wheel that freed the rider from the need to kill (and re-start) the engine if wishing to halt the machine. The same year saw the introduction of the first "one-litre" Harley, the 61-inch X8E, which also featured chain final drive. Although the two capacities were briefly produced in tandem, production of the smaller twin was dropped for 1913. The same year marked the debut of the

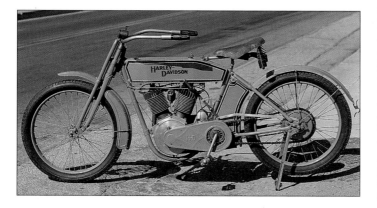

Model G "Forecar", a 61-inch twin with front-mounted luggage box – a sort of back-to-front precursor of the Servi-Car.

By this time, the engine was almost unrecognizable in its internal details from the original twin. Relatively exotic alloy steels were employed in high-stress areas of the engine, such as chrome vanadium steel for the "I" beam connecting rods, while roller and ball crankshaft bearings were widely used. A separate three-quart (2.8 litre) tank held oil for the total-loss lubrication system (used oil was either burnt by the engine or drained by hand from the crankcases). Like most contemporary engines, there was no oil pump: good old gravity and flailing engine parts moved the oil around the engine's internals and all the major bearings were of "self-lubricating" phosphor bronze. An auxiliary hand-operated oil pump had become standard in 1912, crudely metering about 25 "drops" of oil per minute.

Until this time, all Harleys had been single-speed, but in 1914 the Model 10F and Forecar debuted the two-speed rear hub. This astonishingly intricate device comprised no fewer than five bevel gears, yet was replaced by a true three-speed gearbox after only one year.

A measure of the twins' success is that, by 1915 the Harley-Davidson range comprised just two single-cylinder roadsters but six twins, including the three-speed Model K "Stripped Stock" –

■ ABOVE *By the time this twin was built in 1917, three-speed transmission was available for an extra $25.*

■ ABOVE RIGHT *The cam drive is clear in this sectioned F-head twin.*

a race replica for its time. Among six "Speciality" twins were the even hotter "Fast Motor" K12 and out-and-out racers such as the KRH. This elaboration continued throughout the 61-inch F-head's astonishingly long career.

So comprehensive was its evolution that, by the time it was discontinued in 1929, almost no part from the original twin would fit.

■ LEFT *An exquisite 1916 board-racing twin. Note the Bosch magneto and single carburettor.*

■ BELOW *The timing side of a 1917 twin. Note valve-gear cutaways in tank.*

MODEL W SPORT TWIN, 1919–22

■ LEFT *The very Model W machine that set the Three Flag record, riding from Canada to Mexico in less than 75 hours.*

One of Harley-Davidson's most radical machines appeared as early as 1919. Developed during the war years and first shown to the public in 1918, the Model W "Sport Twin" was quite unlike the general expectation of what a Milwaukee twin should be. Its cylinders, rather than being tucked close together in a 45 degree V, were set 180 degrees apart. This was Harley's Boxer twin – but unlike BMW's more modern Boxers, this carried its cylinders fore-and-aft like contemporary British Douglas machines.

In theory, this somewhat unwieldy layout should have made the bike very long, but in practice the new model's wheelbase was actually three inches shorter than that of the existing V-twin – just 53½in (1,360mm). It was also low overall and carried its heaviest components in particular low to the ground – a considerable bonus on the rough roads of the time. It also weighed fully 100lbs (45kg) less than its sibling V-twins. Aesthetically, too, the "Brewster Green" Sport looked low and lean, with an elegance of line rarely achieved by previous V-twins. The engine's horizontally-opposed cylinders bestowed perfect primary balance,

SPECIFICATIONS

Engine	horizontally-opposed side-valve twin
Capacity	35.6 cu in (584cc)
Transmission	3-speed
Wheelbase	53½in (1,360mm)
Top speed	around 50mph (80kph)

making it far smoother than the other big Vs in the Harley range. In fact, this was a most civilized mount all round.

As well as the standard equipment of magneto ignition and gas lights (fed by acetylene gas produced "on the move" by dissolving calcium carbide in water), optional equipment included coil

ignition and true electric lighting. Engine lubrication was taken care of by an automatic pump, freeing the rider from the obligation of injecting just the right amount of oil at just the right time. The three-speed transmission was driven by a multi-plate clutch (albeit hand-operated) running in engine oil, just like a modern motorcycle.

The Sport's drive chain, enclosed in a steel case and lubricated by oil mist from the crankcase breather, was as close to zero-maintenance as chain transmission could get at the time. All in all, the Model W was a neat, light, economical and innovative piece of kit which Milwaukee clearly hoped would find a ready market, as riders were less disposed to the rougher pleasures of previous big twins.

■ LEFT AND ABOVE *It may look ratty, but it still works. The horizontal cylinders and low overall lines of this original Sport Twin are clear.*

Unfortunately the Sport had one major shortcoming – cubic inches, or the lack of them. It was way down on power compared to the existing 61-inch Harley V-twin and similar offerings from Indian. with a displacement of just 35.6cu in (584cc). To compensate, at least in part, it had to be revved hard – indeed it was reputed (very dubiously) to be the highest-revving internal combustion of its time. Yet even when thrashed, power was poor, with a top speed of little more than 50mph (80kph). Then, as now, America's motorcyclists demanded less revs and far more guts. Although its agility made it modestly popular for a while on Europe's more tortuous roads (almost one third of exports to Britain in 1919 were Sport Twins), the Model W was never a success at home. Production ceased in 1922, after just four years on the Milwaukee line.

■ ABOVE *Little can the builders of machines like the Sport Twin have realized the cultural tide they were unleashing.*

MODEL JD & FD BIG TWINS, 1921–9

Milwaukee's first 74-inch model, the so-called "Superpowered Twin" hit America's streets for the 1921 model year. Producing some 18 horsepower, the big engine was intended to compete with Indian's big twins and four cylinder models from Henderson and others. The "74" followed the practice of the "61" from which it evolved, employing inlet-over-exhaust valves (the F-head layout) driven by a single camshaft in a timing cover on the right side of the engine.

However, many major components – crankcases, cylinders and heads – were all new, and both bore and stroke were increased. The transmission was three-speed, the gears and shafts being located in a separate aluminium housing which was connected by enclosed chain to the left end of the crankshaft.

An "automatic" oil pump delivered lubrication for the engine's mixture of plain phosphor bronze, roller and ball bearings. As with almost every other motorcycle of the time, used oil was burned or dripped on to the ground. The multi-plate clutch, on the other hand, ran dry.

■ ABOVE *Sidecars, such as this mated to a Model J, were huge business.*

■ BELOW *An immaculately restored 1928 Model JD, one of the first to feature a front brake.*

Although often referred to generically as the JD, up to 1925 the 74-inch twin might more helpfully be called the Model D, with the addition of essentially the same prefixes as contemporary 61-inch twins. "JD" indicated a complete electrically equipped version, while the magneto model was designated "FD". Where fitted, electrical equipment comprised a six-volt generator, battery, contact breaker points and coil, headlight, tail light and oil

SPECIFICATIONS 74-INCH SUPERPOWERED TWIN	
Engine	F-head V-twin
Capacity	74.2cu in (1,216cc)
Transmission	3-speed
Power	18bhp
Wheelbase	59½in (1,510mm)
Top speed	around 75mph (120kph)

warning indicator light. An additional "S" in the model description indicated a sidecar model, with lower gearing and a 0.12in- (3mm-) thick steel spacer between cylinder and crankcase mouth to reduce the compression ratio. Other subsequent suffixes included such variables as piston material – A for aluminium, B for iron. The lighter weight and improved heat dissipation of the aluminium alloy pistons were particularly beneficial after their introduction in 1924.

A tubular steel, single-loop frame tied the whole thing together, the rider cushioned from the worst road shocks by a "Full-Floteing" Mesinger saddle. Front suspension comprised similar double-sprung girder forks to the smaller twin. Only a rear brake – a 7¼in (186mm) drum actuated by a long steel rod from a pedal on the right footboard – was fitted until 1928 when a front drum brake also became standard. For markets in which a second brake was mandated by law, an additional "stopper" – essentially a parking brake – could also be fitted. Other changes over the "74"'s life span included the use of "Alemite" surfaces for all chassis bearings in 1924. The rider would periodically inject these with grease from a purpose-made high-pressure grease gun, which did much to

■ BELOW LEFT AND RIGHT *A lower frame carrying a teardrop-style tank first appeared in 1925, whilst front brakes finally arrived for the 1928 model year. The example below left clearly has neither.*

extend component life, especially in wet or dusty conditions. Less practical, but carrying echoes into the styling of Harleys today, 1926 found the big twin equipped with broad "balloon" tyres and a curvaceous "teardrop" fuel tank.

Over its eight-year career, the "74" proved itself a brisk performer which enhanced Milwaukee's reputation for building dependable motorcycles.

Some indication of its virtues – and not least of Harley's tradition of sticking with what worked – was that, at 87 x 101.6mm, the "74"'s cylinder dimensions remained almost unchanged up to the Shovelhead models of relatively recent times.

Clearly, the machine that would take its place in the future would have to be at least as special as the present one. Yet to begin with, at least, it would be anything but.

JH, JDH TWO-CAM, 1928–9

Twin-cam and even eight-valve machines had formed the cutting edge of Harley-Davidson's official racing efforts since the First World War, yet the ordinary road-going motorcyclist could only dream of such performance. All that changed in 1928 when Harley offered a two-cam motorcycle to the general public at an affordable price. These special J-series machines were available for two years only, as the 61-inch JH and the awesome 74-inch JDH, which were priced at $360 and $370 respectively.

"The magic words 'two-cam' mean exceptional speed and power," extolled contemporary advertisements, with some justification. Not for the last time, Milwaukee was treading the fine line between effective salesmanship and encouraging public disquiet over bad boys on antisocial machines.

Both twin-cam engines featured inlet-over-exhaust valve operation driven by paired, gear-driven cams in a timing case on the right side of the engine. Instead of operating via Harley-Davidson's customary roller arms, the

SPECIFICATIONS	
Engine	2-cam, F-head V-twin
Capacity	60.33cu in (988cc) or 74.2 cu in (1,216cc)
Transmission	3-speed
Wheelbase	60in (1,525mm)
Top speed	around 85mph (137kph)

cam lobes acted directly on tappets, offering more accurate valve control, higher revs and improved combustion. The height of each cylinder's inlet valve necessitated flamboyant clearance cutaways in the narrow fuel tank, which gave the "JH" its characteristically racy appearance.

The two engines differed in both bore and stroke, as well as in the use of Dow metal pistons, but were built on essentially the same crankcases. These were connected by roller primary chain to a multi-plate dry clutch and three-speed gearbox, which in turn drove the rear wheel by chain.

As well as the choice of capacities, two specifications of the Two-Cam were offered, although numerous racing specials would be created in private hands. As well as the competitive potential of stripped-down Model Js, Juneau Avenue anticipated a demand for an exclusive road version – or "superbike" as it might be known today. Thus the Two-Cam was available with full electrical equipment, carburettor air cleaner, fully valanced mudguards and front and rear brakes.

Echoes of the machine's racing pedigree were retained, however, in the slimline "sport" chassis, single seat and racer-style two-gallon (7.5 litre) fuel tank.

Even as a roadster, the Two-Cam was billed as "the fastest model ever offered by Harley-Davidson" with the JDH specially recommended "for greatest speed and maximum performance."

With an 80-inch version available on special order in 1929, this olive green projectile was no less than the American equivalent of Brough Superior's sensational SS100 in Europe.

Yet even this degree of exclusivity was priced too high for an American market more interested in cars, and the Two-Cams passed into legend after spending a very short two years in the Harley-Davidson range.

■ BELOW *Reflected glory: an Evo-engined Low Rider basks in the setting sun.*

■ BELOW *Reflected glory: an Evo-engined Low Rider basks in the setting sun.*

45-INCH TWIN, 1929–51

One of the most enduring motorcycles in Harley-Davidson's history was announced in October 1927, hitting the road just over 12 months later. The Model D, as it was first styled, was the first of a new generation of side-valve "flathead" V-twins – far cheaper to create than the relatively complex F-head engines. Not much more than a pair of 21-inch "Ricardo" singles on a common bottom-end, it featured three-speed transmission and a spindly frame almost identical to the little single's.

If the beginnings were lacklustre, improvements came fast. Within a year, the "45" benefited from a sturdy new frame with lower saddle but increased ground clearance. It was now available in four guises: D (low compression solo), DS (sidecar), DL (high compression Sport Solo) and DLD Special Sport Solo. Two years later, it emerged from a comprehensive redesign as the Model R. This included aluminium pistons in place of Dow metal (with magnesium offered as a special option from 1933), new crankcases with improved oiling and a sturdier frame.

■ LEFT *An early Model D "45". The unfinned timing cover is one obvious difference from the later Model W.*

SPECIFICATIONS:
1929 MODEL DL

Engine	side-valve V-twin
Capacity	45.3cu in (742cc)
Transmission	3-speed
Power	around 22bhp
Weight	395lbs (179kg)
Wheelbase	56½in (1,435mm)
Top speed	around 65mph (105kph)

In 1933, of course, the Depression was at its deepest. A sign of these cash-strapped times was that this much-improved machine now cost just $280 – $10 less than the Model D had at its introduction. After a further steady regime of continuous improvement, the "45" was transformed once again to become the Model W in 1937. Although the most obvious difference was the adoption of styling from the Knucklehead released the previous year, there were numerous engine

■ LEFT AND
RIGHT *The
inspiration for the
"flathead"
nickname is
obvious (left).
Note the
streamlined
instrument console,
which remains a
Milwaukee hallmark.*

improvements as well, with its troublesome crankcase oiling and breathing system getting the lion's share of attention.

The range now comprised not only standard (W), sidecar (WS), Sport (WL) and Special Sport (WLD) models, but also the WLDR Competition Sport Special, a mean-looking stripped-down racer – though by 1941, the WLDR machine was a "Special Sport" roadster, the racer being known by a simple "WR". Four-speed transmission, adopted from the bigger twins, appeared in 1938 and by 1940 the WLA Army version was on the books. By now, the

WLD and WLDR versions carried light alloy cylinder heads with more fin area and a larger carburettor, improvements that would not reach the base models for another five years.

Indeed, the engine would receive almost no more significant changes during the WL's final decade – a far cry from the 1930s when anything from 15 to 30 modifications were made each year. Instead, Harley-Davidson directed its efforts into its overhead-valve models, confining the "45" mainly to cosmetic revisions, partly inspired by the Hydra-Glide. Civilian production of "45"s ceased after 1951, although some

military versions were produced later, and the same side-valve engine would continue to power the Servi-Car into the 1970s. The WL is – and was for most of its life – a crude, heavy machine better suited to the American Prairies or war-torn battlefields than any road with bends. By the time it went out of production, it was a motorcycling dinosaur. Though it was slow, outdated and cumbersome, it was also strong as an ox and almost indestructible: this model had proved itself to be a tough old Hog that for more than two decades had dependably delivered the bacon for Harley-Davidson.

■ OPPOSITE BOTTOM LEFT AND
RIGHT *Art-deco influences are clear
in the styling of these two striking
WL45s. The inspiration for modern
Springers is clear in the girder forks,
especially on the chrome-plated
example on the right.*

■ LEFT *A 1942
WL45, one of the
last pre-war
civilian models.
The "Boat-tail"
rear fender
appeared in 1939.*

74-INCH SIDE-VALVE TWIN, 1930–48
80-INCH SIDE-VALVE TWIN, 1935–41

Far from being the dependable machine the market required, the model which propelled Harley's big-inch fortunes into the troubled 1930s was even more bothersome than that very first V-twin of 20 years earlier. Launched just in time to see the New York stock exchange collapse in 1929, the Model V "Big Twin" began life as a fiasco.

With the original twin, valvegear was the problem. With this new 74-inch model it was almost the entire machine. As William H. Davidson recalled: "bad engine... bad clutch... flywheels too small... frames broke... mufflers became so clogged the engine lost power."

It's a mystery now – and probably was for Harley at the time – why the first of this line were so very poor. The cylinder heads, though now of side-valve layout, retained the proven "Ricardo" pattern of the earlier single.

At 87.3 x 101.6mm, the bore and stroke dimensions were unchanged from the Model D. As before, a single dependable Schebler carburettor metered fuel via a forked manifold. Testing showed that power was up 15 per cent on the old "74".

SPECIFICATIONS: 74-INCH (80-INCH) TWIN	
Engine	side-valve V-twin
Capacity	74.2cu in/1,216cc (78.9cu in/1,293cc)
Transmission	3-speed (4-speed from 1937)
Wheelbase	60in (1,525mm)
Top speed	up to 90mph (145kph)

There were novelties, of course, but nothing suggesting the trouble to come. Primary drive was now based on duplex chain, far stronger than the single chain used previously. Revisions to the oil-circulation system promised the rider a less oil-soaked time, as did full enclosure of the valvegear, which was impracticable on the old ioe twin. Other improvements that ought to have been welcomed by serious users included interchangeable quick-release wheels (at a time when punctures were a

■ ABOVE *The mighty VL, the top of the Milwaukee range before the arrival of the Knucklehead.*

■ LEFT *A 1936 VLH 80-inch twin. The spring shield on the girder forks was new for that particular year.*

■ ABOVE LEFT *Hand gear-change would remain a Milwaukee norm until the 1950s. The foot pedal operates this VL's "suicide" clutch.*

■ ABOVE RIGHT *A drab army 74-inch twin. Note the metric engine capacity in the "1200" on the tank.*

NAME GAMES

Not for the first time, Harley-Davidson's model nomenclature looks confusing viewed from decades distant. Sometimes called the "VL", the 74-incher was available from the outset as a straight Model V, with "VL" representing the high compression version, "VS" the sidecar puller and "VC" signifying the use of nickel iron rather than light alloy pistons. This continued until 1934, when options included the VLD ("Special Sport solo" with TNT motor), VD (low compression, solo), VDS (low compression, sidecar gears) and VFDS (heavy duty commercial, TNT motor). In 1935, the 80-inch model appeared and was dubbed VLDD (Sport solo) or VDDS (sidecar), alongside existing 74-inch models. This all changed for the 1937 model year, with "U" replacing "V" (alphabetically backwards). From then on, all the big side-valve twins' model designations began "U-" (80-inch models were indicated by a subsequent "H"). Thus a simple "U" indicated the basic 74-inch model and the plain "UH" was the equivalent 80-inch model.

daily hazard) and an improved electrical system with better weather protection. The frame, too, was new: lower, heavier and reputedly sturdier than before.

For a company trading on unsurpassable reliability, the "74"s problems were serious indeed. No matter how handsome the new

■ ABOVE AND BELOW *With the change to four-speed transmissions in 1937, the Model V became the Model U, one year before this handsome 80-incher was built. Note the revised timing cover.*

machine was, dressed in olive green with red pin-striping, no-one would buy it if it didn't work. To its credit, Milwaukee dropped everything to fix all the faults and the Model V proved dependable for the rest of its days.

Having benefited from the fixes applied to the 74-inch model, the 80-inch model released for 1935 proved almost completely problem-free. The bigger engine was substantially similar to the contemporary "74", the extra capacity resulting from an increase in stroke from 101.6 to 108mm.

For 1937, the V-series gave way to the U-series big twins, with four-speed transmission, improved engine oiling and both the running gear and styling from Knucklehead twins. Both were capable of up to 90mph (145kph), had vestigial brakes and no rear suspension. Production of the "80" effectively ceased after 1941.

WLA & XA

■ LEFT *The redoubtable WLA. Note the large auxiliary air-cleaner to prevent the motor choking in dusty conditions.*

■ WLA, 1940–5

If the Willys Jeep was the archetypal American military four-wheeler during the Second World War then Harley-Davidson's rugged old 45-inch flathead twin was its two-wheeled equivalent. By the time the United States entered the war in December 1941, the "45" had proved itself during a dozen years of civilian development and was the obvious choice for an army workhorse. The first example, dubbed WLA (the A stood for "army") appeared in 1940 and was initially scarcely more than a drab green WL. By 1941, it had acquired blacked-out auxiliary lights, an oil-bath air-cleaner (intended for North African conditions) and a quieter fishtail exhaust. Depending on the precise military requirements, luggage racks were added, front and rear, plus a gun scabbard and under-sump bash plate.

That pivotal year also brought the first of around 18,000 WLC models built for the Canadian military, which differed principally in having a foot-operated gear change on the right, rather than hand-change on the left. Anti-hertz suppressors and more comprehensive

blackout gear were added later, and by late 1943 – the year in which WLA/WLC production peaked, at over 27,000 – even the crankcases were painted olive drab. Each machine bore a plate warning the rider not to exceed 65mph (105kph), not that the WLA was capable of very much more. Of around

■ BELOW LEFT AND RIGHT *The key to the WLA's success was its low-tuned, dependable engine, which had already enjoyed over a dozen years of development since the original Model D of 1929. Later examples had slotted "black-out" lights.*

SPECIFICATIONS: WLA	
Engine	side-valve V-twin
Capacity	45.3cu in (742cc)
Transmission	4-speed
Power	around 22bhp
Weight	varied with specification
Wheelbase	59½in (1,510mm)
Top speed	limited to 65mph (105kph)

■ LEFT *Although American-liveried models are best known, over half of military WL production went to other countries' armies.*

SPECIFICATIONS: XA	
Engine	side-valve horizontally-opposed twin
Capacity	45.1cu in (739cc)
Transmission	4-speed
Power	around 25bhp
Wheelbase	59½in (1,510mm)
Top speed	around 65 mph (105kph)

■ LEFT *Most observers would fail to recognize this as Milwaukee iron: the horizontally-opposed XA twin.*

88,000 WLs produced for war-time service, many went to Russia, of which later examples were specified WSR models. It is reputed that some 30,000 Red Army Harley-Davidsons entered Berlin as the war in Europe drew to a close. Milwaukee's contribution to the war effort was marked by no fewer than three Army/Navy "E" awards for excellence in military production – although this was to backfire commercially on the company when thousands of WLAs were sold as war surplus after 1945, damping-down the post-war recovery.

■ XA, 1942–3

Although Milwaukee built some military versions of the 74-inch side-valve twin (UA) and even fewer ELC Knuckleheads for the Canadian forces, the factory's second-string army model was the curious XA. Powered by a horizontally-opposed 45.1cu in (739cc) twin with shaft final drive and plunger rear suspension, the XA was expressly

■ BELOW *Note the shaft drive coupling and large air-cleaner on this flathead XA.*

■ BOTTOM LEFT *Although most XAs were intended for North African use, this example is painted in non-desert livery.*

■ BOTTOM RIGHT *Note the instruction plate: the military ensured that as little as possible was left to chance.*

designed for use in the North African desert. The transmission was four-speed, with foot change and twin carburettors feeding the two side-valve cylinder heads. This may seem reminiscent of contemporary BMWs: this was a direct copy of the German machine. Juneau Avenue did not copy the opposition's dependability, for it reputedly suffered serious bearing failures due to the Sahara's heat and sand. As a result, only around 1,000 XAs were built, all during the years 1942–3, though this may have been because the North African campaign was drawing to a close. There was also a rare XS variant with sidecar. A civilian prototype derivative of the XA was tested during 1946 but failed to reach production.

SERVI-CAR, 1932–74

Although we think of them now as kings of style even when carrying the Highway Patrol along California's freeways, in their earlier years Harley-Davidsons were no strangers to humble workaday vehicles. As early as 1913, the range included a "Forecar" delivery van, the Model 9-G, essentially a 61-inch F-head twin with front-mounted luggage box. Sidecars and sidecar accessories had been an integral part of the Milwaukee range since 1916, with a huge sidecar production facility in operation at Juneau Avenue since 1926.

With the Wall Street Crash and its aftermath placing a particular premium on cheap, dependable commercial transport, it was perhaps no surprise that 1932 marked the debut of one of the strangest – and most enduring – Harleys ever produced. The Model G Servi-Car was a more-or-less conventional V-twin from the saddle forward, but the rear looked for all the world like an ice-cream van. Although it resembled a car rear axle crudely

■ LEFT *Servi-Cars proved adept at many tasks, although cooling ice cream in an inferno probably wasn't one.*

grafted on to a conventional bike (and topped off with a metal and fibreglass boot (trunk), the Servi-Car was a practical and cheap working vehicle which found a steady market in Depression-torn America.

Some suggested that it was inspired by Far East rickshaw-style machines; however, the Servi-Car was initially

■ ABOVE LEFT AND LEFT *A Servi-Car kitted out for police duty, as so many examples were. Note the additional lights and large siren on the front mudguard.*

SPECIFICATIONS	
Engine	side-valve V-twin
Capacity	45.3cu in (742cc)
Transmission	three forward speeds, one reverse
Power	around 22hp
Wheelbase	61in (1,550mm)
Width	48in (1,220mm)
Top speed	around 60mph (96kph)

■ RIGHT *Proving that any Harley can be customized, although tassels were never a Servi-Car factory option.*

intended for the recovery of broken-down cars – hence the tow-bar and huge 60 amp/hour battery fitted as standard. Perhaps surprisingly, given the fraught circumstances of the time, it combined both sound design and solid engineering – so tough and enduring in fact that it remained in production from 1932 until 1974. From the outset, it employed a purpose-built frame with chain drive from the gearbox turning a car-type rear axle complete with differential. It enjoyed conventional drum brakes in each wheel, plus a parking brake mounted inside the rear axle housing. Power came from the same 45.3cu in (742cc) flathead V-twin fitted to the Model R. It may have been sluggish but it was undeniably dependable.

The first examples had the same three-speed gearbox as the roadster solo but within two years a reverse gear (not

to mention contemporary art-deco styling motifs) had been added. By this time, the three-wheeler range was popular with police, garages, motoring organizations and small businesses alike and comprised no fewer than five models. In fact it was almost everything such enterprises needed: practical, reliable and cheap.

Above all, it was easy to drive, so there was usually need for only a minimum of operator training. One clever and user-friendly touch was the adoption of the same 42in (1,067mm) wheel track as the typical car – inexperienced Servi-Car drivers would not need to forge their own ruts in mud and snow. At its introduction, it was priced at just $450; by 1969 this had risen to $2,065.

With such a lengthy life-span, inevitably there were other changes too

numerous to list. A radical styling change was introduced in 1937, echoing the new 61-inch Knucklehead (indeed the factory briefly dabbled with a prototype shaft-driven Knucklehead Servi-Car). This included a white-faced speedometer calibrated to 100mph (161kph), which would have been terrifying were it not at least 35mph (56kph) over the machine's capabilities.

At the same time, the revised flathead twin from the Model W provided the power – and would continue to do so for the rest of the Servi-Car's days.

Electric start was finally added in 1964 and rear disc brakes toward the end of 1973, at which time annual sales still exceeded 400. Volume production of Servi-Cars ceased after 1973, although some were made to order the following year.

The Model G's most obvious drawback – the absence of heater and roof – had finally brought about its demise, although it could still be seen in service with United States' police forces well into the 1990s.

■ RIGHT *This is a more original example, and here it is painted in colours of the fire department.*

MODEL K, 1952-6

If a single model demonstrated Milwaukee's problems during the post-war years, it was surely the Model K, unveiled in November 1951. Virtually a technological throwback, the "K" was born into an age when competition from Europe was intensifying almost monthly. Opposition machines offered high-performance overhead-valve engines with 100mph- (161kph) plus performance and the finest chassis ever built. In response, Harley-Davidson offered as its premier model an antiquated, long-stroke, side-valve twin as its premier sports model, which struggled to reach 80mph (129kph).

Advertised as "America's Most Sensational Motorcycle", the "K" was "designed to outperform, outride, outlook, outvalue ... any motorcycle in its class." Of course, this was only true if a class existed for absurdly slow and out-dated machines – which it might if Milwaukee's plea for a 40 per cent tariff on imported motorcycles had succeeded in May 1951. Harley literature claimed 30 horsepower for the Model K, only a little less than the contemporary 650cc Triumph Thunderbird. Whether true or not, the V-twin was no match for the

SPECIFICATIONS	
Engine	side-valve V-twin
Capacity	45.3cu in (742cc)
Transmission	4-speed
Peak power	30bhp
Wheelbase	60in (1,525mm)
Top speed	around 80mph (130kph)

103mph (166kph) Britisher. Yet remarkably, Joe Leonard became first American national champion in 1954, on a machine substantially derived from the K. Its other saving grace was that it was the only large-capacity motorcycle Hollywood stars could be insured to ride – in other words, the K was so slow, it was considered safe.

True, the K was the first Harley-Davidson twin to feature suspension at both ends: "easy riding" double-action telescopic forks up front with a swinging-fork rear end (oddly, a sprung seat was retained.) By the standards of Triumph, BSA and Norton in particular, the handling was ponderous and mushy, although the eight-inch (200mm) brakes weren't bad for the time. It offered a hand-operated clutch and in a demonstration of supreme optimism, its speedometer was graduated to 120mph (193kph).

Nor was the K dependable, at least initially, as it was beset by a variety of performance and reliability problems. Perhaps the worst was its habit of breaking its "large, rugged" transmission gears, until a switch to forged parts after 1954. In many other respects, the bike was sturdy and sensibly conceived, such as in the use of taper-roller bearings for the swing-arm pivots. Bore and stroke were identical to the WL's: 70 x 97mm. The four-cam, air-cooled engine enjoyed generous finning to its aluminium heads and iron

■ TOP *Aided by a 30.5cu in (500cc) limit for ohv engines, the side-valve 45.3cu in (742cc) Model K fared better on the track than on the street.*

■ ABOVE AND LEFT *The best of the breed: a KHK in strident yellow.*

barrels, and it featured in-unit construction of engine and gearbox, with triplex chain drive, long before this became widespread among competitors.

Some years after the age of the K, Harley revealed what many had suspected – that it was only a stop-gap model to see the company through until something better could be developed. Although history records that the Model K was superseded by the Sportster, something more radical was envisaged originally. The familiar 45-degree V layout was dropped in favour of a wider 60-degree engine to be known as the KL, with "high" cams, twin carburettors and side-by-side rather than forked connecting rods. This would have increased secondary vibration, although the wider V angle would have gone some way to reducing primary imbalance.

Evidently, the KL project ran into patent conflicts with Vincent and ran out of development time, although it is possible that the progress of European machines convinced Harley that something even more potent was required. By way of a stop-gap to the stop-gap, a drastic 19mm increase in stroke raised the Model K's capacity to 55cu in (883cc) for 1954, and power to a claimed 38bhp, in an attempt to stay at least within sight of the Brits. The cover of *The Enthusiast* showed one Elvis Aaron Presley on board just such a machine in 1956, by which time work on the model's successor was already well in hand. As well as the basic KH, a tuned Super Sport Solo KHK model with high-lift camshafts, polished ports, leaner styling and lower handlebars arrived in 1955. Though they were ostensibly intended for racing, most found their way on to America's streets where they proved far more acceptable to American sports riders – their top speed exceeded 90mph (145kph). After 1956, the old flathead expired and was replaced by the first of the overhead-valve Sportsters. As the KR and KRTT, it soldiered on for more than a decade as Milwaukee's principal racing iron.

■ TOP *Pictured here is a handsome example of a 1956 Model K.*

■ LEFT *The K probably looked cooler than it went, especially here at Daytona Beach, Florida.*

Overhead-valve Twins

Knucklehead, Panhead, Shovelhead – these familiar names represent almost half a century of Milwaukee overhead-valve twins and many motorcyclists' idea of the quintessential Harley-Davidson.

Yet the career of each of these stalwarts was blighted. The Knucklehead project began in 1931 and may well have reached fruition in 1934 but for government restrictions aimed at reducing unemployment. When it finally arrived in 1936, the 61-inch twin was a sensation, not least when Joe Petrali hurtled one along Daytona Beach at a staggering 136.183mph (219.16kph). No sooner was a 74-inch version released than the Second World War halted civilian motorcycle production in its tracks. By the time the dust had settled, the age of the Panhead had come, making the Knuckle "74" one of the rarest and most prized Milwaukee twins of all.

The Pan offered more power and refinement, plus the distinction of propelling one of the most celebrated Hogs – the first ElectraGlide – and yet, during this period, Harley's sales slid to their lowest since 1921. Next, the Shovelhead which was better still, but coincided unhappily with a revolution in motorcycling with which it was ill-equipped to compete. Both the Pan and Shovelhead have their fans, but they almost rang the death-knell for Harley-Davidson.

KNUCKLEHEAD, 1936–47

It's difficult to appreciate the impact Harley-Davidson's first overhead-valve roadster twin must have had on a motorcycling public that was emerging groggily from six long years of Depression. In fact, no Milwaukee model before or since was ever quite so comprehensively new. Even the latest Twin Cam, remember, is installed in largely familiar running gear.

Not so with the legendary Knuckle. Not only was the engine a major departure, but it sat in an equally new twin-cradle frame, with just the mudguards and generator remaining from the flathead VL. Its striking styling owed much to the art-deco innovations of the Depression years, capped by a teardrop-style tank, complete with an audacious white-faced Stewart-Warner speedometer calibrated to 120mph (193kph). Fanciful, perhaps, but factory

■ LEFT *The overhead-valve Knuckle was the biggest development in years*

■ ABOVE *Milwaukee makes metal come alive.*

■ BELOW *This 1946 FL Knucklehead looks better now than it did when new.*

SPECIFICATIONS	
Engine	ohv V-twin
Capacity	60.32 or 73.66cu in (989 or 1,207cc)
Transmission	4-speed, hand change
Power	40 or 45bhp
Weight	565lbs (256kg)
Wheelbase	59½in (1,510mm)
Top speed	up to 90mph (145kph)

■ LEFT AND BELOW *A finned timing cover (left) identifies this as a post-1941 Knucklehead. Compare this with the "smooth case" example below. A host of other changes also came in for 1942.*

testers had reported 100mph (161kph) during development. Little wonder that would-be owners queued in droves when the first examples were shipped to dealers in January 1936, despite the $380 Knuckle costing $40 more than a contemporary 80-inch twin.

Designed by William S. Harley and Lothar A. Doerner (the latter tragically killed while testing a 1937 model), the 60.32cu in (989cc) twin underwent no fewer than 70,000 hours of testing, according to contemporary claims. As with previous mainstream models, the Knuckle was initially available in three guises: E (standard, discontinued after 1937 but restored during the Second World War), ES (sidecar) and EL (high-compression sport). All proved free-revving and eager, while the EL in particular – with 40 horsepower at 4,800rpm – offered a huge performance increase over the laggard side-valvers. Even the mighty 80-inch VL couldn't come close to an ohv twin.

Yet despite the time-consuming route to production – and not for the first time – there were initial problems. Many changes were implemented during the first year of production, including frame reinforcing and revisions to the kick-start gears. The rocker assemblies

became enclosed for 1938, by which time the patented tank-mounted instruments also included warning lights for low oil pressure and generator output.

But the 61's worst fault concerned its dry-sump lubrication. Some parts got too little oil while others – including the road underneath – got too much. A partial fix was introduced in 1937 but the glitch was not completely solved

until the arrival of the centrifugally-controlled oil pump bypass of the 74-inch (Model F) Knuckle of 1941. The crankshaft main bearings had been up-rated in 1940, perhaps in anticipation of the extra loads on the bigger engine. The arrival of the more potent "74" also brought larger 8½in (216mm) diameter flywheels, revised crankcases, an up-rated seven-plate clutch and a carburettor choke increased to 1⅛in (28.6mm). By now, the two ohv models combined were comfortably out-selling Milwaukee's established range of side-valve twins. Given further development, the Knuckle could surely have become better still, but with the outbreak of war in December 1941, production concentrated almost exclusively on military side-valve twins and development of the ohv models all but ceased.

Milwaukee lore has it that the very best of the big Knuckles were those built in that final pre-war year, but hostilities meant that relatively few Model Fs reached the road until 1947, when the line's reign was almost over.

Not surprisingly, that first overhead-valve "74" remains one of the most prized Harley roadsters of all.

By 1948, however, a new pretender was on the scene: the age of the Panhead had arrived. At last it was goodbye, finally, to oil leaks from the rocker box, which was a problem that had never been completely solved on the Knucklehead.

HYDRAGLIDE, 1949-57

■ BELOW RIGHT *Although the Panhead shared its bottom-end with the Knuckle, the heads, valve-gear and oil feeds were new.*

■ BOTTOM *The HydraGlide name came from the bike's new telescopic front forks, then becoming widespread on motorcycles worldwide.*

For the 1948 model year, Harley-Davidson had unveiled its new Panhead engine, mating it to a revised "Wishbone" frame with characteristic "dog-leg" front downtubes. Within a year, it had been eclipsed by the first of Milwaukee's "Glide" models.

Although retaining a rigid rear end, the HydraGlide broke with the company's usual reliance on leading-link sprung forks. Instead, here was a Hog with a modern oil-damped telescopic front-end. As if to compensate for this fit of novelty, the Hydra persevered with a uniquely American hand-change gearbox until 1952 and even later as an option for true die-hards.

For the present, however, it was as close to modern as heavyweight Harleys would get. Billed with characteristic restraint as "the nearest thing to flying and as modern as a spaceship," the first HydraGlide was, in truth, only a relatively slight departure from the model that went before.

SPECIFICATIONS	
Engine	ohv V-twin
Capacity	60.32 or 73.66cu in (989 or 1,207cc)
Transmission	4-speed, hand change
Power	around 50/55bhp
Weight	560lbs (254kg)
Wheelbase	59½in (1,510mm)
Top speed	around 95mph (152kph)

As was company tradition, a host of detail changes would follow year-on-year. Many of these would be cosmetic (the speedometer alone received an astonishing degree of attention), but most concerned the internal workings of the engine and chassis, making the final HydraGlide of 1957 very different from the first. It should be remembered, however, that in the American automotive industry in general, the 1950s and 1960s were characterized much more by developments in styling than in functional engineering.

In essence, the Panhead engine comprised new cylinders and heads grafted on to the Knucklehead bottom end. The heads were now aluminium with hydraulic valve lifters (tappets), and internal oilways had replaced the Knuckle's external lines.

Like the Knucklehead it replaced, this new Panhead was produced in both 61- and 74-inch (989 and 1,207cc) versions, designated models E and F respectively. Six versions comprised the initial range: Model F Sport Solo, FL Special Sport Solo and FS Sidecar twin, with the designations repeated for the 61-inch motor. All featured four-speed transmission, while sidecar models had lower gearing and reduced compression ratios. At their launch, all sprung-fork Model Es cost $635, with the larger engine adding a mere $15 to the price. Within a year, the introduction of the HydraGlide had upped those figures by precisely $100. Just to be on the safe side, sprung-fork models – designated ELP and FLP – remained in the range for one transitional year.

Of literally hundreds of detail changes, the first major improvement came in 1950 when revised cylinder

heads with larger ports added a claimed ten per cent more power. The 61-inch Model E was dropped for 1953, by which time annual sales of the smaller Panhead had slumped to below 1,000. The same year – the company's fiftieth anniversary – brought about Harley-Davidson's familiar "mid-series" bottom-end redesign. This included major changes to both crankcase halves as well as the relocation of the hydraulic lifters from top to bottom of the pushrods. A new "straight-leg" frame was brought in for 1954, followed by the FLH Super Sport model (the "H" stood for "hot") 12 months later, with gas-flowed heads and 8:1 compression ratios.

Even the FLH was no tyre-shredder, though, retaining the low-revving, high-torque virtues of every Milwaukee V-twin. These were very much machines in the American tradition, having ponderous steering, limited ground clearance, marginal brakes and hand gear change.

In terms of styling, the HydraGlide was pure 1950s – or perhaps pure 1990s, since so many modern Harley models echo its visual themes. Central to this was its low-slung profile with "Air-Flow" front and rear fenders (mudguards).

A chrome-plated tubular steel front "safety guard" was offered as an option from 1950, with "HydraGlide" emblems available one year later – both mimicking those gracing the very latest FLs.

It had some early "innovations" – like black silencers and fork sliders – that did not last, but overall the Hydra-Glide made an impact that is still very much with us today.

■ LEFT *Yes, this 1953 HydraGlide could almost be a year 2000 Softail. That's precisely the point of Retro-Tech.*

FL DuoGlide, 1958-64

■ BELOW *It was still a Panhead, but with the arrival of the DuoGlide the FL had springing at both ends.*

By 1958, Harley-Davidson was already in grave difficulties as annual sales hovered around a paltry 12,000 under intense competition from European machines. To make matters worse, the start of the Japanese invasion was just one year away – though no-one knew it at the time – with the arrival of Honda into the American market.

One way in which the company responded was through increased diversification of its range – first the Model K, and then the Sportsters took different directions from the heavyweight twins. But by the late 1950s, the latter – the FL models – were woefully outdated and badly in need of a major overhaul. Instead, they got little more than a facelift.

After the HydraGlide, the DuoGlide was the logical next step. As well as real, oil-damped telescopic front suspension, the Duo floated on a swinging-arm rear end, hence the name. This was a major improvement on the face of it, even though the Model K had beaten it comfortably for the distinction of being the first Harley-Davidson twin

SPECIFICATIONS

Engine	ohv V-twin
Capacity	74cu in (1,207cc)
Transmission	4-speed
Power	55bhp
Weight	575lb (261kg)
Wheelbase	60in (1,525mm)
Top speed	around 95mph (152kph)

with rear suspension. By the time it appeared in 1958, however, pretty much everything it offered had already been done – and done better – by every other major motorcycle manufacturer, with the exception of the Duo's hydraulic rear brake. Unfortunately this was little more than a gimmicky novelty, since both hubs contain tiny, ineffective single-leading shoe drums.

With major engine revisions having been implemented in 1953 and in 1956, the DuoGlide's engine might as well have been called the "Panhead Mark

II". It also benefited from more generous finning than previous Pans for 1958, as well as an up-rated generator. With the 61-inch Pan long departed, all DuoGlides enjoyed 74-inch (1,207cc) power. The range offered a choice of hand or foot gear-change and Sport or Super Sport ("H") tune, making four models in all. In 1958, the hotter specification added $65 to the standard $1,255 purchase price.

Central to the machine's layout was a new "Step-down" frame with larger diameter backbone and attachment

■ ABOVE *The distinctive speedometer is original; the handbag is not.*

■ LEFT *The chrome crash bars, fender rails and panniers were available as part of 16 Harley-Davidson option groups.*

■ **RIGHT** *As soon as Milwaukee installed rear suspension, some riders wanted to take it off. This hardtailed 1958 DuoGlide is similar to Hopper's* Easy Rider *mount.*

■ **BELOW** *An original 1961 example shows how Harley intended it to look.*

points for the twin rear shock absorbers. These incorporated oil-damping (typical of the time, for rebound only) and their springs were enclosed in gleaming chrome-plated shrouds. The new frame necessitated many other modifications – to the oil tank, toolbox and fork yokes – although the first Duos looked rather like soft-tailed HydraGlides.

If the Duo's looks weren't enough for aspiring owners, 1958 also introduced a huge expansion in the number of factory "option packs" including no fewer than nine for the new DuoGlide. These comprised accessories groups for "Chrome Finish", "Road Cruiser" and

"King of the Highway", with a bewildering array of lights, luggage items and other paraphernalia. The "King of the Highway" package included front and rear nudge bars, twin rear lights and a dual exhaust system.

Unfortunately it didn't sell very well, being particularly unsuited to most export markets, although it accounted for around 40 per cent of Milwaukee's sales at home. The Duo didn't much like corners, and was woefully under-braked. Even the "H"-designated Super Sports models, with optional high-lift camshaft and higher

compression pistons, weren't rapid. Vibration was intense at high engine speeds, leaving much of their potential power unused most of the time, except by the most determined riders – who would probably seek the high-rev thrills of a Triumph Thunderbird anyway.

Then, as now, the DuoGlide was about a different sort of motorcycling, with its big, slow-revving engine and charismatic looks. It was indisputably a Harley, with all the attributes and vices of the breed. And it was also indisputably beautiful.

FL ELECTRA-GLIDE, 1965

Of all Harley-Davidson models, surely the enduring FL ElectraGlide is the one that best epitomizes the breed. The "FL" designation actually arrived with the first 74-inch Knucklehead of 1942 and has since been ever-present in the Milwaukee range. The model that has carried those laurels with the greatest distinction has been the thundering ElectraGlide – the quintessential model since its 1965 debut.

Yet for all its lusty pedigree, that first ElectraGlide was little more than a DuoGlide with the addition of 12-volt electrics and an electric starter which – initially, at least – did not prove altogether very dependable.

Just as there was a 12-month hiatus between the introduction of the Panhead and the HydraGlide, Harley-Davidson waited until 1966 before giving the Glide something new. From its second year of production, it was powered by the new Shovelhead mill with its (relatively) more efficient "Power-Pac"

■ ABOVE *The first of the breed, the 1965 ElectraGlide. The large battery box distinguishes it from earlier DuoGlide.*

heads. Initial examples used the alloy-headed Panhead engine which had first appeared in 1948 and gone on to propel the first Glide (the HydraGlide of 1949) and the DuoGlide of a decade later. The Hydra- had been the first big twin with telescopic forks while the Duo- added swinging arm rear suspension.

The starter motor itself lived behind the rear cylinder and engaged on the rear of the primary drive. The DuoGlide frame had to be opened up slightly to accommodate it, yet still there was no room for the earlier model's tool kit. Surprisingly for a unit "borrowed" from an outboard motor, the first starters were

SPECIFICATIONS: 1965–1970	
Engine	ohv V-twin
Capacity	73.66cu in (1,207cc)
Transmission	4-speed
Power	around 55bhp
Weight	595lbs (270kg)
Wheelbase	60in (1,525mm)
Top speed	95mph (152kph)

■ ABOVE LEFT *It would do considerably more than 12mph (20kph), but in Harley-land style counted as much as numeracy.*

■ LEFT *For little more than $1,500, this Milwaukee dream could be yours – in 1965.*

■ RIGHT *As leaps forward go, the ElectraGlide was conservative: both hand-change and foot-change versions were available until 1972.*

■ BELOW *The last of the Panheads: in 1970 the Shovelhead took its place.*

troublesome when damp and the kick start was prudently retained. Harley later adopted Homelite starters, which proved much more reliable.

Like all Harley big twins, the ohv engine ran forked con-rods to eliminate rocking couple (so the rear cylinder was precisely, rather than roughly, masked by the front). Primary drive was by chain to a four-speed box (with a sidecar option, up to 1980, of three forward and one reverse). Capacity was 74cu in (1,207cc): the current 81.74cu in (1,340cc) dimensions didn't arrive until 1970 with the new generation of "alternator" Shovelheads. The rest was almost unchanged from the DuoGlide, complete with five-inch (127mm) whitewall tyres and running boards, although for the first time a five-gallon (19-litre) "Turnpike" tank was fitted. Of

the four-model range, two versions retained hand gear change, which would remain an option until 1972.

In short, this was never a state-of-the-art machine. Indeed the "King of the Road" touring pack offered in 1966 required the rear shock absorbers to be relocated forwards, to the detriment of the Glide's handling, which had already proved to be rather pedestrian.

For all that, it's a strikingly handsome machine – one which looks far better than it performs. Like most Harleys, the rear brake is good but, prior to the arrival of a front disc in 1971, no prudent rider would choose to stop a Glide in a hurry.

This is a device for getting into top gear and staying there as you cruise serenely to the next horizon.

FX SUPERGLIDE, 1971–84

In the late 1960s, customizing was king. In California in particular, Harley-Davidson owners were tearing their machines to pieces, discarding one piece and adding another to produce unique examples of what were to become known as "blend" bikes. Nowhere was this more publicly demonstrated than in the film *Easy Rider*, with Peter Fonda cruising to New Orleans on the outrageous "Captain America" alongside Dennis Hopper's hardtailed DuoGlide.

Milwaukee's response was as startling as it was controversial. When the SuperGlide was unveiled for the 1971 model year, it was the first example of a genre quickly dubbed "factory custom". The influential *Cycle* magazine's misgivings were typical.

"Is the American motorcyclist ready to ride around on someone else's expression of personal, radical tastes?" it asked, before testing the newcomer and answering its own question enthusiastically in the affirmative. Such was the SuperGlide's impact that almost every major motorcycle manufacturer has since produced its own interpretation of the "factory" custom – invariably to less

■ LEFT *By the 1970s, customs were all the rage. Willie G.'s official version was less flamboyant than this "Captain America", but its impact was more enduring.*

■ BELOW LEFT *Part Sportster, part FL, the SuperGlide was an instant hit, with 4,700 built in the first year.*

effect than Harley's original. From a modern perspective, taking into account models such as the Springer Softail, the FX wasn't actually all that radical. Styled and conceived by Willie G. Davidson, it was essentially a combination of heavyweight FLH frame, 74-inch Shovelhead engine (which still

carried "FLH" on the timing cover) and running gear, with the front end from the existing XLH Sportster. The rear end's styling was dominated by a fibreglass boat-tail stepped seat and integral rear mudguard which had debuted as an option on the Sportsters the previous year. Although widely viewed as a defining element of the model, this lasted for only one year and was quickly replaced by a more conventional rear mudguard.

Compared to the FLH, the SuperGlide also had pegs in place of footboards, with foot controls revised to suit. Both exhausts were low-level feeding paired silencers on the right hand side. Wheels were 19in (483mm) front, 16in (406mm) rear, both equipped with fairly feeble drum brakes. The 3½ gallon (13 litre) fuel tank included a built-in speedometer. Functionally, it was a far from perfect machine, although it went and handled far better than the FLH

SPECIFICATIONS: 1971–80	
Engine	ohv V-twin
Capacity	73.66cu.in (1,207cc)
Transmission	4-speed
Power	around 60bhp @ 5400rpm
Weight	590lbs (267kg)
Wheelbase	61in (1,550mm)
Top speed	105mph (169kph)

from which it was derived, not least because it was more than 66lbs (30kg) lighter. The hybrid instantly struck a chord and sold well – 4,700 units in its first year, almost as many as the established FLH ElectraGlide. After two years, it acquired hydraulic disc brakes at both ends and improved suspension with stiffer springs. A year later, an electric start option, the FXE, was added. Japanese Showa forks were added in 1977, electronic ignition in 1978 and twin front discs in 1979, before it developed 80-inch Shovelhead power for 1981. For the final year of production in 1984, five-speed transmission was added; the FXR and FXRS Super Glide II models were also

on the Milwaukee stocks, comfortably out-selling the old stager. Although almost two decades would pass from the SuperGlide's launch to the turnaround in the company's economic fortunes, it's impossible to overstate the effect the model has had on Harley-Davidson's affairs. The FX invented the concept of the factory custom and led to landmark models such as the FXEF Fat Bob in 1979 and Sturgis 12 months later.

POLICE BIKES

The first police Harley was bought by the city of Detroit in 1908. Specially equipped machines took a little longer, but by 1924 more than 1,400 police forces across America had at least one Harley-Davidson in their ranks. Two years later, an office was established at Juneau Avenue to handle fleet sales to police forces, and it was from this that the first factory police option packs began to emerge. Previously, most modifications had been undertaken by the customers themselves. Incidentally, the first order from CHiPs – the California Highway Patrol – was for the 74-inch Model JD in 1929. Twelve months later, bikes could be equipped with that most vital piece of law-enforcement equipment: the Police Special speedometer. By 1935, two police option packs were available for inclusion on any of the big-twin models.

During the 1950s, the HydraGlide and then the DuoGlide – fitted with one of three option groups – became the "standard" police two-wheeler (for a time the Servi-Car had up to four distinct option packs). The arrival of the

Shovelhead in 1966 continued the theme, until the first specific Police model hit the stocks for 1974. The FL-Police was essentially a 74-inch ElectraGlide with basic police equipment included as standard. Almost 800 were sold that year.

From 1979, the 80-inch Shovelhead FLH-80 began to displace the old FLH-1200 as the standard police model and, by 1982, Harley's law-keeper was known simply as the FLHP, available variously with chain, enclosed chain or belt final drive.

Today's police range comprises the FXRP CHiP and FLHT-Police, which are based on the Evo-engined Low Rider and ElectraGlide respectively, and each has special equipment, including an up-rated electronics system, coloured pursuit lights, radio carrier and siren switches (the siren is optional, though).

An indication of the importance of the police market can be gleaned from the sales figures for 1991, when more than 1,500 police machines were sold.

■ BELOW *There are limits. Unless their riders are off-duty, these Harleys are definitely not police machines.*

FXS LOW RIDER, 1977–85

■ BELOW *The Low Rider was built by Milwaukee, but born in the biker heaven of the United States.*

These days, the Low Rider range is as essentially Harley-Davidson as the Sportsters and heavyweight Glides, yet it wasn't until 1977 that Willie G. brought us the first Low Rider model. The FXS Low Rider was, in essence, another reworking of the seminal Super Glide theme, which in turn was to spawn yet another dynasty of Milwaukee hardware.

Described as "one mean machine" in Harley-Davidson's own publicity, the FXS was a new type of custom cruising model, intended to be as content cruising wide-open prairies as downtown avenues. It was finished in menacing gunmetal grey with flat, drag-style handlebars on pulled-back risers, resonating echoes of the choppers that countless enthusiasts had created in the past. The laid-back name came from a seat height of just 27in (686mm), a characteristic which would appear again in the Huggers of the future.

Although the 80-inch Shovelhead first appeared on the FLH ElectraGlide in the Low Rider's debut year, the FXS was initially powered by the established 74-inch Shovel. The engine came

SPECIFICATIONS	
Engine	ohv V-twin
Capacity	73.7cu in (1,207cc)
Transmission	4-speed
Power	60bhp
Weight	550lb (249kg)
Wheelbase	63in (1,600mm)
Top speed	98mph (158kph)

finished in crinkle black paint with highly polished outer covers. Both exhaust pipes curved back along the right side below a new "1200" air-cleaner cover, before thumping the atmosphere through a single chromed muffler. The revised frame was heavily raked and fitted with highway pegs, allowing the rider to stretch out, like the latter-day *Easy Rider* styling sought to emulate.

Chassis components included Japanese Showa telescopic forks, chromed twin rear shock absorbers and dual

front disc brakes. Sadly, the stoppers were still disconcertingly feeble in their effect, although the rear was relatively fierce with massive leverage available at the pedal. The puny forks, too, were prone to flex while the short-travel rear suspension units were at the same time

■ LEFT *The FXS-1200 Low Rider was described as "one mean machine" when it first came on to the scene.*

■ BELOW *This 1985 FXRS Custom picks up the tradition of V-Twin power that was started by the Knucklehead, Panhead and Shovelhead.*

every succeeding year. Along the way, they've spawned eye-catching sister models, such as the 80-inch FXB Sturgis of 1980 – the year after the FXS itself was first offered with the larger Shovelhead mill.

The biggest novelty came in 1983 with the much revised FXSB Low Rider. The "B" represented the adoption of the Aramid-fibre toothed belts first seen on the Sturgis for both primary and secondary drive.

A small number of late-1984 examples may have received the new 80-inch Evolution motor, but it wasn't until the FXRS "Custom Sport" Low Rider of 1985 that this much-improved engine became widespread. By the time five-speed transmission was grafted on to the same model 12 months later, the modern Low Rider series had arrived.

both harsh and under-damped. It would be a while before any heavyweight Harley aspired to even the sketchiest handling prowess.

Quicksilver handling, though, wasn't what the FXS was all about. The model was an instant success, hitting the public's wish-list almost as soon as it was unveiled. It was comfortably out-selling the SuperGlide by its second year, with almost 10,000 examples built. Clearly, the Low Rider concept was here to stay and the breed has benefited from a steady stream of improvements in

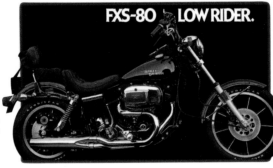

FXS-80 LOW RIDER.

■ ABOVE AND LEFT *The FXS caught on almost instantly, becoming Milwaukee's best-selling model by 1978.*

■ BELOW *Although built in 1992, this Low Rider Sport displays features similar to the original FXS.*

FLT TourGlide, 1980

Like most things Harley-Davidson, the TourGlide didn't suddenly appear out of the Milwaukee ether, it just sort of evolved. One fundamental element, the 80-inch Shovelhead engine – a long-stroke derivative of the old "74" – first appeared on the 1978 FLH Electra-Glide. Another arrived one year later with the FLH Classic, offered as standard with special paint and wheels as well as a complete set of "Tour Pak" touring extras. The Tour Pak was ultimately to become the heavyweight long-haul norm, comprising saddlebags, luggage rack, "batwing" fairing and chromed crash bars.

In 1980, Harley bundled the two together, adding a few other choice ingredients for good measure, and the FLT TourGlide was born. The most obvious change was the replacement of the ElectraGlide's handlebar-mounted fairing with a bigger, more protective frame-mounted fairing, now equipped with twin headlights. There was an improved new frame with "sport bike"

SPECIFICATIONS	
Engine	ohv V-twin
Capacity	81.6cu in (1,338cc)
Transmission	5-speed
Power	65bhp
Weight	765lb (347kg)
Wheelbase	62½in (1,590mm)
Top speed	100mph (161kph)

■ LEFT *Additional long-distance kit allowed heavyweights such as this late-1970s ElectraGlide to evolve into the TourGlide series.*

geometry and a box-section backbone. Fabricated from both tubes and forgings, the frame was further modified at the rear to increase suspension travel. At the front, it now extended forward of the head-stock for more secure fairing mounting.

Less obvious – unless you were riding one – were a host of engine improvements also bestowed on the FLT. Rather than existing separately, the engine and transmission were now bolted rigidly together, gaining the benefits of unit construction without the drawbacks. The transmission itself was now five-speed for the first time on any big twin Harley-Davidson roadster, permitting even more long-legged gearing than before. A new Motorola electronic ignition virtually guaranteed dependable running at all engine speeds (or perhaps not: within a year it gave way to the superior V-Fire II system).

Final drive was still by roller chain but now fully-enclosed in its own oil-bath, a useful asset on any long-distance machines. Chain was superseded by a toothed belt drive on the FLTC Classic of 1984, which became standard across the FL range the following year.

Despite some initial scepticism, the Aramid fibre belts – made from a similar material to that used in bullet-proof vests – had worked well on the lighter V-twins, lasting four times as long as a chain, at similar cost but without the mess. By 1993, they would be a welcome feature on every Harley-Davidson model.

If that particular virtue was still in the future, an equally compelling one first appeared on the inaugural TourGlide. In contrast to previous rigidly-mounted engines, for the first time the FLT engine was installed using a clever three-point rubber-mounting system designed to isolate the rider from the worst of the big V-twin's vibration. In essence it couldn't be simpler, but the effect transformed the machine, making it smoother and more usable than any previous big twin.

Anyone with $6,013 to spare in 1980 could buy what was undoubtedly the smoothest, most comfortable and lavishly-equipped motorcycle Milwaukee had ever produced, a machine tailor-made for demolishing large distances.

The TourGlide might not be everyone's idea of motorcycling but it launched a generation of Milwaukee luxury tourers to which rival manufacturers have yet again paid the ultimate compliment: most of them have since tried to copy it.

■ LEFT *All Tour-Glides enjoyed five-speed transmission and rubber engine mounts. The Evo powerplant brought further refinement from 1984.*

Sportsters

If the original Model K was behind the times, the machine that superseded it has become a legend. Launched in 1957, the 883cc XL Sportster was a much finer machine in every respect. Where the Model K was a flathead, the Sportster featured overhead valves. The engine and gearbox were now in-unit (a refinement to which Harley beat much of its opposition) and there was full swing-arm rear suspension with car-type shock absorbers, allowing early Sportsters to be sold as suitable for both on- or off-road use. The XL was an instant hit, accounting for one fifth of Harley-Davidson's total production in its first year on sale.

As well as meeting performance expectations, the Sportster also looked the business. Its lean, purposeful lines, capped with a minimalist fuel tank and raucous "shorty" exhausts are little changed even today.

Having learned its lesson with the Model K, Milwaukee didn't stand still with its new Sportster, introducing improvements year on year. The first electric-start model was brought in for 1967, more power in 1968 and more again with the first 1,000cc version of 1972, culminating in the delicious XR1000 of 1983. By the time Evolution-engined models arrived in 1986, there was a choice of either 883cc or 1,100cc engines, the latter eventually growing to 1,200cc.

THE FIRST OF THE BREED

■ RIGHT *In 1957 the first of the Sportsters proved to be a giant leap forward from the primitive side-valve Model K.*

After the debacle of the side-valve Model K, the Sportster series roared across America like a refreshing gale. At its heart was an overhead-valve engine displacing the same 883cc as the XLs of today. In those days, however, both the cylinder barrels and heads were of heavy cast iron, the latter with a hemispherical combustion chamber.

Each valve had its own gear-driven camshaft, operating the valve via "High Speed Racing" roller tappets and solid push-rods. A single Linkert carburettor fed mixture into the cylinder, where shallow domed pistons offered a compression ratio of 7.5:1. In 1957, peak power was around 40bhp but this rose considerably with the ported, high-compression "H" and "CH" versions, reputedly reaching 58bhp at 6,800rpm by the mid-1960s. By then, a good one could exceed 110mph (177kph).

Cosmetically, even fully-equipped versions of the XL were as lean as motorcycles can be – an attribute most retain to this day. Not so much as a pillion seat was permitted to mar their purposeful lines. The chassis was adequate if altogether less persuasive. A

SPECIFICATIONS: XL SPORTSTER 1957	
Engine	ohv V-twin
Capacity	883cc
Transmission	4-speed
Power	40bhp
Weight	438lbs (199kg)
Wheelbase	58.5in (1,485mm)
Top speed	95mph (152kph)

■ ABOVE RIGHT *The mercurial "H" stood for high-compression and was intended to signify that this machine was hot.*

■ BELOW *By 1970, the Honda CB750 had arrived, yet the XL had feeble brakes and relatively lacklustre performance.*

combination tubular steel and cast iron frame married "easy riding" telescopic forks and twin rear shock absorbers, with the swing arm pivoting on taper roller bearings. Each 18in (457mm) wheel held an underwhelming eight-inch (200mm) drum with shoes one inch (25mm) wide.

In truth, the handling wasn't great, although (for a Harley) the Sportster was light and low enough for a good rider to manhandle it into shape. An improved front fork helped matters from 1968 but the XL only really began to behave with the appearance of a lighter and stiffer frame, universally praised in press road tests, in 1982. By this time, the old one was very much feeling its age. Those first Sportsters were comparable with almost anything on the road and, at $1,103 apiece, sold like "Competition Hot-cakes". By the late 1960s, this was comfortably Harley's best-selling range.

■ LEFT *The XLCH, which is commonly dubbed "Competition Hot". Sportsters remain the only Harleys to use unit construction engines.*

■ SPORTSTER EVOLUTION

Since its introduction in 1957, the XL Sportster has been the bread and butter of the Harley-Davidson range. Within a year, the stock Sporty had been joined by the high-compression XLH Sportster Sport, the legendary XLCH "Competition Hot" (as it is commonly called, although it actually meant "Competition High-compression") and the stripped-down XLC Sportster Racing. Perhaps surprisingly, the latter, intended for off-road use, lasted for only one year.

Originally marked for a life on dirt, the XLCH featured the 1.8 gallon (8.2 litre) "peanut" tank (standard was 3.5 gallon /16 litres), big valves,

magneto ignition – and neither lights, speedometer nor battery. It was superseded by a fully road-equipped XLCH one year later. Detail changes included a switch to 12-volt electronics in 1965, two years before the first Sportster electric start – or "Push the button... ZAP... and away you go" as Milwaukee promoted it.

For 1971, the previous dry clutch gave way to a wet one. The first 1,000cc examples were the XLH/XLCH Super H and Super CH of 1972, the extra displacement coming from a 4.5mm increase in bore size to offer around 60bhp. (The captivating XLCR and XR1000 are dealt with in

detail later.) Another spin-off from the Sportster line was a series of hybrid models, hoping to hit any untapped market niche. The XLT Touring came out in 1977, equipped with saddlebags, high bars and a thicker seat. More than 1,000 were built in the first year, a mere six in the second, giving way two years later to the XLS Roadster, with extended forks, highway pegs and a 16in (406mm) rear wheel. That year might be remembered as the last year of the legendary XLCH. A lasting hybrid was the optional Hugger package of 1980, offering shorter shocks and a thinner seat – this was a precursor of the true Hugger models of today. The equally far-reaching XLX61 came out in 1983, a stripped-down, budget-priced version of the XLH1000 aimed at cash-strapped riders. It has been Milwaukee policy ever since to produce a cut-price "entry-level" model. When the 883 and 1,100cc Evolution models arrived for 1986, it was to be the beginning of a new chapter in the Sportster story.

■ LEFT *The very first of the Sportsters, from 1957. The Model S-inspired fuel tank came later.*

XLCR CAFE RACER, 1977-8

If black truly is beautiful, then the XLCR was sublime. So dark, it practically drank in the light, the Café Racer was another of Willie G. Davidson's variations on an old theme, in this case re-working the basic 1,000cc Sportster which had first appeared in 1972. When it arrived for the 1977 model year, the XLCR looked revolutionary – the most unashamedly different Harley-Davidson yet.

At its heart was the then biggest XL engine grafted into a redesigned frame, with extended rear frame rails allowing more vertical shock absorbers than before. Most striking of all was the "Black-on-Black" paint job. This included gloss black bodywork, crinkle-black engine finish and a black Siamesed exhaust which snaked together below the air-filter housing – which, naturally, was black.

The 3.8 gallon (14.5 litre) fuel tank – black, of course – was unique to the XLCR, as were a fibreglass "bikini" fairing and single seat. The latter ended with a

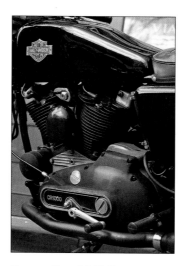

■ ABOVE *The stylish XLCR, with its "race replica" footrests, did not produce the kind of sales that Harley had hoped for.*

racing-style "bum stop" – although a dual seat option was available for 1978, the model's second and final year of manufacture. Cast aluminium Morris wheels, as well as rear-set "race replica" footrests and controls, were also provided as standard.

The move to more vertical shock absorbers was a not particularly successful attempt to improve the Sportster's habitually sloppy handling.

At the same time, twin hydraulic front discs were fitted in much-needed pursuit of improved braking. They proved moderately powerful, if rather lacking in feel.

SPECIFICATIONS	
Engine	ohv V-twin
Capacity	992cc
Transmission	4-speed
Power	around 60bhp
Weight	540lbs (245kg)
Wheelbase	58.5in (1,485mm)
Top speed	110mph (177kph)

■ BELOW *In truth the XLCR looked better than it went.*

25mph (40kph) slower than rival sports machines, with equally inferior handling and braking. Worse still, the XLCR bore all the worst hallmarks of the AMF years. Contemporary road tests might praise the marque's "indefinable magic" but they would equally slate the Café Racer (and its siblings) for being "appallingly built and hideously unreliable," to which was usually added "prohibitively expensive".

By the end of the model's brief reign, Harley-Davidson's share of the American motorcycle market had slumped to a paltry four per cent, yet it would be several years before the reborn company would seriously set about tackling its manufacturing shortcomings. This wasn't specifically the fault of the XLCR, of which just 3,124 examples were built, but this model did illustrate Harley-Davidson's problem – that beauty had to be much more than skin-deep.

Visually, this "top Sportster" was superb. True, it wasn't to everyone's taste, but most bikers would cast admiring glances at this stylish symphony in black. For all its eye-grabbing credentials, however, the XLCR was far from a runaway success.

On the one hand, most Harley die-hards found it visually too radical. On the other hand, more neutral buyers found sport-bike image and performance far more effectively packaged in Japanese and Italian machines. For all that, the XLCR is a desirable classic now, though at the time it was neither a vintage Harley-Davidson model nor a competent sports machine.

With around 60bhp and a top speed close to around 110mph (177kph), the XLCR was certainly no slug, but the bald truth was that it went at least

XR1000 SPORTSTER, 1983-4

Unveiled at Daytona in March 1983, the XR1000 was the closest Harley-Davidson fans would ever get to a road-going XR racer. Even this far on, it's still many people's idea of the ultimate Harley Sportster. This should have come as no surprise because the big XR roadster was designed (and the prototype built) in the official factory race shop under the direction of Dick O'Brien. The 1000 could scarcely have enjoyed a better pedigree – O'Brien had managed Harley-Davidson's racing efforts since 1957 and overseen every moment of the XR750's career. Fittingly, O'Brien retired in the same year as the XR1000 roadster was released, making it an appropriately snarling swansong.

The $6,995 1000 wasn't quite a big-bore factory racer with lights but it was pretty special all the same. The engine employed a normal Sportster bottom end capped by special cylinder barrels, heads, fuel and exhaust systems. The aluminium heads were based on those of the racing

■ ABOVE *Not quite a racing XR750 for the road, but visually the XR1000 came pretty close.*

SPECIFICATIONS:	
Engine	ohv V-twin
Capacity	998cc
Transmission	4-speed
Power	70bhp
Weight	487lbs (221kg)
Wheelbase	59.3in (1,505mm)
Top speed	115mph (185kph)

XR, each reputedly shipped to Los Angeles to be ported and polished by legendary tuner, Jerry Branch (although it's likely that Branch simply oversaw the work, since a total of 1,777 XR1000s were built).

Induction was in the capable hands of twin 1½in (36mm) Dell'Orto carburettors with accelerator pumps, each breathing through huge, free-flowing K&N air filters stacked, flat-track style, on the engine's right side. Although stock Sportster camshafts were employed, valve-lash was adjusted by

■ RIGHT *Possibly the most prized of all AMF-era models, the XR1000 was race boss Dick O'Brien's major contribution to Harley roadsters.*

■ RIGHT *This example has been customized to superb effect with a flat-track style rear mudguard and seat.*

■ BELOW RIGHT *That's better: the same colours flown by Jay Springsteen, Scott Parker and the rest of the champion racers.*

harsh, making the XR nervous when ridden hard on bumpy surfaces. The brakes, however – twin 11½in (292mm) front discs – were surely the best Harley-Davidson had put on any roadster model up to that time and improved even further for 1984.

During the model's second year, it was offered with optional black and orange "factory" racing paintwork as well as the original steel grey. This seemed to be a suitably fitting livery for such a great machine.

The XR1000's reign as the ultimate sporting Harley-Davidson ever to have been produced by Milwaukee came to an end when production of this model ceased in 1984.

racer-style eccentric rocker shafts. The push-rods, too, were special lightweight alloy components. Lumpy pistons gave a 9:1 compression ratio. Paired high-level black megaphone exhausts growled back along the machine's left side.

This bespoke engine was red-lined at 6,200rpm but there was no earthly need to spin it that high, since the spread of power was immense.

Peak power – a claimed 70bhp – arrived at 5,600rpm but the engine pulled strongly from as few as 2,000rpm. Maximum torque was 48lb/ft (65Nm) at just 4,400rpm. The speedometer was calibrated only to 110mph (177kph), a figure a good XR could reach comfortably.

With optional performance kits offering more than 90bhp, the sky was almost the limit.

In truth, the XR's chassis was far less impressive than its engine. The frame and running gear were based on the XLX61, which was also new for 1983,

with a nine-spoke, cast 19in (483mm) front wheel and 16in (406mm) rear. Rear suspension was in the hands of twin shock absorbers of no great quality, adjustable only for spring pre-load. Travel was quite short and the action

XLH883, 1986– PRESENT

■ LEFT *The 883 is just the coolest thing on the road.*

With a price tag of just under $4,000 when introduced as the XLX61 in 1983, the basic Sportster was precisely the type of entry-level machine so conspicuously absent from the Harley-Davidson stables in the past. This was a piece of genuine Milwaukee hardware at a price almost anyone could afford. In 1986, the deal was made even better with the appearance of Evolution engines across the Sportster range and the arrival of the XLH883. Then, just 12 months after that, would-be 883 owners got an even more irresistible package with the announcement of Harley's innovative buy-back scheme: "Trade in your XLH against an FX or FL within two years and we'll guarantee $3,995 on your old machine." How could anyone lose?

The smallest Sportster was the last model to benefit from the wave of refinements sweeping through the Milwaukee range. But in two short years from 1992, Harley-Davidson's bargain-basement superbike progressed from being the runt of the Harley-Davidson litter to become a thoroughly competent

SPECIFICATIONS	
Engine	ohv V-twin
Capacity	883cc
Transmission	5-speed
Power	52bhp
Weight	489lb (222kg)
Wheelbase	60.2in (1,530mm)
Top Speed	103mph (166kph)

■ BELOW LEFT *No frills, no tassels and bereft of baubles, the 883 is the most honest-to-goodness model in the Milwaukee range.*

■ BELOW RIGHT *The least expensive, lightest and easiest Harley to handle is popular with male and female riders alike.*

machine. There were dozens of detail changes over those two seasons, but two stand out. First came five-speed transmission for 1992, followed 12 months later by belt final drive.

The extra gear transformed the smallest Harley from a relatively buzzy, busy machine into a far more laid-back device, with the bonus of a better gear-shift. The tooth-belt drive made it smoother still, with the added benefits of low maintenance and cleanliness.

The first belts – pioneered by Harley-Davidson and the Gates company that manufactures them – aroused a degree of suspicion. However, thanks to space-age Aramid fibre reinforcement (similar to Kevlar – they last at least four times as long as a chain, cost about the same

and are practically unknown to fail. This was to make the XLH slightly more of what it was always good at – being a lean, spare and handsome means of filling practically all the space between headstock and rear spindle. There are no tassels, no gratuitously shiny but ultimately useless bits – just plain, single-seated function.

Of course, like all Harleys, the function in question has relatively little to do with sheer speed, handling or stopping. The 883 is essentially a cut-down cruiser, its low-profile Hugger stablemates all the more so. It looks cool while allowing its rider to appreciate, with as little intervening sanitation as possible, the most intimate doings of the internal-combustion engine.

Peak power from the 883cc engine is around

52bhp at a distinctly unruffled 5,500rpm – 1,000rpm after the arrival of maximum torque of 52lb/ft (70.5Nm). Acceleration is brisk rather than vivid, although the ample torque means there's always power on hand.

This motorcycle might be smaller than any other that Harley has produced, but crank open the throttle at almost any revs and the Sportster lunges forward on the same irrepressible wave of power. Without the rubber-mounting available on some larger models, engine vibration can be intense at high revs. There is no question that the 883 series represents good quality and value.

As well as the basic 883, there's also the

Hugger – a variant dating back to 1979 and so called because it squats even lower to the ground.

They hardly depreciate and, with a bit of care, they can all last practically forever. Best of all, however, more than 40 years after the introduction of the original XL, the 883s continue to embody the same frill-free virtues.

For a chunk of a legend, the 883 really is a steal.

■ LEFT *A 1996 Hugger 883, even lower to the ground than the stock Sportster.*

XL1200S SPORTSTER SPORT, 1996–PRESENT

By the mid-1990s, the redoubtable Sportster family was approaching its fortieth birthday – and beginning to show it. True, Evolution V2 engine technology had reached the old XL steeds on the 883 and 1100 Sportsters for the 1987 model year. Twelve months later, Milwaukee unleashed the first of the family's 1,200cc models, the XLH. Essentially this was the old 1,100 engine with the bore increased from 85.1 to 88.8mm. The stroke remained unchanged at 96.8mm, the same as the 883. Other than a change to five-speed transmissions and belt drive across most of the Sportster family in 1991, the range remained largely unchanged until the appearance of the 1200S in 1996. Along the way, it had definitely lost some of the fire that had burned in the first of the breed all those years before.

Those first Sportster Sports were perhaps a case of "close, but no cigar." Initially, their chief distinction was the adoption of improved, fully-adjustable suspension components at both ends, mated to softer, grippier tyres – but the engine remained stubbornly unmoved.

SPECIFICATIONS	
Engine	ohv V-twin
Capacity	1,203cc
Transmission	5-speed
Power	75bhp
Weight	518lbs (235kg)
Wheelbase	60.2in (1,530mm)
Top speed	110mph (177kph)

Sportster fans had to wait another two years before the model truly reached its peak, but the 1998 Sportster Sport was surely worth the delay. In broad terms, the engine was little changed from previous Sportsters, with its hydraulic tappets, dry sump and triple-row primary chain driving a wet multi-plate clutch and toothed-belt final drive. Naturally, the 1200S carries higher overall gearing: 2.103:1 compared to 2.259:1 on the 883.

However, a comprehensive engine revamp had raised torque figures by an average of 15 per cent throughout the twin's 2,000–5,500rpm operating range. The model now had both the chassis and the engine to justify its "Sport" aspirations at last.

Essential to these improvements was an all-new ignition pack igniting not one, but two spark plugs in each cylinder, promoting quicker, more efficient burning of the incoming fuel/air charge. Although a conventional carburettor was retained – a 1½in (40mm) constant velocity Keihin instrument equipped with an "accelerator" pump – combustion control was further improved by an

electronic management system even more sophisticated than the V Fire III set-up fitted to its sister models. The system, incidentally, also affords high-tech electronic diagnostic capabilities. These measures allowed Harley-Davidson's engineers to bump up compression from 9:1 to 10:1, offering a substantial increase in mid-range power.

As well as lumpier pistons, the revised powerplant benefited from a larger, less restrictive exhaust system and new camshaft design. The camshafts offer both higher lift and longer duration, again with the emphasis on enhancing mid-range torque. Harley can claim a peak torque figure of 78lb/ft (106Nm) at 4,000rpm, over 50 per cent higher than the 883. With not only much improved power characteristics but better throttle response as well, the Sport feels even stronger than the figures might show. The 1200S looks every inch as mean and muscular as a Sportster should, with its clean lines and understated black engine highlights. Nor is this a deception, for the twin-plug Sport package delivers genuine punch. Better still, it stops and handles in a most un-Milwaukee-like manner – a

mantle several more recent models have since adopted, to welcome effect.

In short, this not only proved to be the best XL for years, but perhaps was also the model with which Harley rediscovered the Sportster's roots, and made a great addition to the range.

■ ABOVE LEFT *One of the first examples of the 1200S. Later versions were better.*

■ ABOVE RIGHT *The Sportster is really a joy to ride.*

■ LEFT *Getting back to its roots: the XL1200S.*

Softails

It is a typical Harley irony that the Evolution V2 engine, unveiled in 1984, brought about a revolution in the company's fortunes, whereas the Twin Cam engine launched in 1998 was truly revolutionary in engineering terms. Then came the Twin Cam 88 and its balance-shafted brother, the 88B – so revolutionary that it might aptly be dubbed the Revo V2. It took four years and 2.5 million test miles (4 million km) to bring the project to fruition, resulting in an engine with 18 of 450 components in common with the 80-inch Evo motor. The result has as many benefits over its predecessor as the Evo had over the Shovel. If it does half as well Harley-Davidson can look forward with confidence.

If the Evolution V2 engine was a success, then so was the model in which it first appeared. Softails are the glittering style kings of the Harley range, and the first of these was the seminal FXST Softail of 1984. "Retro-Tech" is something modern in concept but executed and styled in a recognisably "classic" way. To achieve the hardtail illusion, Harley-Davidson engineers designed a massive triangulated rear swinging fork, with twin shock absorbers hidden from normal view beneath the engine. The clean overall lines of the machine emphasized the elegant sweep from head stock to rear wheel spindle, heightening the hardtail effect. Visually, however, the origins were the 1949 HydraGlide, the first Harley model with telescopic front forks. If any modern motorcycle belonged outside a 1950s American diner, the Softail was surely it, until the even more eye-grabbing 1988 Springer Softail brought the same throwback concept to the front end as well. Retro-Tech has since established itself as the fourth major theme in the Milwaukee menagerie, alongside the Sportsters, Dynas and Glides. Indeed, of all Harley models, Softails are invariably in the shortest supply.

FXST SOFTAIL, 1984

Certain motorcycles have stood out as memorably special over the years, mobbed for days on end at motorcycle shows. Honda's original CB750F was one, as was Ducati's sensuous 916. In recent years, the Milwaukee equivalent has surely been the first Softail, from 1984. True, all Harley-Davidsons are someone's idea of beauty but the FXST had a quality all its own.

Based on the existing FXWG Wide-Glide – somewhat loosely, to judge by appearances – the Softail had bikers not knowing quite where to look. Did they focus on the all-new Evolution V2 engine or eyeball that strangely elegant rear end? Most probably they did both and Softails are still being eyed covetously to this day.

The Softail's rear suspension was a clever piece of lateral thinking based on an old theme, created for Harley by consulting engineer Bill Davis. The inspiration almost certainly came from custom craftsmen such as Arlen Ness – and even carries a distant echo of the Goudier-Genoud endurance racing Kawasakis. Essentially, it's an inverted cantilever rear end (as per Vincent and

SPECIFICATIONS	
Engine	air-cooled ohv V-twin
Capacity	81.6cu in (1,338cc)
Transmission	4- (later 5-) speed
Power	69bhp
Weight	604lbs (274kg)
Wheelbase	66.3in (1,685mm)
Top speed	106mph (170kph)

■ TOP RIGHT, CENTRE RIGHT, RIGHT AND ABOVE *The earliest versions of the Softail featured Evo engines with four-speed transmissions, although contemporary FLs enjoyed five speeds. Even a kick start was originally retained.*

Yamaha) in which a triangulated assembly pivots at the top, near the seat, rather than at the usual place. Paired, gas-charged Showa shock absorbers lie unobtrusively under the engine. The layout has little to do with function but a lot to do with style, something it

■ LEFT *With its fake hardtail rear end, the 1984 FXST was the first true "Retro-Tech" model. The series has since become the most stylish and desirable in the range.*

demonstrated superbly. Despite the space constraints inherent in the twin-damper system, Softails in fact boasted more rear suspension travel – 4in (103mm) – than any other models in the Harley range.

Maybe the Softail look wasn't keenly anticipated, since most people didn't know it was coming, but the engine certainly was. Although a few very early 1984 Softails may have been built with Shovelhead engines, every one since has had belt-driven Evo power. With its all-new light alloy top end, the new big twin produced around 70bhp at 5,000rpm and a withering 84lb/ft (114Nm) of torque at just 3,600rpm. Indeed, the spread of power was so immense that almost no-one complained that 1984 examples had to make do with four-speed gearboxes. A five-speed cluster was installed for 1985, by which time a lighter diaphragm spring clutch had also appeared.

The chassis is characterized by an immense 66.3in (1,685mm) wheelbase and a seat height of 1in (25mm) lower than even a Low Rider's seat. Fuel is carried in the familiar, bulbous, two-piece Fat Bob tank, split across the mid-line, with a speedometer set in the centre. Wheels are wire-spoked, 21in (533mm) front and 16in (406mm) rear, carrying a single hydraulic disc apiece. Unlike contemporary Glides, the 80-inch engine is solidly mounted, although rubber-insulated handlebars and footrests compensate to some extent. Softails may be stylish, but smooth they are not.

The low saddle and forward-mounted "highway" pegs impose an appropriately laid-back riding position. As for handling: well, the Softail doesn't – it just sort of rumbles from A to B and all the better if that doesn't include too many fast corners. The suspension at both ends is woefully under-damped, the front forks are characteristically soft and woolly, and the rear is, frankly, harsh. Nonetheless, the expansive wheelbase and conservative steering geometry keep things more or less in line. Besides, this is a bike for cruising.

It's a measure of the overall rightness of the concept that, superficially at least, Softails appear little changed to this day. This disguises the vast improvements Harley-Davidson has made in build quality and detailing since the time of the FXST's launch.

Above all, there's the inescapable fact that this inspired piece of post-modern design was a huge and instant success.

Although not the most practical model that Harley-Davidson has ever built, it certainly can be said that Softails are the most eye-catching and, above all, the most prized.

■ LEFT *The Softail Custom introduced in 1987 was the first of many models inspired by the original FXST.*

FXSTS SPRINGER SOFTAIL, 1988–PRESENT

In late 1987, the motorcycle world took one look and pinched itself – twice. The Springer Softail unveiled for the 1988 model year looked like no new motorcycle of the previous 40 years. Gone were the telescopic front forks to which we had become accustomed. In their place was a trellis-work of bright-chromed steel members, linkages and springs. It was called "Springer", and was as audacious as it was surreal.

As Harley said at the time, the new front-end wasn't just reborn, it was re-invented. The Springer front end was styled along the lines of the girder forks seen on almost every make of motorcycle from before the 1920s until the late 1940s, but the technology and the detail were all-new. Using computer-aided design (CAD) and the latest materials, Milwaukee had created a system which not only afforded an acceptable level of wheel travel (around

4in/100mm) and suspension control, but which freed its designers to make the styling statement of the year.

We now had Retro-Tech at both ends: Springer at the front to accompany Softail lines at the rear. The engine,

naturally, was the doughty 80-inch Evo, styled for its new role and fitted with staggered shorty dual exhausts.

Like all "conventional" Softail models, the new Springer offered defiantly lazy steering geometry. In this case, a shallow 32-degree steering head gave a generous 5¼in (133mm) of trail. The wheelbase was a lanky 64.6in (1,640mm). Unlike standard Softails, Springers roll on slow-steering 21in (533mm) front wheels, with a 16in (406mm) hoop at the rear. Inevitably, the result isn't quite at the cutting edge of modern suspension performance. Any Softail rear end can be harsh, especially

■ ABOVE *A modern damper unit (with Harley sticker) controls the movement of the Springer forks.*

■ LEFT *No-one pretends Springers give state-of-the-art handling, but who needs it on a cruise in the sun?*

SPECIFICATIONS	
Engine	air-cooled ohv V-twin
Capacity	81.6cu in (1,340cc)
Transmission	5-speed
Power	69bhp
Weight	625lbs (284kg)
Wheelbase	64.6in (1,640mm)
Top speed	100mph (161kph)

■ BELOW RIGHT *Optional screen, trim and running lights give the owner of this Springer even more to polish.*

■ BOTTOM *Aftermarket fishtail silencers and two-tone paint contrive to make this Springer look for all the world like a 1946 FL.*

over freeway seams, and the latter-day girders lack the control of even Fat Boy's massive telescopic forks. Such judgements miss the point, however. Of all the Milwaukee models, Springers are unashamedly machines for stately cruising – and are as far removed from a Japanese "crotch rocket" as a 1959 Cadillac.

If 1987 marked the Springer's debut, then 1997 marked what many regard as its finest hour. As well as offering practical accessories such as leather saddlebags as standard, the 1997 FLSTS Heritage Springer Softail went

further down the classic road, combining even more vintage styling with today's retro-technology. "Loaded with chrome and leather," publicity material hailed at the time, "the Heritage Springer Softail screams nostalgia." And so it did, from its bright-chromed fishtail mufflers to its deeply-valanced mudguards and whitewall tyres. Even at first glance, the result is sublime, the level of detail extraordinary. Note the nostalgic front fender-tip light and the "retro-1940s tombstone tail-light once commonplace on Harley-Davidsons decades ago." Admire a seat with a leather fringed valance "embossed with a basket-weave pattern and accented with conchos".

The ultimate factory custom had come a long way from the original SuperGlide. As the man said: "Is it a motorcycle or is it art?"

FLSTN HERITAGE SOFTAIL NOSTALGIA, 1993

Dubbed the "CowGlide" on its release for the 1993 model year, the limited-edition Heritage Nostalgia was the fanciest incarnation of Milwaukee's fanciest line. The nickname came from its hairy, black-and-white natural cowhide seat and saddlebag inserts, but there were plenty more cosmetic tricks where they came from. Little wonder its creators described it as: "Without doubt, the most distinctive-looking motorcycle in Harley's 1993 line ... nostalgic-looking ... but thoroughly modern." It had already proved a winning formula.

Modern, of course, means something else in Harley-Davidson's wondrous time-warp world – like whitewall tyres and forks straight out of the 1940s. Ever since beginning life in 1986, the Heritage Softail package attempted to re-enact the look of the 1949 HydraGlide, with its "hardtail" rear and gleaming metal fork shrouds.

Fine detail isn't something you'd normally expect from a device scaling almost one third of a ton, but this is a Harley, so the tank badge is a specially fired enamel named "jewelled

■ ABOVE *The engine was an 80-inch Evo like any other, but the Nostalgia package set it apart.*

■ BELOW *The "CowGlide" was derived from the stock Heritage Softail, here seen cruising in company with a LowRider.*

SPECIFICATIONS	
Engine	air-cooled ohv V-twin
Capacity	81.6cu in (1,340cc)
Transmission	5-speed
Power	69bhp
Weight	710lbs (322kg)
Wheelbase	64.2in (1,630mm)
Top speed	100mph (161kph)

cloisonné." Yet at heart, it's essentially an even more customized variant on the Heritage Softail Classic, available only in Birch White and Black two-tone, with black and chrome engine trim. Power comes from an identical 80-inch Evo engine booming out the same 69bhp at a mere 5,000rpm and a mammoth 70-or-so pound-feet (95Nm) of torque at an even lowlier 3,500rpm. Like the rest of the 1993 range, the Nostalgia benefited from a taller final drive (61-tooth rear pulley) for lower revs at cruising speeds. Improved brake and clutch levers, master cylinder sight glasses and a new, neater engine-breather system also arrived for the same model year.

To ride, it's inevitably much like any other Softail, particularly the Classic or Fat Boy (with which it shares wheel sizes), steering geometry (32-degrees rake, 5.8in/147mm trail), forks, footboards, handlebars and almost every other relevant dimension. The only significant differences are a fuel tank almost ¼ gallon (1 litre) larger and the addition of a hefty 93lbs (42kg) of mass compared to the basic Softail model.

With suspension springing as soft as the CowGlide's considerable weight will allow, handling falls somewhere between sedate and ponderous. Over bumps, the steering is vague and

factory floor – to be either the real 1949 McCoy or a bespoke special that had been put together at huge expense by one of Hollywood's celebrity custom farms. Harley-Davidson's retro illusion was that good, yet only 2,700 examples of the limited-edition Nostalgia were ever built.

Even at $13,000 – just $3,100 less than the most lavish Glide – demand for these highly-desirable models far exceeded supply.

Second-hand "CowGlide" Nostalgias were soon changing hands at far more than list price. Mark up another masterpiece for Willie G. Davidson and his men.

accompanied by a slow weave whenever the road turns lumpy. As with the brakes, it's adequate if it is ridden with prudence.

Since Softail engines are not rubber-mounted, the vibrations intrude towards the top of the rev range even with its higher overall gearing – or as its makers prefer, the bike "rumbles with the echoes of Harleys past."

At a first glance, most onlookers took the Nostalgia – which was fresh from the

■ BELOW *They say that nostalgia isn't what it used to be. No, in this case it's much better.*

FLSTF FAT BOY, 2000

The irreverently-named Fat Boy has held pride of place in Milwaukee's custom line-up since its debut in 1990. The FLSTF could claim to be the coolest of all the Retro-Techs, with its 16in (406mm) solid-disc wheels, elegant lines and bold but understated paint. For the year 2000, Fatso and its fellow Softails got the biggest shake-up since the line began back in 1984, with only a handful of parts retained from the old model. The new millennium marks the end of the noble 80-inch Evo engine and the adoption of the Twin Cam 88 across the entire heavyweight range.

This is no ordinary Twin Cam, though. Designated the 88B, the engine was developed in parallel with the "stock" 88 and uses essentially the same top ends, including the same 88.42cu in (1,449cc) displacement from identical bore and stroke dimensions. The bottom-end, however, features hardware never seen on any previous Harley: twin counter-rotating balance shafts. The eccentrically weighted shafts, tightly-packed inside the crankcases, rotate in

■ LEFT *Solid disc 16in wheels have distinguished the Fat Boy since its launch for 1990.*

■ BELOW LEFT *Only Harley could get away with such a derogatory title – and make it sell.*

the opposite direction to the crankshaft to eliminate primary engine vibration.

This is necessary because the Softail rear suspension pretty much demands that the engine be mounted rigidly in the frame. As a consequence, the rubber mounting used to such good effect on other heavyweight models is not a practical option.

Since their inception, Softails have been marred by punishing vibration, especially at high revs, reducing their long-haul capability. Rideability has been dramatically improved with the 88B, offering true long-distance comfort. In keeping with this, fuel capacity was increased to 5 gallons (19 litres) and the tank is now one-piece, obviating the irritation of earlier twin fillers.

Although somewhat less powerful than Twin Cam Dynas and Glides, the 88B also offers more power and torque

SPECIFICATIONS

Engine	air-cooled ohv V-twin
Capacity	88.42cu in (1,449cc)
Transmission	5-speed
Power	63bhp
Weight	666lbs (302kg)
Wheelbase	64.5in (1,637mm)
Top speed	106mph (170kph)

■ LEFT *The first of the breed. Fender trim, backrest and saddlebags are non-standard.*

■ RIGHT *The Fat Boy is actually no more of a fatso than other Softails, and its lines are cleaner, as these late-Evo versions clearly show.*

with substantially improved tractability. Maximum power is some 63bhp at 5,300rpm, with torque peaking at 78lb/ft (106Nm) at 3,500rpm. Uprated gearbox internals offer slicker, lighter gearshifts, easier neutral-finding and less transmission noise.

At the rear, a new drive belt is stronger and longer-lasting than before yet, at 1⅛in (28mm), almost ¼in (6mm) narrower in section. This permits a wider rear tyre, although – with less than 30 degrees of lean angle on offer – this is scarcely likely to promote scratching.

In addition, year 2000 Softails ride on an all-new frame, stiffer than before but fabricated from half as many parts – just 17 – as previous models. This is complemented by a redesigned swing arm which also contributes to a more stable ride. When it comes to hauling this 666lb (300kg) brute down from speed, even the brakes – long a Milwaukee blind-spot – have been substantially improved. Four piston callipers now grace both ends of the Fat Boy, and the disc rotors are more resistant to heat distortion. The effect is

■ LEFT *The very first FLSTF in metallic grey was widely considered the most handsome.*

■ BELOW *For year 2000 the Fat Boy benefited from the new 88B balance-shafted Twin Cam engine.*

improving braking power and a 20 per cent reduction in brake-lever effort.

This is a considerable catalogue of real improvements on any model, let alone one cherished more for its looks and style than its functional elan. The 2000

Fat Boy has received a few cosmetic touches – notably, restyled exhausts and rear mudguard – without losing any of its essential character, but Milwaukee has surely got it right by making it work far better, too.

Low Riders and Dynas

It's the Milwaukee way to create blend bikes which take on their own identity over the years, and these are a case in point. DynaGlides evolved from Low Riders, which evolved from SuperGlides, which in turn evolved when the factory first grafted a Sportster front end on to an ElectraGlide. The very first Low Rider, the FXS, appeared in 1977. At heart it was little more than a FXE SuperGlide, complete with 74-inch Shovelhead engine, yet within four years it had soared to become Harley-Davidson's best-selling non-Sportster model.

In 1980, the FXB Sturgis – essentially a Low Rider with belt drive and extended forks – was added to a growing FX series which now included SuperGlide, Low Rider, WideGlide and Fat Bob models. Despite their popularity, these were the last to receive the Evolution V2 engine, making do with Shovelheads until late in 1984.

Five-speed transmission was added model-by-model throughout 1985–6, but the most significant novelty was the appearance of a new chassis with the limited-edition FXDB Sturgis of 1991. Incorporating a magically effective, new two-point engine-mounting system, this has progressively replaced the old Low Rider frame on all FXD-series models. The family now comprises perhaps the most practical and versatile workhorses in the Harley-Davidson range.

FXRS-CONV LOW RIDER CONVERTIBLE, 1989–93

■ BELOW *The Convertible became the ultimate Harley all-rounder upon its launch for 1989.*

Characterized by their brutal, low lines, fat rear wheels and skinny front ends, Low Riders represented one of the core "families" of Milwaukee models from 1977 until the mid-1990s. Beginning with the 74-inch Shovelhead FXS in 1977, the range grew to include seminal spin-offs such as the FXEF Fat Bob and FXB Sturgis. Along the way, Low Rider capacity grew to 80cu in (1,338cc) for 1980 and adopted toothed-belt final drive for the FXSB of 1983. The first Evolution-engine Low Rider, the FXRS Custom Sport, appeared for the 1985 model year, gaining five-speed transmission one year later. By 1987, Harley's "broadest and most versatile range" included Standard, Custom and Sport Edition models, as well as sister models such as the quintessential Super-Glide and SportGlide.

Harley-Davidson literature was always keen to stress Low Riders' unrivalled "combination of style and comfort", and it was certainly true that the range always veered towards the practical end of the style scale: cruisers that are as adept on the open road as on the city streets.

"They're in their element anywhere there's pavement" was how the brochures put it. It was no idle boast.

This was never more apparent than with the Low Rider Convertible released for the 1989 season.

Although not exactly a convertible in the Cadillac sense, this model was as close as any two-wheeler needed to be. No longer did owners need to lash luggage wherever they could – this Convertible came complete with leather saddlebags. There was a large, wind-cheating Lexan screen, too. The real beauty of both was that they were detachable, and quickly. Riders setting out for the long haul could leave them on – or, in just a few moments, whip them off for a cruise downtown.

■ LEFT AND ABOVE LEFT *Easily detached screen and saddlebags made the FXRS equally at home in the western deserts as cruising city streets. The 1991 model (above) is en route from the Harley factory at York, Pennsylvania to San Francisco.*

SPECIFICATIONS

Engine	air-cooled ohv V-twin
Capacity	81.6cu in (1,340cc)
Transmission	5-speed
Power	69bhp
Weight	585lbs (265kg)
Wheelbase	64.7in (1,643mm)
Top speed	106mph (170kph)

■ BELOW *Successor to the FXRS-Conv is the DynaGlide Convertible, now with 88 Twin Cam power.*

■ LEFT *Hot dry air and stinging dust make the screen essential in desert conditions.*

■ BELOW *Possibly not the most handsome chunk of Milwaukee iron, but very definitely one of the most practical. This is a 1992 example.*

As a touring alternative to Electra-Glide overkill, the Convertible was supreme. Its plush seat, standard sissy bar and highway pegs offered reasonable comfort (although the pillion pad was always something of a style-dictated joke), while the screen kept off the worst of road grime and weather. It handled tolerably well, too. The 1½in (39mm) front forks featured air-adjustment and anti-dive. For a heavyweight Harley, ground clearance was also good. Stopping was better than the Milwaukee norm – courtesy of twin hydraulic discs at the front and one at the rear.

The Low Rider look came largely from the choice of wheels: a 19in (483mm) front rim with a 100/90 tyre, compared to a 16in (406mm) rear hoop with a fat, 5⅛in- (130mm-) wide tread. Power came from the Evo 81.6cu in (1,340cc) mill. Although the rubber-mounting wasn't quite in the same league as modern Dyna models, it was pretty good. For five years until it gave way to the Dyna series at the end of 1993, the Low Rider Convertible was perhaps the most practical Harley-Davidson model. It was a neat adaptation of a well-sorted design, so there were few improvements during the time. A 1⅝in (40mm) Keihin carb and improved clutch were introduced in 1990, and other minor details, but essentially the first one was as good as the last. In 1994, the FXRS gave way to another Convertible, the Dyna-series FXDS.

FXDB STURGIS, 1991

On the face of it, the "Mark II" Sturgis added little to the Low Rider family from which it sprang. Named after the annual North Dakota bike rally, the FXDB looked like little more than a midnight-black FXRS with modest changes to its rear shocks and oil tank. Indeed, the two models shared the same front end. The major attributes of the FXDB Sturgis were simplicity itself – just two hard-to-spot pieces of rubber – and with them, a motorcycle was transformed. The Sturgis was a limited-edition model – just over 1,500 were produced – but its impact lives on in every DynaGlide built since. The frame itself, an all-steel structure developed by advanced computer-aided design, is fabricated from a mixture of tubular and forged components with a large-diameter box-section backbone.

The engine isolation system differed from the existing Glide series and Low Rider mounts. These had used three location points with rubber-bonded

SPECIFICATIONS	
Engine	air-cooled ohv V-twin
Capacity	81.6cu in (1,340cc)
Power	69bhp
Transmission	5-speed
Wheelbase	65.5in (1,665mm)
Weight	597lbs (271kg)
Top speed	106mph (170kph)

bolts, rather than the two more sophisticated composite blocks of the Sturgis. The result was startling. The big twin's effective rev range had been limited by low-speed shudders at the bottom end and intrusive vibes at the top. With the Sturgis, that all changed. One could now happily ride at engine speeds where other Hogs would rattle. Softails have the highest overall gearing of any model to reduce revs to comfortable vibration levels at cruising speeds. Fittingly, another Sturgis, the FXB, had been associated with two other momentous bits of rubber a decade earlier – the toothed rubber belts of its revolutionary primary and final drive.

■ ABOVE TOP AND CENTRE *Named after a major motorcycle rally, the Sturgis was a major leap forward in Harley affairs. It was to give rise to the stunningly successful Dyna-Glide series.*

■ LEFT *Stars and stripes had less to do with the Sturgis legacy than did two deceptively simple rubberized blocks.*

FXDWG DYNA WIDEGLIDE, 1993–PRESENT

By 1992, the Sturgis no longer existed, but it had spawned a growing DynaGlide family – first the Dyna Daytona, then the SuperGlide Dyna Custom. By 1993, the Dyna Low Rider was closer to the original but the WideGlide harked back to its namesake of the 1980s. Both, however, went one stage further than the Sturgis in the anti-vibration stakes, with revised "directionally-controlled" mounting blocks.

Harley's idea was "to combine the look of Low Riders of the late 1970s, with the handling and rubber-mounted ride of today", and it worked startlingly well. The 1993 DynaGlides were the smoothest Hogs yet, by a margin. Milwaukee's engineers had made a good bike better, even more than they had with the Sturgis. Without so much as laying a hand on the engine, the company had broadened the big V's effective powerband by a quantum amount – a bigger bonus than adding another ten horsepower.

Much of the rest, as is Harley's way, was in the hands of the blend-men and cosmetic engineers. There are "factory ape-hangers", a "tucked-in tail light", "air-foil directionals" and a wide front fork (hence the "WideGlide") with a 21in (533mm), wire-spoked front wheel, as well as a new, one-piece Fat Bob

■ RIGHT *An original 1993 WideGlide, so named because of the obvious width between the fork legs.*

■ BELOW *The badge might be fiery, but the vibrations were not, thanks to a revolutionary system of engine mounting.*

tank, which removed the need of having to fill up two separate fuel tanks each time you ran short on petrol (gas).

To ride the WideGlide is to marvel at the unprecedented smoothness of the experience – especially after you've grown accustomed to having only forward-mounted footpegs and controls. The ape-hanger handlebars tower somewhere above you, but after a couple of miles it all feels fairly natural and comfortable.

In that uncanny Harley-Davidson way, the steering is light with excellent low-speed balance.

Turns, however, reveal a lot about the WideGlide. Even by Harley-Davidson standards, ground clearance is poor. The stand scrapes on the left, the muffler on the right, both with sufficient force to pitch you off line.

But on the straight, wide highway, it's great to ride.

■ BELOW *For 1999 the new Twin Cam 88 engine was bestowed upon the redoubtable WideGlide.*

SPECIFICATIONS	
Engine	air-cooled ohv V-twin
Capacity	81.6cu in (1,340cc)
Transmission	5-speed
Power	69bhp
Weight	598lbs (271kg)
Wheelbase	66.1in (1,680mm)
Top speed	106mph (170kph)

FXDX DYNA SUPERGLIDE SPORT, 1999–PRESENT

The FXDX Dyna SuperGlide Sport is much more than just the first model to be fitted with the new Twin Cam powerplant. True, the 88.42cu in (1,449cc) engine will attract the most fuss and gives the latest Dyna more get-up-and-go than any previous Milwaukee model, but the rest of the bike offers even more surprises – this is a Harley that stops and handles. For once, the "Sport" in the title means what it says.

Compared to the 80-inch Evo, the Dyna's blacked-out Twin Cam 88 engine runs a bigger 3⅜in (95.25mm) bore with a shortened 4in (101.6mm) stroke. Despite a ten per cent increase in capacity, the result is a powerplant that spins up faster yet with less vibration and a higher rev ceiling of 5,500rpm. The high-pressure, die-cast aluminium crankcases possess a strengthened vertical rear face across which four high-tensile bolts connect the engine to the five-speed transmission. The resulting structure is more rigid than before, reducing stress on the inner

primary drive and reducing overall vibration levels. The crankcases themselves are lighter and stronger due to design changes in high-stress areas, redesigned tappet guides and the relocation of the oil pump. Chain cam drive, in place of the previous straight-

cut gears, is not only cheaper to produce but also one of several measures aimed at reducing mechanical noise in the face of increasing environmental concerns. Great effort has also been put into improving even the Evo's record of durability, with the all-new pressed-up

■ ABOVE *The FXDX was the first Harley to be fitted with the Twin Cam powerplant, the chain drive to which can be seen here.*

■ LEFT *The Dyna can be adjusted to suit any riding style.*

■ RIGHT *Gliding along on the open road.*

crankshaft featuring new forged flywheels, beefier connecting rods and an uprated crank pin – all of which should easily withstand the Twin Cam's prodigious torque – over 78lb/ft (106Nm) at a mere 2,900rpm. O-rings replace the Evo's cylinder base gaskets, allowing a sturdier and more oil-tight joint between the crankcase and

SPECIFICATIONS

Engine	air-cooled ohv V-twin
Capacity	88.42cu in (1,449cc)
Transmission	5-speed
Power	86bhp
Weight	614lbs (279kg)
Wheelbase	64in (1,623mm)
Top speed	115mph (185kph)

cylinders, as well as enhancing temperature tolerance and reducing bore distortion. Of course, Harley's trademark air-cooling is retained, but a 50 per cent increase in fin area on the cylinders and cylinder heads improves its effect.

If the 88's eager power makes it a real joy to ride, the chassis is at least as rewarding. The frame is substantially similar to previous Evo-engined Dynas, with the same highly effective rubber mounting system insulating rider and passenger from vibration. By the standards of many Harley-Davidson heavyweights, the Dyna runs relatively little trail at just over 4in (104mm) and thus turns more eagerly, but it's the suspension that makes the difference – as big a departure as

was the DuoGlide's more than four decades earlier. Both the forks and the Japanese Showa rear shock absorbers now feature full adjustment of preload, rebound and compression damping. Whatever type of riding you have in mind, the Dyna can be adjusted to suit.

Winding up the damping at both ends won't turn the 614lb (279kg) FXDX into a sports bike, but it certainly allows it to corner like no previous big Hog. It still wallows to a degree through fast, bumpy turns, but handles with reassuring precision even at three-figure speeds. Ground clearance is also better. When the time comes to slow down, the latest Dyna is up to the challenge, thanks to a trio of four-piston Hayes calipers biting hard on 11½in (292mm) discs.

Cosmetically, the newcomer sports the same understated lines as previous Dynas, with flat, dirt track style handlebars, a low-line saddle, acres of moody black and a relatively restrained sprinkling of chrome.

Maybe that's just how it should be, for perhaps more than any other Milwaukee musclebike, this is the one that least needs to shout about its virtues.

■ LEFT *The Twin Cam FXDX – a thoroughly modern Harley.*

Glides

For more than half a century, the Glide series has stood at the pinnacle of the Harley-Davidson hierarchy — the plushest, best equipped and most expensive models. The line began with the 1949 HydraGlide, a long, low cruiser of which the current Heritage Softail is more than faintly reminiscent.

With their big, slow-tempo engines and long, slow-steering chassis, Glides have always been the long-haul kings of America. In the old days, though, the rider needed to be at least as tough as the Hog, for the bikes had few concessions to comfort. The 80-inch Shovelhead on the FLH-80 was introduced in 1978. Twelve months later, essentially the same machine metamorphosed into the ultimate grand tourer as the FLHC. As well as a luxurious frame-mounted saddle, standard equipment included a fairing and windshield, saddle bags, crash bars, luggage rack and running boards — previously available only as "Tour Pak" optional extras.

At the time, no other motorcycle in the world was so comprehensively equipped, but the Glide story hasn't stopped there. Subsequent models have added a bewildering array of touring extras to top-of-the-range touring models. At the same time, other models have moved nearer to the family's roots with leaner, stripped-down variants, such as the Road King.

FLTCU TOURGLIDE ULTRA, 1989–96

After the ElectraGlide, Sportster and SuperGlide, the TourGlide was one of the most enduring packages in the entire Milwaukee line up. The concept – the most "loaded" machine Harley-Davidson engineers could imagine – began with the basic FLT TourGlide of 1980. At the time, the TourGlide offered the nearest thing you could buy to a two-wheeled limousine. Small refinements to the already profoundly refined machine followed year-on-year, not to mention the adoption of belt final drive and Evo V2 power in 1984. The basic concept was still fine, but as the decade was drawing to a close, an even more luxurious carriage was needed. It arrived in 1989 with the awesome TourGlide Ultra Classic, 81.6cu in (1,340cc) of imposing, luxurious brawn. As well as obvious features, such as new fairing "lowers" to protect the rider, a welter of electronics graced the big Glide. From the saddle, the rider now had control of

a mouth-watering array of on-board refinement. At the rider's fingertips, there was now electronic cruise control, CB radio and a sophisticated stereo hi-fi system. Even the pillion was provided with separate speakers and a built-in intercom allowed rider and passenger to chew the fat. A cigarette lighter was

■ ABOVE *A 1991 TourGlide in its element, easing across the high desert plateau of Utah, in the south-western United States.*

■ LEFT *The last of a majestic line, a fuel-injected FLTCUI Ultra Classic TourGlide from the 1996 model year.*

■ LEFT *Copious luggage capacity and excellent rider protection are clear from this image of a TourGlide crossing Nevada's wide-open spaces.*

In 1990, I rode a TourGlide from the Harley-Davidson factory in York, Pennsylvania, to San Francisco, California, on America's west coast. Along the way, the big Glide had thumped up endless gradients to more than 11,000ft (3,300m), rumbled across baking deserts for hour after hour, splashed through thunderstorms and scarcely missed a beat. It carried me and everything I needed for 4,000 miles (6,500km), and everyone I met smiled in appreciation. For this sort of experience – traversing the vast emptiness of the United States – no other motorcycle comes anywhere close to it. It was almost as though the TourGlide evolved there – which, come to think of it, it did.

The TourGlide story has ended – for the time being, at least. After 16 years as the long-haul king of America's open roads, the name was dropped from the Harley line-up after the fuel-injected FLTCUI model of 1996. However, its spirit still lives on in the extravagantly equipped Ultra Classic ElectraGlides.

SPECIFICATIONS	
Engine	air-cooled ohv V-twin
Capacity	81.6cu in (1,340cc)
Transmission	5-speed
Power	69bhp
Weight	765lbs (347kg)
Wheelbase	63in (1,600mm)
Top speed	105mph (169kph)

standard and even the self-cancelling indicators were microprocessor-controlled. To cope with this plethora of added electrical demands, a new high-output 32-amp alternator was also fitted.

Overkill? Perhaps, but profoundly practical too. The panniers and capacious "Tour-Pak" top-box easily swallowed two weeks' luggage. The plush, upholstered saddle was good for long, long days on the road, while the screen kept dust and dry desert winds at bay. True, a sound system as good as the one at home isn't strictly necessary on a motorcycle, but who can resist cruising enchanted landscapes to a favourite blues tune, all to a backbeat of a thundering Milwaukee twin?

■ ABOVE *The rider's cockpit perspective of the Ultra Classic TourGlide.*

■ BELOW *The majestic spirit of the Glides lives on in this 1992 TourGlide.*

FLHR ELECTRAGLIDE ROAD KING, 1994–PRESENT

As standard equipment became even more comprehensive at the top of the ElectraGlide range, there came a demand for a model more like the stripped-down FLs of the 1960s. Harley-Davidson's response was the FLHS Sport of 1987 – a real lightweight at "only" 690lbs (313kg). Today's handsome FLHR Road King is in much the same mould.

Launched for the 1994 season, the Road King was an attempt to bridge the gap between Milwaukee's custom and touring models. Although in essence a full-on ElectraGlide minus the fairing, with a "retro" chromed headlight and tank-mounted speedometer, its long, low silhouette belied its super-heavyweight roots. Here was a machine that could hit the highway with the same authority as any other Glide – once the detachable windscreen was installed. As well as the QD windshield (an idea borrowed from the Low Rider Convertible), the panniers and pillion perch were also easily removed, changing the machine's profile and character in the wink of an eye. Thus

■ ABOVE *Cleaner, lower lines distinguish this king of the road from other heavyweight FLs.*

■ BELOW *Adding a few of Milwaukee's many accessories can undermine the effect.*

stripped, the King had all the languid grace of a custom cruiser.

To most eyes this is the best looking of all the Glides, the normally ponderous lines replaced by a machine which, if not exactly svelte, has a certain grace. Where fully-loaded FLs tend to obesity, the Road King has style. It's a Harley-Davidson for those who want their heavyweight cake in custom clothes.

Equally, its touring roots make the King an eminently practical custom bike. Six hours in the saddle is hard work on any Softail but a Glide can comfortably knock that off – and more.

SPECIFICATIONS	
Engine	air-cooled ohv V-twin
Capacity	81.6cu in (1,340cc)
Transmission	5-speed
Power	69bhp
Weight	692lbs (314kg)
Wheelbase	62.7in (1,590mm)
Top speed	100mph (161kph)

■ LEFT AND BELOW *The "Road King" badge and overall detailing is pure 1960s, although the other chromework (below) is aftermarket kit.*

The rubber-mounted Evo engine keeps vibration at bay but lets that evocative rumble pour through. Parked anywhere it looks good; on the open road, it works.

The first fuel-injected Road King, the FLHRI came in 1996, although carburetted versions continued to be produced in parallel. The ESPFI (Electronic Sequential Port Fuel Injection) system is based on a similar Italian Magneti Marelli design to that of Ducati V-twins, although in this case the emphasis is on user-friendliness rather than sheer power. Though some owners may prefer the reassuring simplicity of a stock single carb poking out of the right-hand side, the new fuel-injection system is a major bonus. As well as improving emissions, it offers slightly higher torque

(83lb/ft rather than 79lb0/ft) and much better driveability, particularly at high altitude. The fuel system was improved across the Injection range for 1997.

High-tech is largely absent elsewhere, except of course for Harley-Davidson's trademark belt final drive. Suspension is adjustable only for air pressure in the twin rear shock absorbers. Both wheels are cast light alloy, 16in (406mm) in diameter, wearing characteristically fat Glide rubber.

Twin hydraulic disc brakes grace the front, with a single disc at the rear. All three of these brakes have a lot of work to do on a machine that scales 692lbs (314kg), but these days, Harley-Davidson

stoppers work fairly well. Like most of the Glide family, the Road King's top speed is maybe a shade over 100mph (161kph), although screaming the big twin that hard is a futile pursuit.

The Road King is happiest when it is ambling along at a disdainful 75mph (120kph); if you travel at much above 85mph (140kph), a disconcerting weave has sometimes been known to intrude.

To be king of the road the Milwaukee way, you don't need to be the fastest – just the coolest.

■ LEFT *A 1996 Road King – or should that be FLHR-Convertible? Both the windshield and pillion seat are quickly detachable.*

FLHTCU-I ULTRA CLASSIC
ELECTRAGLIDE, 1997–PRESENT

For a supposedly conservative model from a fairly cautious company, the top ElectraGlide has undergone a relentless battery of changes during the past few years. Fuel injection (ESPFI) first hit the family on the FLHTC Thirtieth Anniversary in 1995, before becoming standard on Road King and top-of-the-range ElectraGlides for the following model year. Then, scarcely had 1997 brought a new frame with lower saddle height (27in/685mm) and many other detail changes, than Harley-Davidson's first new engine for 15 years graced the good old ElectraGlide.

The Twin Cam 88 is not only "glittering with chrome" but gives the massive ElectraGlide a welcome boost to more than 80bhp, with a prodigious peak torque of 86lb/ft (117Nm). With a wider spread of torque and the driveability that only fuel injection brings, the big Glide's legendary ability to gobble up countless miles is

■ ABOVE *With its luxuriously cushioned seat, riding the Ultra Classic is a dream.*

■ BELOW *An Evo-engined predecessor to the full-on Ultra Classic 88. But who'd want his electricity bill?*

improved. Now it shrugs off gradients and altitude with even greater ease than before. Everything about the big Glide, from its fat tyres and sofa-like saddle to lazy, laid-back steering geometry, marks it out as the grandest of open-road tourers.

Scaling a thundering 776lbs (352kg) without so much as a drop of fuel in the tank, this is the heaviest Hog of them all. Most of that weight is good, solid Milwaukee metal, but much of the rest aims to pamper the rider like no other bike known to humanity. The amply

SPECIFICATIONS	
Engine	air-cooled ohv V-twin
Capacity	88.42cu in (1,449cc)
Transmission	5-speed
Power	80bhp
Weight	776lbs (352kg)
Wheelbase	63in (1,600mm)
Top speed	105mph (169kph)

■ RIGHT *With plenty of room to store luggage, this is the ultimate long-haul Hog.*

padded seat is huge and welcoming, while the adjustable footboards give room to move and relax. Harley's neat method of rubber mounting the engine in the steel square-backbone frame ensures that engine vibration is enough to say "Harley" but not so that it will intrude. Meanwhile the panniers, fairing pockets and copious, carpet-lined "King Tour-Pak" top box simply swallow up luggage.

Harley-Davidson describes its top model as "fully loaded" and you'd better believe it. Depending on the market, it comes with passing and running lamps, more instruments than a Boeing and even a cigarette lighter. There's a voice-activated intercom, CB radio and electronic cruise control complete with "Resume" and "Accelerate" modes. The 40-watts-per-channel AM/FM cassette radio contains weatherband, four speakers, separate passenger controls and dual antenna, all controlled

from a myriad of switches on the left handlebar and able to respond automatically to ambient noise levels.

If any Harley-Davidson is as much fantasy as motorcycle, this top ElectraGlide takes the dream to the next level. Imagine cruising over Arizona's high plateaux, the warm desert wind tugging at your sleeves and caressing your designer sunglasses. Slip in your favourite blues cassette or tune in to a passing country music station, and the

Glide will transport you to Hog heaven. Come service time, it can even talk to Harley-Davidson mechanics as well, since the engine management system contains full diagnostic capability – and that's only part of the story.

Some bikers mock the ElectraGlide as a two-wheeled Cadillac de Ville. Certainly, it's as far from a sports bike as it is possible for a motorcycle to get.

Absurd, to some.

Over-the-top, probably.

But glorious – definitely yes.

■ LEFT *The biggest, most expensive and most magnificent model in the Harley-Davidson range, the mighty fuel-injected ElectraGlide Ultra Classic.*

FLHRCI ROAD KING CLASSIC, 2000

■ BELOW *The aristocratic Road King Classic, a new breed of style machine.*

The Classic version of the Road King takes up where the standard model left off. In terms of straight specification, there is little to set the two models apart. Yet the Classic, as the name suggests, is a different sort of hybrid: a full-on tourer which is also a custom machine.

With laced (spoked) wheels and fat whitewall tyres, chrome-fringed saddlebags and swept-back lines, the King Classic is almost as svelte as the ElectraGlide is gross – or, as Harley puts it, "has enough traditional styling to drop jaws throughout the continent". Indeed, throughout any continent.

So, for a tourer, the Classic screams "style". As well as those wheels and tyres, it's in the custom metal emblems on the tank, fender tips and seat. It's in that bold trademark , chromed headlamp and twin 35-watt passing lights. It's in the chrome dual mufflers and stainless-steel "Buffalo" handlebars and – new for 2000 – in classic two-tone paint.

As with all year 2000 big-twin models, power comes from the Twin Cam 88 engine first unveiled the previous year. The 88.42cu in (1,449cc) ohv V-twin features electronic fuel injection via 1½in (38mm) inlet stacks – and, not least, an attention-grabbing chrome-and-black engine finish. Other than its

SPECIFICATIONS	
Engine	air-cooled ohv V-twin
Capacity	88.42cu in (1,449cc)
Transmission	5-speed
Power	80bhp
Weight	710lb (322kg)
Wheelbase	63⅖in (1,612mm)
Top speed	110mph (177kph)

long-legged lump, the King's touring credentials lie with its leather saddlebags (with rigid inserts to prevent their going out of shape), well-upholstered seat, Lexan windshield (quickly detachable for town riding) and 5-gallon (19-litre) fuel tank. In addition, both rider and pillion foot-boards can be adjusted to the right height.

Once upon a time, Milwaukee might have been content with leaving it at that, but not any more. In recent times, it has actively sought greater user-friendliness and better performance on all fronts. So, in common with its fellow heavyweights (except the Springer Softail), the feeble old brakes give way to four-pot calipers

(heavy-weights have two at the front), squeezing uprated friction pads on to much-improved 11½in (292mm) rotors. Both braking power and feel are improved as a result, while lever effort is reduced substantially.

There are new wheel bearings, maintenance-free for 100,000 miles (160,000km). The same goes for the new sealed, long-life, 28Ah battery.

The King Classic is built as vast as only Harley-Davidson knows how, scaling over 700lbs (320kg) without so much as a drop of fuel in its Fat Bob tank. Tying the plot together is a massive mild-steel frame with heavyweight box-section spine and twin tubular cradles.

Suspension at both ends is air-adjustable, although wheel travel is less than generous.

The HydraGlide-style forks offer 4.6in (117mm) of movement while the twin rear shock absorbers afford (3in) 76mm. The King Classic will change direction in its own good time, and has 6.1in (155mm) of trail and a gargantuan wheelbase of 63⅖in (1,612mm). Which is precisely the point: where's the dignity in rushing?

■ ABOVE *An Evo-engined 1997 Heritage Springer Softail. The latest version benefits enormously from the smoothness of the Twin Cam 88B powerplant.*

Buell

The name might be unfamiliar and Buell may not have the length of pedigree of the Harley-Davidson company, but they do have deep and fertile roots. The breed arose from the efforts of former racer Erik Buell, who began creating his idiosyncratic line of racing specials in 1983. The first of these, the RW750, had a four-cylinder 750cc two-stroke engine and was capable of around 180mph (290kph) – very un-Harley fare. When this was outlawed by a change in racing regulations, Buell began his first Harley-engined project, the RR1000.

A total of 50 of these XR1000-engined machines were produced during 1987–8, before the focus switched to the new 1,200cc Evolution powerplant and the RR1200 model. Tuned versions of the same 1200 Sportster engine have powered all Buell models since. All bore tribute to Buell's innovative approach to design, particularly with respect to their lightweight monoshock chassis with advanced suspension and braking components.

It is precisely these attributes that now differentiate Buell Harleys from the more traditional Harley-Davidson models. Buell does not build cruisers or customs – or tourers in the heavyweight Milwaukee sense. Buells are sports bikes, sports tourers or "in your face" streetfighter machines. They still have Harley-Davidson soul and presence, but they have added muscle and attitude, too.

M2 CYCLONE &
S3 THUNDERBOLT

■ M2 CYCLONE

"It came from a motorcyclist's soul, not from a product planning committee," is the Buell promotional slogan, and it fits the streetfighting Cyclone to a "T". The base model of the East Troy range when launched in late 1996, the Cyclone is propelled by a tuned 1,200cc Sportster mill. Claimed peak power is a shuddering 86bhp – more than even the new Twin Cam 88. A wickedly broad torque band peaks at 79lb/ft (107Nm) at 5,400rpm.

The Cyclone runs on slightly less exotic chassis components than its siblings, notably conventional Showa teles rather than upside-down forks. All Buell models employ a single White Power rear unit located under the engine. Bodywork is kept to a minimum, showing the chrome-molybdenum steel perimeter frame off to maximum effect. The big twin engine is located using Buell's patented "Uniplanar" mountings, with tie-rods to reduce the effects of vibration. Final drive is via a reinforced toothed-belt similar to the mainstream Harley range. Although

■ RIGHT *The Cyclone has style, speed and attitude. What more could you want?*

■ BELOW *Sleek yet brutal – the Buell Thunderbolt.*

bestowed with only a single front disc, this offers an enormous friction area swept by a huge six-piston caliper. Both wheels are cast aluminium and of lightweight, three-spoke design. With a frame weighing a mere 26lbs (12kg), the Cyclone is fully 77lbs (35kg) lighter and more than 10bhp stronger than a 1200S Sportster. With these impressive numbers and this quality of chassis kit, the Cyclone and its kin handle and stop like no conventional Harley. Soul and speed are not mutually exclusive.

■ S3 THUNDERBOLT

The Thunderbolt, launched for 1997, was based around a chassis assembly similar to the then top-of-the-range S1

Lightning, mated to the Cyclone's 86bhp carburetted big twin engine. The race-bred chassis features fully-adjustable inverted White Power forks and under-slung rear suspension unit, with similar wheels and brakes to the Cyclone's. The Sportster-derived engine produces a claimed 86bhp at a giddy 6,000rpm and 79lb/ft (107Nm) of torque. The motor enjoys the same Uniplanar anti-vibration mountings as other Buell models, allowing plenty of gutsy rumble to reach the rider but damping out more destructive vibes. Visually, the T-bolt is distinguished by its swooping rear bodywork and aerodynamic fairing. Buell produces a sports-touring version, the S3T, with legshields and panniers.

SPECIFICATIONS: CYCLONE (THUNDERBOLT)	
Engine	ohv 45 degree V-twin
Capacity	1,203cc
Transmission	5-speed, toothed-belt final drive
Power	86bhp
Weight	434lbs/197kg (450lbs/204kg)
Wheelbase	55½in/1,410mm
Top speed	126mph/203kph (133mph/214kph)

BUELL HISTORY

Following the modest success of the Sportster-powered RR1200 (of which 65 were built), 1989 marked the debut of the first two-seater Buell, the RS1200 from which the single-seat RSS1200 evolved two years later. By this time, inverted telescopic forks and six-piston disc-brake calipers had become the norm for a marque which was rapidly grabbing the attention of the motorcycle community. By the end of 1992, the company had built a total of 442 machines and brought its founder a solid reputation for engineering and design.

In February 1993, Buell became part of the Harley-Davidson empire when Milwaukee bought a 49 per cent stake in the company. The merger gave Buell access to development funds and Harley-Davidson expertise while offering Harley a direct avenue into Buell's creative engineering. Buell was in fact collaborating with Harley on design as early as the late 1970s when he contributed to the original belt-drive Sturgis project.

■ LEFT *A rare Buell RS1200 from around 1989. Its heritage is evident.*

■ BELOW LEFT *The Buell assembly line in East Troy, an hour from Milwaukee, shown before Harley bought in.*

■ BELOW *The Buell's raw lines and radical engineering are abundantly clear with body-work removed.*

Buells are now built at East Troy, Wisconsin, using engines made at the "small powertrains" plant on Milwaukee's Capitol Drive. Now marketed in parallel with mainstream Harley-Davidson machines, the current generation of Cyclone, Thunderbolt and Lightning Buell models was first launched in the United States in 1994.

BUELL X1 LIGHTNING, 1999

Sharing a name with a 3,000mph (5000kph) jet plane, the X1 Lightning replaced the S-series Lightning when launched for 1999. This is a mean and purposeful "Streetfighter" from the makers of "Harleys with attitude".

The X1 is a truly credible sports machine. It bristles with character, and its power and handling are vastly improved compared to more traditional Milwaukee fare. At the X1's heart is a reworked "Thunderstorm"

SPECIFICATIONS

Engine	ohv 45 degree V-twin with EFI
Capacity	1,203cc
Transmission	5-speed, toothed-belt final drive
Power	95bhp (see main text)
Weight	439lbs (199kg)
Wheelbase	55½in (1,410mm)
Top speed	135mph (217kph)

version of the familiar 1,203cc Sportster engine with higher compression pistons, larger valves and ports re-profiled for improved gas flow. Lighter flywheels improve engine response and at the same time quicken the Sportster's normally leisurely gearchange.

Best of all is the X1's new and ultra-sophisticated Dynamic Digital fuel injection. The system uses state-of-the-art computer control to ensure that the big V-twin delivers its best under all conditions, virtually eliminating flat-spots, improving fuel economy and

cleaning up exhaust emissions. The result is one of the sharpest Harley-Davidson's ever built – and perhaps the most powerful.

According to independent dyno tests, peak power is 85bhp at 5,300rpm – more than any other stock Harley; the X1's torque is even more impressive:

■ ABOVE *The X1 Lightning: a real mean street-fighting machine.*

■ LEFT *With its minimalist seat design, this is a far cry from the ElectraGlide.*

Handling, too, is top notch. With its short, nimble wheelbase and only 3½in (89mm) of trail, the X1 turns quickly by Harley standards, inviting riders to dive hard into turns. Stability, too, is surprisingly good, allowing the machine to be ridden with confidence under almost any circumstances. Its minimalist seat and overall ergonomics may fall a long way short of ElectraGlide territory, but the sort of owners the X1 is aimed at will not mind that.

This impressive package is cloaked in the sort of eye-catching yet understated muscular styling for which the East Troy streetfighting machines have become renowned.

With a Buell, what you see is what you get – and you get the best Buell yet with the X1 Lightning.

92lb/ft (125Nm) at just 3,300rpm, guaranteeing a broad range of solid, usable power (Buell actually claims 95bhp and 85lb/ft (115Nm).

With this engine there is almost no such thing as being in the wrong gear: simply wind open the throttle and the big twin will deliver the goods at almost any rpm. Top speed is around 136mph (220kph), although this can vary as some markets receive models with raised gearing to help meet local noise limits.

Pinning all of this to the road is a rugged tubular steel trellis chassis, with new Japanese Showa suspension components at both ends. At the front are sturdy inverted forks which are adjustable for pre-load, compression and rebound damping.

The monoshock rear end offers built-in rising rate, plus pre-load and two-way damping tuning. The stainless-steel exhaust is tucked tight in, providing maximum room and comfort for one- or two-up riding and giving the best cornering ground clearance of any Milwaukee roadster, allowing the X1 to exploit to the full its Dunlop rubber. Although the Lightning boasts only a single front disc, braking is excellent as well, with a brawny 13.4in (340mm) rotor grabbed by a huge, six-piston "Performance Machine" caliper. A simple single-piston caliper and 9in (230mm) disc adorn the rear.

■ LEFT *Burnouts are easy thanks to tuned 1,200cc Sportster power.*

■ BELOW *Truly awesome: the Buell X1 Lightning.*

Racers

The first Harley-Davidson "racers" were nothing more than standard production machines in the hands of some adventurous private individuals.

These days, although competition is a long way from Harley-Davidson's corporate image, it's still very much part of the company soul. The American motorcycle racing scene was effectively founded by the Indian and Curtiss companies, but Harley soon picked up the gauntlet and eventually became the dominant force. Even some of the founders were keen competitors – Walter Davidson himself recorded the first "factory" win in an endurance trial in 1908. By the First World War, daredevil riders were hurtling along on Harley twins at three-figure speeds – with no brakes and almost no suspension.

Since the innocent enthusiasm of the pioneer years, a wealth of Harley-Davidson racing machines have become legendary, from the first eight-valvers to the booming XR750 which still runs rampant on America's dirt tracks. For Harley-Davidson, as for almost everyone else, racing has improved the breed.

EARLY RACERS

■ EIGHT-VALVE, TWO-CAM
Although a special "7-E" competition
version of Harley-Davidson's first V-twin
was built for selected customers as early
as 1910, the first model created
specifically for racing was the eight-
valve twin which appeared in 1916. The
multi-valve layout had already been
amply proven by the exploits of Indian's
similar engine, already the winner of the
Isle of Man TT.

Displacing 61cu in (999cc), the
Harley-Davidson eight-valve was the
device on which the Harley Wrecking
Crew began their domination of the
American racing scene.

Private individuals were less
fortunate, since the machine's price –
$1,500 – was deliberately inflated to
ensure that it could only fall into
serious hands.

A 65cu in (1,065cc) twin-cam racer
followed. Like the eight-valve model,
the Two-Cam had inlet-over-exhaust
valve layout, no brakes and direct drive
by chain to the rear wheel (although
some examples may have used three-
speed transmissions). Once started – no
easy task due to the use of very high

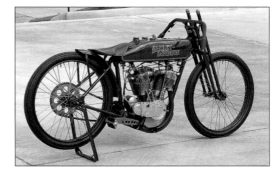

■ LEFT *A
handsome 74-inch
J-series racer
dating from 1924.
Note the total
lack of any sort
of brakes.*

■ LEFT *A 1924
74-inch F-head
racer. Exhaust
silencing was not a
prime concern.*

■ BELOW *Another F-head, a 1920 board
racer ridden by Dewey Sims. The plunger
on the left side of the tank feeds engine oil.*

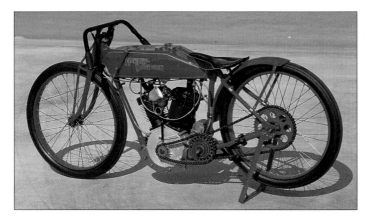

compression ratios – these monsters
were capable of well over 100mph
(160kph). To promote its wares overseas,
Harley-Davidson freighted its top racing
machines all over the world. In Britain,
both Freddie Dixon and D.H. Davidson
took the Two-Cam to numerous records
at the famed banked Brooklands circuit
in Surrey. In September 1923, at
Arpajon in France, Dixon took the same
machine to a world-record speed of
106.5mph (171.4kph).

■ OHV TWINS
During the mid-1920s, the F-head Two-
Cam was the mainstay of Harley-
Davidson's factory twin-cylinder racing
efforts, but they were seriously
hampered when the AMA introduced the
new "Class C" racing formula. This was

for production-based 45cu in (750cc) machines, of which at least 25 had to be built. Overnight, the old Class A and Class B factory specials were relegated to the sidelines in much of American racing – especially in the buoyant "slant-shooting" (hill-climbing) scene.

At the time, Milwaukee produced no eligible machine, but by 1926 it did have the remarkably fast 21-inch ohv Peashooter single, and any darn fool could see that two times 21 wasn't far from 45. It wasn't long before someone investigated the possibility of grafting Peashooter heads on to existing V-twin bottom ends.

The first such ohv Harley-Davidson twin was probably a machine dubbed "Home Brew", ridden with some success by Oscar Lenz in 1927. A similar device, also based on a 61-inch bottom end, was built by Ralph Moore of Indianapolis.

By 1928, Harley-Davidson had given in to popular demand and released "roadster" versions of its Two-Cam racing twins, the 61-inch JH and 74-inch JDH and it wasn't long before Juneau Avenue followed the example of creative privateers with a number of factory specials featuring ohv Peashooter top ends grafted on to JD Two-Cam crankcases.

These first hit the tracks in 1928 at Fond du Lac, just a few miles north of Milwaukee. However, there is some

■ ABOVE *Four overhead valves per cylinder can clearly be seen in this view of the same 1923 eight-valver. Note the single carburettor between the cylinders.*

■ BELOW *Compared to the exotic factory eight-valvers, F-head board racers such as this were relatively low-tech, but still capable of frightening speeds.*

dispute as to whether they were actually created in Harley's competition shop or by a local dealer, Bill Knuth, with the factory's knowledge and support.

In either case, this was an interim measure, because twelve months later a 45-inch factory racer, the DAH, first appeared.

Unlike the Two-Cam-based machines, the DAH was substantially a new engine from the ground up, although it still depended on cylinder heads derived from the Peashooter's.

Displacing 45.44cu in (744cc), the DAH retained the 88.9mm stroke of the JD, but with a bore reduced to 70.6mm.

The DAH was dominant for a while, but Knuth came back with a four-cam hybrid reputed to produce fully 45 horsepower, which continued to give the official factory machines a run for their money. There are even records of a 61-inch ohv racing twin, designated FAR, being built for export.

It is highly likely that, in some measure or other, these exotic racing models were to inspire the later Knucklehead ohv twin. What is for certain is the profound influence that they had on the racing world at large.

PEASHOOTER, 1929

As legendary in its way as was the exotic Two-Cam, the Peashooter began life as a standard roadster model. The Peashooter was based on the overhead-valve Model AA magneto version of the 21.1cu in (346cc) single produced from 1926 to 1935, which proved itself more than amenable to race tuning. Perhaps this was not altogether surprising, as the cylinder head – the most crucial performance element in any four-stroke engine – was designed by the great Harry Ricardo, the British engineering genius. Only a few years earlier, Ricardo had created Triumph's first four-valve motor, the Model R. Sir Harry, as he was later to become, practically invented the art of petrol- (gas-) flowing and, during

■ LEFT *The cylinder head of the Peashooter was designed by Harry Ricardo, a British engineer.*

■ BELOW *This single became a legend on the race tracks of the United States.*

SPECIFICATIONS	
Engine	ohv single
Capacity	21.1cu in (346cc)
Transmission	1- or 3-speed
Weight	290lbs (132kg)
Wheelbase	55in (1,400mm)
Top Speed	over 80mph (128kph)

the course of developing the concept of octane ratings for fuel, gained an unparalleled understanding of the combustion process.

Central to the Peashooter's success were two things. One was the engine's hemispherical "squish" heads, in which the outer portion of the piston crown almost touches the cylinder head as it rises up the bore. This in turn creates a fierce turbulence, promoting fuel/air mixing and combustion. This made the 'Shooter's combustion more efficient than its rivals over a broader range of revs, also permitting the safe use of higher compression ratios. Even in roadster form, the "21" generated only 20 per cent less power than an F-head twin with almost three times the displacement.

The Peashooter's other "ace" was Joe Petrali who (along with Scott Parker) is surely the most successful racer ever to grace the race tracks of America. In 1935, towards the end of the model's racing career, he won every one of the 13 dirt track races in the national series. The diminutive Californian was equally adept whether board racing or tackling towering hill-climbs, proving virtually unbeatable until his retirement in 1938.

Petrali and the single first hit the headlines when the AMA adopted a new

21-inch racing class in 1925. In the first race under the new formula, fittingly held in Milwaukee before a crowd of over 20,000, Petrali, Jim Davis and Eddie Brock simply blasted the opposition into the Wisconsin weeds. Board-racing versions of the ohv roadster were stripped to the bare essentials, with tiny seats, "Speedster" drop handlebars and neither brakes nor mudguards. Such abbreviated devices were easily capable of speeds in excess of 80mph (128kph). Depending on the

type of competition, they were built with single-speed (Model SM) or three-speed (SA) transmission.

Despite the ohv single's instant track success, Juneau Avenue was oddly disposed towards its side-valve sidekick since the flathead roadster was seen as the likeliest seller. However, others quickly saw the potential of high-revving overhead-valve engines, and the Peashooter became the single of choice on the American racing scene (although a speedway version, inspired by the all-conquering British JAP, was far less successful).

The final, flattering piece in the Peashooter jigsaw came with the introduction of the ohv Knucklehead in 1936.

Although the factory was developing overhead-valve DAH competition twins during the late 1920s, the Knuckle bears many detail similarities with the Peashooter top end.

Whether this was by design or accident, no-one can now tell.

■ LEFT
"Speedster" drop handlebars were a feature of the Peashooter.

WR/WRTT, 1940–51

Harley-Davidson's racing mainstay of the 1940s, the side-valve WR, had the humblest of beginnings, evolving by degrees from the unpretentious Model D of 1929. Essentially, this was powered by little more than a pair of Ricardo heads grafted from the 21.1cu in (346cc) single (which had almost the same bore diameter) onto a common crankcase. The machine developed rapidly year-on-year, becoming the Model R in 1932, at which time its hottest roadster derivative was the RLD Special Sport Solo.

Racing efforts at the time, both official and private, were concentrated on overhead valve engines, both singles and 45-inch twins. However, by 1933 the RLDE twin with magnesium alloy pistons was available from the factory by special order.

Two years later still, the Series R range included five models based on the familiar flathead "45", crowned by the lean and purposeful RLDR Competition Special – a snip at $322. For 1937, a

■ ABOVE *This "45" wears telescopic forks manufactured long after the side-valve racer was history.*

SPECIFICATIONS

Engine	side valve 4-stroke V-twin
Capacity	45.3cu in (742cc)
Transmission	3- or 4-speed
Power	40bhp
Wheelbase	60in (1,525mm)
Top speed	around 105mph (169kph)

Knucklehead-inspired restyle and a welter of engine improvements metamorphosed the R into the enduring Model W. Other than the change of prefix letter, the 45-inch range continued as before, now with the WLDR Competition Special at its head – a WR in all but name. Harley-Davidson put this right in 1941: the WLDR still existed, but now as a mere Special Sport Solo roadster.

Taking its place as the hottest 45 was the plain WR, a race machine available only to special order. Initially, availability was poor – just 36 WRs were produced in 1941 – but both

■ ABOVE AND LEFT *Although substantially similar engines propelled American postmen, the WR carried Harley's racing banner for a decade in both factory and private teams.*

■ RIGHT *The main advantage of the side-valve twin wasn't its potency, but its capacity, which kept it competitive in American racing.*

■ LEFT *A competitor fettles his "45" during a modern classic race meeting.*

■ BELOW *The "pillion" pad helped the rider stretch out to cheat the wind.*

45 inches was unimpressive. Yet this, and sheer weight of numbers, was enough to rival the much more sophisticated but sorely handicapped overhead-valve twins and overhead-camshaft singles from Europe. The brute toughness of the WRTT, in particular, made it a surprisingly capable "Class C" racer. This formula had first been introduced for roadster-based machines in the 1920s to reduce the spiralling cost of Class A and B factory specials.

For more than a decade, these outwardly primitive machines gave a good account of themselves on the race tracks of America – taking 19 out of 23 championship victories in 1948 alone.

This was partly because they were rugged and dependable, and partly because the AMA was as eager then as it has been since to adjust the rules in favour of domestic hardware.

In this case the AMA, which is the governing body of American motorcycle sport, greeted the arrival of fast European overhead-valve machines with a decree that said they would be limited to 500cc, while side-valves of 750cc were permitted. And guess who made the only flathead racers in the frame?

demand and supply picked up dramatically in the aftermath of war. A total of 292 were produced in 1948, 121 in 1949 and 23 in the last year of production.

These purpose-built racing machines were, of course, very much stripped down compared to their roadster cousins (the WR had not so much as a front mudguard, and later examples also benefited from a lightweight chrome-molybdenum steel chassis). The WRTT, produced as a specific model only late in the WR's career, retained the heavier roadster frame. Being a flat-track machine, the WR also had no brakes, while the road-racing TT machine was equipped with standard WL wheels and brakes – scarcely state-of-the-art stopping power. The WR's suspension was no more impressive, with old-

fashioned girder front forks and a rigid rear end. For good measure, the gearbox, although available with close-ratio racing cogs, was hand-change. It may have been crude, and 40bhp from

KR/KRTT 1952-69

What Harley-Davidson needed to replace the elderly WR was a machine reflecting the technology of its era. In the KR, the company most certainly didn't get it. What it got instead was yet another long-stroke flathead racer derived from a road bike, in this case the 45.3cu in (742cc) Model K which was about to be so comprehensively licked by British machines on America's streets. In racing, the KR had an edge: the AMA's 500cc limit on overhead-valve engines still applied.

As with the WR a decade earlier, production began slowly, with just 17 KRs built in the first year. Yet by 1955, the special equipment range encompassed no less than five specific models: the KHK Super Sport Solo, KHRM off-roader, KR dirt track racer, and KRTT and KHRTT "Tourist Trophy" machines.

All three KH models boasted the new 55cu in (883cc) long-stroke K-Series engine and were essentially "race replicas" intended as much for the

■ BELOW LEFT *The 45-inch (750cc) engine in close-up. The push-rod tubes to the side valves are clearly seen.*

private enthusiast as the racer. Serious racers remained limited to what the regulations allowed: 750cc.

In 1955, the factory built 90 45-inch competition models, declining to 33 by the decade's end. Unlike the

WR/WRTT, all variants now enjoyed a lightweight racing frame, although only the road-racing TT model received the new swinging-arm rear end.

The flat-track KR had a smaller tank, fatter wheels and tyres and no need of brakes. Bore and stroke were identical to the WR's at 70 x 97mm (the slow-revving 55's stroke was even longer at 116mm).

However, the cylinders were commonly re-bored after bedding-in. By using the maximum permitted piston oversize – more than 0.04in (1.1mm) mechanics could raise the displacement legally to 46.8cu in (767cc).

At 9:1, the compression ratio was high by side-valve standards and a single 33mm Linkert carburettor was

SPECIFICATIONS	
Engine	side-valve 4-stroke V-twin
Capacity	45.3 cu in (742cc)
Transmission	4-speed
Power	48bhp
Weight	377–385lbs (171–175g)
Wheelbase	56in (1,420mm)
Top speed	150mph (240kph) (with road-race streamlining)

■ RIGHT *Rear springing identifies this KR as the TT version.*

standard. Power was around 48bhp at 7,000rpm, with 50lb/ft (68Nm) of torque at 5,000rpm. British Norton, Matchless and Triumph machines, as well as putting out far more specific power than the KR, handled and stopped far better. Yet the old KRs just kept rolling on.

While they were heavy (around 380lbs/172kg) and ill-suited to any circuit with proper corners, they remained surprisingly competitive elsewhere – not least because every race grid in America seemed to be packed with them.

Since a dirt-track KR actually cost $95 less than a stock road-going

Sportster during the mid-1960s, perhaps this wasn't too surprising.

The road racers, too, were capable of surprising feats. At the super-fast Daytona Speedway, streamlined KRs have been recorded in excess of 150mph (240kph), an astonishing achievement for a side-valve machine.

For all their shortcomings, in the hands of racing aces such as Markel and Resweber, they managed to win a round dozen American national titles during their 18 years on the grid.

The KR's astonishing span came to an end in 1969 when the AMA ended discriminatory limitations on overseas machines.

Faced with a level playing field, there was no way that the redoubtable old flathead "45" could compete with the machines that were coming in from abroad.

■ ABOVE RIGHT *A KRTT in Harley's famous orange and black factory racing colours.*

■ RIGHT *This dirt tracker wears TT-type rear suspension and brakes, although both the shock absorbers and front forks are non-period items.*

XR750 FLAT-TRACKER, 1970–PRESENT

To many people's eyes – and ears – the XR750 dirt-track machine is the most handsome, the raunchiest and the most purposeful piece of kit ever to rumble out of Milwaukee. Certainly no other Harley-Davidson has enjoyed so much competition success over so many years as the seminal XR. After almost two decades plugging along on the side-valve KR twin, the arrival of an overhead-valve replacement in 1970 must have been keenly anticipated. Yet its debut year was to prove a deep disappointment when Mert Lawwill and Mark Brelsford could manage only a disappointing sixth and seventh in the AMA championship. Just 12 months earlier, Lawwill had won the title on a side-valve KR.

The problem was the new engine's iron cylinders. They were heavy and conducted heat much less efficiently than aluminium components. This in

SPECIFICATIONS	
Engine	ohv V-twin
Capacity	45.8cu in (750cc)
Transmission	4-speed
Power	around 95 bhp
Weight	290lbs (132kg)
Top speed	130mph (210kph)

turn meant that the motor's compression ratio had to be drastically reduced – to around 8:1 – if fatal breakdowns were to be avoided. With lumpier pistons, the iron XR had proven fast – but it just couldn't last the distance. In 1970, race boss Dick O'Brien admitted to a lowly 62bhp at 6,200rpm. In June 1971, light alloy replaced iron, and the XR750 hasn't looked back.

■ ABOVE LEFT *Despite troubled beginnings, the XR went on to sweep away all before it in American dirt-track racing – with only occasional help from the rules when Honda's RS750 got too close.*

■ LEFT *Only that ugly California-mandated silencer mars the XR750's brutal yet beautiful lines.*

■ LEFT *The XR was also briefly successful in road racing, notably with Cal Rayborn in control. This is the iron-head machine on which he won the 1972 Transatlantic Series.*

On dirt, Mark Brelsford took the XR to the 1972 American Number One plate in its maiden season. At Easter the same year, the great Cal Rayborn whipped all comers in the annual USA v Great Britain road-race series.

At the heart of the XR is that rarest of beasts, a short-stroke Harley-Davidson. "Iron-head" XRs used what were essentially de-stroked 883cc Sportster engines, retaining the road machine's 72mm bore but with a shorter 82mm stroke. The 1972 engine's cylinders measured 79.4 x 75.8mm – by comparison, the side-valve KR measured an ultra-long-stroke 70 x 97mm. This, allied to a much stronger crankshaft, permitted more revs as well as a substantially higher 10.5:1 compression ratio made possible by the use of light alloy. The result was a dramatic rise in power and reliability. Shortly after Rayborn's Transatlantic road-race triumph (which was, ironically, on an iron-head engine), peak power was reputed to be around 80bhp at 8,000rpm. Even so, for many years even the light alloy XR ran dangerously hot – road-racers employed two oil coolers yet were worn out after only 200 miles (320km) – until the internal oil circulation was improved.

At the outset, carburation was by twin 1½in (36mm) Japanese Mikuni instruments (often larger on the road racers). Sparks were provided by a Fairbanks-Morse magneto, an unreliable system sometimes dubbed "Can't Get

■ ABOVE *They still fight for it: the coveted AMA Number One plate.*

■ BELOW *Nine times AMA Number One Scott Parker, here in action at Sacramento. All his titles have been XR-powered.*

Worse" by unhappy riders. The lightweight, high-grade steel frame used Ceriani forks and paired Girling rear shock absorbers. Dry weight was a feather-light 291lb (132kg), although the road racers, with a fairing and brakes, were somewhat heavier.

Almost 30 years of detailed development have left the XR engine little changed visually, but without equal for the demands of dirt-track competition.

These days, power is around 95bhp at 7,800rpm, with a strong spread from 4,500 to more than 8,000rpm. On one mile (1.61km) ovals, this is good for a top speed of around 130mph (210kph), although it's the way that the big twin finds grip that really sets it apart from the others on the field.

True, the XR soon became obsolete as a road racer, but has gone from strength to strength on the dirt tracks of the United States.

In the hands of men like Brelsford, Gary Scott, Jay Springsteen and Scott Parker, the XR has simply swept away all before it, taking three-quarters of all the subsequent AMA championships.

RR250, RR350 1971-6

The twin cylinder, two-stroke racers built at Varese during the 1970s brought Harley-Davidson its sole successes in post-war grand prix road racing. These were state-of-the-art machines, broadly similar to the stroker twins produced by Yamaha and Kawasaki, with fierce powerbands, strident exhaust notes and performance belying their relatively small engine displacement. To cope with the narrow band of usable revs, the gearbox held six speeds – and might well have held more if this were not prohibited by FIM regulations.

The 250's 56.2 x 50mm cylinders were fed via rotary disc valves by twin 34mm Mikuni carburettors. The earliest examples were air-cooled but the factory soon switched to liquid-cooling, bringing far greater temperature stability and reliability during long grand prix races. Primary drive was by gear, to a multi-plate dry clutch and thence to the six-speed "box". Power output was prodigious (particularly by Milwaukee's four-stroke standards), with the 250 producing 58bhp at 12,000rpm and the 350 a dozen horsepower more at 11,400rpm. The 250's figure equates to over 232bhp per litre, compared to a mere 65 for the KR750 which had been Harley-Davidson's racing mainstay at the time RR250 development began.

■ LEFT *The great Walter Villa at speed on the RR250 at the notorious Nurburgring circuit in 1978. He failed to finish. Note that the machine still relies on a drum front brake.*

SPECIFICATIONS: RR250	
Engine	liquid-cooled twin cylinder 2-stroke
Capacity	15.1cu in (248cc)
Transmission	6-speed
Peak power	58bhp @12,000rpm
Weight	230lbs (104kg)
Top speed	140mph (225kph)

■ BELOW LEFT *A disc-braked factory two-stroke twin shares pride of place with a classic four-stroke single.*

■ BELOW RIGHT *Villa on the RR350 at Hockenheim in 1977, carrying the world champion's Number One. He finished third in the 250cc world championship that year, but the 350 proved less competitive.*

The chassis featured a conventional twin cradle of high-grade tubular steel. Italian Ceriani suspension graced the front end with a pair of English Girling shock absorbers at the rear. The whole package weighed just 230lbs (104kg). If the machine had a shortcoming, it was the use of drum brakes (albeit a double-sided twin-leading shoe affair at the front) when hydraulic discs were already in widespread use and far superior. Discs finally arrived in 1976, by which time the great Walter Villa had already taken two 250cc world titles.

With better brakes, he repeated the feat in 1976, adding the 350cc title for good measure. RRs also campaigned successfully in American road races, ridden by Gary Scott, Jay Springsteen, Cal Rayborn and others.

MX250
1977–8

Harley-Davidson's only venture into mainstream motocross produced a highly competitive machine which could have become better still had Milwaukee not severed its Italian links after just two years of MX production. By the time the MX250 came on stream in 1977, Varese had developed a formidable pool of two-stroke know-how, not least from its successful grand prix road-racing experience.

Four years after its official demise, the great Jay Springsteen mischievously used an MX-based machine to win the first AMA event of the 1982 season in Houston. We can only speculate about where this potential might have led.

The single-cylinder stroker used a short-stroke (72 x 59.6mm) engine which drove an integral five-speed transmission via gear primary drive and wet multi-plate clutch – such as you might find on any dirt-bike today.

Initial examples were air-cooled, but a liquid-cooled version came later. A 38mm Italian dell'Orto carburettor provided the fuel (mixed 20:1 with oil for lubrication), while sparks came from a CDI generator on the left end of the crankshaft. During development, peak power rose to a ferocious 58bhp

■ ABOVE AND LEFT *Harley's Italian-designed and built MX250 motocrosser benefited from lessons learned in grand prix road racing and might have gone on to great things had Varese not been sold.*

at a giddy 12,000rpm. Telescopic forks provided a generous 9in (228mm) of travel with a similar degree of movement that came from the twin rear shock absorbers.

Light alloy Akront rims were laced to simple 5½in (140mm) drum brakes (as discs were not yet used on dirt-bikes).

SPECIFICATIONS	
Engine	single-cylinder 2-stroke
Capacity	14.8cu in (242cc)
Transmission	5-speed
Peak power	58bhp @12,000rpm
Weight	233lbs (106kg)
Wheelbase	57.3in (1,455mm)
Top speed	n/a

■ RIGHT *Harley's only current single is this Rotax-engined device.*

AERMACCHI OHV RACERS
1961–78

Originally an aircraft factory – hence the name – Aermacchi diversified into motorcycle production in 1948, in Varese, Italy. Its first models were 123cc (7.5cu in) singles – two-strokes but already possessing the horizontal cylinder which was to become so typical of the marque. Overhead valve four-stroke singles followed, both road bikes and the potent Ala D'Oro (Golden Wing) production racer. A generation of elegant racing models were developed from the late 1950s onwards, based on this Alfredo Bianchi-designed machine.

Although the racers were built in both 250cc (15cu in) and 350cc (21cu in) versions, it was the latter which achieved the greater success. Even during the 1960s, a single-cylinder push-rod machine was an anachronism among the exotica then crowding the grands prix grids, yet the "Macchi" exploited its fine handling, light weight and slim aerodynamic profile to the fullest. Its best world-championship performance came in 1966 when the late Renzo Pasolini – the "Paso" in

■ LEFT *An Aermacchi 250 at speed. Light weight and a slim profile made them astonishingly fast.*

■ BELOW LEFT *A CRTT 250 in factory racing livery.*

SPECIFICATIONS: 350

Engine	ohv horizontal single
Capacity	344cc (21cu in)
Transmission	5-speed
Power	38bhp
Weight	245lbs (111kg)
Wheelbase	not known
Top Speed	130mph (210kph)

the Ducati model of the same name – took third place in the 350cc grand prix championship.

It was as a privateer mount that the little "Macchi" achieved its greatest popularity and success however, although it also had a reputation for being temperamental unless expertly set up. Perhaps its most remarkable performance came in the 1970 Isle of Man TT races when Alan Barnett lapped the daunting Mountain Course at a stunning 99.32mph (159.84kph) on a Syd Lawton 350, recording well over 40mpg (15km/litre) in the process.

Nor were the ohv single's exploits confined to the track. On 21 October 1965, a 250cc Aermacchi established a world mile record of 176.817mph (284.55kph) and kilometre record of 285.21kph (177.225mph) at Utah's Bonneville salt flats. Although nominally a Sprint roadster, the machine in question used a 1966-specification CR racing engine on standard pump fuel. Officially, Milwaukee dubbed its Italian singles CR, CRS and CRTT, although in Europe these designations were largely ignored.

The single was produced with many variations over the years, but the 350's

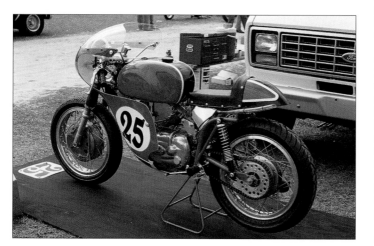

■ BELOW *A brace of ex-factory racers. Note the racing dry clutch.*

■ BELOW *A 350 'Macchi contesting the 1984 Historic Isle of Man TT. Ironically this was the only TT ever won by an American – on a British Matchless machine.*

typical power output was around 38bhp at 8,400rpm. Bore and stroke were under-square at 74 x 80mm, although this incurred a dangerously high piston speed (almost 4,400ft/1,340m) at maximum revs. As a result, other configurations were also built, including short stroke and ultra-short stroke examples. Compression was high – around 11.4:1 – and the engine breathed through a 35mm dell'Orto carburettor tipped almost vertically to feed fuel into the horizontal cylinder. A short megaphone exhaust swept down the right side of the machine.

The racer was available with a choice of "A" or "B" gear clusters, the latter offering the closer ratios, although the engine delivered a reasonable spread of power considering its high state of tune.

The chassis was simple in the extreme, using a large-diameter tubular steel spine, which was reputed to flex but in a controlled, user-friendly way which gave the rider ample feedback.

A variety of suspension and brake components were employed, invariably with telescopic forks (usually Ceriani), twin rear shock absorbers and drum

brakes. On later versions, the front drum was often twin-sided.

A measure of the machine's excellence is the sheer joy – and speed – with which many contest classic races today.

■ LEFT *Pictured here, the engine of a 1969 350 Aermacchi.*

■ BELOW *In the USA, Aermacchis derived from the Sport roadster were also popular for dirt-track racing.*

LUCIFER'S HAMMER, 1983

■ BELOW *Lucifer's Hammer's engine was based on that of an XR750 competition model.*

In the spring of 1983, Lucifer's Hammer was the first big twin for a decade to carry Harley-Davidson's famous black and orange racing livery on to the Daytona speed bowl. It certainly did so with distinction, taking the great Jay Springsteen – better known as a dirt-track rider but certainly no slouch on tarmac – to victory in the Battle of the Twins event. In October of the same year, Gene Church began a love affair with the same machine when he rode it triumphantly in the BoT finals, also held at Daytona.

The Hammer represented one of those bouts of enthusiasm and expertise with the big twin that were often typical of Harley-Davidson. The germ of the project began when Dave McClure rode a prototype XR1000 street bike at Daytona the previous autumn, which

SPECIFICATIONS	
Engine	ohv V-twin
Capacity	60.9cu in (998cc)
Transmission	4-speed
Power	104bhp
Weight	286lbs (130kg)
Wheelbase	56in (1,420mm)
Top speed	158mph (254kph)

suggested that a full-on racer project might succeed. Once race-boss Dick O'Brien got the go-ahead to build what would become the Springsteen machine, he set his hand-picked team into action. Engine work was put in the hands of Don Habermehl, while racing legend Carroll Resweber (four times AMA

champion for Harley, 1958 to 1961) put his considerable talents into the chassis, and Peter Zylstra oversaw the design. To some extent, the machine was also a test-bed and publicity statement for the XR1000 roadster unveiled at the same Daytona meeting, another project which very much carried the O'Brien imprint.

The engine consisted of a modified competition XR750 bottom end and light alloy heads mated to iron Sportster barrels. Twin 42mm smoothbore Mikuni carburettors took care of induction, feeding exotic 110 octane aviation fuel – for nothing less would handle the engine's giddy 10.5:1 compression ratio. To improve combustion, each cylinder boasted twin spark plugs, fired by a total-loss racing ignition system.

In dyno tests, this device had put out a brutal 106bhp at 7,500rpm, but fears

■ BELOW *The Hammer with fairing removed, at Daytona in 1983.*

about reliability caused Habermehl to impose a rev ceiling of 7,000rpm, at which point the big twin was pumping out 104bhp. Since even this equated to a dizzying mean piston speed of 4,430 ft/min (1,350m/min), the precaution

must have been wise. Not only was power prodigious but the spread was enormous, too, coming in strongly by 4,000rpm. A four-speed gearbox was more than adequate. Resweber's chassis employed the very XR750 frame

comprehensively crashed by then-AMA champion Mark Brelsford at Daytona fully ten years before the Hammer's 1983 win. The basic single spine and twin tube cradle was heavily reworked with extra gussets and bracing, mated to an all-new box-section swing-arm.

The rest was essentially an Italian affair: front suspension was in the hands of a pair of 1.57in (40mm) Forcelli Italia forks, with twin Fox gas shock absorbers at the rear. Brembo supplied the brakes: twin 11.8in (300mm) floating-front disc brakes, with a 9.8in (250mm) disc at the rear. These ran on Campagnolo magnesium wheels, 16in (406mm) front wheel, 18in (457mm) rear, both shod with Goodyear racing slick tyres. Dry weight was a remarkably lean 285lbs (130kg) and top speed an even more impressive 158mph (254kph).

After its winning Daytona debut, Gene Church went on to take the HOG-sponsored Hammer to three AMA Battle of the Twins titles.

All of this success was not really too bad for a bike that began its life as a ten-year-old scrap!

■ ABOVE *The Hammer owed many of its engine parts to the XR750 flat-tracker.*

■ RIGHT *The road-going XR1000 (shown here) is blood brother to the awesome Lucifer's Hammer.*

VR1000, 1994– PRESENT

The VR1000, which has been flying Milwaukee's road-racing flag through the latter half of the 1990s is a Harley even the faithful scarcely believe. It's a V-twin, true, but with twin overhead camshafts, and its cylinders are liquid-cooled and splayed at a sacrilegious 60 degrees. True, its four valves per cylinder have been done by Milwaukee before – but not for 70-odd years.

Clearly the VR is not your typical Hog. It's built in the United States, says "Harley-Davidson" on the side, and is decked out in classic black and orange racing livery. But it probably doesn't share a single part with any other Milwaukee model.

The machine uses Harley's own purpose-built powerplant, which looks for all the world like one quarter of a V8 car engine in its design and construction. Almost everything else is bought-in from quality suppliers, such as Swedish Ohlins

■ ABOVE *Chris Carr in action on the VR1000 at Daytona Raceway. In 1999, Carr returned to dirt track and claimed the AMA title.*

suspension and Italian Marchesini magnesium-alloy cast wheels. The whole is tied together, not by American steel, but by a massively stiff twin-beam aluminium chassis. Erik Buell was one of the original development engineers on the project, while the race team is run by Steve Shybee.

In its early years, ridden by the mercurial Miguel du Hamel, the VR proved surprisingly potent, pumping out more than 120bhp at 10,800rpm. Yet it did not make the progress for which Harley fans might have hoped. This was not for the want of talented riders. Among others, the twin has been ridden

SPECIFICATIONS

Engine	dohc V-twin
Capacity	60.8cu in (996cc)
Transmission	6-speed
Power	171bhp
Weight	373lbs (169kg)
Wheelbase	55.1in (1,400mm)
Top speed	179mph (288kph)

■ ABOVE *As brutally black as the old XLCR, the factory racer has failed to live up to expectations on the track.*

■ RIGHT *A private racing VR with special lightweight frame. The 60-degree engine layout is apparent with bodywork removed.*

by AMA Number 1 Chris Carr, Thomas Wilson, Doug Chandler and former World Superbike champion Scott Russell. The bike continued to improve, but not quickly enough. Observers were often surprised at the lack of all-out effort the factory appeared to put into the project. As a racer, it had one fatal and embarrassing flaw: it didn't win. No wonder onlookers – Harley devotees and not – struggled to comprehend quite what the VR1000 was for.

Even the VR's noted tractability could not overcome this sort of deficit. Although it could be competitive in wet conditions, it lacked at least 30bhp compared to similar Ducati twins. During 1998–9, however, an intensive programme of development work began to show startling results. Peak power soared to more than 170bhp, giving a measured top speed of 179mph (288kph) around the Daytona banking. Rider Pascal Picotte, in particular,

posted some impressive results during 1999, although he could manage no better than twelfth place in the American MBNA Superbike championship. Team mate Scott Russell placed twentieth.

Some VRs have been sold to private teams, with an odd route to racing legality. To qualify for competition, these must be street-legal – not necessarily in the USA, but somewhere. The United States is a very expensive place to make any motorcycle legal, so a limited-edition run of 50 "roadster" VRs flew a flag of convenience. No, not Liberia, but the truth is almost as absurd. The VR1000 met the relevant standards for road-going motorcycles – in Poland.

Nonetheless, this high-tech device – the only racer in the world, for instance, to run a carbon multi-plate clutch – remains a puzzle. What is the purpose of the VR1000? Is it a rolling test-bed for hardware that might appear on future roadsters? Or is it the basis for a future roadster model? Racing people close to the factory team have suggested that a road-going liquid-cooled sports bike may be a genuine possibility. Some even believe that such a device could blow away even a Ducati V-twin; traditional Harley die-hards must throw up their hands in horror at the very thought. Wherever you stand, like the rest of us, you'll just have to wait and see.

■ FAR LEFT *Note the slim lines of the Superbike VR. The ventilated dry clutch would later be replaced by an exotic multi-plate carbon assembly.*

■ LEFT *What the future might hold: a sneak shot of a prototype roadster VR1000.*

HARLEY-DAVIDSON MODEL CODES

The Harley-Davidson company has always favoured a particularly cryptic method of model designation, although the system is in most cases quite simple once the "code" is understood. The first model made in any numbers was the 1908 Model 4 – indicating the fourth year of production. A suffix letter identified the precise model type, such as "A" for magneto ignition, with the most basic model simply known by its model year number. The first "suffix" was actually a prefix: in 1912, "X" before the model year indicated a rear wheel clutch.

Thus, the Model 5 followed in 1909, the Model 6 in 1910 and so on, until all models adopted the last two digits of their year of manufacture from 1916 (Models 16). Thus, Model 16B was a base-model 1916 single, a 16E was the most basic twin and a 16J was a three-speed twin with full electrical system. Unfortunately, Harley's long-standing habit of having lead times – by which you could buy most "year 2000" models in late 1999, for instance, often creates additional ambiguity.

Later, as the range became entirely composed of V-twins, the suffix letters became more elaborate and numerous but the basic year-prefix system continued publicly until 1969 (and technically still does). Initially, there was little attempt to marry a suffix letter logically with what it represented,

although in recent times the connection has – usually – been more clear.

Not quite every letter of the alphabet has been used ("Y" is the exception) which would be daunting enough, but several have enjoyed different meanings at different times. Equally, the same "feature" has also commanded different code letters. Thus, electric start has been indicated variously by "B" and "E", while the latter has also represented the 61-inch Knucklehead and Panhead engines (as opposed to "F" for the 74-inch models) and even police spec. In recent times, "B" has variously represented Belt drive, Daytona and Bad Boy, to name but three.

All current Harley-Davidsons start with a pair of letters, denoting certain engine and chassis combinations.

■ ABOVE *Daytona Beach, Florida, has been the scene of many record-breaking attempts by Harley over the years.*

■ LEFT *A classic Harley-Davidson: the ElectraGlide. "FL" is the suffix that now identifies this model.*

Therefore, XL is the Sportster range, with solidly-mounted 883cc or 1,200cc engines. The suffix dates back to the original 55-inch XL Sportster of 1957.

"FX" first appeared for the 1971 SuperGlide when the "X" indicated that the model had borrowed the lighter Sportster front end. The FX suffix now refers to a welter of models with Twin Cam or 81.6cu in (1,340cc) Evo engines. FXD now represents the Dyna series with two-point rubber-mounted engines dating from the FXDB Sturgis frame of 1991. FXST denotes Softails, with engines rigidly mounted in a chassis that is based on the previous FX range.

"Heavyweight" models (not that most others are light) have enjoyed the FL suffix since 1941, when "F" indicated the new 74-inch Knucklehead engine, of which the Special Sport version was designated "L". These days, it refers to rubber-mounted big twin engines: Electra and TourGlides. Exceptions to this are rigidly-mounted FLST Softail models, such as the Fat Boy and Heritage Softail.

The table on the right outlines a selection of the suffix letters that have been employed.

Suffix	Modern meaning	Historical meaning
A	–	Army (military spec)/without tow bar (on Servi-Car)
B	Bad, as in Bad Boy, Belt drive and Daytona	Electric start/previously aluminium piston(s)
C	Custom, Classic, Café (as in Café Racer)	"Competition"/Commercial/Canadian spec
CH	–	"Competition Hot": super sports with magneto
D	Dyna, Daytona	At least four other uses
DG	Disc Glide	–
E	(Formerly) electric start. Previously 61-inch ohv engine and some police models	–
F	Fat Boy	As a prefix, 74-inch ohv engine; as suffix, foot change
H	Notionally extra power but largely redundant	Extra power/high compression/larger engine
I	Fuel injection	–
J	–	Battery electrical system (as opposed to magneto)
L	–	Sports specification; "LD" signified Special Sports models
LR	Low Rider	–
N	Nostalgia	Iron piston
P	–	Police model/sprung fork on 1949 ohv models
Q	–	Two passenger sidecar
R	Road King	Racing/pseudo racing (XR1000)
S	Springer, as in the last letter of FXSTS (Springer Softail) or Sport, as in FLHS (ElectraGlide Sport)	Sidecar specifications/ sometimes Sport
SP	Sport Edition, as in FXRS-SP Low Rider Sport Edition	–
ST	Softail	–
T	Touring, with frame-mounting fairing	Reverse gear/Twin
U	Ultra	"Restricted" engines
WG	WideGlide	–
X	Some Sports models	Rear wheel clutch

 GLOSSARY

Adjustable engine pulley: The first method of adjusting gear ratios; belts were changed on a movable pulley with variable diameter.

Air cleaner: Filter for removing dust from the air entering the carburettor.

Air-cooled: An engine which is cooled by the air flowing over it, rather than by a liquid-filled radiator.

Alternator: An electrical generator producing alternating current which must then be converted to direct current by a rectifier. It has replaced the dynamo on modern motorcycles.

AMA: American Motorcycle Association (governing body of American bike racing).

Amal: A British make of carburettor.

Aspect ratio: The ratio of the height of the tyre wall to the width of the tread, expressed as a percentage.

Back plate: The plate on which drum brake operating gear is mounted.

BDC: Bottom dead centre, the piston at the bottom of its stroke.

Bearing: Placed between two rubbing or turning components to reduce friction. Can be "plain" or with moving balls or rollers.

bhp (brake horsepower): Engine power as measured by a dynamometer, on which the engine is run against a resistance or "brake". Horsepower is essentially torque times revs.

Big end: The connection between con-rod and and crankshaft.

Bing: A German make of carburettor, popular with BMW.

Blower: A supercharger, or pump

giving forced induction.

Bore: Diameter of the cylinder in which the piston travels.

Bore/stroke ratio: Ratio of cylinder diameter to stroke. "Square" if equal, "oversquare" if bore exceeds stroke.

Bottom end: The engine below the cylinder, containing crankshaft, bearings, oil pump, etc.

Bush: A plain bearing; without rollers or balls.

CAD: Computer-aided design.

CADCAM: Computer-aided design, computer-aided manufacture.

Camshaft: Lobed shaft turning at half engine speed which operates valves.

Carburettor: Instrument that mixes fuel and air for combustion.

Choke: A device that enriches the fuel and air mixture to facilitate cold starts; also the carburettor venturi.

Clutch: A device that allows the rear wheel to be isolated from the turning of the engine.

Coil: An electrical device that turns low-voltage current into high voltage for the spark plug.

Combustion chamber: The area between piston and cylinder head where the fuel/air mixture is compressed and ignited.

Compression: The extent to which the piston "squeezes" the fuel and air mixture, expressed as a ratio of maximum to minimum volume.

Con-rod (connecting rod): A usually steel member connecting the crankshaft to the piston.

Crankcases: The usually aluminum housing containing the bottom end components. Commonly in pairs.

Crankshaft: An eccentric (cranked) shaft on which con-rods run, held in the crankcases by main bearings; it turns the piston's reciprocating motion into rotary motion.

Cylinder: A cylindrical "barrel" in which the piston moves up and down.

Cylinder head: Covers the cylinder at the top end; in four-stroke engines it

contains the valves.

Dellorto: An Italian carburettor.

Disc: A type of brake in which friction "pads" are squeezed against rotating disc(s) attached to the wheel.

Displacement: An engine's capacity, i.e. total volume displaced by an engine's pistons.

DOHC: Double overhead camshaft.

Dope: Fuel other than gasoline, such as methanol or methyl alcohol.

Drum: A type of brake in which a mechanism forces "shoes" against the inside of a drum in the wheel hub.

Dry-sump: An engine in which lubricating oil is located in a separate tank rather than the sump.

Earles forks: Old front fork design with long leading link and rigid pivot through both links at the back of the wheel. Used by BMW among others.

Evo: The 1,340cc V2 Evolution Harley-Davidson engine produced from 1984.

Exhaust valve: Valve which opens once every two revs allowing spent gases to escape.

FIM: Federation Inernationale Motocycliste, governing body of motorcycle sport worldwide.

Fins: Ribs on a cylinder barrel which help to dissipate heat.

Fishtail: A wide, slotted end to an exhaust.

F-head: An ioe cylinder head.

Flathead: side-valve engine.

Flat twin: An engine with two horizontally opposed cylinders.

Float chamber: Part of the carburettor which houses the fuel awaiting use.

Flywheel: A heavy disc spinning with the crankshaft which stores engine inertia and "smooths out" any power impulses.

Friction drive: An ancient form of drive, which used discs rubbing

against each other rather than chains and gears.

Fuel injection: A method of introducing precise amounts of fuel into the engine without the use of a carburettor. Borrowed from car technology, most of the leading manufacturers have tried it, with varying degrees of success.

Gasket: A washer placed between metal components to produce a gas-tight seal.

Gearbox: A housing in which lie the shafts on which run the transmission gears.

Hardtail: A rigid, i.e. unsprung, Harley-Davidson motorcycle rear end.

High camshaft: A camshaft mounted high up on the engine (ohv) which shortens the push-rods.

Hog: Nick-name given to any Harley-Davidson model.

HOG: Harley Owners' Group.

Horsepower: Torque times revs, the power output of an engine; in the early years, horsepower was just an expression of engine displacement.

Hydraulic: Operated by pressure in a fluid, as with disc brakes or hydraulic "lifters".

Induction: The sucking in of the fuel/air mixture in to the engine.

ioe (inlet-over-exhaust): An early type of valve arrangement, with a side-exhaust valve facing an overhead inlet valve. The latter could be "automatic" or mechanically operated.

Knucklehead: Harley-Davidson's first ohv engine, 1936–47.

Layshaft: Secondary shaft of the gearbox running parallel with the main shaft carrying some of the gears.

Lifter: A push-rod. Also called hydraulic lifters.

Magneto: An early, free-standing device which generated (and timed) the ignition spark.

Main bearings: The bearings in which the crankshaft is situated.

Manifold: The pipes which supply the fuel/air mixture or take away the exhaust fumes.

Master cylinder: Sends fluid to the wheel cylinders to operate the brakes.

Mikuni: A Japanese carburettor.

ohv (overhead valve): Both valves contained in the cylinder head and activated by rockers.

Panhead: Harley-Davidson's ohv engine, 1948–65.

Pinion: The smaller gear in a pairing, e.g. crown wheel and pinion.

Piston: An inverted cylindrical "tub" in the cylinder which transmits combustion forces to the crankshaft via the con-rod.

Piston ring: A flexible iron or steel ring located in a groove near the top of the piston which seals against the leakage of combustion gases or oil.

Pitch: The distance between the rollers on a chain.

Plenum chamber: An extra reservoir for fuel or gas to help feed the engine.

Port: An opening, e.g. an inlet port, leading to the valve.

Post-vintage: A motorcycle built after 31 December 1930 and before 1 January 1945.

Push-rod: A metal rod which transmits camshaft motion to the valve via the rocker.

Rake: Effective angle of the front forks, expressed as degrees from the vertical.

Ram effect: A crude kind of supercharging, using wind pressure caused by the bike's progress.

Retard: Setting the ignition back so that it occurs just before top dead centre. Excessive retard causes overheating, but it can increase the engine's performance.

Retro-Tech: Modern technology which mimics old, such as Springer forks on Harley-Davidsons.

Rising rate: A type of rear suspension

in which the spring "reacts" at an increasing rate in comparison with the movement of the wheel.

Rocker: A rocking arm which transmits motion from lifter to valve.

Scavenging: Clearance of fumes from the combustion chamber after combustion; can be assisted.

Seat angle: The valve seat angle in a cylinder head, normally 45 degrees.

Shovelhead: Harley-Davidson's ohv engine, 1966–84.

Side-valve: "Flathead" engine, where both valves are below the level of the cylinder head.

Sleeve: Cylinder liner, either "wet" (in contact with coolant) or "dry."

Slickshift: An arrangement on some Triumph machines whereby the gear lever also operated the clutch.

Small end (little end): The connection between the piston's wrist pin and the con-rod.

Softail: Rear suspension on a Harley-Davidson with swing arm and underslung shock absorbers, designed to look like a hardtail.

Sprung fork: Pre-1948 (on Harley-Davidsons) front suspension with solid legs and (usually) coil spring(s) at the top.

Steering head: Where the front forks join the frame.

Stirrup brake: One just like that on a bicycle, with a stirrup rubbing on the wheel rim.

Stove enamel: A method of painting frames or other components in which the enamel is baked to a hard finish.

Stroke: The distance travelled by a piston between its top-most and bottom-most points. Multiply this by the bore to give capacity.

SU: A distinctive British carburettor with a movable needle rising in the jet.

Subframe: On some machines this carries the seat and rear suspension components, on others the engine.

Sump: An extension at the bottom of the crankcase containing oil.

Swing-arm: A pivoting suspension member allowing the rear wheel to move up and down.

Tachometer (rev counter): An instrument that measures engine revs.

Tappet: A rod which transmits cam action to the valves. This facilitates adjustment.

Telescopic fork: Front suspension in which one tube (containing a spring) slides within another, damped by oil.

Thermal efficiency: Measure of an engine's efficiency, i.e. how much work done for fuel consumed. Internal combustion engines are surprisingly inefficient; about 35% useful work is average.

Throw: Crankpin travel.

Timing: Arranging that the spark is delivered, or the valves open and close, at the correct time.

Top end: The engine above the base of the cylinder, including the cylinder head.

Torque: Turning force applied to the crankshaft (and ultimately the rear wheel) by the force of combustion on the piston.

Torque converter: With automatic transmission, replaces the clutch to transfer the drive through a fluid coupling.

Trail (castor): The extent to which the front tyre's contact patch trails the point at which the steering angle intersects the ground. High trail figures give slower steering but greater stability.

Trailing link: Front suspension with a pivoted link ahead of the axle.

Transfer port: In a two-stroke engine, it allows fresh fuel/air mixture to be transferred from one side of the piston to the other.

Turbocharging: Supercharging by making the inlet pump a turbine, to be driven by another turbine spun by the escaping exhaust gases.

Turbulence: The swirling of gases in the combustion chamber; it is

desirable for an efficient burn and can be artificially induced.

Two-stroke: An engine without valves, firing on every other stroke, unlike the four-stroke Otto-cycle type.

Universal joint: This permits movement between two shafts but can still transmit power through them.

Unsprung weight: Parts of the motorcycle that are not supported by the suspension.

Valve float: When an engine is overrevved, the valve springs cease to function.

Venturi: The part of the carburettor through which incoming air passes; also its diameter.

Veteran: Strictly, a machine built before 1 January 1931.

Wankel engine: A valveless and pistonless engine in which all primary functions – induction, compression etc. – are performed by a rotor revolving in a chamber. Looked great on paper, but never quite came off. Tried by several motorcycle manufacturers, notably Norton.

Wheelbase: Distance between the front and rear wheel centres.

Worm gear: Gear system using a gear wheel and an endless screw on a shaft.

Wrist pin: A steel tube connecting the piston to the small end.

ACKNOWLEDGEMENTS

The Publisher would like to thank the following for their kind permission to reproduce their photographs:

Martyn Barnwell/EMAP and EMAP Archives
12 (all), 13tl, 14tr, 17bl/br, 20b, 21tl, 28b, 35tl/m, 42 (all), 65tl/tr, 66t, 84t, 90t, 91ml, 93, 94, 100t/b, 118t, 126 (all), 127b, 134b, 153bl, 154t, 155t, 156 (all), 191tr, 194t, 196m, 203t, 209m, 210ml, 212t, 213tl, 214 (all), 215tl/ml, 216 (all), 218 (all), 220t, 224t, 234m, 245mr, 246t, 247t/r 3 down, 396b, 432b, 450b, 451t.

John Bolt
292tr, 293tr, 297b, 307br, 325b, 332bl, 348 (all), 349tl/tr/br, 358–9, 360 (all), 361 (all), 362 (all), 363tr/b, 398–9, 401tl, 414t, 416b, 430t.

British Film Institute
29b, 30 (all), 31t/b, 34lm.

Roland Brown
21tr/bl, 23t/m/b, 24b, 25m, 33tr, 44b, 51tl/b, 54tr, 55t, 61tmr/tr/b, 72t, 73bl, 76t, 87br, 91mr, 96b, 97b, 103t, 104–5t/b, 109tr, 111tl/bl/br, 121tl, 123bl, 129b, 130b, 132m/b, 137t, 140t, 147 (all), 148t, 157ml/ml/mr, 161tl, 163ml, 166b, 167b, 169bl, 175b, 179br/bm, 182 (all), 185t,

186t, 190 (all), 195b, 196t, 206t/b, 212m/b, 215tr, 217t, 219br, 227bl, 228 (all), 229tr, 231b, 232b, 233b, 237m, 241tl/b, 243 (all), 245b, 248m, 249m, 252t/b, 253m.

Roland Brown/Graeme Bell
153t.

Roland Brown/Jack Burnicle
102t/m, 128t/b, 129tl.

Roland Brown/Gold & Goose
61tl, 72b, 73t, 97tl, 121tr, 130t, 131tr, 139t, 191tl/l 3 down, 239b.

Roland Brown/Mac McDiarmid
24m, 43b, 197b, 199b.

Roland Brown/Phil Masters
44t, 69tr, 101b, 105b, 108t/m, 163r, 191l 2 down/l 2 down, 200b, 221b, 236t, 240b.

Roland Brown/Oli Tennent
17t, 21br, 26–7, 33b, 57tl, 58b, 59t, 61tml, 92, 103b, 123br, 133tl/ml/b, 159tml, 160 (all), 174m/b, 176 (all), 177tl, 178 (all), 180t, 181tr/tl/m, 193b, 198 (all), 199tl/m, 204t, 223 3 down, 231tl/tr, 238 (all), 241tr/m, 248t/b.

Roland Brown/Riders for Health
25t, 58t, 59b, 73br, 77t, 96t, 109tl/b, 111tr, 120t/b, 122b, 131tl/br, 150t/b, 161tr, 166t, 167mr, 186b, 188t/bl/br, 189, 191bl, 201tl, 207ml, 213b, 232t, 242t/b, 252m, 253t/br.

Jack Burnicle
80 (all), 82b, 83t, 102b, 137bl, 158b.

John Caroll
341b, 350t, 408br, 412t/mr/b, 413bl.

Alan Cathcart
376tl, 498, 499t.

Roland Brown/Graeme Bell
153t.

Bob Clarke
278m, 282t, 289tl, 291t, 312t, 332tr/br, 333bl, 337m/b, 344bl, 350bl/br, 351 (all), 353t, 371b, 373bl, 374ml, 388 (all), 411tr, 413m, 416t, 417b, 429b, 436–7, 457m, 479 (all), 482–3, 488t, 489t/b, 491t/m, 493t, 494bl, 496b, 501 (all).

Neil Dalleywater
291br, 322br, 408bl, 440t, 481t.

Kel Edge
8, 25b, 40–1, 59m, 60, 61tm, 79 (all), 124t, 155tl, 167tl, 170t, 181bl, 185ml/mr, 201tr, 213ml, 225b, 231m 3 down, 237b, 253bl.

John Freeman/Anness Publishing
32m/tr/b, 35tr.

Gold & Goose
20t, 22t/b, 46b, 47tr, 50b, 51tl/m, 62–3, 65ml, 70t, 71b, 74–5b, 77t, 97tr, 110, 122t, 131bl, 164b, 165tl, 168, 171tl/tr, 173b, 180b, 183bl, 184–5b, 227t/m, 251tl.

Hulton Deutsch Collection
14tl/b, 18t, 27tl/b, 43tr, 64 (all), 65b.

Imperial War Museum
48 (all), 49tl/tr/b.

Kobal
344t/m, 345tr, 375t, 375br.

Mac McDiarmid
1, 2, 3, 4, 5, 6 (all), 7b, 19t/m, 24t, 32b, 35br, 36 (all), 37 (all), 38, 39t/b, 43tl, 46m, 55b, 57tr, 58m, 68b, 69tm, 85t/m, 86b, 87tl/tr/bl, 88t, 101tl/tr, 111m, 112 (all), 113bl/br, 116m,

118m/b, 124b, 125tm/bm, 127tr, 140b, 155m, 157b, 158t, 165b, 187l, 193tr, 195tl/tr, 197m, 205tl/tr, 211b, 219l, 222t, 223 2 down, 226m/b, 234t, 235tl/b, 237tl/tr, 244 (all), 246m/b, 256–7, 276t/b, 281, 283b, 289tr, 293b, 295tl/b, 297t, 308t/m/br, 309tr, 310 (all), 311tl/b, 312b, 313 (all), 314 (all), 315 (all), 319 (all), 320t, 321br, 322t/bl, 324t, 326t, 330 (all), 331 (all), 332tl, 334–5, 342–3, 345tl/bl/br, 349bl, 353b, 354 (all), 355 (all), 356tr/b, 357 (all), 363tl, 368b, 370t, 371tl, 372 (all), 373m/br, 376b, 383tr, 386t, 394b, 395tr, 400t, 401tr/b, 405t, 418–9, 420 (all), 422t, 423tl, 425t, 426m, 427t, 430m/b, 441t, 442t, 443tl, 444bl/br, 445tr, 454 (all), 455t/m, 458–9, 460m/b, 461m, 462t/m, 463t/m, 466–7, 468t, 469t, 476–7, 492 (all), 493m/b, 495m, 497tl/m, 499bl/br, 502t, 505, 507t, 512.

Phil Masters
22m, 45tr, 52–3, 67t, 113tr, 125m, 149b, 153m, 162 (all), 200t, 229b, 240t, 249b, 250, 251b.

Don Morley
10–11, 13tl/m/b, 14m, 15t/b, 16, 18b, 30tl, 32t, 33tl, 46t, 47tl/b, 49bl, 50t, 51tr, 56tl/tr, 57b, 65mr, 66b, 67tl/tr, 68t, 69tl, 70b, 71tl/tr/m, 75tr, 77m, 82t, 83b, 84b, 85b, 88b, 89tr, 90b, 91t/b, 93, 95 (all), 97m, 98 (all), 99t/b, 101 (all), 105m, 106, 107 (all), 108b, 114 (all), 115 (all), 117 (all), 118t, 119 (all), 121m/bl, 123tl/tr, 125tl/tr/2 down, 129tr/m, 132t, 133mr, 134t/m, 135, 136 (all), 137ml/mr/b, 138m/b, 139bl/br, 141m/br, 145t/bl, 152t, 153br, 154b, 155b, 157mr, 159tr/m, 161bl/br, 163tl, 165tr, 169tl/tr/m/br, 170m/b, 171m/bl/br, 172t, 175tl, 177tr/b, 183br, 187tr/mr, 191br, 192 (all), 193tl/m, 194b, 195m, 196b, 197t, 201bl, 202 (all), 203m/b, 204b, 205m/b, 207mr/b, 208 (all), 209tl/tr/b, 210 (all), 211t/ml/mr, 213tr, 215mr, 217tl/ml/mr, 219t, 220b, 221t, 222b, 223t/b, 224b, 225t/m, 227br, 229tl, 233tl/tr/ml, 234b, 235tr, 236b, 239t/ml/mr, 245t/ml/lmr, 247tl/r 2 down, 249tr, 261br, 269b, 283t, 290b, 307tl, 376tr, 380–1, 389, 403, 431, 494t/br, 495b, 496t, 497tr, 502b.

Nick Nicholls
69b, 74t, 75tl, 141t, 215b, 249tl, 369t, 374b.

John Nutting
167tr, 183t, 201br, 207t, 230 (all), 251tr/tm.

Dick Parnham
89tl/b.

Quadrant
378, 428t, 475.

Tony Stone
298–9, 407.

Garry Stuart
7t, 28t/m, 44m, 45tl/mr/b, 146 (all), 148b,

149t/m, 152b, 172b, 173t/m, 174t, 175tr, 217b, 259t/ml, 260tl/tr, 261bl, 262bl/br, 263t, 264t/bl, 266b, 267(all), 268 (all), 269t, 270t/b, 271t, 272 (all), 273 (all), 274 (all), 275 (all), 277 (all), 278t/b, 279 (all), 280 (all), 282b, 284 (all), 285 (all), 286 (all), 287 (all), 288 (all), 289b, 290t, 291bl, 292tl/b, 293tl, 294 (all), 295tr, 296 (all), 298tl/b, 306b, 308bl, 309tl/b, 316–7, 318 (all), 320b, 321t/bl, 323 (all), 324b, 325t, 326b, 333tl/tr/br, 336br, 338 (all), 339tl/m, 340t/b, 341t, 346 (all), 347 (all), 352b, 356tl, 364–5, 367t/b, 369b, 370b, 371tr, 373t, 374t/mr, 377tr/b, 382 (all), 383tl/b, 384 (all), 385 (all), 386b, 387 (all), 390–1, 392 (all), 393 (all), 394t/m, 395tl/b, 396t, 397, 400m/b, 401m, 402 (all), 404t/b, 405m/bl/br, 406t/b, 408t, 409 (all), 410 (all), 411tl, 412m/ml/b, 413bl, 414m/b, 415t/b, 416m, 417t, 421t/b, 422b, 423tr/b, 424 (all), 425b, 426t, 428b, 429tl/tr, 434 (all), 435 (all), 438 (all), 436 (all), 440b, 441b, 442b, 443tr/b, 444t, 445tl/b, 446t, 447ml, 448–9, 451b, 452 (all), 453 (all), 455b, 456m/b, 457t, 461b, 462b, 470 (all), 471 (all), 472bk, 484 (all), 485 (all), 486 (all), 487 (all), 488bl, 489m, 490m/b, 491b, 495t, 497, 500, 503.

Phillip Tooth
142.

Oli Tennent
78, 138t, 164t, 184t, 231m 2 down.

Thanks to BMW, Ducati, Harley–Davidson Inc., Honda, Moto Guzzi, Kawasaki, Suzuki and Yamaha for supplying photographs, and Frontiers Motorcycles Ltd for loaning the clothing on p. 34.

KEY
t=top, b=bottom, l=left, r=right, m=middle, tr= top right, tl=top left, ml=middle left, mr=middle right, bl=bottom left, br=bottom right, lm=left middle, tmr=top middle right, tml=top middle left.

INDEX